THE DYNAMICS OF
RUSSIAN POLITICS

THE DYNAMICS OF RUSSIAN POLITICS

Putin's Reform of Federal-Regional Relations

Edited by
Peter Reddaway
and
Robert W. Orttung

ROWMAN & LITTLEFIELD PUBLISHERS, INC.
Lanham • Boulder • New York • Toronto • Oxford

ROWMAN & LITTLEFIELD PUBLISHERS, INC.

Published in the United States of America
by Rowman & Littlefield Publishers, Inc.
A wholly owned subsidiary of The Rowman & Littlefield Publishing Group, Inc.
4501 Forbes Boulevard, Suite 200, Lanham, MD 20706
www.rowmanlittlefield.com

P.O. Box 317, Oxford OX2 9RU, UK

Copyright © 2004 by Rowman & Littlefield Publishers, Inc.

All rights reserved. No part of this publication may be reproduced, stored in a retrieval
system, or transmitted in any form or by any means, electronic, mechanical,
photocopying, recording, or otherwise, without the prior permission of the publisher.

British Library Cataloguing in Publication Information Available

Library of Congress Cataloging-in-Publication Data

Dynamics of Russian politics : Putin's reform of federal-regional relations, vol. I / edited
by Robert W. Orttung and Peter Reddaway.
  p. cm
Includes bibliographical references and index.
  ISBN 0-7425-2643-7 (cloth : alk. paper) — ISBN 0-7425-2644-5 (pbk. :
alk. paper)
  1. Central-local government relations—Russia (Federation) 2.
Regionalism—Russia (Federation) 3. Russia (Federation)—Politics and
government—1991–I. Orttung, Robert W. II. Reddaway, Peter.
  JN6693.5.S8D86 2004
  320.447'049—dc21

                                                  2003011934

Printed in the United States of America

♾™ The paper used in this publication meets the minimum requirements of American
National Standard for Information Sciences—Permanence of Paper for Printed Library
Materials, ANSI/NISO Z39.48-1992.

Contents

Acknowledgments

THIS BOOK, WHICH IS THE FIRST OF TWO COMPANION VOLUMES, was funded by a generous grant from the Russia Initiative of the Carnegie Corporation of New York to George Washington University. Preparatory work included three conferences: in September 2001 in Bol'shoe Boldino (Nizhnii Novgorod Region), in March 2002 in Washington, and in June 2002 at the Golubaya Rechka center just outside Moscow.

The editors and authors are indebted to a large number of people who contributed to the development and production of the book. Deana Arsenian and David Speedie at Carnegie invited us to take on the project and have provided valuable moral support. Suzanne Stephenson at George Washington University labored mightily to deal with many of the project's organizational, bureaucratic, and logistical issues. Lilia Troshina likewise provided enormous support in making the necessary conference arrangements in Moscow, and Sergei Borisov was most helpful regarding the conference in Bol'shoe Boldino. As discussants, Petr Kozma, Steven Solnick, and Julie Corwin shared their insights with the authors in order to improve the chapters. And the authors as a group did the same thing for one another by engaging in a lively, free-flowing, sometimes fierce but always constructive debate at the conferences, and also via electronic "mutual aid." (Kropotkin would have approved of at least this aspect of modernity.)

While the authors deserve credit for the insights that their chapters provide, the editors naturally take their share of the blame for any mistakes that may have crept into the texts.

The editors are grateful to Nikolai Petrov for editing the Russian edition of this book, to Petr Kozma for doing the translation and indexing, and to Vladimir Benevolensky of the Moscow Public Science Foundation (MONF) for publishing it.

Robert Orttung would like to dedicate this book to his children, Nicole and Joseph, because they kept the noise level down while he was working on it. Peter Reddaway is grateful to his wife, Betsy, for her forbearance throughout, and to Robert Otto for invaluable intellectual stimulation.

A Note on Terminology

IN THIS TEXT, wherever possible we have tried to provide English equivalents of Russian geographical terms, titles, parties, movements, and companies to make the book accessible to non-Russian-speaking comparative scholars. In translating Russian terms into English, we have sought consistency. Thus, we call the seven men Putin appointed to oversee the eighty-nine regions "envoys," or in rare cases "polpredy," a Russian term deriving from the title *polnomochnyi predstavitel' prezidenta*. In particular, we have distinguished them from the eighty-plus presidential representatives of the Yeltsin era.

Russian geographical terms can be very bewildering. To ensure there is no confusion about the seven territories into which Putin divided Russia, we use the same word that is used in Russian—that is, "okrug." To translate the word *oblast* we use "region." In all cases "region" refers to "oblast," except, occasionally, in a phrase like "the eighty-nine regions of Russia," when it would be pedantic to list all six categories that make up that total of eighty-nine—that is, regions, krais, republics, autonomous okrugs, the two federal cities of Moscow and Saint Petersburg, and the Jewish autonomous region. We decided to adopt into English the Russian word "krai." A territory called a "krai" has the same status as an oblast, but at some point in history it acquired the designation "krai" (meaning "edge") because of its location on Russia's border. For the *avtonomnyi okrug*, the anomalous geographical division that denotes an area that is simultaneously one of Russia's eighty-nine regions and a component part of one of the other eighty-eight, we use "autonomous okrug."

We've kept the term "military district" because this translation has been used in the Western literature for so long. And we've translated the term *raion*, which designates a division within an oblast, as "district." Also, we use the word "area" where the sense is vaguer and bigger than just one oblast or republic but doesn't refer to an okrug.

In this book we usually use the words "procurator" and "general procurator," rather than "prosecutor" and "attorney general," as in the United States, to highlight the different duties these officials perform in their respective countries.

We have also used the term "power ministries" to translate the Russian *silovye ministerstva*. These ministries are often grouped together to designate ministries and other agencies whose personnel are armed. There are almost twenty of them, the best known being the Ministries of Defense and Internal Affairs, and the Federal Security Service (FSB).

The 7 Federal Districts of the Russian Federation

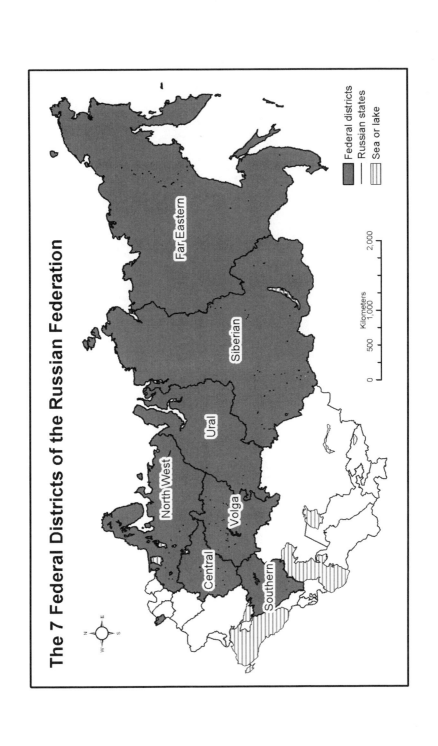

Far Eastern

Siberian

Ural

North West

Central

Volga

Southern

Federal districts
Russian states
Sea or lake

Kilometers

0   500   1,000   2,000

1

Historical and Political Context

Peter Reddaway

THIS IS A BOOK PRIMARILY OF EMPIRICAL INQUIRY, not theory. It seeks to measure the impact on the polity, economy, and society of Russia of three years of efforts to reform the relationships between the federal government and the country's eighty-nine regions. To help the reader, in particular the nonspecialist reader, to understand this complex subject, some historical and political context may be useful.

The context offered below presents my views in summary fashion to show:

- how weak were the first roots of regional self-government in Russia, planted as late as the 1860s;
- how these roots were destroyed by the early 1920s and replaced by a centralized, totalitarian, initially unique party-state system of administration that reached down to every village;
- how the system ensured—until it gradually decayed over the post-Stalin decades—that regional autonomy was virtually nonexistent;
- how the brain, the backbone, and the muscles of this system—the Communist Party's nationwide structure, or apparat—weakened and collapsed very rapidly from 1989 to 1991;
- how the gaping vacuum of authority that resulted was, beneath a thin veneer of democratic government, filled—in both Moscow and the regions—by the more dynamic members of the communist elite, or "nomenklatura," along with—and often in association with—aggressive business and criminal elements;

- how in the 1990s many of the regional governors took advantage of this development and the increasingly dysfunctional nature of President Yeltsin's regime, to head their own nomenklatura/business/criminal clans and become largely autonomous rulers of their own domains;
- how the Putin administration's reaction against the governors, designed by hardliners, supported in varying degrees by most of the national elites, and launched in 2000, has scored some points, but has inevitably been hampered by the deep corruption of Russia's weak governmental institutions and the low level of the new system's popular legitimacy;[1]
- how the emergence of new alliances, notably those between various governors and big business, have been further hindering the Kremlin's efforts to "bring the governors to heel";
- and finally, how big business, most federal and regional leaders, and their bureaucracies have, despite hardline pressure and the many tensions and rivalries between them, cooperated extensively with one another to try to preserve the status quo in society's power relations.

Running through these themes is my belief that studies of contemporary Russia do not give enough weight to the issue of popular legitimacy. In particular, can reforms like those analyzed in this book, survive and bring some social benefit, if they do not increase the legitimacy of the political and economic order? And if they do not, are they almost exclusively, perhaps—in effect, if not necessarily in intention—maneuvers for factional advantage among the groups that make up the Establishment? And also a symptom of the state's ongoing loss of legitimacy?

Only by having some grasp of the broad historical and political context sketched below will it, I believe, be easier to understand the otherwise confusing processes set in motion by the Putin administration's attempts to reform federal–regional relations.

Without possessing not just formal legitimacy, but also a reasonable level of popular legitimacy (see endnote 1), no polity is likely to be stable or long-lasting. This is especially the case with multiethnic countries of great territorial size, which, naturally enough, are particularly difficult to rule. In today's world, such states include India, China, the United States, and—the largest of them all in territory—Russia. Legitimacy can derive from a variety of sources, such as tradition, ideology, good government performance, and a charismatic leader. The now rapidly waning legitimacy of communist rule in China has been based on a communist ideology tinged with nationalism, and also on the erstwhile charisma of its first ruler, Mao Tse-tung. By contrast, the legitimacy of the Indian and American governments, and in theory of the Russian government too, rests on the principles of popular sovereignty, federalism, and what Weber called "rational-legal" ideology. To understand why it is hard for Russians to turn federal theory into practice, let us turn to some history and examine the important issue of legitimacy and the varying ways in which Russia's leaders have ruled its vast regional expanses.

In the wake of the "Time of Troubles" of the early seventeeth century, when the Russian state began to fragment, the tsarist autocracy that pulled the country together again established its legitimacy by basing itself on principles that had gained value through the force of tradition: autocratic rule, dynastic succession, Orthodox Christianity, and Russian culture. By contrast, throughout the three centuries of its existence the autocratic system of the Romanov dynasty threw up only one charismatic leader, Peter the Great. And only toward the end did it produce a feeble sort of state ideology, summed up as a combination of autocracy, Orthodoxy, and *narodnost,'* or national tradition. To this ideology the idea of imperialism became loosely and uneasily attached. However, the ideology never had more than a limited appeal, because by the time in question—the middle and late nineteenth century—anti-autocratic ideas were gaining ground, and the regime's imperialist aspirations were increasingly threatened, in different ways, by the emergence of Russian and minority nationalisms.

From the time of the Muscovite state in the sixteenth century right up to the present day, one can trace in Russian history a succession of rather similar political cycles. In these cycles, strict authoritarianism gives way to reformism, which then generates political instability, which in turn provokes a return to one or another form of authoritarianism. On three occasions, an additional stage has occurred in the cycle—between the instability and the return to authoritarianism: the political system has suffered a major collapse. This happened in the Time of Troubles, in the twin revolutions of February and October 1917, and in the double collapse of 1991, when communist rule imploded and, simultaneously, the USSR fragmented into fifteen independent states. These three occasions demonstrated, though in very different circumstances, that key principles on which the state system was based had finally lost their legitimacy.

To gain insight into the federal reforms with which this book is concerned, let us look more closely at why successive state systems finally lost their legitimacy, first in 1917 and then in 1991. Under the tsars, the rulers' periodic impulse to reform the autocratic system stemmed from a variety of motivations: to obtain more reliable funding for the state's regular activities; to strengthen Russia's security against the threat of invasion across its long and vulnerable borders; to compete effectively in the nineteenth-century race for empire; and, more generally, to head off the sort of deterioration in all-round "state performance" that could lead to a decline in the system's legitimacy—a legitimacy that came under increasing attack over time, both from Russia's emerging intelligentsia and from the West.

The choice regarding what sort of reforms to adopt was simplistically but suggestively summed up in Lenin's formula, which juxtaposed the "Prussian" and the "American" models of development.[2] The former implied that the fiscal crisis of the moment should be resolved by squeezing resources of labor and cash out of the most vulnerable sections of society, and by fashioning an elite with which to do this. To squeeze the numerous victims, rulers like Ivan the Terrible, Peter the Great, and Joseph Stalin employed various methods of extreme coercion. By contrast, the "American" model implied opening Russia up, relaxing censorship, looking for reform models, usually in the West, and drawing a wider range of people into the affairs of the polity.

When Alexander II, humiliated by Russia's defeat in the Crimean war, took the latter path in the 1860s, he was sufficiently influenced by his westward-looking advisers to introduce the principle of popular election into the new system of local government with which, after abolishing serfdom in 1861, he replaced the semifeudal rule by landlords. In this way he undermined his dynasty's bedrock principle of autocracy, which was the absolute rule of one man, sanctioned by God. In theory, autocracy was simply not compatible with the principle of popular sovereignty. Nonetheless, from 1864 on, the latter principle gave legitimacy to the new organs of regional and town government known as the *zemstva*.

Not surprisingly, many of the *zemstva* took advantage of their opportunities and became, among other things, seedbeds of revolutionary ideas like constitutional democracy and socialism. Partly in response to such trends, a worried government put an increasing number of regions under various forms of emergency rule. In sum, the liberalism of the *zemstva*, along with other factors like the corruption of the state bureaucracy and the church, and the economic plight of most of the peasants and urban workers, was contributing significantly to the country's drift toward revolution. The fact that Alexander and his two successors continued to insist that their autocratic power remained "unlimited" *(neogranichennaya)* only eroded the legitimacy of their rule still more.

For our purposes, it is important to note at this stage, first that the tsars' experiment with devolving limited political authority to elected local governments came very late, was widely disrupted, and did not last long; second, that when the loss of legitimacy by the whole tsarist system eventually precipitated the dual revolution of 1917, Russia quickly fragmented territorially; third, that it took the Bolsheviks four years to reincorporate—by a mixture of wile and armed force—the majority, but by no means all of the lost territory into their new state; and fourth, that by the early 1930s they had taken an extremely tight political grip on every corner of the land.

The ability of the Bolsheviks to establish their rule derived from a variety of factors, including strong leadership, much good fortune, the Allies' counterproductive intervention, and a powerful ideology of social justice that appealed to a significant proportion of the population. This ideology, plus the charismatic leadership of Lenin and, as the Second World War developed, Stalin too, plus the titanic victory of the Soviet armies over the Germans, gave the Soviet regime, by 1945, enough legitimacy to survive for another forty-six years.

Thus in the seventy-odd years from 1860 to the early 1930s the Russian regions went from having erratic, semifeudal administration by a class of widely differentiated landlords, to rule by a shifting mixture of quasi-martial law and weak, much disrupted *zemstva*, to a stifling system in which every territorial and economic unit down to the villages was ruled by the interlocked and centralized hierarchies of the state administration and the Communist Party: the latter made all the key legislative, executive, and judicial decisions, while the former obediently carried them out through routine, day-to-day administration. To generalize, then, the regions went in a few decades from being underadministered to being suffocatingly over-administered. The complex Soviet system of authoritarian over-administration was one of the main factors that eventually eroded the legitimacy of Bolshevik rule. To work effectively, and above all to avoid the onset of endemic corruption and localism (i.e., officials putting their own or local convenience above party priorities), the system required a variety of centralized hierarchies to inspect, supervise, and discipline the state hierarchy's administration of the entire economy and the whole of society. These hierarchies were tightly controlled by the most important inspecting and supervising hierarchy of all, the Communist Party's "apparat." To make sure that the party leaders' will was obeyed, the apparat's disciplinary arm, the secret police, often practiced terror and murder.

Under Stalin, this system worked reasonably well. Since the gigantic, countrywide bureaucracy was successfully terrorized, corruption and localism remained relatively minor problems. When, however, on Stalin's death, Khrushchev and his party colleagues abandoned mass terror, these problems soon became more serious. The party's half-hearted efforts to deal with them did not resolve them. Eventually, Gorbachev's more radical steps had the completely unintended effect of bringing party rule crashing down, along with the mighty USSR.

Khrushchev's rule illustrates the postterror problems. His typically Stalinist restructuring of the government in 1957, which involved sending thousands of comfortable Moscow bureaucrats into the uncomfortable provinces to run regional economic councils, provoked serious discontent among them. In the absence of a terror machine, officialdom's unpunished discontent with this and other reforms spread, until in the end he had alienated all sections of the elite, including his bastion, the party. He was removed from power.

His successors promptly reversed his reforms and instituted a long-term policy of placating the legions of party and state officials he had upset. Inevitably, in such a huge and bureaucratized country, corruption and localism began to thrive. Gradually the whole political and economic system lost its dynamism. The inspection and supervision hierarchies, including the party, became lax, as the practitioners of localism in its many forms insured themselves against punishment by bribing the inspectors.

In fall 1988 a desperate Gorbachev, whose initial economic reforms had not worked to his liking, tried to kick-start a new system of market socialism by, among other things, abolishing the party's role of policing the economy. So now the second of the two powerful hierarchies that had monitored and controlled "USSR Incorporated" had been removed from the job—the secret police by Khrushchev and the party by Gorbachev. The ministerial bureaucracies suddenly became relatively autonomous.

Inevitably, corruption, localism, and economic disruption accelerated rapidly, fired also by Gorbachev's creation of a small private sector. The furtive appropriation of state assets by private interests became widespread. And—out of self-defense against the disruption of normal distribution mechanisms—some republics, regions, and cities began to behave autonomously and to practice a degree of economic autarky. The level of popular legitimacy enjoyed by the party sank below the critical minimum, and in the years 1989 to 1991 the whole system of communist rule unraveled.

Its lynchpin, the party, had been emasculated vis-à-vis the economy, and regionalism and republican nationalism, unleashed by Gorbachev's glasnost' and democratization, undermined its political control. His attempts to replace its economic monitoring role with popular pressures mobilized through newly created, semidemocratic legislative bodies did not work. But these bodies did promote the centrifugal forces that began to pull the country apart. In general, Gorbachev's reforms, as they stumbled, revealed the system's low level of legitimacy, and simultaneously drove it still lower. They also showed how easily in Russia the loss of legitimacy leads to territorial fragmentation.

When Boris Yeltsin started undermining Gorbachev's all-union government in 1990 by urging the Russian regions to "take as much sovereignty as you can," and when, after facing down a hard-line coup attempt in August 1991, he banned the still ruling Communist Party and closed its offices in every Russian city and town, he took actions that, while politically rational, also helped to create major administrative problems. These were only exacerbated by his subsequent policies. For, as we have seen, the state's officials had been trained through their whole careers to be passive executors of the will of the party. They did what the party body responsible for supervising them at their level in the hierarchy told them to do. And suddenly the party no longer existed. From where, then, were the political directions, the daily guidance and hand-holding, and the policing, to come?

In some measure, of course, the directions came from the ministers in Yeltsin's government. But the ministers had no partylike hierarchy to give the bureaucrats at all levels the detailed instructions, or the daily guidance, or the policing, that the communist apparat had provided. Worse still, Yeltsin decided—after some hesitation—not to set up a presidential political party (and his successor, Vladimir Putin, has so far taken the same course).

One might have thought that, with the transition from a state-owned to a mainly privately owned economy, the number of functions for state bureaucrats to perform, and therefore the number of officials too, would sharply decline. Surely the market's "invisible hand" would carry out many of these functions spontaneously? Such an outcome was, of course, what the bureaucrats feared. Not surprisingly, then, they have worked mightily ever since to create new functions for themselves, such as licensing and inspecting everything they could think of, not giving up even when new laws sharply reduced the number of such functions. Thus Prime Minister Sergei Kirienko complained to parliament on April 10, 1998, that the number of staff employed by the federal and regional governments had, far from decreasing, actually increased—by 1.2 million—between 1992 and 1997. In April 2001 President Putin made the same complaint to parliament: the number was *still* increasing.

To put things simply, the collapse of the communist apparat, plus the large-scale indulgence of Yeltsin and the governors in patronage politics (jobs for their cronies, and then more jobs for their cronies' cronies) has caused the Russian bureaucracy to get out of control. Quite apart from the exorbitant cost to the taxpayer of thousands of unneeded bureaucrats, and the baneful effect on business of their excessive regulatory activities, the politicians' failure to control the bureaucracy has had the even more insidious effect of facilitating its now endemic cooperation with a wide range of business interests. This cooperation is based primarily on the routine exchange of bribes for administrative favors. Through their corrupt activities, the national or regional interest is sacrificed to private interests. We shall return to this topic at the end.

To understand better how all this came about and to focus more exclusively on regional issues, let us return to 1991. This was the year after Yeltsin had, as noted above, appealed to the regional, city, and local governments of Russia to take their fill of sovereignty. This appeal stemmed primarily from the sudden collapse of the Communist Party as the animating force in all three branches of power in Russia's government, and from the resulting vacuum of authority. This created an especially big problem in Russia, as opposed to the other fourteen republics, because the Russian Soviet Federated Socialist Republic's (RSFSR) government enjoyed less autonomy from the all-union government than the other governments did, and also because the RSFSR was the only republic endowed with neither a party central committee nor an associated apparat. In other words, Yeltsin's government simply did not have the administrative resources to ensure that federal institutions would go on working adequately in the regions. Many of these institutions were not operating effectively without the Communist Party's animating force and daily supervision. Nor did the government have the "transmission belt" of an elaborately structured pro-government party that might have conducted some supervision through legislative bodies.

Thus Yeltsin found it essential to urge the regional, city, and local governments to assume substantial responsibility for, and control of, many of the federal institutions on their territories, so that he and his government could concentrate their limited resources on trying to play the role of the old central committee departments of the party. His government had to animate those federal ministries that were important to them—that is, get them to work effectively at the national level. Naturally, Yeltsin's forced expedient damaged vertical authority relations within the ministries, and thus tended to exacerbate tensions between them and the regional governments.

To act as his agents in each region (though not in the republics), Yeltsin appointed a governor to be the chief regional executive, and a "Representative of the President" to play a delicate complementary role as a two-way mediator. The latter's mission was first to ensure that federal policy was carried out properly by the governor and the executive apparatus in his region (under communism, this had been the top-priority role for the old party regional chiefs). But he also had to check that federal ministries did not infringe on the prerogatives of his region. This was important, given that Russia was now, unlike in the past, a democratic and supposedly genuine federation. In addition—as if this dual role were not hard enough already—he had to perform it with virtually no budget and a staff of only one or two assistants.

While a few of the presidential representatives achieved a considerable amount, not surprisingly many of them became frustrated, reduced as they were to writing regular reports to Moscow, listing problems that Moscow usually had no resources to handle—reports that might, indeed, never even be read.[3]

We see, then, that Yeltsin's broad political response to the disintegration of the USSR and the old communist order was, of necessity, a liberal one. However, his economic policy, which was also highly political, was authoritarian. The "shock therapy" medicine applied to the Russian economy on the recommendation of the International Monetary Fund and Western governments involved imposing "one size fits all" nostrums about privatization, deregulation, and so forth, on a country that was quite unprepared for them.[4]

This had serious political as well as economic consequences. For Yeltsin's sovereignty appeal required coordinated action by his appointed governors and the regional Soviets that had been elected in semifree elections in 1990. In the period 1992–1993, most of these Soviets, which varied widely in their political complexion, sided with the parliament (the Supreme Soviet) in Moscow, as its leaders tried to mobilize them against Yeltsin. The parliament needed their help to resist the unpopular economic policies of the government and Yeltsin's efforts to browbeat parliament into submitting to him. Needless to say, this bitter conflict, which lasted a year and a half, greatly damaged the already complex relations, mentioned above, between the federal ministries and the regional governments.

The conflict came to an end in October 1993, after military clashes in Moscow had killed several hundred people in an incipient civil war. The parliament and the regional and other Soviets were all abolished by Yeltsin, and in December a new constitution was announced as having been approved by a popular referendum (the results of which were apparently falsified). The political outcome of all this represented a massive gain for the executive branch at every level, whose powers were greatly increased, and a major setback for all legislatures and for Russian democracy.

In the regions, the appointed governors had often, up to now, had to face elected and independent-minded Soviets. These had sometimes been headed by able and respected chairmen, and supported by lively sections of the regional media. Now, by contrast, the governors were able to fashion a new division of power, new executive bodies, and new electoral procedures that were highly advantageous to themselves. The much weakened legislatures lost most of their authority, and could no longer hope for help from the parliament in Moscow, which was now made up of a reconfigured lower house called the Duma, and an upper house called the Federation Council, both—especially the latter—with very limited authority.

Above all, though, as a result of these authoritarian changes the governors were freer than before—now being clearly the biggest fish in their ponds—to exploit to the full the power vacuum left behind by the meltdown of the party apparat. In particular, they could exploit more blatantly the opportunities to operate with near impunity in the newly privatized and yet-to-be-privatized sectors of the regional economy. After all, Yeltsin was keen that they should establish strong, authoritarian administrations that would marginalize the groups that had—prior to October 1993 and again in the parliamentary elections and constitutional referendum of December—organized opposition to him, whether in the regional Soviet, the political parties, or other bodies. He would not object to governors and their cronies taking a tight grip on political and economic power in their regions. This was exactly what Yeltsin himself was trying to do at the national level.

In 1995, with Duma elections due again in December and a presidential election the following June, and with Yeltsin's approval rating falling dramatically, partly due to the unpopular Chechnya war, the governors' position improved still more. Yeltsin needed their services more urgently than ever. Their job now was to organize support first for the parties he favored for the Duma and then, more important, for him personally in June 1996. So he did them two huge favors. He changed the electoral law, so that this time the Federation Council would not be popularly elected, but made up, ex officio, of the governors and the heads of the regional legislatures. This meant that the governors would become, automatically, national legislators able to influence laws affecting their own regions—in addition to continuing to be regional chief executives. Furthermore, Yeltsin also decided that they should in future, starting in 1996, be elected, not appointed. Thus, if they could get themselves elected, as nearly half of them did, they would gain not only greater independence from Moscow but also increased personal authority and prestige, at both national and local levels.

All this was royal treatment indeed. However, it put them under a strong obligation to throw their considerable weight behind Yeltsin's electoral goals, unpopular as these were with most voters. In the event, while the outcome of the Duma vote greatly disappointed the Kremlin, Yeltsin's gambit with the governors, along with many other electoral ploys and dirty tricks, made the crucial difference in taking him to victory over the reluctant communist candidate Zyuganov in the second round of the presidential election.[5]

Once this critical task had been achieved, the Yeltsin forces were soon compelled to pay the political price. The first payment regarding the governors was the Kremlin's disappointment when almost half the governors who were duly elected in the period 1996–1997 proved to be in varying degrees oppositionally inclined. And of course most of them took advantage of their new independence from Moscow and the new prestige of their elected office. With these priceless assets, many of them had the skills needed to build tight-knit oligarchic groups of cronies, and in general to maximize the groups' near monopoly on political and economic power in their princedoms. In so doing, the governors of the economically stronger regions in particular antagonized not just the federal authorities but also the emerging class of national "oligarchs," many of whom wanted to extend their business empires into the provinces, only to find themselves shut out by regional oligarchies.

It took the ailing Yeltsin and his own oligarchic circle until early 1997 to appoint a new team of "young reformers" to the government. One of their main tasks was to devise an urgent strategy to beat back the rise of gubernatorial independence that the Kremlin had just—using legally grounded structural reforms, not mere cash—so generously engineered. The central thrust of the chosen strategy was to beef up the powers of the presidential representatives in the regions, to force some particularly objectionable governors out of office, and thereby to intimidate the others into being more submissive to Moscow. Another thrust was to induce the mayors of capital cities in regions with obstreperous governors, to assert their powers to the maximum, and generally harass and threaten their governors. This approach brought few political dividends, and not surprisingly damaged the overall quality of administration in the relevant regions.

There was also much discussion and planning among the architects of regional policy about the radical, rational, but politically explosive idea of reducing the number of federation subjects from eighty-nine to, for example, twenty-four.

In May 1997 the Kremlin launched an offensive against one of the most corrupt and unyielding governors, Yevgeny Nazdratenko of Primorskii krai. First, Yeltsin appointed the head of the krai's security police, General Kondratov, to the additional post of presidential representative (PR). Then in June he decreed extra PR powers for Kondratov. In response, Nazdratenko appealed to his fellow governors to defend him, and in early July, with an unprecedented show of corporate solidarity, they voted unanimously in the Federation Council in his support. Thus, when another presidential decree widened the powers of all the PRs a few days later, it was psychologically too late. The governors had staged a successful collective revolt against the Kremlin, which soon decided to leave Nazdratenko alone.[6] The degree could not now be seriously implemented, even by the new and tougher PRs who were appointed to twenty-one regions at about this time to do precisely that. Nor were the PRs able to implement effectively a further decree of May 1998 that created regional boards *(kollegii)* of the heads of key federal institutions in each region, to be run by the PR as chief executive. If these boards had been funded and got off the ground, they would have constituted a rival government in each region, parallel to the governor's administration and well placed to monitor and harass it.[7] In the event, they later proved to be something of a precedent for the activity that Putin's envoys were instructed to engage in—at the higher level of specially created federal okrugs—in 2000.

Although the Kremlin's offensive of 1997–1998 against the governors made some advances in the important field of fiscal federalism, in most respects it soon fizzled out. This was mainly because the years 1998–1999 were a period in which the state's financial crises, Yeltsin's repeated dismissals of his prime ministers, and the spate of corruption charges against his family and their associates became increasingly frenzied. It was impossible to implement any difficult reforms.[8]

Naturally enough, this fizzling-out emboldened the governors, who began fixing their sights on the upcoming Duma and presidential elections, due in December 1999 and June 2000. They founded several "governors' parties" to run for the Duma, two of which merged to form "Fatherland—All Russia" under the leadership of Moscow mayor Yuri Luzhkov and former prime minister Yevgeny Primakov. These two heavyweights made fairly clear their shared intention that one of them would run for president. In addition, the governor-dominated Federation Council refused to back down, when it vetoed Yeltsin's efforts to dismiss the prosecutor general who had been embarrassing him and his family by doggedly pursuing investigations of high-level corruption.

In these circumstances, Yeltsin, his cronies, and their small army of "political technologists" hit back at the mushrooming opposition with all the dirty tricks they could think of. In particular, Luzhkov and his wife were routinely smeared on the major television station controlled by the oligarch Boris Berezovsky, and various explosions and gang fights rocked Moscow, creating an atmosphere of violence, instability, and xenophobia in which a state of emergency could if necessary be imposed and the elections cancelled.

The turning point in the struggle was the Kremlin's depiction of an old enemy, Chechen separatists, as a new threat of such proportions that the country had to rally round the government to defeat it. This maneuver was successfully performed, after some apartment houses were blown up in September 1999 in four bombings, two of them in Moscow, and over three hundred people were killed. Without any evidence, the Kremlin blamed the Chechens for this terrorism, and then successfully whipped up popular fever to support the launching of a new war in Chechnya in October.[9]

The surge of patriotic fervor enabled the Yeltsin camp to create the pro-Kremlin party Unity at the last moment, and to beat off the challenge of Fatherland–All Russia in the Duma elections. It also enabled Yeltsin's latest prime minister, Vladimir Putin, appointed in August, to ride the surge of war fever, and, in the wake of Yeltsin's unexpected early resignation, be elected president in March 2000. In this way, the governors' electoral challenge at the national level was defeated, and they found themselves thrown on the defensive.

After Putin's election, the mood of Russia's political and economic elite comprised two main emotions. They were almightily relieved that they and their wealth and power had survived through the chaotic last years of the ailing Yeltsin's erratic, roller-coaster rule. But they were also desperately anxious that this wealth and power be secured and guaranteed, that the state and the elite be consolidated and strengthened after all the confrontations and dislocations of the Yeltsin years. They wanted all-round consolidation, but not at the price of any major new conflict.

In August 1999 a small, informal, inner group of the elite had selected Putin for the job of prime minister, seeing him as potentially capable of performing as president the tasks just described. They saw him, I believe, as a rather junior member of the Establishment, without a strong personal power base, and with the right qualities as a mediator, conciliator, and balancer of rival forces; as a man who, as he himself has said, listens to many points of view and then has the task of coming up with something as close as possible to a consensus; as a man who could be expected to promote some of his former colleagues from the security forces, a development that would assuage the popular desire for law and order and also intimidate, usefully, any oppositional forces that might be set on changing the status quo; as a man, finally, whom it would not be too difficult to keep under the elite's control, partly perhaps because, as the Russian media have speculated, the elite possess—as insurance—materials with which to blackmail him, if this should prove necessary.

From Putin's personal perspective in early 2000, he needed to pursue a strategy that would simultaneously achieve three broad goals. It had to strengthen both the funding and the operational workings of a floundering, disorderly state, and thus reassure the ruling elite. It had to convince ordinary people that their new leader would, unlike the last one, impose order and pay them their wages and pensions on time. And it had to strengthen Putin's own position vis-à-vis the existing power groups, and thus give him at least some chance of maneuvering between them.

Fortunately for him, he could address the first two goals with one set of policies. He could adopt "strengthen the state" as his main slogan, he could tighten various institutional controls in a firm, but not too threatening way, and he could appoint to public office a number of people with police and military backgrounds. All this would enable him to claim that he had reversed the dangerous trends that were moving Russia toward fragmentation, and that this complemented his determined new effort, begun in October, to return Chechnya to Russian control through military force.

As for his third goal of strengthening his own position vis-à-vis the existing power groups, the federal reform that he launched in May was tailored for the job. First, the reform would be powered mainly by officers from the Federal Security Service (FSB),[10] the institution he had served in and later headed. This group of loyalists, indebted to him for their promotions, would work both to bring the other power ministries under his control, and also to strengthen vertical discipline in all the federal ministries. These tasks would be achieved, first by creating a new second-level structure of seven federal okrugs to strengthen the rather weak hierarchy of the presidency, second by staffing it in significant measure with FSB officers, and third by tasking it to monitor and supervise the operations of all the federal institutions in the regions. The okrugs, under the presidential envoys who headed them, would also be charged to supervise the taking back of power from the governors for the benefit of the federal government, a process facilitated by other aspects of the federal reform discussed in this book.

By creating this new structure, Putin cleverly fashioned for himself an administrative instrument directly subordinate to himself, independent of existing institutions, empowered to monitor and if necessary harass these institutions, and staffed by hand-picked individuals whose political and administrative skills he could now test out before deciding whether to promote them to higher office. He possessed an instrument, albeit with limited executive powers, that he could wield to the degree needed—though with no guarantee of success—against recalcitrant governors or ministers or oligarchs or politicians.

Nearly three years after Putin launched the federal reforms, this appears to be a reasonable assessment of his original goals and intentions.[11] It is the prism through which the broad concluding thoughts that follow are presented. Hopefully they will be a useful backdrop to the subsequent chapter by Robert Orttung, which elaborates on the detailed features of the reforms.

First, although Putin announced his regional reform program in May 2000 without prior public discussion, the ideas underlying it had been discussed for a long time. Indeed, as we have seen, a model not so different from what emerged had actually been launched in the period 1997–1998, only to quickly lose steam in face of the unprecedented governors' revolt, and because the Kremlin was too distracted by financial crises and the turmoil caused by the succession struggle and high-level corruption charges. We should also note that Putin himself had been directly involved in the formulation of regional policy in the Presidential Administration in the years 1997–1998, prior to his appointment in summer 1998 to run the security police, or FSB.[12]

More importantly, perhaps, the reforms he adopted in 2000 to claw back a substantial amount of power from the governors for the benefit of the federal government found more resonance among the national elite in 2000 than such ideas possessed in 1997. The governors had just shown in the run-up to both the elections that they aspired to play a major role on the national stage—as candidates for the presidency, and through their own parties in the Duma, as well as through collective action in the Federation Council, where they were already entrenched. This was the group, the national elite felt, that had got too big for its boots and was trying to change the status quo in power relations. Therefore it was violating a sacred taboo.

Thus Putin's goal of eliminating the governors from the Federation Council over a couple of years was widely seen as a good one, as was his plan to put an end to their habit of passing laws and regulations that conflicted with federal legislation. Also, threatening some of them with jail, and making them all removable by the president in extreme circumstances—these too were sensible ideas. Such threats would hardly ever need to be carried out. As for creating seven federal okrugs and putting Putin's envoys in charge of them, this too would probably be useful for cutting the governors down to size, even though the okrugs would probably not be desirable as a long-term institution.

Most of the elite seems to have thought like this. At the same time, those members of the Yeltsin camp who were potentially most vulnerable to any campaign of de-Yeltsinization that Putin or his successor might launch—figures like Chubais, Berezovsky, and Gusinsky—were certainly worried that the appearance among the seven envoys of five men from the power ministries presaged a trend by Putin to rely increasingly on such people in the future. This made them wary.

However, their fears cannot—prior to July 2003—be said to have come to pass on a major scale. To the frustration of the envoys, Putin did not significantly increase their powers between May 2000 and March 2003. In particular, they have been denied the executive powers vis-à-vis the economy and financial flows that they have clearly asked for. Also, it does not appear, at least so far, that the extensive work done by the "Kozak Commission" on defining the powers of the different levels of government favors any expansion of their role.

In any case, it does not seem logical in my view for the envoys' position to remain unchanged for the indefinite future. As this book shows, some of their tasks have been at least formally accomplished, while others concerned with promoting greater integration between the regions of their okrugs appear hard to push forward without their being given a serious budget so that they can fund more than just their staffs' salaries. Also, most of the governors appear to have learned over time how to get along with, or around, their envoy, and, noticing that he does not really bite, have lost their fear of him. In short, logic seems to point to the envoys' jobs being *either* abolished, as envoy Kirienko has repeatedly predicted, or gradually reduced in size and given to less senior figures, *or* steadily expanded, with an appropriate budget.

The latter course would be undesirable from the viewpoint of creating an up-to-date administrative system for Russia. The envoys' offices constitute an administrative anomaly, clumsily grafted onto existing institutions and without constitutional status. Also, any expansion of their role might presage an attempt to impose a more thoroughgoing form of authoritarianism on Russia than it has at present.

Maybe the federal reforms have done some good in the short term, stabilizing the regional situation and tempering the ambitions of the governors.

And maybe this good has outweighed the cost of the bureaucratic confusion they have caused in the regular chains of administrative command. But it seems most unlikely that they are helping to cure the underlying problems of today's Russian polity.

These concern the postcommunist order's loss of legitimacy in the eyes of much of the population. Reasonably enough, ordinary people see the elites as being mainly preoccupied with their own personal interests, at the expense of the national interest. In particular, government has become an activity dominated by intensive collaboration between businessmen on the one side and bureaucrats and politicians on the other. The goal is mutual private enrichment. The victims are the national interest and the well-being of ordinary people. As the political sociologist Igor Klyamkin has recently written in a major analysis based partly on interviews with businessmen, "The civil service has become a form of private business: officials display their administrative services on the gray market, and businessmen have to pay for these services illegally. Otherwise, their businesses would be threatened."[13] Klyamkin argues further, and I agree with him, that the liberal laws on deregulation and related issues that have been passed in the last few years have had little or no effect. The existing patterns of behavior appear to be too deeply engrained to be changed by laws, at least for the foreseeable future. And they mean that no president or prime minister or governor can rely on any part of the bureaucracy to carry out any reform that goes against the interests of either big business, or the top officials of the ministry concerned, or, more likely, both.

If this interpretation of the current state of the Russian polity is somewhere near the mark, then the federal–regional reforms are not likely to change anything very much. Even though the state badly needs to become more cohesive, and business urgently requires a level national playing field, and responsible fiscal federalism is essential to the pursuit of even a minimum of social justice, the reforms seem unlikely to do more than adjust the balance of power within the elite groups. The governors have lost a bit, while the power ministries have gained a bit.[14]

In general, the elite groups see a powerful common interest in limiting their natural rivalries and preserving the current power relationships in society. These relationships mean that virtually all political and economic power is concentrated in the groups' hands, and only a small residue remains for everyone else. Certainly these elite groups, which include the governors, have, to preserve the status quo, colluded in recent years to buy off political and labor opposition, and erode the fragile democratic structures and civil freedoms that emerged in the wake of communism's decline and fall.

The danger of this mind-set to the Russian state is that the elites as a whole will be so focused on their own political and economic interests that they will neglect the state to the point where it functions less and less well, loses its last elements of legitimacy, and eventually breaks down through fragmentation or revolution. Ultimately, as we saw earlier, this is what happened in both 1917 and 1991. On each occasion, the erosion of viable relations between the central government and the regions played a critical role in the process.

Whether this book provides evidence for or against an unhappy scenario of this sort, readers can decide for themselves. But in any case the book presents an overview, followed by detailed surveys from seven geographic angles, of how federal–regional relations have developed over the last three years. Thus it illuminates an extremely important dimension of Russia's national life, which needs to be studied intensively, even if the outcome in terms of reform that is helpful to ordinary Russians should turn out to be minor or even negligible.

Notes

1. By this phrase I mean that the majority of ordinary Russians do not see the institutions of government and the economy as being built on socially just foundations. In this connection they see them as operating in ways that are often detrimental to ordinary people—for example, when elections are rigged, wages are low or paid late, real unemployment is high, social welfare, education, and health systems decline, public officials need to be bribed, and so forth.

2. This particular point, and the whole argument of this section, comes largely from the ideas of Dmitri Glinski, as presented in P. Reddaway and D. Glinski, *The Tragedy of Russia's Reforms: Market Bolshevism against Democracy* (Washington, D.C.: U.S. Institute of Peace Press, 2001), 18–27.

3. This was the message I received during a lengthy interview in Krasnoyarsk in October 1994 with presidential representative Yuri Moskvich.

4. On these complex and contentious issues see Reddaway and Glinski, chapter 5. For a contrasting interpretation see Anders Aslund, *How Russia Became a Market Economy* (Washington, D.C.: Brookings Institution, 1995).

5. On these extraordinary episodes see Reddaway and Glinski, 491–530.

6. On his eventual removal in 2001 through the device of giving him a lucrative post in Moscow, see Elizabeth Wishnick's chapter on the Far East okrug below.

7. On the trends discussed in this section see the detailed and valuable articles by Rostislav Turovskii, "Otnosheniya 'Tsentr-Regiony' v 1997–1998 gg. : mezhdu konfliktom i konsensusum," *Politiya*, no. 1 (7) (Spring 1998), 1–20; and Eugene Huskey, "Political Leadership and the Center-Periphery Struggle: Putin's Administrative Reforms," in *Gorbachev, Yeltsin, and Putin: Political Leadership in Russia's Transition*, ed. Archie Brown and Lilia Shevtsova (Washington, D.C.: Carnegie Endowment for International Peace, 2001), 113–41.

8. For details on the events summarized in this section, see Reddaway and Glinski, chapters 8 and 9.

9. It is still not known who was behind the bombings. While some Karachais have been named as suspected participants, a significant proportion of Russians, and many foreign observers, believe that circumstantial evidence points to the authorities themselves having had some involvement in them.

10. See the appendix to this volume, where this is made clear in a long and unusually frank interview by the chief federal inspector of the Perm region in the Volga federal okrug. He says that the only institution that okrug personnel do not supervise as regards top personnel appointments is the FSB: "Of all the federal bodies, this one is special. It monitors the state apparatus for the bane of corruption. . . . Thus it's not I who supervises them, but they who supervise me." Interview of Nikolai Fadeyev, "Tret'ii chelovek," *Zvezda* [Perm], December 20, 2002.

11. I have argued this interpretation in two articles, "Will Putin Be Able to Consolidate Power?" and "Is Putin's Power More Formal than Real?" in (respectively) *Post-Soviet Affairs*, no. 1 (2001): 23–44; and no. 1 (2002): 31–40.

12. See the testimony of Sergei Samoilov, head of the Main Territorial Directorate in the Presidential Administration until December 2000, in Marina Kalashnikova, "Sergei Samoilov: Gossoviet budet rabotat' v Kremle," *Nezavisimaya gazeta*, August 2, 2000.

13. I. Klyamkin, "Byurokratiya i biznes v Rossii," typescript paper to be published in a forthcoming book on contemporary Russian bureaucracy edited by Marie Mendras, 23. See also Mendras's own paper to appear in the same book, which, from a somewhat more theoretical perspective, takes a similarly dire view of the problems posed for Russian government by bureaucratic corruption: "The State Is Weak, Administrations Are Strong: Assessing the Functionality of Bureaucracies in Russia," 24 pp.

14. However, the governors are not stupid, so, finding themselves forced in many cases to lift the blockade against big business coming into their regions, they have promptly made deals with it, and these are not always to the Kremlin's advantage.

2

Key Issues in the Evolution of the Federal Okrugs and Center–Region Relations under Putin

Robert Orttung

A S SOON AS VLADIMIR PUTIN WON Russia's March 26, 2000, presidential election, he focused with special intensity on the central question of how best to rule Russia. The power of the federal government had deteriorated extensively under the care of his predecessor Boris Yeltsin, who had spent much of his second term in the hospital. Putin believed firmly that he had to strengthen the authority of the federal government and take back much of the power that the regional elites had grabbed during the 1990s, when central control was weak.[1] The most immediate major task was to improve the efficiency of the Russian state and ensure that decisions adopted in Moscow were actually implemented in the regions.

During Yeltsin's decade in power, the regional elite had grown strong while the capacity of the federal government shrank. Yeltsin relied on the regional leaders for much of his power. In 1991, Yeltsin needed the support of the regional elite to undermine the authority of USSR president Mikhail Gorbachev to set up Russia as a state independent of the Soviet Union. Yeltsin sought the aid of the regional leaders again in 1993 to defeat his opposition, most dramatically in the shelling of the Russian parliament, and in 1996 to beat back a communist threat in the presidential elections.

To secure the support of the regional elite, Yeltsin made numerous concessions to the governors, and the Russian government lost the extensive control its Soviet counterpart once held over the regions. At the federal level, the regional leaders joined the Federation Council in 1996 and had a direct voice in the key political and economic questions facing the country. Between 1994 and 1998, the federal government signed forty-two power-sharing treaties with forty-six of the eighty-nine regions, in some cases handing over lucrative privileges. At the regional level, governors were often able to co-opt federal officials, including law enforcement agents, and entice them to work for regional, rather than federal, interests. Within their own regions, the elite governed with little regard to federal guidance, frequently adopting laws that violated Russian legislation. The governors set up autarkic economies, with a variety of regional barriers that often blocked the import and export of goods. The result severely restricted the development of a common Russian market. By the late 1990s, the governors had gained inordinate control over Russia's financial flows and natural resources, although the federal government managed to claw back some control of fiscal levers from 1997 on. In many cases, the governors repressed popular demands for more accountable government and personally controlled many aspects of day-to-day life at the regional and local level. The typical governor dictated his preferences to the regional media, courts, and local governments as a way of perpetuating his own power and blocking any incipient opposition from encroaching on it. Many argued that by the end of Yeltsin's term, the country was in serious danger of falling apart.

President Vladimir Putin launched his presidential term with a package of initiatives aimed at strengthening the power of Russia's federal government in its relations with the regions. Putin's first task was political: Taking back the federal powers that the governors had captured during the previous decade. His second task was largely economic: Removing the various interregional barriers and trade impediments that had appeared during these years. These goals fit with Putin's overall efforts to integrate Russia into the world economy.[2] Putin's reforms

- divided the country into seven okrugs, each under the control of a presidential envoy;
- changed the way members are chosen for the Federation Council, the upper chamber of the national parliament;
- gave the federal authorities the power to remove governors and disband regional legislatures;
- created a consultative State Council, whose membership included the president and all eighty-nine governors;
- breathed new life into the Security Council; and
- reorganized the country's finances in favor of the federal government.

Putin imposed some of his reforms by presidential decree and passed others through the national legislature in the form of new laws. Although the regional elite objected to many of Putin's reforms, they lacked the political resources, particularly a strong party organization, to oppose them.[3] Moreover,

Putin introduced his reforms on the eve of the fall 2000 gubernatorial election cycle, a time when the governors were particularly vulnerable and wanted Moscow's support. Above all, the president benefited from the fact that the regions are divided in their perceptions of his reforms, with the poor regions viewing them more favorably than the rich ones, because they hoped to receive more federal subsidies and had fewer benefits to lose.

This book provides a midterm assessment of Putin's reforms, seeking to show what their impact has been after two and a half years of implementation. This introductory chapter lays out Putin's intentions and his overall reform program, identifying the key issues that the substantive chapters of the book discuss. This chapter also provides the overall context for understanding what is happening in each of Russia's seven federal okrugs. The seven main chapters of the book examine how the reforms have been implemented on the ground in the seven newly established federal okrugs that Putin created. It is in the okrugs where Moscow's dictates meet regional reality and the real machinery of governing Russia must do its work. The concluding chapter provides an overall assessment of Putin's reforms, comparing his original intentions with how they have been implemented—with many regional variations and varying degrees of success—across the seven okrugs.

Seven Federal Okrugs

On May 13, 2000, Putin issued a presidential decree that radically restructured his administration, abolishing the more than eighty presidential representatives to Russia's eighty-nine regions and replacing them with seven envoys who would be responsible for greatly expanded federal okrugs.[4] Through this reform, the two-headed federal executive—the Presidential Administration (PA) and the Cabinet of Ministers—sought to regain control of federal functions they had lost to the regions during the Yeltsin era, arguing that they needed to keep the country from splitting apart. Putin complained that the earlier presidential representatives, based in almost all of the regions, had come under the influence of Russia's governors. Rather than represent federal interests in the regions, they were lobbyists for regional interests in Moscow. Putin hoped that the new presidential envoys with responsibility for numerous regions would stand above the governors and operate independently of them. Thus, a central question this book addresses about the envoys is whether they represent federal policies in the regions or are again becoming regional lobbyists in the capital. In other words, how far does the president's power really extend in Russia?

Putin's decree stated up front that its main purpose was to "ensure the realization of the president's constitutional powers, increase the effectiveness of the federal agencies, and improve the system of monitoring the implementation of their decisions." The decree subordinated the envoys directly to the president and they serve at his discretion. He assigned his envoys the tasks of:

1. ensuring that the president's domestic and foreign policies were being implemented;
2. guaranteeing that appropriate personnel were appointed to federal office; and
3. reporting to the president regularly about the national security, political, social, and economic situation in the federal okrugs and making appropriate recommendations.

In carrying out these tasks, the president gave his envoys a variety of functions, including:

1. coordinating the activities of the federal agencies working in the okrug;
2. analyzing the effectiveness of the law enforcement agencies, including their personnel policies, and making appropriate recommendations;
3. organizing the interaction of federal agencies with regional and local authorities, political parties, and other social and religious organizations;
4. preparing socioeconomic development plans for the okrugs in coordination with the eight existing interregional economic cooperation associations (since the membership of the eight interregional associations does not correspond with the borders of the seven federal okrugs, this provision of the decree seems to show that the text was prepared hastily and that initially its authors had considered founding eight okrugs following the borders of the associations);
5. approving the appointment of personnel to federal agencies in the okrug;
6. organizing a process of monitoring to ensure that federal laws and other executive acts are implemented;
7. signing off on federal projects that affect the interests of the okrugs;
8. participating in the work of regional and local governments;
9. organizing conciliatory procedures at the president's direction to resolve disputes between federal and regional agencies;
10. making recommendations to the president about canceling the orders of governors if they violate the Russian constitution, federal law, Russia's international obligations, or human rights; and
11. working with the Presidential Administration's Main Monitoring Department and the procurator to ensure that federal laws and acts are being implemented.

Once they began working in the new system, the envoys complained repeatedly that they did not have enough power to carry out their responsibilities. In particular, they frequently sought to win the power to determine how federal money was spent. All of their numerous attempts to secure this right failed.

Despite assigning them extensive tasks, Putin gave his envoys very few actual resources. Unlike the tsars' governor-generals, they do not have real executive powers. Nor did the seven okrugs replace the eighty-nine regions with the envoys as appointed leaders usurping the power of the governors as some speculated in the early days of the reform. Instead the envoys hold a poorly defined position within the federal executive branch and have few formal levers to influence federal bureaucrats or regional leaders. Each envoy has a small staff, usually totaling about one hundred individuals. This number includes chief federal inspectors (CFIs) and federal inspectors assigned to each region or a small group of regions. Often the staff has to rely on the governors' administrations for office space and other logistical support. The Finance Ministry handles decisions on how to spend federal money. Governors and regional legislatures are responsible for defining and executing regional budgets. Moreover, the envoys do not implement laws or prosecute legal violations, since other institutions exist for these purposes. Unlike governors, whom they are supposed to stand above, the representatives are not elected by popular vote. Unlike government ministries, whom they are supposed to coordinate, they are not legitimized or defined by the constitution.[5] In effect, the presidential representatives are an extra layer of state bureaucracy with very poorly defined powers. This vagueness leads to persistent rumors that the entire institution will be abolished.[6] It has also led commentators to suggest that the authors of the reform intentionally left the envoys' powers vague because they wanted to use them in a variety of ways against the regions.[7]

Nevertheless, the envoys have considerable informal powers. The main resource they wield is their direct relationship to the president. Nobody wants to cross an official who speaks for Russia's most powerful man. But this lever of influence is severely constrained, as the envoy cannot run to the president every time a midlevel official ignores him.[8] Moreover, unlike Putin personally, the envoys have little public support. Only 24 percent of those asked said that the institution was useful in November 2000, down from 44 percent in June.[9] Their popularity did not grow in subsequent years. In an August 2002 poll by the All-Russia Center for the Study of Public Opinion (VTsIOM) only 30 percent of the respondents expressed confidence in the envoys, compared to 73 percent for Putin and 50 percent for the governors.[10]

The envoys are all members of the Security Council and meet there regularly with Putin. From 2000 to 2002, this body met seven or eight times a year.[11] Usually, sessions focused on general security issues; but since the envoys were appointed, two sessions were devoted exclusively to Chechnya, and one each to Kaliningrad and the Far East. Under Sergei Ivanov, a close friend of Putin, this body was considered to be very influential. Since the appointment of Vladimir Rushailo as secretary following his removal as minister for internal affairs in March 2001, its importance has dropped considerably.

One key power the envoys do have is the ability to sign off on federal appointments. In 2000 there were 374,400 federal civil servants working in the regions, according to the World Bank.[12] In the same year, the regional governments employed 624,800 people. Since the personnel that make up a bureaucracy play an extremely important role in defining how such state institutions function, the main chapters will pay attention to this issue.

One of Putin's key goals was to set up a uniform system of administration, essentially appointing intermediaries to deal with Russia's vast territory. In practice, however, each of the presidential envoys has defined his tasks differently. Their activities range across a variety of fields, including sponsoring candidates in gubernatorial elections, meeting with federal representatives in the regions, disposing of chemical weapons, fighting the drug trade, seeking foreign investment, and trying to reshape regional media. The envoys' different interpretations of their responsibilities partly reflect their different personalities and the different challenges they face in the territories under their purview. However, the differences also, to some degree, reflect the vagueness with which their tasks were defined in the first place.

In some cases it is hard to tell if the president originally meant to sanction activities that the envoys ultimately engaged in. For example, the decree authorizes the envoys to make recommendations on the political situation in their okrugs and to establish ties with political parties. It is not clear, however, that these passages meant that the envoys should sponsor specific candidates in gubernatorial elections. That is exactly what happened though.

As his envoys, Putin named Federal Security Service (FSB) general Georgii Poltavchenko, FSB general Viktor Cherkesov, army general Viktor Kazantsev, army general Konstantin Pulikovskii, Ministry of Internal Affairs (MVD) general Petr Latyshev, former prime minister Sergei Kirienko, and diplomat Leonid Drachevskii. Putin's decision to appoint men with military or security backgrounds to five of the seven posts suggests that his main priority in choosing personnel was personal loyalty rather than public sector managerial experience. Naming a general as presidential representative makes practical sense in the southern okrug, where the ongoing fighting in Chechnya is the top priority for federal authorities. In the other okrugs, however, most of the envoys seem to lack the skills and career backgrounds to deal with the kind of complex economic and political problems facing Russia's regions. His choice of personnel for the seven positions reflects the larger problem of Russia's inability to carry out a civil service reform that would improve the qualifications of those working for the state. The unreformed bureaucracy is increasingly prominent as one of the main obstacles to reform, a situation Putin himself complains about. But Putin seems to lack a team of officials capable of addressing this problem effectively.

The single exception is the Volga's Kirienko, who, in contrast to the other envoys, has managerial experience in the banking and energy sectors, and briefly served as prime minister before the 1998 financial crash. Kirienko has tried to improve the level of civil servants working in his okrug by choosing at least some of his staff through competitive examinations. On the other hand, his technocratic and invasive approach to government has its own drawbacks.

A key area for investigation in the main chapters of this book is the relationship between the presidential envoys and the other state institutions. As new institutional players, the envoys are understandably locked in conflict with some of the existing players on Russia's political stage: the governors, the government ministries, and the Moscow-based PA.

The envoys have the greatest impact on Russia's eighty-nine governors. At the federal level, the governors (with a few exceptions) no longer have the access to President Putin that they enjoyed to President Yeltsin. Rather, they must work through the envoys and the okrug staffs in their dealings with the highest levels of the federal government. The envoys also make it harder for the governors to influence federal officials in their regions than it was in the past. At the regional level, the governors no longer are the single dominant figure in their regions, since they have to share the stage to some extent with the envoys. The decision to set up the okrugs destroyed the governors' monopoly on power in many regions and created more competition on the regional political market.[13] Businessmen and other citizens can now complain about the governors without having to go to Moscow. Finally, the envoys intervene directly in gubernatorial elections, meaning that they can use the federal government's resources to remove—or at least try to remove—governors from office through the ballot box. This power is one of the reasons why Novgorod governor Mikhail Prusak, who has been one of the most vocal critics of the okrugs, has spoken for many governors by denouncing them as an unnecessary intermediate structure.

However, there are clear limits to the envoys' power. The governors are public politicians backed by the mandate of popular election, while the envoys are appointed representatives of the Kremlin. The October 1999 federal law on regional political institutions defines the governors' powers, and any change in those powers would require new legislation. Putin's decree defines the envoys' authority, and he can revise it at any time. The governors deploy staffs that are much larger than the envoys', control regional budgets, hold the loyalty of mayors elected with their support, and can direct local media how to portray important events.[14] The governors have close relations with local and national business (in particular because they control shares in some regional companies), help set prices for key commodities such as electricity, determine regional taxes, have the power to issue licenses, influence the courts, set conditions for debt restructuring, and have an impact on bankruptcy procedures.[15] In some cases, the regional administrations sign bilateral agreements with certain corporations. Many citizens, such as teachers and pensioners, are dependent on the governors for supplemental income, while contractors and construction workers rely on their orders.[16] Most important, governors who can secure their own election most likely have the power to help the president win reelection and place his allies in the State Duma. Therefore the president is reliant on them to some degree for electoral help, thereby giving them some leeway to run their fiefdoms as they see fit to win their electoral backing.[17] At a Kremlin meeting on December 25, 2000, Putin specifically warned his envoys not to encroach on powers that rightly belonged to the governors. Thus, despite the creation of the envoys, the governor's office remains extremely important and powerful.

Additionally, the envoys have had to work out by trial and error their relationship with the Russian government and the PA. The envoys are supposed to coordinate the actions of federal ministries in the regions, ensuring that they represent federal interests outside of Moscow, rather than serve as lobbyists for the governors within the federal government. However, the ministries, which are vertically organized with their top officials in Moscow, resent outsiders telling them what to do. The result has been a battle over the limits of the authority of various institutions.

As noted above, during the first two years of their existence, the envoys have repeatedly, and fruitlessly, sought a presidential decree that would give them power over some of the country's financial flows.[18] The Finance Ministry, which currently has the power to control these flows, jealously seeks to hold on to it. Unlike some other ministries, it has not set up okrug-level offices, because the envoys might have been able to bring them under their influence. The Federal Security Service (FSB) has also not set up okrug-level offices.

Many other ministries did set up okrug level offices, adding a new layer between the federal and regional offices, and the envoys do seem to have some power over their operations. Ministries that set up such new divisions include, among others, the Ministry of Internal Affairs, the Justice Ministry, the Procurator General's Office, and the Federal Tax Police Service.[19] The envoys particularly had a voice in who would be appointed to head these new offices.[20]

The envoys' efforts to expand their powers also brought them into direct conflict with the PA. However, these attempts met with failure when Putin issued a decree on January 30, 2001, that subordinated them directly to PA head Aleksandr Voloshin.[21] Until this decree, Putin himself had served as the envoy's boss. To partially compensate them for this loss, Putin fired Sergei Samoilov, the head of the PA's Main Territorial Department, who had coordinated the seven representatives from Moscow, and cut its staff 40 percent, transferring twenty-eight employees to the staff of the envoys.[22]

Although the envoys won a fairly hefty increase in funding for their offices in the 2002 federal budget, they received much less than other parts of the PA. Overall, Putin secured an 87 percent increase in funding for his administration, from 4.6 billion rubles in 2001 to 8.6 billion rubles in 2002.[23] Funding for the envoys increased by just 32 percent, from 342 million to 452 million rubles. Up to now, they have had extremely inadequate staff resources to deal with their assigned jobs of coordinating federal activities and monitoring regional governments; so the increased funding is unlikely—especially when reduced in value by continuing high inflation—to make a very large impact.

Reforming the Federation Council
and Establishing the State Council

Putin's reform of the Federation Council took full effect on January 1, 2002, when the last of the governors and regional legislative speakers gave up the seats they had held ex officio since 1996 in favor of delegates from each region appointed by the regional executive and legislative branches.[24] Most observers believe that the current system for choosing the delegates—known as senators—is transitional, and debates are already well under way on how to change the system. According to the current system, the governor appoints his senator by decree, and only a two-thirds vote in the legislature can block him. The legislature appoints its senator by majority vote. The regional authorities can remove their appointees by similar procedures.

The current method of choosing Federation Council members represents a compromise by the Kremlin that gives the governors considerably more power than Putin had originally intended.[25] In Putin's initial proposal, the regional legislature would have appointed each region's two representatives and have the ability to recall them.[26] Giving the governors the power to recall their senators apparently provides them with a way to keep their representatives on a short leash. However, the governors may be hesitant to recall a senator who votes against their interests, if such a move would anger the Kremlin.

Putin's purpose in reforming the upper house of the national parliament was to reduce the power of the governors to influence federal policies. He feared that the governors, in expressing the particular interests of their regions and themselves, were preventing the country from pursuing its national interests and those of the federal government. He also sought to take away the governors' legislative immunity from criminal prosecution, making it possible to threaten them with legal sanctions that they had been able to ignore in the past. Finally, Putin sought to limit the ability of the Federation Council to organize politically against the president.

Putin's reforms have succeeded in knocking the governors out of the national political elite. In its April 2002 monthly survey of Russia's elite, *Nezavisimaya gazeta* noted that the governors were no longer listed among Russia's twenty most influential people, except for Chukotka governor Roman Abramovich, whose authority came from his personal wealth rather than his office.[27] What is less clear is what kind of Federation Council Putin created in place of the one that existed from 1996 to the end of 2001.

The key question here is where the primary loyalty of the senators lies, since there are numerous competing pressures on them. The governor or regional legislature appoints the senators, but this does not mean that other influences are not more important. The senator, however, has a stake in the governor or legislature that appointed him because the senator's term lasts only as long as that governor or legislature is in power. A wealthy or well-connected senator will use his financial and other resources to ensure that the governor or his allies in the legislature will win their next elections. In this sense, the Federation Council reform gives the governors access to extra resources that they can use to fund their reelection campaigns.

Although the senators formally represent the regional executive and legislative branches, Putin's PA has often pressured these nominators to appoint "appropriate" senators who would in fact pursue the interests of the Kremlin. A large percentage of the senators are from Moscow rather than the regions they are supposed to represent, indicating that they often have closer ties to the federal government than to the regions. However, governors and legislatures appoint such senators to improve their regions' ties to the Kremlin. If the senators vote against regional interests, the possibility always exists that the governor or legislature will remove them if the regional officials are willing to risk a confrontation with the Kremlin.

Also, many of the senators have strong ties to big business. Governors appoint such senators because they want to improve their ties with the companies and seek economic benefits for themselves and their regions. At the same time, the companies use a senatorial position to lobby regional and federal governments for their particular interests.[28] This can be valuable to them. In 2002 *Moskovskii komsomolets* cited "well-informed and trustworthy" sources who said that senatorial status initially cost $500,000 to buy, but the price rose to $4 million when most seats had been filled and few were left.[29] To pursue their corporate interests most effectively, such senators are likely to back the Kremlin's overall political goals so they can avoid any political controversy. Such general political compliance is, when accompanied by cash, expected to open the doors of the federal executive branch for help on specific issues of concern to a company.

In a few cases, a senator might pursue his party's ideology in the upper chamber if he should belong to a party (many do not). Some communist-dominated regions have sent communists to the Federation Council in the hope that they would oppose some of Putin's liberal economic reforms.

Senators also may be expected to pursue their own personal interests in the Council. In some cases, governors appointed their political enemies to the upper chamber to remove them from the region and make it harder for them to compete in future gubernatorial elections. Such senators can be expected to use their positions to further their careers, even at the expense, sometimes, of the governor who appointed them.

Finally, in spite of these competing pressures, some senators may actually pursue what they see as the policy interests of their regions. Some senators, for example, have said that they would seek investment capital for their regions. The chapters on the seven okrugs look at the way the senators were appointed to determine their primary allegiances. Naturally, if a senator is primarily loyal to the Kremlin, he still may be able to pursue other interests. Both the governor and Kremlin will use any or all of this sample of instruments—money, perks of many sorts, kompromat, and promises of future elevation—to win the loyalty of the senators. Senators, of course, may try to play off the governor and the Kremlin against each other to win the best deal, and their loyalties may switch back and forth over time in ways that would be unpredictable to outsiders.

Although the creation of the State Council as partial compensation to the governors for their loss of a direct national role in the Federation Council allowed them to save face after departing the parliament's upper chamber, it gave them little actual influence on federal policies. Putin clearly preferred "a powerless and unconstitutional" State Council to the old Federation Council.[30] The membership of this new body includes the president and all eighty-nine governors (and some former governors) in an organization that meets once a quarter to discuss important issues facing the country. Its establishment partially answers the governors' complaints about their removal from the national parliament by giving them direct access to Putin. However, the new body has considerably less power and influence than the Federation Council. It was established by presidential decree and can be abolished at any time at the president's whim.[31] It is merely an advisory body. Since the seven governors sitting in the State Council presidium rotate once every six months, obscure regional officials often dominate the body's leadership council. In contrast, the Federation Council's role is defined in the constitution, and it has veto power over important pieces of Russian legislation such as the budget.

Although the State Council discusses important issues, it has little impact on actual policy. For example, Prime Minister Mikhail Kasyanov rejected its plan for the Unified Energy System (EES) electric monopoly (prepared by Tomsk governor Viktor Kress), in favor of one sponsored by EES head Anatolii Chubais. Also, the PA blocked the body from hearing proposals on Russian federalism by Tatarstan president Mintimer Shaimiev. In another typical case, the government completely gutted State Council proposals for education reform.[32]

Firing Governors and Disbanding Regional Legislatures

The third major innovation Putin introduced at the beginning of his term gave the federal authorities the power to fire governors who violated the law and to disband regional legislatures that adopted unconstitutional laws. In both cases, the regional authorities would receive opportunities to revise their actions after warnings from the courts and federal authorities.[33] By taking this power to intervene at the regional level, the Kremlin sought to persuade the regional elite to behave in a way that it found acceptable—under threat that recalcitrant officials would be removed. In practice, the procedures of this system appear too cumbersome to implement, and they have not to date been used. On April 4, 2002, the Russian Constitutional Court confirmed the power of the federal authorities to fire governors and disband regional legislatures, but it made the procedures even more difficult to implement, thereby signaling that they may never be used.[34]

The Putin administration's initial attempts to replace opposition-minded governors with more pliant alternatives through elections often proved ineffective.[35] The presidential envoys played the lead role in many of these efforts. Such official federal interference in regional elections is controversial both in society at large and among the envoys themselves. The main chapters in the book lay out the different approaches of the envoys. Federal efforts to influence the regional elite were further set back when the Kremlin and the Duma eventually allowed the vast majority of them to run for a third, and even fourth, term. Moreover, incumbents won two-thirds of the gubernatorial elections contested between 2000 and early 2002. However, we should note that in some cases the envoys have played a role in getting the Kremlin's preferred candidates elected, although a caveat is needed here: it is often difficult to be sure about the relative weight of various factors that may have contributed to any particular victory.

Other Policy Initiatives

President Putin has made a number of other policy initiatives that go beyond these three major reforms. While these new policies do not receive as much attention as Putin's more visible changes, they have caused real shifts in the balance of power between the center and the regions. This section lays out the key changes to provide context for the subsequent chapters examining the seven okrugs and to identify some of the key issues for discussion.

Fiscal Federalism

As part of his overall effort to strengthen the federal government, Putin has significantly changed the way Russia's tax revenues are divided between the center and the regions, thereby shifting a much greater share of the country's income from regional governments to the federal government. In addition, the latter is working to reduce the possibility of corruption at the regional level by requiring the use of the federal treasury system established in 1998. Since Moscow now has direct control over a greater share of state resources and since it is doing a better job keeping track of these funds, it naturally has more leverage over all regions. As a commentary in *Nezavisimaya gazeta* put it: all regions are now seeking aid from the federal government, whose main principle is "from each according to his ability, to each at the discretion of the center."[36] By April 2002 numerous commentators noted that regional budgets did not have sufficient funds to meet their various obligations, and public sector wage arrears were starting to pile up in many places.

By the end of 2002, when the federal budget was in surplus, regional budgets had a deficit of 44.12 billion rubles ($1.4 billion), or 0.4 percent of gross domestic product (GDP). As a result of Putin's various reforms, regional tax revenues fell by 0.2 percent of GDP, while wages of state-sector employees rose by 70 percent during the course of 2002.[37]

Russia's policy deviates sharply from the approach that China is taking toward reform. There, according to one observer, the "central government has moved from a policy of control through direct management of the economy to one based on macroeconomic controls. In the process, fiscal relationships between the center and provinces have changed dramatically, with the latter gaining control of a higher proportion—in some cases, a dramatically higher proportion—of their revenues."[38]

In its February 2002 report on the Russian economy, the Organization for Economic Cooperation and Development (OECD) acknowledges that some centralization of funds is necessary for a comprehensive reform of Russia's fiscal federalist system.[39] However, the OECD stressed that the government had not fully implemented such a program: it centralized control over resources without developing genuine subnational budgetary autonomy. The report argued that regional and local officials need to have greater taxation authority so that they will feel more incentives to develop their local economies and thereby generate the revenue they need to provide public services. The current system does not provide such incentives.

According to article 48 of the Russian Budget Code, the regions should receive at least 50 percent of Russia's overall tax income. The Audit Chamber claims that in 1997 the regions received more than 60 percent of the tax revenues.[40] However, for 2001 and 2002, the federal government was able to get around this requirement by adopting laws to suspend this article temporarily (by a separate December 27, 2000, law for 2001 and as part of the federal budget law for 2002 through a provision buried in appendix 17, paragraph 37). In 2001 the federal government–regions' split was 51:49. In 2002 the difference widened to 62:38.[41] On April 25, 2002, Finance Minister Aleksei Kudrin said that he saw no need to change this ratio.[42]

Several changes in Russia's tax legislation have further constrained regional autonomy and raised questions about the regions' ability to meet their obligations to provide public services. Most regional revenues come from taxes whose rate and proportion received locally are set at the federal level. The largest single source of income for regional and local budgets is transfers from other levels: nearly 30 percent for regional budgets in the first quarter of 2002 and more than 40 percent for local budgets. The second part of the tax code that came into effect at the beginning of 2001 made its most important change for the regions by sending 100 percent of the value-added tax (VAT) revenue to the federal budget, depriving the regions of the 15 percent that they had received in previous years.[43] To make up for this loss, the governors are supposed to gain the revenue from other taxes.

Reform advocates believe that this system of "one budget, one tax" is a step forward in assuring that subnational governments will have a predictable and sufficient source of tax revenue that will not be subject to shifting federal policies. However, regional leaders point out that the taxes they are assigned are harder to collect than the VAT, and thus the revenue they supposedly receive on paper might not materialize in reality. Specifically, the governors believe that the new 5 percent local profit tax will be extremely hard to collect since most Russian enterprises claim to be working at a loss or with no profit so that they can avoid paying taxes. Another problem is that Russia's tax collectors are all federal agents and therefore give priority to federal, rather than regional taxes. In other words, if the collectors do not gather all the money due, they pay the federal government first and the regions second.

The situation is similar with a variety of other taxes. The loss of the 1.5 percent turnover tax designated for housing will also mean that much less revenue will come into the regions. The same is true with the reduction of the road tax. The initiators of the tax reform wanted to abolish the road tax all together, but the governors temporarily were able to save a 1 percent tax for this purpose. That 1 percent represented about 130 billion rubles.[44] However, the government abolished even that last 1 percent on January 1, 2003. Currently the regions can set sales tax up to 5 percent, and all of it goes into regional budgets. However, on January 1, 2004, the government plans to abolish the sales tax as well. This tax represents 3 percent of the regions' overall income, valued at about fifty billion rubles a year.[45] Additionally, the federal government has taken over taxes from tobacco producers that used to go to regional governments.

In April 2002 deputy PA head Dmitrii Kozak announced that the government wanted to assert its ownership of all of Russia's natural resources, including oil, gas, diamonds, iron ore, and forestry products. It planned to take all the taxes garnered as a result of exploiting these resources so that it could redistribute the income more fairly among regions—that is, reduce differentials in living standards.[46] In 2002, the regions expected to receive 150 billion rubles from these taxes, so the loss of that sum would have a significant impact on some well-endowed areas. Such plans are naturally controversial, and they arouse strong opposition from the rich regions that stand to lose, though poor regions can be expected to applaud the changes. The constitution currently assigns joint ownership to both the federal and regional levels, so the changes sought by Kozak may require a constitutional amendment.

In some cases, the government's tax policies may benefit the regions. Since the beginning of 2001, 99 percent of the income tax has gone to subnational governments, meaning that the government's decision to lower the tax from a 12 to 30 percent regressive scale to a 13 percent flat tax has helped the governors directly. The lower rate has increased compliance by encouraging more people to pay their taxes and, therefore, has increased revenues. During the first quarter of 2002, income tax generated 15 percent of regional budget revenue and 24 percent of local budget revenue. At the beginning of 2002, the government reduced corporate profit tax from 35 to 24 percent and cut the regions' share from 24 to 16.5 percent.[47] In the first quarter of 2002, corporate profit tax made up 18 percent of regional income and 11 percent of local income, down from the first quarter of 2001. As with the personal income tax cut, over time this tax cut may stimulate business and thus increase revenue. Additionally, to offset partially the adverse tax consequences for the regions, federal transfers to them have increased during the last several years, while not as much as the money flows in the other direction.

The regions have not yet felt some of the pain to come from the new tax policies, because Russia's economy recorded strong growth in 2000 and 2001 and somewhat weaker growth in 2002. While the regions are getting a smaller share of Russia's overall tax revenue, they often receive more money in absolute terms because of the expanding economy. However, many regions are predicting severe problems in the years ahead, as economic growth slows. So they are planning for major deficits in their budgets.[48]

Beyond taxes, the federal government also sets salary levels for public sector employees. On December 1, 2001, it raised their salaries by 89 percent, representing a burden on the budget of 120 to 150 billion rubles, or 1.5 percent of GDP. In many regions, the government did not provide enough funds to meet this increase, so the regional budgets had to make up the difference. Many regions have simply not possessed the money to pay these costs, so the level of wage arrears to public sector employees has been increasing. Even in areas where the regions do have sufficient funds to pay public sector salaries, the share of regional budgets devoted to salaries is increasing, meaning that the regions have less money to spend on other things and therefore have fewer levers of influence over their own economies.

The government of Prime Minister Mikhail Kasyanov has eliminated some of the exceptional tax benefits that the most powerful republican governments won from Yeltsin. For example, Tatarstan and several other republics secured the right to retain federal taxes within the republic for use on federal programs carried out there. The government has greatly reduced the extent of these special deals.

It is also using the federal treasury system created in 1998 more systematically. The goal is to deprive governors of access to money flows, which they frequently diverted for their own purposes. For example, in the past the government sent money for veterans' benefits to the regional administrations, with directions on how it should be spent. Regional leaders would then—illegally—use it for other purposes. Now the treasury transfers the money designated for medications, for example, directly to pharmacies, so that the benefits have a better chance of reaching their intended recipients, although the pharmacies are not always honest. The governor's administration no longer plays a role.

Once it is fully implemented, housing reform should also distance governors from a lucrative stream of money. Currently, regional and local governments provide housing and municipal services, relying on substantial federal support. In 2002 these subsidies were expected to amount to 130 billion rubles.[49] Since the federal money flows through the regional governments, the governors can illegally divert it to programs they deem more important than housing. Under the new system, most of the population will ultimately be responsible for 100 percent of its housing costs. As regards the very poor, rather than transferring money through the regional or local government, Moscow will send nontransferable credits directly to needy citizens, who will be able to use them only to pay for the municipal services they need but cannot afford.

The federal government is also strengthening its management of the tax police. In the past, regional leaders like Bashkortostan's Murtaza Rakhimov used the republican branch of the tax police to fill the republic's coffers and pressure political opponents with tax inspections. Now, Moscow has asserted greater control over the institution. It is prioritizing issues of federal taxes and staying out of intrarepublican political battles.[50] The result is to weaken Rakhimov's powers within his own republic.[51]

In the area of fiscal federalism, the government's reforms address real abuses that were taking place at the regional level. Many governors were using federal and regional money inappropriately, often building up their own power at the cost of the public good. The reforms address these problems because they help make the actions of the regional leaders more transparent. However, by concentrating power in federal hands, the government has probably opened the door for still more abuses at the already corrupt federal level. It has also failed to make the necessary complementary reforms that would give subnational governments the kind of autonomy and incentives they will need to develop their local economies, rather than merely seek to use state funds for the private gain of public officials.

Crime, Corruption, and Law Enforcement

While Russian cities compare favorably to their Western counterparts in terms of street crime, the country faces a variety of problems. Organized crime groups control important parts of the economy. Contract killings are widespread. In various regions, criminals make off with contraband fish supplies, forestry products, metals, and many other natural resources. Drug flows from Afghanistan through Central Asia have been increasing, as have the problems caused by human trafficking.

The Putin administration has adopted a variety of measures to reform the country's judicial system. In particular, it has pushed through new versions of the criminal procedure code and the arbitration procedure code, as well as legislation affecting the status of judges. Additionally, it has made provisions for introducing jury trials for serious cases in all Russian regions. However, these reforms have a long way to go. Regional courts still depend heavily on funding from regional administrations to pay for their buildings, electricity, and other needs. Such dependence naturally makes them vulnerable to manipulation by the regional authorities and seriously limits the independence of the court system.

The administration has also pushed a number of anticorruption efforts. Most of these have not addressed the underlying causes of corruption, such as the centralized structure of Russian administration. They are, rather largely aimed at weakening the political opponents of Putin or of people close to him.[52] According to Transparency International's Corruption Perceptions Index 2002, Russia remains "seriously corrupt," scoring less than three out of a possible ten on the group's scale.[53]

One of the key failures of the Russian state in the 1990s was that it allowed the governors to capture the police, which are technically under federal control. Thus the MVD has been a central focus for Putin's reform efforts. By the end of the 1990s, the governors had a voice in appointing and (as of March 1999) dismissing regional police chiefs. The result was that they were often able to put one of their close allies in this position, thus inoculating themselves from the possibility of criminal prosecution. The de facto subordination to them of police and other power ministry officials was strongly suggested by surveys of the regional elite in the late 1990s. The surveys found that these officials were not seen as "influential regional political players," because they were under the authority of the governors.[54]

The tussle between the governors and the MVD's national leadership for the loyalty of the MVD's regional bosses was symbolized by a major confrontation between federal and regional authorities over who should be the Moscow city police chief. This took off in December 1999, when the Kremlin fired Nikolai Kulikov, Moscow mayor Yurii Luzhkov's ally as police chief, and sought to name its own replacement in Viktor Shvidkin. Luzhkov then blocked Shvidkin's appointment, setting the stage for an eighteen-month standoff. Ultimately, Luzhkov conceded that the federal government could appoint the Moscow city police chief, but he managed to impose a veto on Shvidkin. So a compromise figure was chosen. The result was a typical Putin-era deal in which the federal government won in principle, but the regional leader retained extensive influence in practice.

As this example suggests, the Putin administration has gradually chipped away at the governors' formal control over the police. First the government amended the law by removing the governors' voice in dismissing police chiefs, making this a purely federal prerogative. Then, formally at least, it deprived the governors of a voice in appointing police chiefs. According to a law that went into effect on August 4, 2001, the president appoints the regional police chief at the recommendation of the minister of internal affairs.[55] The law requires the president only to determine the opinion of the relevant governor, not necessarily to take his opinion into account.[56] In the past, the minister appointed the head of the regional police after taking his opinion into account. The change here is formal, and it is not yet clear how much it means in practice. Additionally, at the end of May 2001, Interior Minister Boris Gryzlov announced that Putin would appoint chiefs to head the new police administrations in each of Russia's okrugs. These seven officials are directly subordinate to the interior minister.[57] Since they stand above the governors and the regional police chiefs, they should in theory not be susceptible to gubernatorial influence or control.

Additionally, in September 2002 the MVD announced a new reform that would divide the country's police force into three parts: a federal police dealing with serious crimes; a municipal militia financed from regional budgets and focused on preserving public order; and a new Federal Guard, which will fight organized crime. The federal government hopes that the formation of the federal police force will further remove the police from the governors' control.[58]

While Putin has been successful in changing some of the laws that govern the police, it is too early to say whether the new legislation will actually change police practices. In early 2002 federal officials were complaining about rising crime rates and the state's declining ability to fight corruption.[59] In regions with strong governors, moreover, the federal government still has to pay careful attention to the governor's opinion. Observers in Irkutsk in summer 2001, for example, did not think that the federal government would have much influence over the police in the region. They noted, for example, that simply changing the law does not alter the regional police's dependence on governors and mayors for such necessities as buildings, cars, gasoline, heating, and other equipment and services to carry out their normal functions.[60] Since the police depend on this aid from the governors, we may reasonably conclude that they will be careful not to cross their interests.

Putin's reforms in this area also raise constitutional issues, since article 72 of the constitution clearly states that law enforcement personnel are under joint management by the federal and regional governments. Thus the reforms may be open to a court challenge by regional leaders.

Business Groups

So far, this chapter has focused on interactions between the federal and regional governments without paying attention to nonstate actors. This section examines the role of big business and regional business. Since the 1998 financial crisis, the role of business has evolved considerably from what it had been for most of the 1990s. There are, of course, complex ties among the president, the governors, big business, and regional businesses. The following analysis will unpack these relationships in a simplified way to lay out the most important trends.

The relationship between the president and big business has enormous implications for how the federal and regional governments interact. When Putin came to power, he claimed that he would hold the oligarchs "at an equal distance" from himself. In fact, he has forced into exile two of the most prominent magnates and set up a close working relationship with many of the others. He has essentially made a deal with big business: as long as Russia's largest magnates do not oppose him politically, and as long they invest a good share of their resources in Russia, he will not block their efforts to retain and expand the enormous wealth they gained during the 1990s.[61] The current relationship between him and big business is mutually advantageous. Putin needs the oligarchs to generate capital to stimulate the Russian economy and, he hopes, make it easier to reform, while the oligarchs need Putin to guarantee a stable polity and protect their property rights.

Probably, though not certainly, Russia's magnates are reasonably happy with the current system and will bankroll Putin's campaign for a second term so that they can maintain the status quo. Of course, the system may not be as stable as it seems. One enormous problem, briefly discussed earlier, is "the financial sub-version by rich businessmen . . . of key bureaucrats at all levels of govern-ment."[62] Russia's leading businessmen have extensive financial, administrative, media, and political resources that could overwhelm Putin if he sought to as-sert state power over the interests of big business. Another potential source of change is Russia's planned, but not yet agreed entry into the World Trade Or-ganization, which would adversely affect some oligarchs and could drive them into opposition. Some analysts already see an alliance forming among big busi-ness, the regional elite, and some elements of the law enforcement agencies, which may be severely limiting Putin's power.[63] The most concrete manifesta-tion of this emerging alliance is the decision of many governors to appoint powerful businessmen to represent them on the Federation Council.

At the regional level, the governors and regional businesses were closely connected in the 1990s. Under Yeltsin, governors relied on close links with im-portant regional businessmen to maintain their power. The two sides had common interests. The businessmen needed capital from the central govern-ment to keep their often loss-making enterprises afloat and, at least poten-tially, invest in renovating their facilities. Until the rise of big business in Rus-sia, the state was the only major source of such capital.[64] The governors helped to obtain these federal resources for the main enterprises in their region, and they also provided other aid in exchange for the political support of the busi-ness class. Close ties with large enterprises ensure governors that they would have the votes to win elections.

Thanks to the 1992 privatization scheme, enterprise managers were often able to become the owners of their factories. Governors liked this arrangement, because it ensured that no outsiders could interfere in the regional economy and thereby threaten their political power. They worked to tamp down unemploy-ment and social tensions, while regional industrialists were often able, through various sorts of bribery, to secure favorable legislation or buy off law enforce-ment agencies. Kathryn Stoner-Weiss presents evidence suggesting that the re-gions that complied the least with federal policy were the ones where business interests had the greatest influence on gubernatorial administrations.[65]

The economic conditions created by the 1998 ruble devaluation, which stimulated import substitution and thus revived domestic industry, increased the oligarchs' incentives to start investing seriously in the regions. From 2000 on, Putin tacitly encouraged them to do so, hoping it would help him to weaken the governors. Thus, having focused on other ways of making money through most of the 1990s, the oligarchs began buying up enterprises that had previously been controlled by the regional elites.

An illustrative example is Oleg Deripaska's purchase of the Gorkii Auto-mobile Factory (GAZ) in Nizhnii Novgorod: a major outside oligarch displaced elite local businessmen. Siberian Aluminum purchased the plant for a variety of reasons. One was to gain favor with Putin. Certainly from an economic point of view, it seemed odd for a highly profitable aluminum company to invest in automobile production, which has traditionally been unprofitable and will face withering competition if Russia enters the World Trade Organization. But the deal has a certain economic rationale. If Deripaska is able to make the plant run more efficiently, it will create a larger domestic market for Russian aluminum than exists now. Also, he has been investing money in a determined campaign against any WTO accession by Russia in the near future.

As Sergei Porshakov has pointed out, the oligarchs' move into the regions divided the regional elite into two camps: isolationists and globalists.[66] Isolationist governors and regional business elites opposed the arrival of big business in their regions, because it pushed them out of their traditional domain and sharply limited their previous power and access to wealth. In particular, the arrival of outsider owners for a region's large enterprises threatened a governor's ability to control the votes of that enterprise's workers. On the other hand, some "globalist" members of the regional elites welcomed the wealthy outsiders because they saw them as the only source of capital to expand the local economy, especially given the weak financial situation of the state. The "globalist" changes are most visible in regions like Nizhnii Novgorod, Irkutsk, and Rostov.

This transformation in the way Russian business works places a major constraint on the power of many governors. The oligarchs often control considerably more resources than the average governor. Now the latter must take big business into account when he is making his policies, not just the more manageable regional businesses.

When they purchase a factory, big businesses often send more than just capital to the region. In most cases, they replace the old directors with young specialists who are much more adept at working in the new economic conditions. The new owners are interested in running their businesses to make a profit, rather than maximizing regional employment or reducing social tension, goals that remain important to the governor.

In the past, the factories had supported the region's social public welfare system, providing things like day care and health services. The new managers have shed these functions from the factories and placed the burden on municipal governments. Where the old managers sought to preserve as many jobs as possible, the new ones focus on profits and are keen to dismiss unnecessary workers. They want to get away from the old situation, where the factories did not have enough resources to pay local taxes and therefore accumulated huge debts.

The new factory owners have set up a somewhat different kind of relationship with the authorities. Rather than depending too much on close personal

ties with the governors, the new bosses have tended to establish more institu-
tionalized ties. They pay their taxes and promise to pay off accumulated factory debts over time. Rather than directly support the governor, most of them
prefer to maintain—at least on the surface—political neutrality. Thus, the authorities can often not be sure if the factory directors are with them, against
them, or simply apolitical. As one LUKoil official in Perm explained, "We want
to be in a position where it does not matter who the governor is,"—that is,
where business can go on as normal through any change.

In some cases, the Putin administration is helping to create big businesses
that can limit gubernatorial power. In the military–industrial sector, it is com-
bining regional defense plants into a small number of large interregional
holding companies. Thus, for example, the Irkutsk airplane manufacturer
IAPO is no longer mainly under control of the governor, but part of the larger
Sukhoi Aviation Military Complex.[67]

Big businesses have used many different strategies in establishing their relations with governors. One is "domesticating" the incumbent governor.[68] In
Irkutsk, for example, Governor Boris Govorin has replaced members of his
staff with representatives of big businesses that have bought important factories in the region.[69]

In a few cases magnates have themselves become the governors, effectively
creating "corporate regions" (Chukotka, Evenkiya, Taimyr, Sakha, and Krasnoyarsk). Isolated regions with abundant resources but small and poor popu-
lations were the initial target for this strategy. The firms want one of their representatives as governor to ensure close cooperation with the regional elite.
Voters electing oligarchs as governors generally hope that the magnate's individual wealth will help the region.

This trend seemed to reach its limit when the Kremlin successfully blocked
an effort by Vladimir Lisin, general manager of the Novolipetsk Metallurgical
Combine, to seek the governorship in the April 14, 2002, Lipetsk election.
However, the election of Aleksandr Khloponin as governor of Krasnoyarsk in
September 2002 suggested that it would continue. With Khloponin's election,
a corporate executive has taken over a region with a much larger population
and a more diversified economy than a place like Chukotka, suggesting the
trend could spread to a variety of other regions.

Predominantly agricultural regions are one place where neither the Kremlin nor the oligarchs have extended their power. Here, usually, the alliance between the governor and local businessmen remains strong and has successfully opposed potential intrusion of these sorts. At the federal level, the Putin
administration would like to adopt a new land code that allows the buying
and selling of farmland. The main opponents of this reform are communist
governors of rural regions, who have spent most of their career in the farm

sector. They want to preserve generous state subsidies for agriculture; and to block change, they work closely with the managers of the large state agricultural enterprises that benefit from these subsidies.[70] Thus the land code that Putin signed into law at the end of October 2001 only allows for the privatization of nonagricultural land, which makes up a tiny proportion of the total. In some regions, however, the governors have supported local legislation that that has allowed certain sorts of buying and selling. This has led to a surge by big business into these regions.

Political Parties

Creating a powerful national political party that could win gubernatorial elections would greatly enhance the Kremlin's ability to control the regions. However, Putin has so far failed to do this. Although he inspired the setting up of a superparty by merging the pro-Kremlin Unity party and Moscow mayor Yurii Luzhkov's Fatherland party into United Russia, this new organization has little clout at the regional level. Even in the Altai Republic, a remote Siberian region heavily dependent on federal subsidies, the party candidate lost badly to Agrarian party leader Mikhail Lapshin in the January 6, 2002, gubernatorial elections.[71]

However, the Putin administration has had legislation passed in an attempt to strengthen the role of parties in public life. The goal of the law on political parties adopted on July 11, 2001, is to create a more predictable and manageable political system, with only three or four big parties and a legislature that is firmly under the executive branch's control. The new law severely limits the number of parties by requiring each one to have at least ten thousand members. In addition, parties must have branches with no less than one hundred members each in more than half of the eighty-nine regions, and their other branches must have at least fifty members each. Thus the law effectively bans the regional parties that some governors had established.[72] Critical observers believe that these requirements are draconian and infringe on voters' rights. The governors naturally oppose the establishment of national parties that would subordinate them to a party discipline dictated by Moscow and as a consequence work to undermine them.

In the face of this resistance the president responded by seeking to ensure that parties play a larger role in regional life. In 2002 he signed a new law requiring that regional legislatures elect no less than half their members on the basis of party-list voting.[73] This provision took effect on July 14, 2003. At a meeting between regional legislative chairmen and Putin on February 18, 2003, the regional officials complained bitterly about the required party list voting, but Putin made clear that he had no intention of changing the system.[74]

The combination of these two laws should, in theory at least, make it easier for Moscow-based officials to control regional legislation and budgets. Under the new system, Moscow-based parties will, the Kremlin hopes, gain political influence that they do not presently wield because deputies selected from party lists will give the regional legislatures more party structure than exists today. Additionally, since party leaders are based in the capital, even if they are not inherently loyal to the Kremlin, the latter may be able to exert more influence over them than it currently does over the regional legislatures. Today, the Kremlin has little influence in regional legislatures because there are simply too many deputies for it to be able to communicate with all of them.

In general, governors have been wary of adopting party-list voting for their legislatures. They fear their influence over them will decline and that of the Kremlin will increase. However, manipulating electoral outcomes is not an exact science where institutional reform has effects predicted by all observers. In Pskov, for example, Governor Yevgenii Mikhailov made a maverick prediction, believing that he, not the federal authorities, would gain from the adoption of party-list voting. He thought that it would help him gain greater control over the legislature,[75] and so far he has been proved right.

Another innovation gave the Central Electoral Commission greater control over the regional electoral commissions.[76] Under the old system, the governors had extensive control over these bodies because they appointed half of the members while the regional legislature, which is often under the governor's control, appointed the other half. The members of the commission then elected their chairman. According to the new law adopted in 2002, the Central Electoral Commission has the right to appoint the chairman of the regional commissions as long as the commission members approve. Additionally, the higher standing commission has the right to appoint two members to the regional commissions. (An earlier proposal had suggested giving the central commission the power to appoint one third of the members of regional commissions, but this was dropped.)[77] Although these changes did not go as far as they might have, they will probably reduce the governors' ability to control regional elections.

However, parts of the new legislation appear to *reduce* the influence of the federal government in regional elections. Now the courts alone have the authority to remove candidates from an election, and they must act at least five days before voting day. In past elections, the rules have been laxer: electoral commissions have removed candidates, and courts have disqualified leading contenders, no more than a day or two before the ballot. However, only time will tell whether the new rules, taken as a whole, will make elections fairer.

Local Government

After paying little attention to local government issues during the first part of his tenure, Putin made this issue one of his top priorities for 2002. In mid-2001 he assigned deputy PA head Dmitrii Kozak to set up a committee to examine how best to divide responsibilities among the federal, regional, and local levels of government; and to issue a report by July 1, 2002. Kozak missed his deadline, and the president did not submit legislation on this issue to the Duma until the beginning of 2003.[78] It remains unclear when a new system will go into effect and what its features will ultimately be.

Russian mayors believe that new policies are needed immediately. "If the tendencies of the last two years continue . . . it will lead to the collapse of Russia's cities," Tomsk mayor Aleksandr Makarov told *Nezavisimaya gazeta* on February 11, 2002. Mayors are responsible for basic aspects of life for the average Russian, including roads, personal security, housing, heating, health care, schools, and public transportation. At the beginning of 2002, local governments devoted more than 70 percent of their expenditures to education, housing, municipal services, and health care.[79]

The federal budget reforms adopted during Putin's first two years have effectively transferred money from the regional to the federal level, with a resulting squeeze on local governments. Over the last decade, the tax system has changed so frequently that it is extremely difficult for local governments to estimate their revenues. Today they are struggling with a chronic shortage of funds. In many cases they are required to provide services, but not given the necessary resources to do so (unfunded mandates). For example, the federal government has required that Russian citizens pay for a larger share of their housing and municipal service costs. But it has not provided sufficient funds to support poor families who cannot afford these higher charges, and the burden of doing so is inevitably falling on local governments.

Another key problem for local governments is that they are often at the mercy of the governor who controls their region. In many of Russia's twenty-one republics and in regions like Novosibirsk, the regional president or governor has simply appointed mayors, violating the federal laws that require mayoral elections. The federal government has tried to end this practice and has taken steps to force regions to hold elections.

However, as it strives for a countrywide standard in holding local elections, some governors are moving in the opposite direction. In 2001 Orenburg governor Aleksei Chernyshev signed a regional law that requires mayors in the region to be elected by members of local councils at the recommendation of the governor.[80] The governor has a much easier time controlling such elections than he did with mayoral election, in which the population could choose its mayor directly. His new power to select his own mayors increases his capacity to rule the region unchecked by other elected officials who may oppose his policies. Additionally, Chernyshev won regional approval for mayors to serve simultaneously in the regional legislature. This further consolidated his power by boosting his control over that legislature.

As already indicated, Chernyshev's moves were not only undemocratic, they violated constitutional and legal norms. This was even more the case after the Russian Constitutional Court, in a case concerning Tatarstan, determined that mayors cannot sit in a regional legislature: to serve in both capacities at the same time violates the separation of power between the executive and legislatives branches.[81]

If adopted in the form that Kozak presented them at the beginning of 2003, his reforms would continue trends already visible by giving the governors even more extensive powers over the mayors and concentrating financial resources at the federal level while shifting down responsibility for social issues to lower levels. However, there is strong opposition to these reforms from regional officials and public sector employees; and the legislation will likely be watered down considerably before passing through the national legislature. The Kozak reforms seek to include Russia's local governments into Russia's hierarchical state structure even though the constitution formally separates them from the state.[82] In so doing, the reforms seek to give the federal government much greater control over the regional governments, which in turn would have much greater control over the local government. While each government would have a clearly defined set of responsibilities, the new law does not identify specific sources of income that would allow each level of government to pay for the services it would have to provide. Thus, the reforms do not address the problems that currently plague Russia's system of fiscal federalism. At the time of this writing, it is too soon to say how these reforms will evolve, but they certainly deserve further attention.

Mayors also face problems when Russia's big businesses buy up local factories as part of their expanding empires. In Irkutsk region, big corporations took over the key factories in company towns like Bratsk, Ust-Ilimsk, Angarsk, Usole-Sibirskoe, and Sayansk. In those cities, the corporations work hard to get their own representatives elected as mayors.[83]

When they succeed, they protect themselves from the kind of criticism they have previously received. Such criticism was voiced, for example, after Russian Aluminum bought the Bratsk Aluminum Factory. Bratsk mayor Aleksandr Petrunko complained that the firm had taken several actions that harmed the city, including cutting salaries despite increased output at the factory, ignoring environmental concerns in drawing up plans for refurbishing the factory, and cutting tax payments by seventy million rubles a month during 2001. Petrunko also accused Russian Aluminum of reneging on a pledge to move seven hundred residents from the village of Chekanovskii, located in an area directly affected by the plant's pollution, to a site with a cleaner environment.[84]

If big business creates problems for mayors, they in their turn, desperate for cash, seem to cause the most problems for small business. According to official statistics, the number of small businesses in Russia stopped growing in the mid-1990s—at about nine hundred thousand. In 2000 this number had not changed. However, the precise state of the small business sector is hard to assess because of problems collecting data about it. It may actually be much larger and growing more quickly than statistics show because many firms work in the gray economy.[85] However, Russia would still compare poorly to the developed economies, where small businesses employ at least 40 percent of the workforce, and also to countries like Poland.

The OECD confirmed that one of the main obstacles Russian small businesses face is the ability of public officials in charge of inspections and licenses to extract bribes from entrepreneurs. "Despite the well-intentioned changes in federal laws and regulations, state officials, particularly at the regional and local levels of government, will continue to possess various means for gaining leverage on small businesses for purposes of extortion," the February 2002 report notes. Until this situation is changed, small business will not be able to serve as an engine of growth for a strong middle class and a healthy civil society.

Civil Society

In focusing on the state, the Putin administration has neglected the need to develop a vibrant civil society in Russia. Facing an increasingly globalized, high-tech world and the need to compete in ever more sophisticated markets, Russia needs public policy that promotes individual freedom to develop innovative responses.[86] In strengthening the power of the state, however, the Kremlin has weakened the institutions of civil society, most visibly in the area of the media. Moreover, its decision to shift some authority from the regions up to the seven okrugs has helped to weaken or sever existing links between state and civil society.[87]

Despite Putin's policies, though, an admittedly weak Russian society is quietly evolving. Fed up with the status quo, ordinary people are starting to organize groups to address their most immediate concerns and are making increasing demands on local government to meet their needs. In the long run, these developments will have important implications for Putin's strategy of centralization, because the activists seek to place as much power as possible in the hands of society.

This new demand for responsive government is apparent in a number of regions across Russia and in various aspects of public life. In a style reminiscent of New England's town meetings, well-off dacha owners in the suburbs of Vladivostok are organizing home-owner groups to build better roads in their immediate communities and organize better security to protect their property when they are absent. These associations collect "taxes" from residents to pay for the roads and to hire watchmen to guard their houses.

While such activities are focused on addressing basic economic problems in a particular community, they could have political implications. By making demands on local government officials, citizens will encourage these officials to become more assertive in their relations with regional leaders.

Such citizen-driven local government activism is also visible in the Komi Republic. There citizens concerned about ecological issues have pressed their local governments to seek greater power from regional leaders. Until the end of 2001, Komi local government was under the firm control of republican authorities; but under public pressure, local officials began to assert themselves politically.[88]

Additionally, Russian voters are starting to use their votes to reward and punish gubernatorial candidates for their actions in office. Systematic research by Andrew Konitzer-Smirnov demonstrates that the more elections Russia has, the more its voters start to cast their ballots in an economically rational way.[89] They are often trying to replace poor leaders with ones they think will be more effective. In practice, though, there is little actual leadership change, because incumbents set the voting rules in such a way as to prevent their being removed from office. Thus, existing political institutions often do not allow voters to translate their preferences into changes in the political leadership.

Unfortunately, Putin's policies seem to be aimed at controlling the activities of societal groups, rather than encouraging their flourishing. He has inspired a series of organizations to coordinate and manage these groups: the Russian Union of Industrialists and Businessmen (RSPP) for the oligarchs; Delovaya Rossiya and the Association of Russian Entrepreneurial Organizations (OPORA) for medium and small business; Media Soyuz for journalists; and the Civic Forum for the majority of nongovernmental organizations (NGO). These new organizations sponsor meetings between their officials and political leaders, with varying results. Thus, through the RSPP, the oligarchs have a forum for meeting with the president a few times a year and for presenting their proposals on issues that concern them. This gives them a measure of formal political legitimacy and probably serves their purposes well. By contrast, the Civic Forum brought five thousand NGO representatives to Moscow to meet with high-level officials on November 16–17, 2001, and promised to organize more such encounters. While there may be some minor policy benefits from having this kind of structured interaction between the state and NGOs, the attempt to centralize and coordinate so many different groups can only reduce their diversity and vitality. It also leads to justified charges that the state is co-opting some groups and marginalizing or even outlawing others.

Media[90]

Under Yeltsin, while Russians benefited from a wide freedom of speech, the freedom of the media became less extensive after the abolition of the old parliament by armed force in 1993. At the national level, the government and a small number of politically active oligarchs controlled the major publications and broadcast media. None of the big news-gathering organizations was able to turn a profit just from selling ads. The state owned 80 percent of the typesetting plants and more than 90 percent of the mass communications' infrastructure. While national television penetrated most of the country and was particularly important, the major national newspapers were rarely available in the provinces on a timely basis. Regional audiences usually turned to local broadcasters and press for their news.

At the regional level, as at the national level, the broadcasters and newspapers were generally loyal to one or another group—either the ruling authorities or powerful business groups that had strong political interests that were sometimes opposed to those of the governor. In regions where the governor had been able to marginalize his political opposition, he had almost exclusive control over the media. Often the regional authorities paid the salaries of the major broadcasters and received in return television and radio coverage that supported their point of view. Additionally, they usually controlled newspaper office buildings and the only printing press in the region, with the result that they could expect favorable coverage in the press as well. By accrediting some sources and not others, and by doling out information to favored journalists, the authorities could put the rest at a disadvantage.

In addition, the governors often used their control of regional media to blame federal authorities for the many unresolved problems in their regions. Such tactics gave them some popularity at home and helped them in their struggle to extract resources from Moscow. With few exceptions, the press suffered from a lack of legislative support, poor backing from the courts, little public demand for better analysis, and low levels of professionalism among journalists. Many of the latter, with low incomes, have been happy to take money from government bodies, according, for example, to Dmitri Strovsky, a journalism professor in Yekaterinburg, and Robert Coalson, who headed the National Press Institute's office in Saint Petersburg.

Predictably, the Putin team's strategy vis-à-vis the media has been to centralize control, a process begun in 1999. It has been working to put the Kremlin's stamp on the major television channels. At the regional level, each of his seven envoys has been setting up a "unified information space" in his okrug. Each okrug is opening a federal center for information and analysis, which will be supported by the local branch of the state-owned news agency RIA Novosti. Additionally, Putin has decreed that the envoys, not the governors as in the past, will approve the appointment of the regional chief for the country's second most important state-owned national television network, Russian Television. On September 28, 2000, the government, working closely with Gleb Pavlovsky, a long-time political strategist and organizer of dirty tricks for the Kremlin, set up a new current events website (www.strana.ru) that provides a uniform source of news and analysis for the okrugs. This effort appears to be only one part of a multipronged strategy for introducing government censorship of the major media. For example, the biggest television network, recently renamed First Channel, had by 2002 become subject to regular and detailed censorship of its news programs by officials in Putin's PA.

Also, since the loyalty of the media is determined primarily by who pays the bills, the Putin team has been emphasizing to the regional editors of state channels that their paycheck comes from the federal government, not the governor. In July 1999, the State Press Committee was upgraded to the status of a ministry. It has offices in every region. Now federal media subsidies are passing through the ministry rather than, as before, the regional administrations. The Kremlin is also tightening media licensing procedures to further insure that the press and broadcasters do not exceed narrow limits in criticizing state bodies. Since the federal government owns the regional printing presses that have hitherto been controlled by the governors, it is likely to reassert its full ownership rights.

As their partners in controlling the media, the Putin team looks to such giant semiprivate corporations as the gas company Gazprom. Gazprom appears to own as many as two hundred regional television stations and one hundred newspapers. In the past, the company has purchased media outlets and then turned control over to mayors in exchange for behind-the-scenes support. Under Putin Gazprom has apparently turned over control of this network to the PA, in exchange for concessions to Gazprom's business interests.

In these circumstances, the Internet becomes more important as an outlet for independent news analysis. But here too the FSB has been active, taking measures to monitor and potentially control electronic information flows.

In sum, then, the Putin team's reforms do not seek to make the media freer. Rather, the president is trying to replace the control once exercised by the governors and some national oligarchs with levers more easily and aggressively exercised by the Kremlin and its surrogates.

Notes

1. See Putin's comments making this point in his interview with ORT, RTR, and *Nezavisimaya gazeta* in *Nezavisimaya gazeta*, December 26, 2000.

2. Jeronim Perovic, "Regionalization Under Putin: Old Models and New Trends," paper prepared for the seminar at the Davis Center for Russian Studies, Harvard University, March 19, 2002.

3. See Alla Chirikova and Natalia Lapina, "Regional Elite: A Quiet Revolution on a Russian Scale," Working Paper no. 4, February 2001, Center for Security Studies and Conflict Research, Zurich, 67 (www.isn.ethz.ch/russia/).

4. "Polozhenie o polnomochnom predstavitele Prezidenta Rossiiskoi Federatsii v federalnom okruge," May 13, 2000, in *Rossiiskaya gazeta*, May 16, 2000.

5. An August 12, 2000, government decree defines how the envoys interact with the government. For the text, see *Rossiiskaya gazeta*, August 22, 2000.

6. See, for example, the interview with Kirienko in *Nezavisimaya gazeta*, December 3, 2002, and *Argumenty i Fakty*, no. 20, 2002.

7. *Ezhenedelnyi zhurnal* (www.ej.ru), April 29, 2002.

8. Before his appointment as a cabinet secretary, Tom Ridge faced similar problems in his efforts to coordinate U.S. federal agencies as the director of homeland security, *New York Times*, February 7, 2002.

9. Yuri Levada, "The Year of 'Symbolic Order,'" *Russia on Russia: Administrative and State Reforms in Russia*, no. 5 (June 2001): 3.

10. RFE/RL Newsline, August 7, 2002.

11. At www.scrf.gov.ru/Documents/Sessions.htm.

12. Neil Parison, "Civil Service Reform: For Real This Time?" *Moscow Times*, May 17, 2002.

13. *Vremya MN*, March 29, 2002.

14. See Rostislav Turovskii, "Itogi i uroki gubernatorskikh vyborov," in Tsentr politicheskikh tekhnologii, *Politika v regionakh: gubernatory i gruppy vliyaniya*, Moscow, 2002, 38.

15. Organization for Economic Cooperation and Development, *Economic Survey of the Russian Federation*, February 2002 (www.oecd.org), 156.

16. See Duma Member Vladimir Ryzhkov's article "Novyi zastoi," *Vedomosti*, July 23, 2003.

17. *Argumenty i fakty*, December 4, 2002.

18. Olga Petrova and Yelena Tregubova, "Semero po vertikali," *Kommersant Vlast'*, December 12, 2000.

19. The others are the Media Ministry, the Health Ministry, the Pension Fund, KFKM, the Customs agency, Tax Collection Ministry, Federal Bankruptcy Service, Securities and Exchange Commission, Goskomstat, Ministry of Natural Resources, Property Ministry, Transport Ministry, and FAPSI.

20. *Izvestiya*, May 12, 2002.

21. "O vnesenii dopolneniya i izmeneniya v Polozhenie o polnomochnom predstavitele Prezidenta Rossiiskoi Federatsii v federal'nom okruge, utverzhdennoe Ukazom

Prezidenta Rossiiskoi Federatsii ot 13 mai 2000 g. No. 849" (accessed at http://president.kremlin.ru/pressa/2001013003.html).

22. Deputy head of the PA Aleksandr Abramov replaced Samoilov. See Irina Isakova, *Regionalization of Security in Russia,* Whitehall Paper Series no. 53, Royal United Services Institute for Defense Studies, 2001, 15.

23. The full text of Russia's budgets are available online at www.budgetrf.ru. The 2001 figure for the administration's overall expenses came from Vladimir Ivanov of the East-West Institute's Moscow Center.

24. For the text of the law defining these changes, see "O poryadke formirovaniya Soveta Federatsii Federalnogo Sobraniya Rossiiskoi Federatsii," *Rossiiskaya gazeta,* August 8, 2000.

25. Matthew Hyde, "Putin's Federal Reforms and Their Implications for Presidential Power in Russia," *Europe-Asia Studies* 53, no. 5 (2001): 719–43.

26. See *Russian Regional Report,* May 31, 2000.

27. *Nezavisimaya gazeta,* April 30, 2002, and Rodion Mikhailov, "Kto upravlyaet Sovetom Federatsii: Kreml, FPG, KPRF, ili regional'nye elity?" SMI.ru, March 12, 2002.

28. For a list of the various industries represented in the Federation Council, see Aleksei Makarkin, "Sovet Federatsii: Novyi sostav, novye problemy," in *Politika v regionakh: gubernatory i gruppy vliyaniya* (Moscow: Tsentr politicheskikh tekhnologii, 2002), 59–68.

29. *Moskovskii komsomolets,* March 26, 2002.

30. Andrei Zakharov and Alexander Kapishin, "The State Council in the Russian Power System," *Russia on Russia,* no. 5, "Administrative and State Reforms in Russia," June 2001, 14.

31. *Rossiiskaya gazeta,* September 5, 2000.

32. *Nezavisimaya gazeta,* February 27, 2002.

33. *Rossiiskaya gazeta,* August 1, 2000. President Yeltsin vetoed a bill in 1998 that would have given the president this power. See Vladimir Lysenko, "The Federation Council Fails to Become a House of Lords," *Russia on Russia,* no. 5, "Administrative and State Reforms in Russia," June 2001, 19.

34. *Russian Regional Report,* April 10, 2002.

35. *Kommersant Vlast',* June 26, 2001.

36. *Nezavisimaya gazeta,* January 28, 2002.

37. RFE/RL Newsline, February 5, 2003.

38. David S.G. Goodman, ed., *China's Provinces in Reform: Class, Community, and Political Culture* (London and New York: Routledge, 1997), 1–2.

39. Organization for Economic Cooperation and Development, *Economic Survey of the Russian Federation,* February 2002, (www.oecd.org).

40. RFE/RL Russian Federation Report, September 24, 2001.

41. Communication from Vladimir Ivanov, EWI Moscow Center, March 1, 2002. Nikolai Petrov estimates the federal take at 63 percent (Carnegie Endowment for International Peace Meeting Summary, "Russian Federal Reform: Implications for Security, Civilians, and the State," December 5, 2002, www.ceip.org). While the actual number is in dispute, the trend line is clear.

42. Prime-Tass, April 25, 2002.

43. For a history of Russia's key taxes, see *Federal'nyi byudzhet i regiony: struktura finansovykh potokov*, (Moscow: Institut Vostok-Zapad, 2001), 54–56. From 1994 through the first quarter of 1999, the regions received 25 percent of the VAT.

44. *Ekspert*, July 24, 2000.

45. Polit.ru, January 30, 2003.

46. Polit.ru, April 25, 2002, quoting that day's *Vedomosti*.

47. Moody's Investors Service, *Russian Regions: Outlook 2001*, November 2001.

48. See *Russian Regional Report*, September 5, 2001.

49. *Russian Regional Report*, February 27, 2002.

50. *Russian Regional Report*, August 29, 2001.

51. Accounting Chamber head Sergei Stepashin was seeking a larger role for his agency in monitoring interbudgetary relations, but in many cases he lacked regional agencies that were truly independent of the regional authorities. He also faced opposition from the Finance Ministry, which did not want to be subject to outside oversight. In the Volga okrug, Stepashin set up his office in Ufa and worked closely with Rakhimov. *Kommersant Daily*, January 29, 2002, and *Nezavisimaya gazeta*, February 12, 2002.

52. Virginie Coulloudon, "Putin's Anti-corruption Reforms," in *Putin's Russia: Past Imperfect, Future Uncertain*, ed. Dale Herspring (Lanham, Md.: Rowman & Littlefield, 2003), 85–105; and Virginie Coulloudon, "Russia's Distorted Anti-corruption Campaigns," in *Political Corruption in Transition: A Sceptic's Handbook*, ed. Stephen Kotkin and Andras Sajo (Budapest: Central European University Press, 2002), 187–205.

53. At www.transparency.org/pressreleases_archive/2002/2002.08.28.cpi.en.html.

54. Alla Chirikova and Natalia Lapina, "Regional Elite: A Quiet Revolution on a Russian Scale," Working Paper no. 4, February 2001, Center for Security Studies and Conflict Research, Zurich, www.isn.ethz.ch/russia/, 16–17.

55. "O vnesenii izmenenii i dopolneniya v stati 7 i 9 zakona Rossiiskoi Federatsii 'O militsii,'" August 4, 2001.

56. L.A. Kravchenko, "Federalnyi zakon 'O vnesenii izmenenii i dopolneniya v stati 7 i 9 zakona Rossiiskoi Federatsii 'O militsii,'" *Sovet Federatsii i konstitutsionnye protsessy v sovremennoi Rossii*, no. 0 *(sic)*, October 2001, www.ilpp.ru/bulletin/index .html.

57. *Izvestiya*, May 31, 2001.

58. Nikolai Petrov, "Power Ministries and Federal Reform in Russia," PONARS Policy Memo no. 282, October 2002.

59. Comments of Deputy Minister of Internal Affairs Vladimir Vasilev reported in polit.ru, February 11, 2002.

60. See, for example, *Nezavisimaya gazeta*, December 11, 2001.

61. See, for example, *Nezavisimaya gazeta*, January 28, 2002.

62. Peter Reddaway, "Is Putin's Power More Formal than Real?" *Post-Soviet Affairs* 18, no. 1 (January 2002): 31–40.

63. *Russian Regional Report*, January 16, 2002.

64. For a discussion of the way the Soviet system worked, see James R. Harris, *The Great Urals: Regionalism and the Evolution of the Soviet System* (Ithaca, N.Y.: Cornell University Press, 1999).

65. See particularly "W(h)ither the Central State? The Regional Sources of Russia's Stalled Reforms," at www.princeton.edu/%7Ekesw/pubs.htm

66. *Izvestiya*, February 18, 2002.

67. *Vek*, June 29, 2001.

68. This analysis and terminology follow Natalya Zubarevich, "Russia's Big Businesses in Regional Elections," *Russian Regional Report*, January 30, 2002.

69. Sergei Porshakov, "'Vrashchayushchayasya dver' ustanovlena," *Izvestiya*, February 18, 2002.

70. See *Russian Regional Report*, October 24, 2001.

71. This is also discussed in chapter 8, on the Siberian okrug by Maksim Shandarov.

72. See the law "O politicheskikh partiyakh," which President Putin signed on July 11, 2001.

73. This law is entitled "Ob osnovnykh garantiyakh izbiratel'nykh prav i prava na uchastie v referendume grazhdan RF."

74. Polit.ru, February 18, 2003.

75. *Nezavisimaya gazeta*, March 6, 2002.

76. *Russian Regional Report*, February 3, 2003.

77. *Kommersant Daily*, February 8, 2002.

78. The outline of the reform appeared in the bills entitled "On the general principles for organizing local government in Russia," and "On the introduction of changes and amendments to the law 'On the general principles for organizing legislative and executive branch state organs in the regions of the Russian Federation.'" These bills were both available on the Duma website: www.duma.ru.

79. Bank of Finland's Institute on Transition, *Russian and Baltic Economies: The Week in Review*, May 10, 2002.

80. *Ekspert*, December 17, 2001.

81. *Russian Regional Report*, December 5, 2001.

82. See *Russian Regional Report*, March 5, 2003.

83. *Nezavisimaya gazeta*, January 24, 2002.

84. Teleinform News Agency (Irkutsk), January 30, 2002.

85. A report authored by the European Commission, the Russian Anti-monopoly Commission, and TACIS came to this conclusion. See Simon Ostrovsky, "Report Finds Small Business on the Rise," *Moscow Times*, July 2, 2002.

86. See the arguments of Lilia Shevtsova in *Obshchaya gazeta*, January 10, 2002.

87. Nikolai Petrov, "Politicization versus Democratization: 20 Months of Putin's 'Federal' Reform", PONARS Policy Memo no. 241, December 2001.

88. *Russian Regional Report*, September 5, 2001.

89. Andrew Konitzer-Smirnov, "Electoral Rules Block Voters from Punishing Bad Governors," *Russian Regional Report*, August 29, 2001.

90. Parts of the section on the media first appeared in an earlier Carnegie Corporation publication: Peter Reddaway and Robert Orttung, "Russian State-Building: The Regional Dimension," *The Russia Initiative: Reports of the Four Task Forces* (New York: Carnegie Corporation of New York, 2001).

3

North-West Federal Okrug

Alexander Duka and Peter Rutland

THE NORTH-WEST FEDERAL OKRUG INCLUDES *the city of Saint Petersburg; the regions of Leningrad, Vologda, Murmansk, Kaliningrad, Novgorod, Pskov, and Arkhangel'sk; the republics of Komi and Karelia; and the Nenets Autonomous Okrug.*

Viktor Cherkesov (born 1950) graduated from the law faculty of Leningrad State University, as did Putin.[1] After a brief spell in the Procuracy, he joined the KGB in 1975 and rose up the ladder of the investigations department of the Leningrad administration.[2] From 1992 to 1998, he headed this administration, during which the organization changed its name several times, ending up as the Federal Security Service (FSB). For many years he was actively involved in the persecution of political dissidents, and in 1996 he led the case against Captain Aleksandr Nikitin, accused of espionage for his work with the Norwegian environmentalist group Bellona. Nikitin was found innocent in the fall of 1999. On August 27, 1998, after Putin became director of the FSB, Cherkesov became one of its first deputy directors, with the rank of lieutenant general, and later was promoted to colonel general.[3] His final job before being appointed as an envoy was directing the FSB's work in Russia's regions: one can also speculate that he may have been involved at an early stage with the designing of the federal–regional reform itself.[4] His wife, Natalya Chaplina, is editor in chief of Chas Pik, *a prominent Saint Petersburg newspaper; and the founder of RosBalt, an influential news agency. He served as envoy from May 2000 until March 10, 2003, when Putin appointed him to head a new state body for combating the narcotics trade and replaced him with a former deputy prime minister, Valentina Matvienko.*

North West Federal District of the Russian Federation

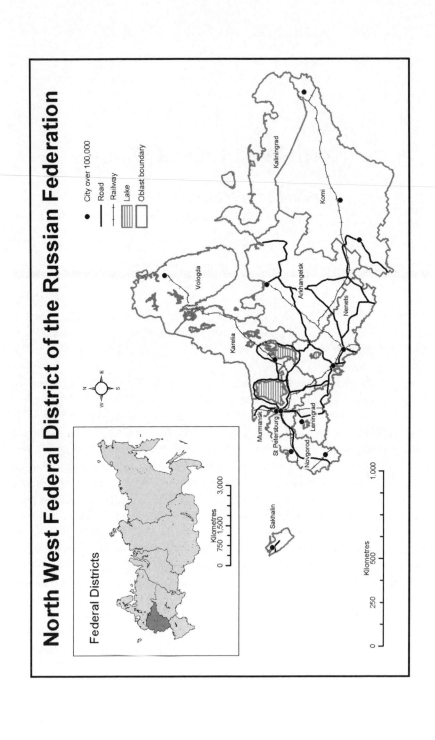

Okrug Overview

The North-West Federal Okrug constitutes 10 percent of Russia's territory, and its 14.4 million inhabitants make up 10 percent of the population.[5] Since the founding of Saint Petersburg three hundred years ago, the region has served as Russia's principal gateway to the outside world: "the window on the West" or, as cynics would have it, the "spy hole on the West."[6] This gateway role is perhaps the chief characteristic governing the priorities given to presidential envoy Viktor Cherkesov. It has both a security and an economic dimension. While the security factor is paramount in two other frontier okrugs—the Southern and Far Eastern—in the North-West both security and economic dimensions are important.

From the economic point of view, the region's proximity and ease of access to Europe mean that it is an important entrepot for exports and imports. It is also second only to Moscow as a favored destination for foreign investors.

From the security point of view, the region has 3,250 kilometers of border with seven states, sixty-five border crossing points, and twenty-two million visitors annually.[7] The okrug abuts NATO member Norway in the far north and is home to the troubled Northern Fleet. It shares a long border with European Union (EU) member Finland. Russia seized a large chunk of territory from Finland, the bulk of present-day Kareliya, at the end of World War II, but Finland does not harbor a claim to the territory (unlike Japan, which still claims the Kurile Islands, seized in 1945). The okrug also neighbors Estonia and Latvia, two countries whose relations with Russia are tense because of the presence of large Russian minorities who have not been granted citizenship. The region also has a frontier and active cross-border trade with Belarus.

The region includes the exclave of Kaliningrad, precariously located between Lithuania and Poland, and physically separated from "mainland" Russia. The geographic isolation of Kaliningrad, together with the preponderance of military facilities in that province, has made it specially prone to economic dislocation, crime, and corruption. The question of transit for Russian citizens to and from Kaliningrad has emerged as a major bone of contention between Russia and the European Union. In preparation for Poland's and Lithuania's entry to the EU, both countries effectively ended visa-free travel for Russians to and from Kaliningrad in the fall of 2002. Security Council secretary Sergei Ivanov has said that Kaliningrad must not become a "besieged fortress" after the expansion of the European Union in 2003, and he warned apropos of demilitarization of the region that "Russia has no obligations not to have tactical nuclear weapons in the Kaliningrad Region."[8]

For these reasons, the North-West region plays a direct and important role whenever discussion in Moscow turns to questions of border regimes, customs procedures, immigration controls, and the like. Such factors are increasingly important to Russian foreign policy as it seeks entry to the World Trade Organization (WTO) and closer ties with the EU. These issues are of direct concern to the Kremlin, and one can suppose that they are too important to be left to the vagaries of border region governors.

When the plans for the creation of the okrugs were being prepared, the second war in Chechnya was in full swing, and the new Russian president took the threat of separatism seriously. Kaliningrad, obviously, is near the top of the list of regions that could conceivably break off from Russia, simply because it is physically separate from the rest of the country.[9] Hence on July 13, 2002, Putin appointed Dmitrii Rogozin as his special envoy to deal with negotiations with the EU over Kaliningrad. (Chechnya is the only other Russian region to merit such an envoy.) There was discussion in spring 2001 of turning Kaliningrad into a separate, eighth okrug, but the Security Council rejected this idea in a meeting on July 26, 2001. Instead, it decided to launch a special federal program for the region, to be supervised by one of Cherkesov's deputies.[10]

The other salient fact to bear in mind about the North-West is that it is the home territory of President Vladimir Putin. He spent the bulk of his career in Saint Petersburg, first in the KGB (where he also served five years in East Germany), then as an aide to the first postcommunist mayor Anatolii Sobchak. Prior to his appointment as prime minister in 1999, he had only served three years in Moscow. As president, Putin continues to visit Petersburg frequently and has arranged many visits by foreign heads of state to the "northern capital." It has now become a standard stop in either the official or the unofficial part of visits by foreign presidents and prime ministers. This was never the practice under previous Russian and Soviet leaders. Cherkesov has even spoken out cautiously in favor of transferring some capital functions to Petersburg on a permanent basis.[11]

The renewed national and international visibility of Saint Petersburg has a significance beyond mere nostalgia. In Russia's patronage-based politics, Putin has relied heavily on the drafting of personnel from Saint Petersburg to staff his administration in Moscow.[12] This practice suggests that the region probably enjoys privileged access to Putin's ear and correspondingly favorable treatment by the federal government. Such a "special relationship" was underlined by the fact that Putin appointed a close colleague and ally from the Federal Security Service (FSB), Viktor Cherkesov, to head the North-West okrug.

Who Is Viktor Cherkesov?

Cherkesov's KGB career closely parallels that of Putin's. Of all the presidential envoys, Cherkesov probably has the best personal and professional relationship with the president. One of his nicknames is "the second Putin."[13] Dmitrii Oreshkin argues that his "fate was apparently predetermined by the years spent together with Vladimir Putin at the Leningrad University Law School."[14]

In early 2000, when Putin was running for the presidency, Cherkesov took a couple of weeks' formal leave from the FSB in order to campaign for Putin.[15] An interview with Igor Chernyak revealed the awkwardness of the shift from KGB to campaigning:

> QUESTION: You are known as 'Putin's man,' one of his closest confidants. How do you feel about this role?
> CHERKESOV: I do not feel anything about it.
> QUESTION: You must know him very well indeed, after all these years. . .
> CHERKESOV: As I see it, Putin's style is contrary to the labels that some circles are trying to apply to him. . . . So all these speculations about him being a mystery man are rubbish.
> QUESTION: You are playing a key part in the 'St. Petersburg team.' At the same time, this team is gaining dominance in the top power structures. Do you think this state of affairs is appropriate?
> CHERKESOV: I would not say that there are very many people from St. Petersburg near Putin, in the government. . . . Of course, he prefers to work with people he knows, and what is wrong with that?"

Commentators differ about the effectiveness of Cherkesov in his new role. Some say he is clever; others say that he will never overcome his KGB background and proclivity for shadowy "analysis and control."[16] A February 2001 comparative analysis of the seven envoys rated their performance in terms of influence on gubernatorial elections, volume of regional laws changed, and mentions in their okrug press.[17] Cherkesov finished in fourth place overall. For example, he had managed to change 180 out of 280 regional laws that violated federal legislation (i.e., 64 percent, compared to Kazantsev's 78 percent). Similarly, a February 2001 opinion poll found Cherkesov's name was known by only 20 percent of respondents in his okrug, behind Pulikovskii (49 percent), Kirienko (46 percent), and Kazantsev (35 percent), but ahead of Drachevskii (10 percent) and Poltavchenko (3 percent).[18] Surveys of elite assessment of Cherkesov's role within Petersburg see him as politically influential, second only to Governor Yakovlev but marginal in economic terms— variously estimated at ninth to fifteenth in rank, according to polls conducted in mid-2001 to early 2003.[19]

Initially there was much speculation that Cherkesov's job performance was not all that important, since he was being groomed for a Moscow position— perhaps procurator general. Reportedly he was openly critical of Procurator

General Vladimir Ustinov, saying for example "If we look at the future, Ustinov is defending ideas that are on their way out."[20] But it took Putin three years to move Cherkesov.

The most striking characteristic of Cherkesov is his secretive style. He has not tried to establish a very visible presence in the local political landscape. This presumably has something to do with his background in the KGB and FSB, and a penchant for discretion and indirect influence. But it makes it rather difficult for him to do his job as a public official in what is a more-or-less open and democratic society.

In his public comments, Cherkesov talks of the role of presidential envoy in expansive terms. He argues that in 2000 "the threat of the country's collapse was real and high"[21] and that this existential challenge was the fundamental reason for the introduction of the new agency. He told an interviewer that the envoys "were not introduced out of the goodness of life. The hierarchy of political power *(vertikal' vlasti)* had practically disappeared. . . . The country was becoming less and less governable."[22] He continued, "But in order to change this situation a strengthening of power structures is not enough. There must be a change in the moral climate of society. . . . I consider the development of such a dialog between state and society one of the envoys' most important tasks. In my view, this means making the work of all state structures transparent for citizens."

Cherkesov is confident that the envoys have accomplished their primary mission. "Today we can say with certainty that the collapse of the Russian state has been halted."[23] He sees nothing sinister in military and security figures' having a prominent role in the political process, including some who have won elections. "Perhaps they were elected because the electors have lost faith in the ability of classic democrats to provide order and stability."

The Work of the Presidential Envoy

The main tasks of the envoys are supervising the implementation of federal laws and programs, as well as gathering information and making analyses to assist the president with future policy formation.[24] Cherkesov's staff is fairly modest: reportedly about a hundred persons.[25] He has ten deputies, some drawn from the military and FSB, others from the local political establishment.[26] There is an office of six to eight people in each of the eleven regions, and it is not clear how many, if any, of these seventy to ninety people are included in the figure of one hundred given above. Each regional office is headed by a chief federal inspector (CFI).[27] These inspectors replaced the presidential representatives created by Boris Yeltsin in 1991. Mostly new men were chosen: only two of eleven CFIs in the North-West were formerly presidential representatives, a stark contrast with the situation in the Central okrug.

At the end of 2001 Cherkesov saw his two top deputies leave for higher positions. Aleksandr Kuznetsov became first deputy railways minister, and Vladimir V'yunov was appointed head of the Northwest Customs Administration. V'yunov was replaced as first deputy envoy by Mikhail Motsak, former head of the northern fleet.[28] (Another ex-admiral was named as a Murmansk representative in the Federation Council.) Motsak had been among the naval commanders reprimanded in the wake of the Kursk submarine tragedy "for serious errors in the daily and military instruction work of the fleet."

The departments of the envoy's administration are concerned with monitoring regional laws to ensure compliance with federal legislation; economic and financial control; personnel and awards; social, economic, and political monitoring; and military and security coordination. It also contains, as a department, the Okrug Inspectorate of the PA's Main Monitoring Administration.[29] Further, Cherkesov created three advisory councils: Economy and Investment (including federal agencies, regional authorities, business people, and foreign investors); Law Enforcement Agencies and Security; and a Societal Issues Council (to study public opinion).[30] The latter is made up of thirty-three representatives of NGOs and has created eleven working groups.[31]

The broad public expectation was that the okrugs would become power links in a vertical chain of command, superregions that would restore Kremlin control over the multitude of excessively independent governors. However, officials from the envoy's staff explained the rationale for the institution in more straightforward terms.[32] Prior to the appearance of the envoys, presidential power was not really felt at the regional level. All that the former presidential representatives could do was to report back, passively, on what was happening: "Previously, presidential power resided only in Moscow. The presidential representative of that time could do almost nothing, even in the event of serious violations. The job of the new envoy was to create an institutional structure which would bring the presidency closer to the ground and create an instrument that could potentially be used to intervene in local abuses." As Cherkesov himself put it: "Now presidential power has been brought to earth, to the territory of Russia."

Outside observers were expecting a massive centralization of power, like in Soviet times. This has not occurred. Moreover, the fact that the tasks assigned them, and the powers granted to realize these goals, are rather limited suggests that Putin never intended the envoys to become the Leviathan that some commentators suggested.

Their task was simpler: to prevent the break-up of the Russian Federation, to control the governors and presidents who were openly flouting the legal authority of Moscow. The reassertion of Russian state sovereignty required the creation of a unified legal and economic space.[33] A secondary goal was to be the eyes and ears of the president in the regions. (Cherkesov once referred to himself as "the tsar's eye," or *glaz tsarya*.)[34] Both of these were more political propaganda goals than administrative goals. But now that the first goal has been accomplished, it is not clear what follows next.

The envoys were not given a clear position in the chain of command. Their legal and constitutional status is ill-defined.[35] They have small staffs and no direct responsibility for the spending of federal funds or for the implementation of the laws. Organizations already exist to perform these functions, such as the Finance Ministry, the Justice Ministry, and the Procuracy. In August 2000 Sergei Kirienko asked that envoys be given direct control over the disbursement of some federal funds, but Sergei Samoilov, then head of the PA's territorial administration, beat back this challenge to his authority, persuading Putin that the necessary systems regarding spending were already in place.[36] The envoys have not found a clear and recognized niche within the organizational chart of Russian public administration. Rather they are seen as an additional and somewhat superfluous layer of central control.

The main role of the envoys has been to gather information and report back to the Kremlin, and to liaise with the governors. It is also clear that not only the staffing but also the functions of the envoys are to some extent an extension of the FSB—not so much in its repressive functions, but in both its intelligence-gathering and public opinion–influencing functions.

The role of envoys in the central government seems to be less than many observers had anticipated. Their monthly meetings give them direct access to Putin, but they have not displaced the PA's responsibility for regional policy. To an extent they have become players in the national political game as individuals. They are often cited as candidates for federal office, and members of their staffs are tapped for federal positions.

To get some idea of at least the formal façade of Cherkesov's duties, we can examine the official record regarding his meetings and events, as given on the okrug press office website.[37] (See table 3.1.) Scrutiny of the 245 activities reported during the fourteen months from August 2000 to September 2001 reveals that a substantial 34 percent of meetings were devoted to the economy and 15 percent to legal affairs. A surprising 13 percent concerned diplomatic activity, such as a three-day trip to Finland in March 2001.[38] This was about the same as his involvement in security matters (12 percent), which attracted close attention in the press. These economic and diplomatic activities did not figure prominently in the initial rationale for creating the institution of the envoys, nor is there substantial evidence that these activities have produced much in the way of concrete results, as we shall see below. They are perhaps evidence of the sort of "mission creep" often found in bureaucratic agencies.

Based on the experience of the North-West okrug, one can identify the main political tasks of the envoy as these: getting regional laws rewritten to conform to federal law; supervision of security institutions; monitoring elec-

TABLE 3.1
Work of the Presidential Envoy's Staff, August 2000–September 2001

Sphere of Activity	Events/Meetings	
	Number	% of total
Economics	83	34
of which:		
Socioeconomic Situation	12	5
Socioeconomic Cooperation	26	11
Investment	16	7
Relations with Business	4	2
Federal Programs	2	1
Technology	1	
Public administration	36	15
of which:		
Laws and Implementation of Laws	15	6
International Relations, Diplomacy	31	13
Social Policy (including Housing, Health Care)	23	9
Security	16	7
of which:		
Defense	7	3
Border Issues	1	
Law Enforcement	6	2
Customs	1	
Culture, Science, Education	15	6
Military Structures	13	5
Organizational Questions, Honorary Occasions	9	4
Crime	4	2
of which:		
Corruption	2	1
Mass Media	3	1
Elections	3	1
Environment	2	1
Other	7	3
Total	245	100

Source: Derived from information provided by the North-West Federal Okrug press office at http://falcon.sinaps.ru/polpred/news.html

tions and using elections to try to remove objectionable governors; battling corruption; helping economic development; and monitoring the mass media.

Strengthening the "Hierarchy of Political Power" *(vertikal' vlasti)*

The first and most pressing duty was to insist that regional laws be rewritten to conform to federal legislation. This was done quickly and fairly smoothly—although it is an open question whether implementation of the new laws will differ from past practices. In the style of a Soviet era campaign, there was a push to complete as many as possible of the revisions by December 2000, with regions reporting on what percentage of laws had been changed.[39] (The Justice Ministry had already prepared detailed lists of what legal corrections needed to be made in the statutes and laws of each region.) In May 2002 Cherkesov said that enforcing the revision of six hundred deviant laws throughout the okrug was his major achievement.[40] This campaign is now proceeding to a second stage—the cancellation of the bilateral treaties that many regions signed with the federal government during the Yeltsin era. By the end of 2002, Kaliningrad, Saint Petersburg, and Murmansk had still not taken action on this.[41]

Relations with Federal Ministries

With the various federal agencies having, in all, several hundred offices throughout the okrug's eleven regions, one major challenge is to bring about a clear chain of command and minimize the number of structures with "dual subordination," that is, those that are accountable to both regional and federal authorities. A nationwide innovation aimed at achieving this was the opening of branches at the okrug level by various federal agencies, including the Justice Ministry, the Procuracy, Tax Service, Customs Service, and Interior Ministry (MVD).[42] This gave Cherkesov—and the Inspectorate of the PA's Main Monitoring Administration that had been formed to act as one of his departments—direct access to the vertical chains of command in these huge bureaucracies. In principle, therefore, the latter could now be better monitored.[73] On the other hand, the structural innovation also created in these federal agencies a whole new layer of bureaucrats and thus inevitably gave birth to additional opportunities for corruption, delays, and the growth of vested bureaucratic interests.

In a bid to improve coordination of military units in the okrug, Cherkesov created a coordinating council of military management units, which periodically meets and discusses issues such as the impact of military reform.[44]

Gaining control over the appointment of regional police chiefs was clearly a top priority for Putin, who saw a real threat of regional leaders creating their own security networks. This process has apparently gone smoothly in the North-West okrug under the direction of okrug MVD chief Boris Uyemlyanin. In December 2001 a criminal case was launched against the criminal police chief in Murmansk, leading to the prompt resignation of the regional police chief and his first deputy.[45] The new regional chief was brought in from Vologda region, as is consistent with Putin's policy of rotating police chiefs among regions.

In September 2001 the central MVD sent a special five-man team to work closely with the envoy's office on "decriminalizing" the city of Saint Petersburg.[46] On July 9, 2002, Putin appointed Mikhail Vanechkin as the new city police chief, replacing Veniamin Petukhov.[47] Unlike his predecessors, Vanechkin came from Moscow and was an outsider to the Petersburg force. Despite this difference, it is hard to know if the appointment will improve past practices, since Vanechkin was the fourth new police chief in Petersburg in five years, and the sixth in ten years.[48] Following his appointment, the MVD launched a month-long investigation of the Saint Petersburg police by a 120-strong commission, whose members hailed from Moscow and the North-West okrug's MVD branch.[49] It declared the police's work a failure *(neud)*, but limited itself to recommending personnel, not structural changes. Since the Petersburg police had been under special monitoring by the central MVD over the previous four years, following the murder of State Duma member Galina Starovoitova in November 1998, it seems unlikely that much will change with the appointment of yet another police chief and the conduct of one more investigation.[50]

The envoy still has a long way to go to function as an effective monitor and coordinator of federal agencies in the okrug. Such a basic function as recommending (or approving) officials for appointment to federal organs, as was carried out by Communist Party committees in Soviet times, seems beyond his grasp at present, although Putin in his annual address to parliament in April 2002 seemed to place this issue on the agenda.[51]

Relations with the Governors

It was reasonable to expect that the envoys' relations with the governors would be difficult. The envoys represented a new institution that had been injected into political structures developed under Yeltsin, structures that gave Russia's eighty-nine regional leaders considerable political and economic autonomy. The reform's goal was to restore the decayed "vertical hierarchy of political power," with the envoys drawing their authority from their appointment by, and ongoing personal contact with, President Putin. More power for the envoy would presumably mean less power for the governor.

In general, Cherkesov has kept his interactions with regional leaders well hidden. He seems to have good relations with the governors of Arkhangel'sk, Vologda, Karelia, and the new governors of Kaliningrad and Komi; but rather strained relations with Saint Petersburg's Vladimir Yakovlev, Leningrad region's Valerii Serdyukov, Novgorod's Mikhail Prusak, and Nenets's Vladimir

Butov. The envoy would undoubtedly be happy to see Pskov governor Yevgenii Mikhailov go, but the region seems to be too insignificant to attract much federal attention.

The Battle for Saint Petersburg

The key political relationship in the region is that between Cherkesov and Saint Petersburg governor Vladimir Yakovlev. Cherkesov has denied that he is angling to remove Yakovlev, calling himself "neither a governor nor a supergovernor."[52] But the city of Petersburg is the jewel in the okrug's crown, spending half of all the federal budget funds allocated to the okrug's regions. Cherkesov was hopeful that he would be able to take over the expected $1 billion of federal funds spent on preparing the city for its three hundredth jubilee in 2003, but he was, for a long time, frustrated. Some of this money went to the completion of ongoing projects: the ring road, the rebuilding of a collapsed metro line, and the refurbishment of the historic city center.[53] Additionally, in January 2002 the city won a $120 million World Bank loan to spend on jubilee projects.

Yakovlev fought the idea of Cherkesov's moving in on the city. "Consider the project for building a bypass around St. Petersburg," he said. "No one is able to do this without the governor and his staff. How to get a loan, who is to be responsible for repaying it? . . . Do you think the staff of the envoy will handle this?" Additionally, he noted that "During the meeting with President Putin we agreed that the envoys would not interfere with the work of the regions."[54] After some toing and froing over the jubilee spending, Cherkesov and Sergei Stephashin's Accounting Chamber (which is appointed by the Duma) agreed to monitor it jointly.[55]

Despite the heated political rhetoric surrounding the funding flows, the situation was relatively straightforward. There were two sources of financing for the three hundredth anniversary celebration: the federal budget and the city budget. Governor Yakovlev and his deputies executed the city budget and the city's Legislative Assembly monitored how the money was spent. Usually the federal treasury and procurator also play a role in monitoring the governor's use of funds. Additionally the Accounting Chamber and the PA's Monitoring Department can exert oversight. In the middle of 2002, the PA's Monitoring Department uncovered a number of violations in the way that the city was using its money.

Money from the federal budget goes directly from the Finance Ministry to the State Construction Commission to carry out federal programs. The city authorities have no oversight over this money. Rather federal agencies exert oversight. Problems were uncovered in the use of these funds as well, particularly with unused monies.

During a June 8, 2002, meeting with city leaders and representatives of several federal agencies, Putin sharply criticized the city and federal officials for mishandling funds set aside for the jubilee, and some of these criticisms were reported in the press.[56] However, in an interview he gave local television and one local newspaper, the president did not repeat his criticisms and declined to answer provocative questions.[57] At this time the city and federal government agreed to work together in building the ring road around Saint Petersburg. But several days later, the city administration withdrew from the project and agreed only to build access roads to the new highway.[58] Ultimately, at the beginning of 2003, Putin gave Cherkesov oversight over the construction of the ring road and the enormous dam in the Bay of Finland, which is supposed to protect the city from flooding.[59] At the same time, Stepashin seemed to be busy in the city rooting around for incriminating evidence against Yakovlev.[60]

Cherkesov also seems to have got directly involved in the plan to raise funds to rehabilitate the Konstantin Palace for President Putin's use, through voluntary contributions.[61] The first round in the jubilee war had broken out over Yakovlev's plan to move the zoo out of the city, triggering considerable public protests that were supported by Cherkesov. Yakovlev backed off.[62]

The two men compete for the loyalty of local business elites, who are divided into a pro-Yakovlev "left bank" and a Cherkesov "right bank," indicating the location of their respective headquarters.[63] (See also the following section on economics.) Overall, the two men have found an "uneasy symbiosis"[64] and tend to avoid each other at public gatherings whenever possible.[65]

Yakovlev's trump card has been his continued high public-trust rating, which is maintained by skillful patronage politics and the massaging of his image by a mostly compliant local media. He does face strong opposition from the liberal wing of the city's political elite, and he has difficult relations with the city's Legislative Assembly, rejecting almost half the bills it sends him for signature.[66]

In the summer of 2002 Yakovlev announced unambiguously that he wanted to seek a third term in 2004. However, the city's charter currently limits governors to two terms. If he had mustered two-thirds support in the Legislative Assembly, he might have amended the charter and thereby gained the opportunity to compete a third time. Such an extension would not have violated federal law. However, in the body that served until December 2002, Yakovlev did not have sufficient support and was unable to get the necessary amendments passed. In the campaigns for that month's elections, Cherkesov and Yakovlev sponsored opposing candidates in a bitter battle to secure as many legislative seats as possible. Ultimately, most incumbents managed to keep their seats, weakening Yakovlev's position.

Putin finally managed to secure his resignation following the 300th anniversary celebrations.

Relations with Other Governors

Novgorod governor Mikhail Prusak, who clearly has ambitions for a political career at the national level, has been one of the most outspoken critics of the federal okrug reform. He charged: "You can't lump together Karelia and Kaliningrad, or the Komi republic and St. Petersburg, because these are regions with completely different ways of life."[67] He complained also about Cherkesov's meetings with investors. "This is idiocy, a mistake. Why is the envoy organizing meetings on investments? Is he better able than I to attract investments?"[68] As for Cherkesov himself, Prusak said that "in terms of personal relations, Cherkesov is a talented man, he has proved that over the past year. But I think that in a bad system, good relations and good people do not exist."[69] In reply, Cherkesov criticized Prusak's record, arguing that the influx of foreign investment, for which the region has received considerable attention, had not reversed Novgorod's economic decline.

Leningrad governor Valerii Serdyukov is equally critical of Cherkesov. In the summer of 2002 he charged that Putin's decision to create the okrugs had not brought visible results. Instead of administrative procedures, the governor suggested that the federal government establish clear rules and laws. "We need to create the appropriate conditions for business, not set up gosplans [State Planning Commissions from the Soviet era]," he asserted.[70] He also argued that the attempts to pull the police and procurators away from the governors and put them under okrug control did not make sense. He claimed that ultimately these bodies worked in the regions, not in the okrugs. However, he agreed that the president should have the right to fire governors if they are not up to their jobs. Unlike Yakovlev, both Prusak and Serdyukov have good relations with Putin, and these ties to the president apparently enable them to criticize Cherkesov without fear of repercussions.

Cherkesov had testy relations with the governor of Komi Republic, Yurii Spiridonov. In June 2001 the Komi parliament passed constitutional amendments removing claims of sovereignty from Komi laws and agreeing that Komi cannot unilaterally allocate land or resources.[71] These changes were adopted despite protests from the nationalist Komi People's Congress that new federal budget rules would cost the republic 1.5 billion rubles in 2002.[72] Another blow to the region was Northern Oil's (Severnaya Neft's) decision in October 2001 to move its legal registration to Orel, a decision that cost the city of Usinsk a hefty chunk of its tax base. Commentator Yurii Shabaev suggests that the company expects to find more compliant local courts in Orel.[73] However, Spiridonov's electoral defeat in December 2001 brought to power a governor more willing to work with the federal government.

Cherkesov likewise has difficult relations with Nenets governor Vladimir Butov. Butov uses his position to promote the interests of companies close to him—at the cost of companies with ties to the envoy. The main battle is between Lukoil and Northern Oil for control of Nenets's lucrative oil deposits. Northern Oil, controlled by former deputy finance minister Andrei Vavilov, backed Butov for reelection in January 2001, while Lukoil, which is seen as close to Cherkesov, backed his main opponent, Aleksandr Shmakov, the deputy director of Lukoil subsidiary Polar Shine (Polyarnoe siyanie). Between May 2000 and January 2001, Cherkesov never once met with Butov, but he did publicly criticize the anomalous legal situation of Nenets, which is a sovereign subject of the federation but is also part of Arkhangel'sk region.[74] If Nenets were incorporated into Arkhangel'sk, presumably Butov would lose his job. However, Butov won the January 2001 election with 68 percent support and shrugged off a court challenge to the result.[75]

In stark contrast to his attitude to Butov, Cherkesov is fulsome in his praise for Anatolii Yefremov, governor of Arkhangel'sk, a region he has described as his "second homeland."[76] The region needs all the help it can get in dealing with its redundant military bases and decaying submarines, along with new investment for a gas pipeline and the Lomonosov diamond mine.[77] As for Kareliya's Sergei Katanandov, although he supported Moscow mayor Luzhkov's Fatherland party in the 1999 Duma race, subsequently he was demonstratively loyal to Putin to make up for this mistake. As a result, he seems to have been "forgiven" for betting on the wrong horse in what was effectively the first stage of the presidential campaign.

Gubernatorial Elections

In the first six gubernatorial elections that took place in the Northwest after his appointment, Cherkesov played no apparent role in two—those in Arkhangel'sk and Pskov. In one race where Cherkesov signaled that he wanted the incumbent defeated, his wishes were thwarted: as just noted, Nenets governor Butov won reelection. Cherkesov was openly hostile to Kaliningrad governor Leonid Gorbenko, who was defeated in the November 2000 election, as the Kremlin wished. Likewise in a December 2001 election, Cherkesov supported Komi parliament speaker Vladimir Torlopov, who managed to unseat the longtime incumbent Yurii Spiridonov (whose stance was discussed above).

The reelection of Petersburg governor Aleksandr Yakovlev in May 2000, just before Cherkesov's appointment, created, as we have seen, a major political obstacle for him. Yakovlev became governor in 1996 by running against his former boss Anatolii Sobchak, who was Putin's sponsor and mentor. Sobchak was bedeviled by accusations of corruption; and speaking at Sobchak's funeral in February 2000, an emotional Putin claimed that it was the pressure of these political struggles that had brought about his premature death. In April 2000 Putin encouraged Valentina Matvienko to take leave from her post as deputy prime minister for social policy in order to run against Yakovlev. Despite an expensive media campaign, her poor showing in opinion polls (she was barely winning 15 percent support) caused her to withdraw her candidacy a month before the election. Cherkesov was neutral in the subsequent race between Yakovlev and runner-up Igor Artemev, a leader of the local Yabloko party, since Yakovlev's victory was a foregone conclusion. Although it was clear that he wanted Yakovlev removed, Putin, ever the diplomat, never publicly confronted the Petersburg governor. When Yakovlev resigned, Putin appointed him deputy prime minister.

Appointments to the Federation Council

One of the key features of Putin's federal reforms was removing the governors and regional legislative chairmen from the Federation Council and replacing them with delegates from the regions' two branches of government. In the North-West, the PA and Cherkesov had the most impact on the Federation Council choices made by the politically weak regions of the okrug. Pskov appointed former members of Putin's campaign team as its senators, and Nenets appointed Yurii Volkov, a former KGB officer and deputy envoy who had served as Yurii Spiridonov's delegate to the Federation Council from Komi, at Moscow's behest, until Spiridonov lost his reelection bid. The Leningrad legislature also sent a former KGB officer with close ties to Putin, after the regional procurator protested successfully against a controversial attempt to nominate former privatization chief Alfred Kokh, who had a blemished record regarding various financial matters.[78] Additionally, the Saint Petersburg legislature, which often opposes Governor Yakovlev, chose Sergei Mironov, an old Putin ally who became the Federation Council's speaker on December 5, 2001, with the president's clear endorsement.

The PA's influence was much more limited in regions that either were less dependent on federal subsidies or had assertive leaders, such as Komi, Karelia, Murmansk, Novgorod, and Arkhangel'sk. In Komi, newly elected Governor Torlopov appointed Rakhim Azimov, a local businessman who had sponsored his campaign, in place of former deputy envoy Yuri Volkov, who, as we have seen, ended up representing Nenets. In Kareliya, Governor Sergei Katanandov was mostly thinking about the internal political situation in his republic when he appointed his immediate predecessor, Viktor Stepanov, as his delegate to the upper chamber, thereby removing a threat that Stepanov might again try running for governor.[79] Similar thinking was apparently behind the nomination of former regional Duma speaker Valerii Ustyugov from Kaliningrad.[80] Novgorod governor Prusak, in contrast, used his appointment to send an ally, former Duma deputy and Yeltsin aide Gennadii Burbulis, to Moscow. Overall, in the North-West the reform of the way Federation Council members are chosen did not give the PA a powerful weapon to use against regions that had the resources and desire to make their own choices.

Corruption

Successes, and particularly the lack thereof, in the battle against crime and corruption have featured prominently in the rhetoric of both supporters and critics of the envoy. In the North-West, the main crime problems revolve around alcohol, fuel, and the ports, according to a Cherkesov address to the okrug's Coordinating Council for Law Enforcement Activities.[81] Okrug-level agencies for the general procurator and the MVD's unit fighting organized crime have been created.[82] However, it is difficult to discern what concrete actions have resulted from this institutional innovation.

Cherkesov has repeatedly called for a tougher approach toward corruption. He told a March 2001 conference on the subject, pointedly held in Kaliningrad, that there were "no serious blows against corruption in 2000."[83] Cherkesov has also proclaimed his unhappiness with the battle against corruption in Novgorod, Leningrad region, Kareliya, and especially Nenets, whose law organs he wanted to merge with those of Arkhangel'sk.[84] The head of the organized crime unit in Kaliningrad was fired.[85] In Pskov, the regional procurator was fired, and Deputy Governor Dmitrii Dervoed was dismissed for corruption.[86]

Evidence of Cherkesov's willingness, in one case at least, to take on the Procuracy in a high-profile case is the statement issued by his press office after he met with okrug deputy procurator Vladimir Zubrin on December 5, 2000. Cherkesov admonished him for how the Procuracy had handled an investigation of the banking sector. The statement read: "Viktor Cherkesov also spoke about some recent armed operations regarding certain Petersburg banks. Without doubting the legal right of procuracy officials to carry out these investigative actions, the envoy noted that the demonstrative publicity with which they had been conducted had in this case led to negative consequences."[87] This may have been a special case in which Cherkesov acted at Putin's behest to safeguard the interests of Putin and his allies.

The background was that leading city bankers had expressed their displeasure over a search by the Procuracy and special police of the main office of Petersburg's Industrial Construction Bank (Promstroibank) in connection with bribes given to the governor's administration.[88] The search had been followed by the confiscation of documents from a number of banks, including Promstroibank and Baltic Bank.[89] Similar complaints had also been made at a session of the okrug's business roundtable held on December 1, 2000, and attended by Cherkesov and German Gref, minister for economic development and trade, who comes from Saint Petersburg and has interests there. Four days later, Cherkesov summoned the above-mentioned deputy procurator and gave him a lecture. And then the case was transferred from the procuracy to the FSB, where it was quickly put on a shelf.[90]

Observers explained this revealing episode by pointing out that Promstroibank's oversight board is headed by Vladimir Kogan, one of the area's most powerful businessmen, who is closely connected not only with Cherkesov but also with Finance Minister A. Kudrin and, most important of all, President Putin.[91]

Petersburg itself is widely seen as corrupt: according to a Procuracy study, it was ranked the fifth most corrupt of Russia's eighty-nine regions.[92] The city procurator and MVD economic crimes unit have been investigating the city's policies for channeling funds through local banks and its actions in raising a one-billion-ruble loan to construct an ice hockey palace. The Duma's Accounting Chamber found violations in the disbursement of the city's 2000 budget. In fall 2001 the Procuracy started to close in on Governor Yakovlev's inner circle, indicting four of his thirteen deputies.[93] In October 2001 prosecutors filed abuse-of-office charges against Valerii Malyshev, accusing him of receiving soft loans from local banks and improperly fundraising for the All Russia party in the 1999 Duma campaign. A month later, prosecutors charged acting deputy governor Aleksandr Potekhin with illegal financial transactions. And in March 2002 they charged Deputy Governor Anatolii Kagan, head of the city's health committee, with fraud in allocating a nine-million-ruble ($300,000) insulin contract to the local firm Kovi-Farm.

However, one observer noted that despite Cherkesov's promise to "decriminalize the corridors of power," in reality the charges against the deputy governors were rather weak and were going nowhere.[94] Since then, Malyshev has died, and Potekhin, having been amnestied, started proceedings on March 5, 2003, to be fully acquitted. Also, although in January 2003 the Kagan case was handed to a court for trial, on March 4 it was annulled on the grounds that the term of limitation had expired.[95] In addition, one of the owners of Kovi-Farm, Denis Volchek, became a deputy to the city legislature in December 2002. (This meant that out of its fifty members, three have been charged with crimes, a fourth is sitting in prison, and a fifth is under suspicion of links with a major organized crime group.)[96] At the same time an ongoing case against

Finance Minister Aleksei Kudrin was quietly dropped. Kudrin was head of the Petersburg finance committee in 1995–1996, and an investigation was started into its possible abuse of funds.[97]

To conclude, Cherkesov often stated his intention to fight against corruption. He further said (e.g., at a January 2001 session of the okrug's Coordinating Council on Law Enforcement Activities) that "to launch the fight against corruption a very strong political impulse was needed. It has been given by the president, and we'll get the job done." The envoy was specially concerned that the number of bribery cases being pursued had been declining.[98] Later a deputy city procurator noted that in 2000 "all the Petersburg procuracy offices sent to courts only 29 bribery cases. But in the first nine months of 2001, 108 cases of bribery have been registered in the city."[99] However, by March 2003 the situation had not substantially changed, and the ending of the Potekhin and Kagan cases made it appear that the Yakovlev forces were successfully counterattacking. In this connection it was notable that various people close to Cherkesov had turned out to be tied to criminal groups.[100] It may also be that the Yakovlev forces counterattacked when they knew or sensed that Cherkesov was about to leave his job, which he duly did on March 10.

The Envoy's Economic Role

Economic management is not part of the envoy's official job description, nor does he have any specific legal mandate or direct management responsibility for economic affairs. Yet our content analysis of his official engagements revealed that one third of his time is spent on economy-related activity. Why is this so?

It is important to remember the political culture within which the institution of envoy was introduced. In Soviet times there was no separation of political and economic power, quite the reverse, and this tradition of political authorities intervening in economic decisions has continued even in the new conditions of market transition. Thus both elite and popular opinion would find it strange if an envoy with political authority did not also influence economic matters. This assumption was reinforced by the general tenor of Putin's remarks, to the effect that the state ought not to withdraw from certain sectors of the economy.[101]

Similarly, Cherkesov himself stated: "At the beginning of the 1990s there was the popular formula: shrink the state, so as to liberate the individual and the economy. Unfortunately, in freeing ourselves from the state, both individuals and economic structures lost the protection which only the state can provide."[102]

At the same time, Cherkesov has claimed that "I never involve myself in economic management."[103] On the other hand, his words and actions indicate a willingness to take on the sort of economic role carried out in the past by Communist Party regional secretaries—safeguarding the interests of the region vis-à-vis the center and trying to deal with crises as they erupt. Thus Cherkesov has also said: "I propose that today and in the future, our participation in economic procedures will be realized via the activities of crisis managers—in the broad sense of this word. Such measures are needed when conflicts arise in certain strategic sectors of the economy or in the enterprises of company towns."[104] One example: an inspector from Cherkesov's office intervened to end a strike by private pilots, which closed the city's ports for a day. They were protesting against a proposed shift to state employment, which threatened to slash their $1,000-a-month salaries.[105]

Some of this activity is demand-driven: local managers appeal to political figures such as Cherkesov to help solve their problems. As one local factory manager put it, "The newcomers to political office want to win the trust of business. And business, like a prospective bride, is looking the authorities over, trying to see what it can expect."[106] The results are mixed. Thus, for example, the Leningrad region electricity provider, Lenenergo, appealed to Cherkesov (and the region's governor) for help over unpaid bills, before cutting off two communities for nonpayment.[107] And Cherkesov told an energy conference that it was "unacceptable" for the Unified Energy System (EES) to cut off electricity to military bases, and he reportedly took the electricity crisis in Arkhangel'sk directly "under his control."[108] These interventions are less an assertion of power by Cherkesov and more an example of his being dragged into ongoing policy standoffs—examples of a kind of "bureaucratic capture" by local elites. In this complex network of lobbying activities, the envoys' "hierarchy of political power" has to compete with the influence of companies, which network with patrons and allies both "horizontally" (locally, and in other regions) and "vertically" (in Moscow).

Like in Russia as a whole, the North-West's economy has barely started to recover from its decade-long recession. There are pockets of viability—fuel and energy, food, timber—but otherwise the okrug's economy is in rather sorry shape. In 1998 exports averaged $514 per capita across Russia as a whole. Leningrad region was above average, at $904, as was Karelia at $643 (mainly timber), while Novgorod lagged at $354 and Pskov at $99.[109] From 1990 to 1998 the Russian gross domestic product (GDP) fell on average by 54 percent: in the North-West okrug, Leningrad did best, falling "only" 47 percent, while the other regions ranged between Novgorod (48 percent) and Karelia (53 percent).[110] From 1990 to 1998 Pskov lost 29 percent of its jobs; Kareliya, 25 percent; Novgorod, 21 percent; and Leningrad region, 12 percent.

Long-Term Planning

The envoy's ability to participate in long-range development planning is quite limited. For one thing, the national government's economic strategy is not very clear, and it does not command a lot of support among economic managers. The okrug includes a broad swathe of territory with no particular economic logic or institutional structure linking together the economic activities of its component parts. Across Russia as a whole, interregional trade has fallen dramatically since 1991, with the partial exception of food supplies. The North-West is particularly disparate compared to other okrugs, with each part pulled in a different direction—for example, toward Belarus, Estonia, and Finland. "Thus far, the formation of a unified territorial entity in the North-West resembles an experiment in which it is not clear who is accountable, or who will pay for unifying projects, or who will push them through."[111]

In January 1991 the North-West Regional Economic Cooperation Association was formed. It includes Kirov region, which is not part of the okrug and excludes two regions that belong to different associations.[112] At the association's meeting on March 20, 2001, only one governor showed up—its president Vladimir Yakovlev.[113] Cherkesov himself did not attend, although he sent his deputy, whose job includes liaison with the association. A little earlier, another of his deputies had claimed that no more than 5 percent of its decisions were actually being implemented.[114]

However, through various sources and interviews, the full picture regarding the "North-West" association is more complex than this evidence suggests. First, the elites of Petersburg and Leningrad region have had a good opinion of the association, 76 percent considering it to be fully capable of taking sensible provisional decisions on economic issues and 53 percent thinking likewise about political issues.[115] Second, the association has welcomed the okrug's participation in its work. According to our interview in 2001 with one of its officials, either Cherkesov or a deputy had attended its meetings and taken an active part in discussing the topics of the day. Usually their input had been based on points made in the president's latest speeches and by documents prepared by the PA. At the meetings, interregional economic programs were discussed and adopted, and drafts of laws aimed at regulating one or another economic activity were put forward for debate.

However, a contemporaneous interview with one of Cherkesov's deputies suggested that in most respects the association and the okrug staff have worked more in parallel than together. The okrug has focused mainly on collecting and analyzing information, as well as evaluating the viability of development plans. According to the deputy: "For us, the most important thing is the perspective from the viewpoint of the whole area. . . . We operate above the level of a subject of the federation, above local interests, we move almost to a multi-regional level. For us, there's no need to weigh up various points of view." Work of this sort necessitates having your own research unit. To all appearances this unit is run by the envoy's deputy Ye.I. Makarov.

In May 2001 Cherkesov admitted: "There is no okrug-wide economic development program." With eleven federation subjects in the okrug, but no okrug economic body with executive powers, it was impossible to develop unified economic programs.[116] Nonetheless, Minister German Gref's think tank, the Center for Strategic Projects, opened a branch in Petersburg in December 2000, with backing from local businesses such as Baltika brewery, Telekominvest, and Rossiya bank; in July 2001, it presented its development plan.[117] The plan drew harsh criticism from, among others, Novgorod governor Prusak, who said: "We don't want to be associated with this strategy. I ask you to withdraw the plan and not terrorize the okrug."[118] Evidently in response to such criticisms, Cherkesov created a special okrug expert commission to draw up an alternative plan. Headed by economist Yurii Solodukhin, it included representatives of all the okrug's regions. The plan duly appeared in September and adopted an "industrial policy" approach to long-term planning.[119] Thereafter, however, an apparent stalemate ensued, as both this commission and the Gref-sponsored group continued to work in parallel under the general oversight of the envoy.

In regard to strategic policy issues with a strong social component, both Cherkesov and President Putin have sometimes had meetings at the okrug level. In August 2000, for example, Putin met with eight of the okrug governors in Valdai, Novgorod region. The governors urged caution in the planned reform of housing costs, and disagreed with Gref when he proposed eliminating the forestry ministry.[120] Cherkesov, too, got involved with housing, when he attended a major conference on the subject. He joined the governor of Nenets in warning against precipitate increases in the costs charged to citizens. [121]

Relations with Business

Shortly after his appointment as envoy, Cherkesov created an advisory committee of okrug business leaders, to meet on a monthly basis. In doing this, he was emulating his boss, President Putin, who has made regular meetings with leading businessmen a routine fixture of his administration. The first meeting took place in November 2000. Six members of Cherkesov's council are from Petersburg, and one or two from each of the other regions. They come from such leading firms as LUKoil, Baltika brewery, Lenenergo, Northern Steel (Severstal'), Syktyvkar Cellulose, Apatity chemicals, and the Admiralty Wharf shipyard.[122] There were some notable absences from the gathering: no one represented Pskov, and the director of the giant oil refinery at Kirishi (which cooperates with Surgutneftegaz, a LUKoil rival) failed to show up.

Cherkesov's involvement with local business elites takes place in the context of his political rivalry with Petersburg governor Yakovlev. Old adversaries of Yakovlev and those currying favor in Moscow have rallied around Cherkesov: "It seems that the big companies, like Baltika Brewery and Menatep St. Petersburg Bank, or those with powerful mother companies like Lenenergo (under the wing of EES), are Cherkesov's supporters."[123] But Yakovlev has a strong base of support in local construction and retailing companies, and in banks such as BaltOneksim Bank.[124] Yakovlev has day-to-day control over the running of the city: the use of land, the issuance of permits, and the allocation of city contracts, something with which Cherkesov cannot compete. Yakovlev has also earned a reputation as an effective lobbyist for his city on the national stage.[125]

Perhaps the envoy's most visible economic activity is cheerleading for investment projects across the territory, and glad-handing foreign investors such as Totalfina, Dresdner Bank, and the US Export-Import Bank.[126] In February 2001 he presided over a large international conference "Investments-2001: New Realities—New Capabilities of Northwestern Russia," which attracted twelve hundred participants.[127] A follow-up conference was held in March 2001, bringing together officials from the okrug's regions.

Cherkesov has also created an investors' council and a commission for investors' rights. While foreign investors have found conditions attractive in Leningrad and Novgorod regions, many have been stymied by the corruption and licensing regime of Saint Petersburg. Before Cherkesov came to office, the Swedish pulp and paper giant AssiDoman was forced out of the Segezha pulp mill in Kareliya after sinking tens of millions of dollars into the project.

State sponsorship is typically regarded as key for long-term investors. In the words of Leningrad region's deputy governor Grigorii Dvas, "If a project falls under the eye of the state, that means the negotiations go faster and the interest rate is kept to the minimum."[128] But the reality of the new Russian economy is that investment decisions are usually made on commercial criteria, and there is little that regional officials can do to attract investors, apart from not scaring them away with excessive regulation. As Alfa Bank chairman Petr Aven explained to an investment conference in Kaliningrad: "The drowning man has to save himself."[129]

The star performer in attracting foreign investment is Leningrad region. It offers easy access to the Petersburg transport hub, but it does not suffer from the city's Byzantine politics and licensing regime. In 1997 the region copied Novgorod's policies by adopting laws that granted investment-related tax breaks for projects worth over $1 million. In 2001 it secured more investment than Petersburg, including $400 million from foreign investors such as R.J. Reynolds, Philip Morris, Kraft, Henkel washing machines, Caterpillar, Ford (in Vsevolzhsk), Ikea (in Tikhvin), and new pulp mills operated by Knauf, AssiDoman, and International Paper.[130] Two new ports for oil (Primorsk) and coal (Ust-Luga) exports are joining existing facilities at Vysotsk and Vyborg.

Cherkesov has also involved himself in some of the ongoing disputes over privatization and investment projects, supporting such major companies as LUKoil and Northern Steel. The latter began as a massive steel mill located in Cherepovets, Vologda region, but its dynamic young director Aleksei Mordashov has used its $1 billion export revenue to create a powerful nationwide industrial conglomerate, buying iron ore deposits, coal mines, the Vostochnyi seaport, and the Ulyanovsk auto factory. In an interview given toward the end of 2000, Mordashov praised Cherkesov, saying his appointment "meant a new opportunity to build good relations between business and the authorities." He also said, "There has been a big change between the conditions a year ago and conditions today."[131] Mordashov mentioned that he knew Cherkesov's then deputy, A. Kuznetsov, from the time when he ran the Oktyabr railway line, of which Northern Steel was the main customer.

While the Cherkesov–Mordashov relationship appears to be mutually beneficial, one gets the impression that Mordashov is probably big enough to deal directly with the Kremlin without the help of the envoy.[132] Still, Cherkesov helped Mordashov to stop the sale of the Vorkuta coal mine to Aleksandr Mamut's Moscow-based MDM Bank in December 2000. Vorkuta is the source of 80 percent of the coal for Northern Steel, which had managed to buy a 15 percent stake in the coalmine.[133] Northern Steel has also invested in iron ore deposits in Murmansk, the pipe manufacturing Izhorskii Factory in Petersburg, and the chemical port terminal in Vysotsk.[134] MDM was, however, able to buy its way into the Kovdor mineral deposits in Murmansk, despite opposition from Governor Yevdokimov.[135]

Apparently Cherkesov also has good relations with the oil giant LUKoil: one of his earliest meetings, in September 2000, was with its chairman Vagit Alekperov.[136] LUKoil is investing heavily in the North-West, as is Transneft, now completing its $460 million Baltic oil export pipeline. Cherkesov helped LUKoil increase its operations in Nenets, acting against the governor's wishes. The tender to develop the large Gamburtsev Val oilfield in that region was won by Northern Oil, but LUKoil and other oil majors have been disputing the sale.[137] The other companies offered premiums of $100 to $140 million, while Northern Oil won with a bid of just $7 million. Cherkesov said his office was monitoring the procurator's investigation of the tender. In Petersburg, the Lenenergo firm is protesting an August 2001 decision by the city to create a new, city-owned corporation to supply electricity, using assets formerly used by Lenenergo.

It is not clear how much influence the envoy has over decisions regarding issues like federal subsidies, federal orders for goods (an important lifeline for many Russian farms and factories), and the management of federal property. Novgorod's Prusak complained that reforms led to the closing of Novgorod's branch of Sberbank (the huge, state-owned savings bank) and the region's office of the forestry ministry.[138] These federal institutions now perform their functions from their branch offices in Saint Petersburg. Prusak blamed these contractions on the okrug reform, although Sberbank officials said they had made their own decision.

Cherkesov has been quite active in trying to salvage the precarious economy of Kaliningrad, and early in his tenure, he expressed frustration with the lack of a federal program for the region, with clear lines of responsibility.[139] In December 2000 the State Customs Committee (GTK) passed a resolution on the nationwide unification of tariffs, which had the effect of virtually abolishing the Kaliningrad Special Economic Zone. Created by presidential decree in 1996, the zone allowed for tax-free imports and exports.[140] With Cherkesov's support, Governor Yefremov met a month later with the GTK head and prime minister Kasyanov, and then with President Putin. On February 1, 2001, the GTK issued an order withdrawing its earlier resolution.[141] This episode showed how the authorities' style and method of operating have not changed very much from Soviet times: an administrative decision by the GKT; then administrative discussions involving the envoy, a governor, the prime minister, the president, and the GKT head; and then another administrative decision by the GKT.

Cherkesov intervened again later in the year, when he opposed a new plan for reforming the region's economy proposed by Gref. The plan, which would have closed the region's amber mine, was aimed in part at stopping the smuggling of amber and related tax fraud.[142] Cherkesov was reported as saying: "German Gref is a big champion of Kaliningrad. However, his words about developing export industries in the region represent ideas that are incomplete and poorly thought through."[143]

Securing the "Information Space"

Putin has emphasized the state's duty to manage information and has sponsored an "information security doctrine."[144] Cherkesov's office seems to have made work in this field a top priority. His efforts include close monitoring of publications and regular meetings with editors. This kind of "news management" strikes Westerners as sinister and undemocratic, but of course it has deep roots in Soviet political culture.

Cherkesov has stressed that one of his tasks is to overcome the information barriers among the regions. Up to now, people have been living "within the walls of their own [regional] press" and getting very little news about events in neighboring regions.[145] This is a particularly acute problem for the exclave of Kaliningrad, where the neighbors are Poland and Lithuania and where schoolchildren may not even get the chance to visit "mainland" Russia or, for example, tour the sites of Petersburg. They may not even know that the Hermitage Museum exists.[146]

Cherkesov's team has put some effort into promoting news exchange across the okrug via television and news agencies—the latter includes the new Rosbalt agency founded by Cherkesov's wife, Natalya Chaplina, in November 2000. His office has helped set up online and videoconferencing links in Murmansk, Petrozavodsk, Novgorod, Pskov, and Vologda; and radio links to Kaliningrad and Arkhangel'sk.[147] The state TRK television station has set aside thirty minutes a day for a program on okrug affairs.[148] All this means, according to Ivan Moseev, the editor of *Business-Class* in Arkhangel'sk, that the only regionwide information comes with "Cherkesov sauce on it."[149]

Yakovlev had established a firm grip on the local media in Saint Peterburg long before Cherkesov's arrival. The governor's team controls or is supported by the Petersburg television and radio company TRK, the papers *Sankt-Peterburgskie vedomosti, Peterburg-Ekspress, Vechernii Peterburg,* and the local *Izvestiya* and *Komsomol'skaya pravda.* Cherkesov has influence over the local broadcasts of Russia's state television and radio company VGTRK (the RTR television channel and Radio Rossii), the Petersburg branch of ITAR-TASS, *Nevskoe vremya,* and his wife's *Chas Pik.*[150]

The first of several important setbacks to Yakovlev came in spring 2001, when the federal Ministry for the Press, Broadcasting, and Mass Media took the local radio company off the all-important first channel on the city's cable radio service and gave it to the national Radio Rossii. (Nearly half of all listeners had tuned in to the local company.)[151] In October 2001 Petersburg television lost the twenty-fifth channel to Euronews. And a subsequent initiative by Yakovlev to introduce new tax breaks for local media failed to pass the legislative assembly.[152]

Local media have seized on various missteps by Cherkesov to embarrass him, but they have generally found slim pickings. These attacks began as soon as he arrived, with a miniature scandal around his decision to take over an elegant downtown villa, ousting a so-called palace for civic weddings. In March 2001 he was tricked into endorsing a new anti-Semitic magazine *The Admiralty (Admiral'teistvo).*[153] Although he managed to stop a plan by local Unity party leaders to distribute busts of Putin to government offices, he failed to catch a new schoolbook, which featured a young Putin as a model of virtue.[154] It was not only in Petersburg that Cherkesov encountered hostile media coverage. The government-controlled television company in Novgorod, presumably loyal to Prusak, presented a biting piece called "Cherkesov's Letter to Putin," done in the style of Soviet spy films.[155] The journalist imagined Cherkesov writing to Putin, with such phrases as "I have a colorless voice and colorless eyes. Should I also make colorless statements so that no one will understand what I'm saying?"

In October 2000, at a big media conference, Cherkesov helped to set up an Association of Northwest Media, whose leaders then signed a cooperation agreement with him. However, media associated with Governor Yakovlev of Saint Petersburg boycotted the new body.[156] Cherkesov also played a prominent role in launching Aleksandr Lyubimov's Media Union, a rival to the Union of Journalists and an organization apparently keen to cooperate in state regulation of the press.[157] Addressing its founding conference in June 2001, Cherkesov said: "The so-called authoritarian democracy of President Putin has strengthened the country."[158] Putin also spoke to the conference, holding that "a free press is the most important guarantor of our country's irreversible democratic course."[159]

Cherkesov seems to have deliberately avoided the mistake of some envoys in setting up okrug media of his own, preferring—as far as possible—to manipulate the existing ones.[160] The PA's media adviser Gleb Pavlovsky made the president's line clear in June 2001, when he criticized "the epidemic of creating okrug media." This, he said, had been the initiative of certain envoys, not the Kremlin, and they would soon be "gently corrected."[161]

As for how exactly Cherkesov's staff do their manipulating, our interviews with some of them elicited these statements: "When necessary, we knock them into line"; and "We open their eyes to the fact that the media market is satiated with topics that it shouldn't be satiated with." Staff members also supply technical equipment to selected news agencies.[162]

Conclusion

Has the introduction of the post of envoy been a success or failure, based on the experience of the northwest okrug? We cannot give a definitive answer to this question, since Putin's aims in initiating the reform were rather opaque. Unlike some other okrugs, the North-West had not experienced any serious challenges to the integrity and sovereignty of the federation. As for the envoy's achievements in clearing up corruption and improving the routine political and economic life of the okrug, these have been decidedly modest.

The introduction of the envoys seems to have been designed to bring back a sense of coordination and direction to a chaotic and confused society. Also, perhaps, its advocates hoped to discreetly and cautiously smuggle back in some elements of the old communist order, hidden beneath a cloud of democratic forms and rhetoric. One is reminded of former prime minister Viktor Chernomyrdin's favorite saying: "We hoped for something better, but we got the usual."

Notes

1. *Rossiiskii kto est' kto*, August 25, 2000.

2. Among his cases were those of Vladimir Poresh (arrested in 1979), Vyacheslav Dolinin (1982), Rostislav Yevdokimov (1982), Gelii Donskoi (1983), and Dmitrii Akselrod (1984), all of whom were legally exculpated in 1991. *Russian Regional Report* (RRR), May 24, 2000. See also the profile of Cherkesov by Robert Orttung, RRR, May 2, 2001, Cherkesov's interview in *Vek*, February 16, 2001; and Vladimir Voronov, "Former KGB Officials Now in Power," *Sobesednik*, no. 23, June 2000.

3. "Piterskii smotritel'," *Profil*, June 19, 2000; Vera Kamsha, "Ptenets gnezda. Put' Viktora Cherkesova v bol'shuyu politiku," *Nezavisimaya gazeta*, October 10, 2000; "Cherkesov Viktor Vasil'evich," at www.agentura.ru/dosie/people/chercesov/ (May 23, 2001).

4. *Russkii telegraf*, August 29, 1998.

5. "O nekotorykh sotsial'no-ekonomicheskikh pokazatelyakh Severo-zapadnogo regiona," *Ekspert Sevoro-Zapad*, June 18, 2001.

6. Vyacheslav Morozov, "The Discourses of St. Petersburg and the Shaping of a Wider Europe," Copenhagen Peace Research Institute paper no. 13, 2002 (at www.copri.dk).

7. *Chas Pik*, April 24, 2001.

8. Itar-Tass, March 24, 2001.

9. Oleg Odnokolenko, "Oborona Kaliningrada," *Itogi*, May 25, 2001.

10. E. Ozerova, "Massivnoe polpredstvo spaset Kaliningrad," *Peterburgskii Chas Pik*, August 1, 2001; S. Chernova, "Kontroleram ne ponravilsya Kaliningrad," *Kommersant*, July 18, 2001; "Vos'mogo federal'nogo okruga ne budet," *Vesti SPB*, July 28, 2001; V. Abramov, "Kaliningradskaya oblast'," *Konstitutsionnoe pravo: Vostochnoevropeiskoe obozrenie*, 2001, 191–93; E. Krom, "Slishkom malo initsiativy," interview with deputy envoy Andrei Stepanov, *Ekspert Sever-Zapad*, January 14, 2002.

11. *Smena*, August 15, 2000.

12. Konstantin Simonov, "Belyi dom na tri sem'i," *Kommersant-Vlast'*, March 16, 2000; Ivan Trefilov, "Muscovites Swell the Ranks of the People from St. Petersburg," *Vedomosti*, July 2–4, 2001.

13. Dmitrii Pinsker, "Vtorichno legitimnyi," *Itogi*, November 14, 2000.

14. "Vladimir Putin and the Topography of Power," *Moscow News*, May 24, 2000.

15. Interview with Igor Chernyak, *Komsomol'skaya pravda*, March 2, 2000.

16. Aleksandr Chernyi, "Polpred reshil vse zadachi," *Obshchaya gazeta*, May 24, 2001.

17. "Chempionat sredi polpredov," *Kommersant-Vlast'*, February 6, 2001.

18. *Profil*, February 19, 2001. Poll by Fond Obshchestvennogo Mneniya.

19. T. Protasenko, "Vliyatel'nye liudi Peterburga," *Peterburgskii Chas Pik*, June 27, 2001; *Peterburg: elitnoe izmerenie: Barometr mnenii liderov Peterburga* (Saint Petersburg: AMK MarKo, 2001), 46–52; "Sankt-Peterburg. Reiting i otsenka deyatel'nosti politicheskikh liderov Sankt-Peterburga po dannym VTSIOM (yanvar' 2000)," at www.murmannews.ru/allnews/19660; D. P. Gavra and E. V. Shmeleva, *Peterburg: elitnoe izmerenie: Barometr mnenii liderov Peterburga* (Saint Petersburg: AMK MarKo, 2002); "Piterskii gubernator lidiruet po vliyaniyu na politicheskuyu situatsiyu," at http://rb.flb.ru/cgi-bin/iframe/flb?56768696.

20. Vlad Kovalyev, "Is Cherkesov Headed for Moscow?" *Moscow Times*, May 14, 2001.

21. Interview on ORT's news program Vremya, May 7, 2001.

22. Yana Yur'eva, "Interv'yu Cherkesova," *Pravda Severa* (Arkhangel'sk), January 2, 2001.

23. Ya. Yur'eva, "V 'igre bez pravil' pobedit' nevozmozhno," *Peterburgskii Chas Pik*, February 6, 2001.

24. Interview on Radio Mayak, May 12, 2001.

25. "Sankt-Peterburg. Viktor Cherkesov napravil 100 chinovnikov vo Dvorets brakosochetaniya," APN, July 7, 2000 on web at http://flb.ru/material.phtml?id=8464; "V shtate polpreda 80 chelovek," *Vechernii Murmansk*, August 3, 2000.

26. Vyacheslav Chichin, "Nasha zadacha—ukreplenie Rossii," interview with V. Cherkesov, *Petrovskii kur'er*, July 31, 2000; Konstantin Zborovskii, "Novye rabochie mesta na Severo-Zapade," *Profil*, August 7, 2000; "Pis'mo na stol prezidentu," *Vechernii Murmansk*, August 30, 2000.

27. Until May 2001, First Deputy Bol'shakov was simultaneously the CFI for Saint Petersburg.

28. *Versiya*, March 11, 2002; K. Zborovskii, "Na smenu nachal'nika tamozhni dali 'dobro,'" *Profil*, January 14, 2002. Before working for Cherkesov, V'yunov was a Colonel-General of the Border Troops.

29. E. Ragozina, "General Cherkesov stanovitsya publichnym politikom," *Peterburgskii Chas Pik*, July 12–18, 2000.

30. *Vremya novostei*, April 3, 2001.

31. A. Rabkovskii, "Obshchestvennaya palata okruga nachala rabotu," *Sankt-Peterburgskie vedomosti*, March 31, 2001.

32. Based on personal interviews, September 4, 2001.

33. Interview with Cherkesov by S. Shelin, "Ya vernu gosudarstvu gosudarstvennoe," *Delo*, September 18, 2000.

34. Marat Khairulin, "Lyubit' prezidenta," *Novye izvestiya*, February 7, 2002.

35. The relevant government decree is "Skhema vzaimodeistviya federal'nykh organov ispolnitel'noi vlasti s polnomochnymi predstavitelyami Prezidenta RF v federal'nykh okrugakh i razmeshcheniya territorial'nykh organov federal'nykh organov ispolnitel'noi vlasti," issued on August 12, 2000, in *Sobranie zakonodatel'stva Rossiiskoi Federatsii*, no. 34, 2000, art. 3473.

36. O'lga Petrova, Elena Tregubova, "Semero po vertikali," *Kommersant-Vlast'*, December 12, 2000.

37. http://falcon.sinaps.ru/polpred/news.html. Such reports ceased to appear in October 2001.

38. RIA Novosti, March 23, 2001; "Viktor Cherkesov: Nashi partnery v Suomi vidyat, chto situatsiya menyaetsya," *Severnyi kur'er* (Petrozavodsk), March 30, 2001.

39. See, for example, reports on this process from Kareliya: Andrei Raev, "Priem v Tronnom zale," *Severnyi Kur'er* (Petrozavodsk), December 20, 2000; Yekaterina Velikhova, "Granitsy igrovogo polya dlya sub"ekta," *Novaya Novgorodskaya gazeta* (Velikii Novgorod), November 11, 2001.

40. Cherkesov interview, Radio Mayak, May 12, 2001.

41. *Izvestiya*, February 19, 2002.

42. *Izvestiya*, February 22, 2001.

43. Artemii Smirnov, "Predchuvstvie zolotogo dozhdya," *Ekspert Severo-Zapad*, March 5, 2001.

44. *Nevskoe Vremya*, February 22, 2001.

45. E. Denisenko, "Militsiya pod kontrolem," *Ekspert Severo-Zapada*, April 22, 2002.

46. A. Tsyganov, "Pod kolpakom Borisa Gryzlova ostaetsya GUVD Peterburga," *Kommersant-S-Peterburg*, May 29, 2002; A. Smirnov, "Nikolai Vinnichenko: Moi polnomichiya analogichny polpredovskim," *Delo*, May 27, 2002.

47. *Sankt-Peterburgskie vedomosti*, July 11, 2002.

48. *Moskovskie novosti*, July 16–22, 2002, and *Izvestiya*, July 11, 2002.

49. *Izvestiya*, July 9, 2002.

50. *AiF-Peterburg*, no. 32, 2002.

51. "Poslanie prezidenta RF, V. V. Putina," *Rossiiskaya gazeta*, April 19, 2002.

52. Cherkesov interview by Denis Sysoev in *AiF Sankt Peterburg*, December 26, 2001.

53. Interview by Anna Shcherbakova, "Cherkesov Keeps a Hand on State Financing," *St. Petersburg Times*, March 25, 2001.

54. Viktoriya Voloshina, *Izvestiya*, March 28, 2001; Natalya Korkonosenko, "Yubilei v skladchinu," *Versty*, February 23, 2002.

55. Anton Mukhin, "Kontrol' budet tak pri Petre," *Nevskoe vremya*, March 3, 2001.

56. "Voprosov bol'she, chem otvetov," *Nevskoe vremya*, June 11, 2002; V.Petrovskii, "Vysokaya bolezn' i t'ma nizkikh istin," *Nevskoe vremya*, June 11, 2002.

57. "Yubilei obyazan dat' Peterburgu moshchnyi impul's: Interv'yu prezidenta Rossii Vladimira Putina gazete 'Nevskoe vremya' i RTR-Sankt-Peterburg," *Nevskoe vremya*, June 11, 2002.

58. "Kto budet stroit' KAD?" *Nevskoe vremya*, June 14, 2002.

59. Kseniya Buksha, "Cherkesov stroit dambu," *Ekspert Severo-Zapad*, January 20, 2003.

60. Anton Mukhin, "Svyatee Cherkesova," *Izvestiya-Peterburg*, February 11, 2003.

61. Viktoriya Uzdina, "Pomogite Putinu," *Vedomosti* March 12, 2001.

62. *Kommersant*, July 9, 2001.

63. Sergei Shelin, "Shturm Smol'nogo," *Novoe Vremya*, January 6, 2002.

64. Vladimir Kovalev, "Yakovlev and Cherkesov: A Tense 12 Months," *St. Petersburg Times*, May 18, 2001. When Peter Reddaway asked Yakovlev on March 12, 2002, in Washington, D.C., about his relations with Cherkesov, he replied briskly: "I have *no* relations with him. I was elected, he was appointed." Personal information.

65. For example, Cherkesov did not attend the opening of an Aleksandr Nevsky statue. M. Bugrov, "Zdes' kazhdyi kamen' kogo-to znaet," *Novaya gaeta v Sankt-Peterburge*, May 13, 2002.

66. *Kommersant,* July 11, 2002.

67. Vlad Kovalyev, "Is Cherkesov Headed for Moscow?" *Moscow Times,* May 14, 2001.

68. "Nenuzhnyi progress," *Ekspert Severo-Zapad,* December 25, 2000.

69. ORT TV: "Vremena," May 13, 2001.

70. *Ekspert,* June 3, 2002

71. S. Sorokin, "Strasti po konstitutsii," *Molodezh' severa,* July 6, 2001.

72. V. Turkin, "Zdravyi smysl kak moment edineniya," *Krasnoe znamya,* November 1, 2000.

73. Yuri Shabaev, "Important Oil Company Reregisters," RRR, November 7, 2001.

74. Itar-Tass SZ, February 1, 2001.

75. Alla Khodyreva, "Nenetskii gubernator mozhet lishit'sya prava byt' izbrannym," *Kommersant,* February 27, 2001.

76. Sergei Smirnov, "Zampolpreda vstretil Paskhu v Arkhangel'ske," *Troitskii prospekt* (Arkhangel'sk), April 17, 2001.

77. *Volna,* August 8, 2000.

78. *Kommersant,* April 24, 2002.

79. RRR, January 9, 2002.

80. RRR, January 17, 2001.

81. Itar-Tass SZ, January 18, 2001.

82. Itar-Tass SZ, April 24, 2001.

83. Viktor Chernov, "Federaly unichtozhayut korruptsiyu v Kaliningradskoi oblasti," *Komsomol'skaya Pravda v Kaliningrade,* March 27, 2001; Baltic News Service, March 24, 2001.

84. Maksim Timofeev, "Cherkesov Concerned about Poor Law Enforcement in Northwest," RRR, May 30, 2001.

85. Itar-Tass SZ, March 23, 2001.

86. "Tass upolnomochen," *Novaya Novgorodskaya gazeta,* May 23, 2001; *Nezavisimaya gazeta,* July 9, 2001.

87. http://falcon.sinaps.ru/polpred/dec-yan.html (January 2001).

88. V.Novikov and V.Morozova, "Promstroibank slegka 'shturmit,'" *Sankt-Peterburgskie vedomosti,* November 17, 2000.

89. V.Morozova, "Bankiry ne dovol'ny sledovatelyami," *Sankt-Peterburgskie vedomosti,* November 24, 2000.

90. Vadim Nesvizhinskii, "Odnorazovoye delo", *Segodnya,* December 8, 2000.

91. Aleksandr Birman, "Kremlevskie shakhmaty," *Kompaniya,* January 5, 2001; Mikhail Rostovskii, "'Sekretnye druz'ya' Putina," *Moskovskii komsomolets,* April 4, 2001; Vitaliy Antonov, "V 'Severnom Palermo' nespokoino," November 29, 2000 (at http://rb.flb.ru/cgi-bin/iframe/flb?59876969).

92. According to data from the procurator-general's office, *Nezavisimaya gazeta,* September 7, 2001. See also results of the INDEM Foundation research project, "TI-Russia i Fond INDEM predstavlyaiut Regional'nye indeksy korruptsii (October 9, 2002)" (at http://korrupciya.cjb.net/).

93. Vladimir Kovalev, "Third Vice Governor Facing Charges," *St. Petersburg Times,* March 5, 2002; A. Smirnov, "Kontrol'naya dubina," *Ekspert Severo-Zapad,* April 1, 2002; I. Bugrov, "Prokuratura prodolzhaet formirovat' kabinet Vladimira Yakovleva," *Kommersant-St-Peterburg,* May 30, 2002.

94. Nikolai Sokolov, "Mochit' v peterburgskom sortire," *Novye izvestiya*, March 20, 2002.

95. Aleksandr Samoilov, "Odin za vsekh," *Novaya gazeta v Sankt-Peterburge*, January 23, 2003.

96. "God deputata," *Novaya gazeta v Sankt-Peterburge*, January 9, 2003.

97. Andrei Tsygankov, "Aleksei Kudrin ostalsya bez del," *Kommersant*, December 7, 2000.

98. Sergey Slusarenko, "Vzyatok stalo men'she. Viktor Cherkesov nedovolen, emu—borot'sya s korruptsiei," *Kommersant*, January 19, 2001.

99. Interview by M.Rutman with deputy procurator of Saint Petersburg B. N. Salmaksov, "U nikh vzyatki men'she, chem u nas . . . " *Sankt-Peterburgskie vedomosti*, December 6, 2000.

100. Vadim Nesvizhinskii, "Starye druz'ya," *Segodnya*, January 10, 2001.

101. See for example Putin's annual address to the Federal Assembly, "Kakuyu Rossiyu my stroim," *Rossiiskaya gazeta*, July 11, 2000.

102. Interview with Cherkesov by S. Shelin, "Ya vernu gosudarstvu gosudarstvennoe," *Delo*, September 18, 2000.

103. Cherkesov interview by Denis Sysoev in *AiF SPB*, December 26, 2001.

104. Interview with Cherkesov by Anna Shcherbakova, "Cherkesov Keeps a Hand on State Financing," *Moscow Times*, March 28, 2001.

105. Vladimir Kovalev, "Problems of Political Amnesia," *Moscow Times*, October 18, 2001.

106. *Vedomosti*, February 19, 2001.

107. *Nevskoe Vremya*, April 19, 2001.

108. Radio Mayak, October 6 and November 2, 2000.

109. Dmitri Zimin, "Economic Performance, Public Policies and Living Standards in North-West Russia," Saint Petersburg Centre for Russian Studies, June 2001.

110. Accessed at www.gsk.ru.

111. Sergei Ageev, "U semi nyanek," *Ekspert Severo-Zapad*, June 18, 2001.

112. Kaliningrad is also part of the Central association, and Novogorod of the Black Earth association.

113. Artemii Smirnov, "Proshchal'nyi yubilei," *Ekspert Severo-zapad*, April 2, 2001.

114. Artemii Smirnov, "Proshchal'nyi yubilei," *Ekspert Severo-zapad*, April 2, 2001.

115. See the findings in *Regional'nye elity Severo-Zapada Rossii: politicheskie i ekonomicheskie orientatsii*, ed. A. V. Duka (Saint Petersburg: Aleteia, 2001), 277–80.

116. Itar-Tass SZ, May 25, 2001.

117. Konstantin Smirnov, "Ekonomicheskoi politiki Germana Grefa klonirovali," *Kommersant*, November 18, 2000.

118. E. Ozerova, "Razvitie regiona tak vozmozhno. No poka ves'ma slozhno," *Peterburgskii Chas pik*, July 18, 2001.

119. E. Ozerova, "Ekonomicheskie orientiry," *Peterburskii Chas Pik*, August 22, 2001; Yu. Voskresenskii, "Severo-Zapadu nuzhna vera," *Ekspert Severo-Zapad*, October 15, 2001.

120. "Prezident pogruzhaetsya v problemy," *Troitskii prospekt* (Arkhangel'sk), August 8, 2000; Dmitrii Nikolaev, "Za nas reshat bez nas?"; *Kaliningradskaya Pravda*, Au-

gust 5, 2000; Ol'ga Kolotnecha, "Prezident poznakomilsya s Valdaem," *Novgorodskie vedomosti*, August 4, 2000.

121. *Izvestiya*, February 13, 2002.

122. Sergei Slusarenko, "Putinskii podkhod k oligarkham," *Kommersant*, November 25, 2000.

123. Anna Shcherbakova, "Who's Side Are You On? A Matter of Two Governors," *St. Petersburg Times*, March 27, 2001.

124. A. A. Mukhin, *Biznes-elita i gosudarstvennaya vlast'* (Moscow: Izd. GNOM I D, 2001), 51–56.

125. Yakovlev ranked seventh in the nation, according to one expert survey, followed by Novgorod's Prusak at number eight. S. Turanov, "Luchshie lobbisty Rossii," *Nezavisimaya gazeta*, March 20, 2002.

126. "Kto takoi investor?" *Ekspert Severo-Zapad*, April 2, 2001.

127. "Protsess poshel," *Ekspert Severo-Zapad*, March 5, 2001.

128. V. Gryaznevich, "Sub"ektivnyi faktor," *Ekspert Severo-Zapad*, April 2, 2001.

129. A. Denisenkov, "Kaliningrad poluchil shifrovku iz tsentra," *Ekspert Severo-Zapad*, December 17, 2001.

130. Lev Lur'e, "Kolybel' evolyutsii," *Kommersant Vlast'*, February 19, 2002.

131. Ol'ga Romanova, "Dlya vedomostei," *Vedomosti*, November 4, 2000.

132. Oleg Lur'e, "Aleksei Mordashov: portret oligarkha," *Novaya gazeta*, August 16, 2001.

133. Natalya Gotova, "Russkaya chernaya metallurgiya vot-vot ob"edinitsya," *Kompaniya*, February 12, 2001; Natalya Gotova, "Ugol'nye oligarkhi," *Kompaniya*, March 19, 2001.

134. *Ekspert Severo-Zapad*, June 18, 2001.

135. Igor' Korol'kov, "MDM Group," *Moscow Times*, October 31, 2001.

136. A. Klepikov, "Cherkesovskii Forum," *Ekspert Severo-Zapad*, March 5, 2001.

137. *Vremya Novostei*, March 19, 2001; D. Butrin, "Val pretknoveniya," *Kommersant Vlast'*, April 3, 2001; V. Chernitsyn, "Voina s oligarkhami," *Ekspert Sever-Zapad*, May 7, 2001; V. Sunsheva, "Orlovskim neftyanikam sud ne ukaz," *Komsomol'skaya Pravda*, January 31, 2002.

138. "Nenuzhnii progress," *Ekspert Severo-Zapad*, December 25, 2000.

139. Interviewed by Mikhail Kushtapin in *Rossiiskaya gazeta*, April 19, 2001.

140. Konstantin Smirnov, "Osobaya zona upushchennykh vozmozhnostei," *Kommersant Vlast'*, May 28, 2001.

141. V. Bashkanova, "U osoboi zony osobye problemy," *Ekspert Severo-Zapad*, February 19, 2001.

142. *Kommersant Vlast'*, no. 45, November 2001.

143. Vladimir Zhukov, "Peterburg meshaet Kaliningradu," *Kommersant*, April 12, 2001.

144. See the lengthy text in *Rossiiskaya gazeta*, September 28, 2000, 4–6.

145. E. Ragozina, "General Cherkesov stanovitsya publichnym politikom," *Peterburgskii Chas* Pik, July 12–18, 2000.

146. Material in this section is drawn in part from the author's interviews in 2001 with officials in the envoy's office, including with one of the deputy envoys.

147. *Sankt Peterburgskie vedomosti,* May 17, 2001.

148. Itar tass SZ, February 7, 2001.

149. D. Groznyi, "Informprostranstvo dlya Cherkesovykh," *Sreda,* May 1, 2001.

150. Gordon Hahn, "Petersburg Dominates Ineffective Federal District," RRR, October 24, 2001.

151. V. Moskvina, "Radiostantsii Peterburga: 10 let spustya," *Teleskop,* no. 6, 2001.

152. M. Korenevskii, "Deputaty pomeshali Smol'nomy prikormit' piterskuyu pressu," *Peterburgskii Chas Pik,* April 18, 2001.

153. Vladimir Kovalyev, "Racism Controversy Hits Cherkesov," *St. Petersburg Times,* March 2, 2001.

154. *Moscow Times,* August 6, 2001.

155. Elena Rikhovtseva, "Freedom of Thought Flickers through the Regions," *Russian Journal,* July 20, 2001.

156. I. Bugrov, "Viktor Cherkesov zatochil per'ya regional'nykh zhurnalistov," *Kommersant–Sankt-Peterburg,* October 19, 2000; *Vremya MN,* April 17, 2001.

157. Igor Aleksandrov, "Defile chistykh i devstvennykh," *Obshchaya gazeta,* June 26, 2001.

158. "Zhurnalisty zhivut v novoi strane," *Kommersant,* June 14, 2001.

159. *Teleskop,* June 27, 2001.

160. See his interview "Ya ne supergubernator—u menya drugaya rabota," *Argumenty i fakty–Peterburg,* no. 1–2, 2002.

161. M. Ol'kina, "'Zakazukhu' otlovyat v seti," *Kommersant–Sankt-Peterburg,* June 15, 2001.

162. Author's interviews, July 4, 2001.

4

Central Federal Okrug

Nikolai Petrov

*T*HE CENTRAL FEDERAL OKRUG INCLUDES *Moscow city and the regions of Belgorod, Bryansk, Ivanovo, Kaluga, Kostroma, Kursk, Lipetsk, Moscow, Orel, Ryazan, Smolensk, Tambov, Tver, Tula, Vladimir, Voronezh, and Yaroslavl. Georgii Poltavchenko (born 1953) built his career in Leningrad, working closely with Putin from the early 1990s. From 1979 to 1992 he worked in the KGB, reaching the leadership of the Vyborg branch by 1990. From 1990 to 1993 he was an elected member of the Leningrad Regional Soviet. From 1992 to 1999, he headed the Saint Petersburg administration of the Federal Tax Police Service, an administration that Putin, as the city's first deputy mayor, helped him set up. In July 1999, Yeltsin appointed him as presidential representative in Leningrad region.[1] Referring to the time after Putin moved to work in Moscow, Poltavchenko describes their relationship as then taking on a more "personal character."[2]*

Okrug Overview

The Central Federal Okrug is the largest of the seven okrugs; it includes the capital city of Moscow; and in Georgii Poltavchenko, it has an envoy who, like Viktor Cherkesov in the North-West okrug, is a career KGB officer from Saint Petersburg with close personal ties to the president. In fact, Poltavchenko is considered the informal leader of all the envoys and has been discussed as a candidate to head the Presidential Administration. Because it includes

Central Federal District of the Russian Federation

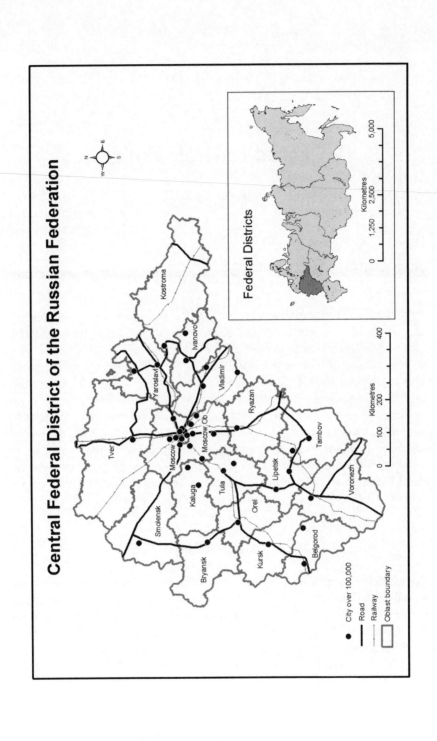

Kostroma

Ivanovo

Yaroslavl

Vladimir

Tver

Moscow Ob

Ryazan

Moscow

Tambov

Kaluga

Tula

Lipetsk

Smolensk

Orel

Voronezh

Bryansk

Kursk

Belgorod

N
W E
S

0   100   200   400
Kilometres

Federal Districts

0   1,250   2,500   5,000
Kilometres

- • City over 100,000
- | Road
- ╎ Railway
- ▢ Oblast boundary

Moscow, the Central okrug covers the country's most strategic region, is highly visible in national politics, and stands astride the axis of Russian political life. Russia's most powerful politicians and a wide variety of economic interests are deeply embedded in the fabric of okrug life. The okrug includes the Moscow-based Russian federal leadership as well as some of the country's most powerful governors, including Moscow mayor Yurii Luzhkov and Orel governor Yegor Stroev, the speaker of the Federation Council from 1996 to 2001.

More than a quarter of Russia's population, thirty-seven million people, live in the Central okrug, which produces about one third of Russia's gross national product (GNP). But the large size of the okrug does not mean that all is going well. Only 30 to 40 percent of the okrug's productive capacity was in use a decade after the collapse of Soviet communism. Despite the significant growth registered in the period 2000–2002, stopping the slide of the 1990s, the okrug's contribution to Russia's overall industrial output has plummeted from 28 to about 21 percent. Its share of agricultural production has also dropped. However, the most ominous indicator is the record low proportion of natural births among the population compared with that of all the other okrugs.[3]

Poltavchenko is new to the okrug and does not have deep roots in it. Before his appointment, he was familiar only with Moscow and Kostroma. During his first six months, he visited all the regions in his jurisdiction except Tver and Smolensk, setting aside three days for each. Usually, during these trips, he held a series of closed meetings with regional officials, visited the major enterprises, and kept contacts with the press and the public to a minimum.

Staffing Policies

In its staffing policies, the Central okrug demonstrates the greatest continuity of all the okrugs between the Yeltsin-era system of presidential representatives and the new institution based on seven envoys. Immediately before becoming Putin's envoy, Poltavchenko served as Yeltsin's representative to Leningrad region. Poltavchenko's first deputy is the former head of the Presidential Administration's (PA) department for coordinating the work of the president's representatives in the regions. Additionally, more than a quarter of the okrug's chief federal inspectors are former presidential representatives in the regions. If one adds in other okrug personnel who moved to the okrug from the PA, the share of holdovers from the Yeltsin era climbs to one half.

While all other envoy staffs were set up largely from scratch and could establish themselves fairly quickly as important new political–bureaucratic actors in their provincial settings, the Central okrug's personnel, based in Moscow, had to fight to establish the status and identity of their institution in a city full of powerful, deeply entrenched federal institutions. The staff's difficulty in carving out a niche for itself has been further complicated by the fact that Poltavchenko's team includes some former employees of the PA's regional staff who, now working for the okrug, are essentially duplicating the work of their successors in the PA, whose offices are located in a neighboring building.

Poltavchenko's staff numbers 123 employees, including thirty-six federal inspectors (including chief federal inspectors) located in the regions and seventeen officials located in the PA's Main Monitoring Department *(Glavnoe kontrol'noe upravlenie)*.[4] By comparison, the staff of the okrug offices of the Ministry of Internal Affairs number 150. Poltavchenko has had six deputies, including three first deputies.[5] Among them are two career employees of the security services, a former member of the PA, a former accountant in the presidential business office, a former businessman from Chelyabinsk, and a former deputy prosecutor general.

Overall, Poltavchenko has placed only a few of his own people in the top echelon of the okrug. His staff is diverse and does not include any public politicians, only apparatchiks, though several of them have run unsuccessfully for public office. Aleksandr Bespalov[6] has been a partial exception, since, prior to his recent departure, he became a leader of the United Russia party and then a senator in the Federation Council. However, despite his leading role in the pro-presidential party, he has yet to win much public recognition.

The envoy has about forty support personnel. This is a relatively small number, though he hopes to take over the staff of the PA's territorial department if it is ever abolished. By the end of 2002, only the PA's office for supervision of the regions had been disbanded, while more than one hundred staff members continue to work in the territorial department, even though this office's official mandate is only ambiguously defined. In order to make up for his lack of staff members, Poltavchenko tries to attract a variety of experts and specialists on a voluntary basis. He has set up various committees to encourage this kind of input.

Of the eighteen chief federal inspectors (CFIs) appointed in 2000, six had already been serving as presidential representatives in their regions. Three additional CFIs came from the PA's personnel reserve, or, like V. Surzhikov in Kursk, had served as presidential representative earlier in their career. Another two were "inherited" from the PA's personnel department, bringing the share of "old" officials among the CFIs to eleven out of eighteen. Generals from the regional branches of the Federal Security Service, the Ministry of Internal Affairs, and the Federal Tax Police Service (Poltavchenko's bailiwick in the 1990s) filled most of the remaining positions. He appointed only two CFIs who were outsiders—that is, who did not already live in the city to which he appointed them: the former head of the Murmansk Tax Police was appointed to Kaluga, and a Saint Petersburg businessman to Tver.

The CFIs in the Central Okrug were extremely stable through the summer of 2002: only one of the eighteen appointed in May 2000 had been removed (in Belgorod region—an FSB general replaced a civilian). However, in September–October 2002, two more departed. Meanwhile, only one was promoted to a more important position, becoming an assistant to PA head Aleksandr Voloshin. As a result of these changes, the share of FSB and other generals remained the same, but the number of holdovers from the Yeltsin administration dropped significantly.

Poltavchenko's Main Functions

The presidential decree establishing the envoys is broad enough so that each can interpret it for his own okrug. In contrast to Kirienko in the Volga okrug, Poltavchenko does not see himself as a public politician and does not seek a lot of publicity. Perhaps for this reason and the lack of public conflicts with the governors in his jurisdiction, there is little information about what goes on within the okrug. The website for the okrug is the least enlightening among the seven okrugs, and little information is otherwise available. The envoy's staff explains this dearth of data by claiming that Poltavchenko's deeds speak for themselves. An alternative explanation is that he is simply following the Chekist approach of limiting information flows, a management style that has become extremely popular in Putin's Russia. Most tellingly here, the envoy has issued strict regulations limiting contacts between his staff and the media.

Many of his duties focus on his role as middleman between the president and the governors. According to his assistants, usually any governor can meet with him, given one or two days' notice. However, the governors cannot meet with the president unless they work through the envoy's office. Before the president and a governor meet, the envoy's staff secures a date on the president's calendar, prepares a short briefing paper for him about the situation in the region, lists the problems to be discussed, and proposes solutions for him to recommend.

Like the other envoys, Poltavchenko would like to expand his authority into other areas. He has suggested that he could play a role in distributing federal funds to the regions. For example, he has proposed that if a governor asks the Finance Ministry for funds from the federal budget, the request would only be considered in conjunction with an explanation provided by the envoy's staff.[7] Currently, the envoy can ask for money from the president's reserve fund to meet a concrete request from a specific region. Thus in September 2002, Putin ordered that more than three million rubles be transferred to Tambov region, for extensive repairs to the Michurin Lyceum and the purchase of an X-ray machine for the regional children's hospital.[8]

Also like the other envoys, Poltavchenko has played an important role in bringing regional laws into line with federal norms. In February 2002 he announced that the process was nearly complete and that only thirty-four or thirty-five more regional laws needed attention. His task was perhaps easier than that of the other envoys, since the Central okrug does not include any of Russia's twenty-one ethnically defined republics, where the largest numbers of legal violations have occurred. Of course, this issue is hard to quantify, so the real meaning of such official figures is difficult to estimate.

The situation in Moscow city suggests the nature of the progress being made and the difficulties the envoy faces. On one hand, Poltavchenko's statements about putting an end to Moscow's procedures for registering citizens remain unfulfilled. Even though the Russian Constitutional Court has ruled repeatedly that forcing Russian citizens to have a permit *(propiska)* to live in the capital is unconstitutional, Mayor Luzhkov continues to require one, arguing that otherwise new residents would overrun the capital. On the other hand, the process of bringing Moscow city legislation into line with federal norms in other areas is moving slowly forward: changes have been made in the city charter; and several laws, some relating to self-government in the city's boroughs, have been revised. However, in the summer of 2001, the envoy determined that more than five thousand subregional executive and legislative acts violated the constitution and federal legislation. While many of these transgressions have been corrected, the process of searching for new violations continues all the time.[9]

An important part of the envoy's work is his participation in resolving crisis situations in the okrug. Since the federal authorities are based in the okrug, his role is less visible than that of the other envoys. Nevertheless, he took part in the work of the response team during the October 2002 hostage crisis in Moscow. Also, other members of the okrug leadership helped deal with both the numerous forest fires around Moscow during the summer of 2002 and the energy crisis in Smolensk region during the winter of 2001–2002.

In fact, much of the work of the envoy is reacting to events in the regions. Thus, for example, in Smolensk, gubernatorial elections took place in 2002, and the Kremlin decided to back the head of the regional Federal Security Service (FSB) as its candidate. Two months before the elections, Deputy Envoy A. Fedorov held a special meeting of the law enforcement agencies to discuss efforts to ensure law and order during the elections. Shortly after the FSB chief won election as governor, assassins murdered his first deputy governor. Two months later, the okrug organized a meeting with governors, CFIs, and ministerial officials to discuss better coordination among the law enforcement and military agencies in the okrug.

Relations with the Power Ministries

Judging by the career backgrounds of his top staff members, working with Russia's "power ministries" is Poltavchenko's main priority. Unfortunately for outside observers, however, this work is the underwater part of the iceberg, and one can try to divine what exactly it consists of only by studying small scraps of evidence. It is well known, for example, that the okrug has a Collegium on Cooperation with Law Enforcement Agencies and Power Ministries. Its members include the chairman of the Okrug Council of FSB regional branches, V. Zakharov (who was appointed head of the Moscow city and regional FSB when Putin's federal reforms were launched), okrug MVD head Sergei Shchadrin, okrug deputy general procurator N. Savchenko,[10] and the head of the Justice Ministry's okrug office, I. Ivanov. The media have mentioned the collegium only a few times, but otherwise there is little publicly available information about its work. In the summer of 2002, the okrug organized an antiterrorism commission, which, in addition to officials of the same federal agencies, includes deputy governors representing the regions.

In order to better understand the work of the two key power agencies in the okrug, the MVD and FSB, we examined the Russian Authorities (Rossiiskaya vlast') website (vlast.rambler.ru) as it stood at the end of August 2002, and the ITAR-TASS publication *The Center of Russia 2002: Official Personnel (Tsentr Rossii 2002: Deistvuyushchie litsa)*. Unfortunately, even though these two sources provided relatively comprehensive personnel lists, they did not contain entries for all of the offices.[11] Nevertheless, the overall picture is relatively clear.

The Ministry of Internal Affairs (MVD)

The first and most striking feature of the recent history of MVD personnel in the okrug is the lack of turnover. Less than one third of the current police chiefs have been appointed during the Putin era and since the most recent gubernatorial elections. The rest were appointed under Yeltsin or, in the case of Ivanovo, under Gorbachev. Of the five appointed during the Putin era, only two—the most visible, since they are serving in Moscow and Moscow region—were appointed after Boris Gryzlov became interior minister and after the amendments to the federal law on the upgrading of police monitoring by the federal government were passed.[12] The other three chiefs were appointed early in the Putin era by former minister Rushailo. These included the new chief in Tambov, where Putin had just appointed his predecessor as the region's CFI.

In short, even though Putin got the federal law amended so as to take from the governors the power to appoint and fire regional police chiefs, he has not in fact used this power in the okrug to put new police chiefs in place.

The case of the Moscow city police provides an especially graphic illustration. As discussed in Robert Orttung's introductory chapter, the federal leadership removed Moscow city police chief Nikolai Kulikov in the fall of 1999, on the eve of the elections for city mayor and the State Duma. The federal and city governments then fought for more than two years over who should take his place. Ultimately the two sides had to settle on the compromise figure of Lieutenant General Vladimir Pronin, former police chief of one of the capital's boroughs. The objections of a powerful governor (in this case the mayor of Moscow, who has gubernatorial status) blocked the federal leadership from doing what it wanted to do. Beyond the political scandal, Pronin's appointment was unusual also because, in the past, new Moscow police chiefs had come from jobs in ministry headquarters.

The second conclusion to be drawn from the MVD's recent personnel records is that police appointments in the okrug have been closely tied to the federal and regional political calendar. Most of the appointments of current chiefs were made in 1996–1997, after the presidential elections and on the eve or just after the first round of gubernatorial elections. This was a time when the power of the federal government was at its height, and when that of the governors was, in contrast, relatively weak. About half of the police chiefs serving in August 2002 were appointed at that time. Between then and the next presidential election in 2000, a period when the governors grew stronger and were able to protect their allies, no police appointments took place at all.

Third, the small "Putin era" group of police chiefs differs fundamentally from those appointed during the Yeltsin era. While those named in between 1990 and 1997 had spent their whole professional life in their native regions, the more recent appointees came from leadership posts in other regions. In Moscow region, the new police chief had previously been the chief in Vologda. In addition, the man appointed to the newly created position of okrug police chief was an outsider, Sergei Shchadrin, who had spent the previous two years as the chief in Rostov-on-Don.[13] Thus we can discern a gradual transition from a Yeltsin model of personnel policies (reminiscent of Brezhnev's "era of stagnation"), where there was little movement between regions, to a pre-Brezhnev rotation model, under which personnel rose up the career ladder by moving from region to region.

Finally, many of the regional police chiefs serving in the summer of 2002 were reaching the age of fifty-five, which had recently been set as mandatory for retirement (though exceptionally the minister can still prolong a chief's career through a special decision). The average chief was 52.5 years old[14] and had served five years in his post. Through the introduction of the new rule, the Kremlin has obtained a new mechanism with which it can—potentially—weed out many of the current chiefs in the near future.

Curiously, however, a fourth of the regional police chiefs in the Central okrug (in Kursk, Belgorod, Bryansk, and Tver) had passed the age limit by the middle of 2002, and another three reached it at the end of the year or the beginning of 2003. Yet none of them has so far been replaced. If all these men should be forced to retire, about half of the police chief positions would become vacant. If, however, they stay, they are more likely to be loyal to the minister on whom their job depends than to their region's governor, regardless of whether or not they are serving in their native region.

This analysis suggests that the ministry may not have a sufficient reserve of reliable, qualified officers with whom to replace the existing chiefs. The question is, then, whether it will nonetheless use this opportunity to replace many incumbent chiefs with younger officers or seek to increase the loyalty to the ministry of the incumbents by allowing them to serve past the fifty-five-year age limit and then continue the pattern by replacing them with officers who are quickly approaching that critical line. In either case, on the eve of the 2003–2004 parliamentary and presidential electoral cycle, the center appears to have a powerful lever it can use against the governors. Up to now, though, Putin's Kremlin has been unwilling or unable to use the tools available to it.

The Federal Security Service (FSB)

The FSB is a completely different type of institution from the MVD and never came under the same kind of gubernatorial influence that the other power ministries did. Logically then, with the strengthening of the central government, one would not expect to see many personnel changes within its ranks. In fact, though, many changes have occurred, and half of the okrug's regional FSB leaders have been replaced since Putin came to power. However, the reasons differ from those that led to changes in the MVD. Instead of being replaced as "bad" leaders, the heads of the regional FSB branches have, with other senior colleagues, been advancing through appointment to a wide variety of other jobs, from presidential envoy, to CFI,[15] to governor.[16]

Several trends are visible within the FSB beyond the widespread leadership turnover. First, the turnover in the okrug seems more evenly spaced and less politically motivated than is the case with the MVD, especially regarding the transfer of FSB chiefs to the post of CFI. Such transitions happened in Belgorod and Ryazan. Nevertheless, there are some connections between FSB appointments and the political calendar, with the election of the heads of the Voronezh and Smolensk FSB chiefs as governors and the removal of the Moscow and Lipetsk FSB chiefs immediately after the gubernatorial elections in those regions.

The second major trend is the frequent movement of FSB officers horizontally, following the kind of pre-Brezhnev era career path introduced by Stalin.

Only a quarter of the okrug's FSB chiefs are local and have made their career in the region where they are serving. The others are outsiders, evenly split between those who have served in one region that is not their native one and those who have moved from region to region. Interestingly, as happened earlier in the Communist Party of the Soviet Union, many have served in the Moscow headquarters staff before being appointed regional FSB leaders.

The average regional FSB chief is fifty-two years old and has been in his job four years. This means that the current crop of FSB regional leaders is part of the Putin generation. The age range is very small, spanning between forty-seven and fifty-five. Two reached the fifty-five-year marker in 2002, and one will in 2003.

Another significant distinction between the FSB and MVD pyramids is that the FSB does not have an intervening link between the center and the regions in the form of an okrug level of representation. From the perspective of 2002, it is hard to determine the exact implications of this difference for the okrug's envoy and his staff. But let us try.

In the case of the MVD, Shchadrin was appointed okrug police chief in August 2001, and by November, 85 to 90 percent of his okrug staff were in place. He said that the staff was likely to grow rather than shrink.[17] Overall, the okrug MVD deals with organized crime, economic crimes, and the narcotics trade; and it has special divisions for coordinating and analyzing the okrug crime situation and overseeing the okrug's battle against organized crime. The okrug MVD works closely with the presidential envoy, but it is not directly subordinate to him. According to Shchadrin, the okrug MVD "feeds the envoy information."[18]

In the case of the FSB, it may be that the envoy's staff, with its strong FSB representation, plays this role by serving as a channel of information. Alternatively, Putin and his presidential bodies are themselves liaising with both the federal and the regional levels of the FSB hierarchy.

Surveying the various law enforcement agencies in the summer of 2002, Poltavchenko cited the general procuracy as the most effective one, especially in its efforts to bring regional laws into line with federal legislation and to deal with criminal cases that involved more than one region.[19] He described the other agencies as "on the right path." He said that he had no serious criticism of the okrug MVD and especially noted its efforts in dealing with interregional crime.

Relations with the Governors

Poltavchenko spends a considerable amount of his time traveling throughout the okrug, which, let us recall, contains Moscow city and seventeen regions. He appears to feel more at ease doing this than staying in Moscow. Unlike his fellow envoys, he can only feel like an important boss when he is traveling. In

Moscow, he is a relatively lightweight official caught between two bureaucratic juggernauts, that of the federal government and that of what is in some respects its rival—Moscow city.

Poltavchenko's relations with his governors are, in general, significantly less conflictual than the corresponding relations of his fellow envoys. On the one hand, he does not seek conflict by temperament, and on the other, he is dealing with individuals of very different political weights. Mayor Luzhkov of Moscow considerably outweighs him, whereas the other governors weigh in lighter than he does. His relations with the "former heavyweight" Yegor Stroyev, who continues to govern Orel after giving up his speakership of the Federation Council, remain cordial. Also, Stroyev continues to chair the Okrug Council, which meets almost monthly, usually not in Moscow.

Poltavchenko has traveled particularly often to the Tambov, Kaluga, Lipetsk, and Belgorod regions. He has chosen Tambov for many important meetings and conferences—on topics ranging from regional investment to science and technology, to agricultural land use, to the military–industrial complex. Sometimes he talks about these trips in public, as in these comments: "I try to visit one or another region at least once a week. Above all, I go where there are problems, and where there's the potential for more effective development."

In this connection, he finds Tambov "extraordinarily interesting":

> Earlier it was considered backward, but I think the reason was the ineffectiveness of the previous leadership. The current governor Oleg Ivanovich Betin is a very qualified person, both as a manager and as an economist. He recently defended his doctoral dissertation. Betin is focused on concrete tasks, on developing the region's economy. In Tambov there are real points of growth. One wants to help such people.
>
> There are, of course, more complex regions, which I have to visit to resolve various serious problems. But it's always more pleasant to go to places where life is on the upswing.[20]

Gubernatorial Elections

Between 1999 and 2002, gubernatorial elections took place in all eighteen regions of the okrug. In Moscow city and the regions of Moscow, Belgorod, Tambov, Tver, and Yaroslavl, they took place in 1999, just before Putin became president. As in 1995, the incumbent governor won another term in most cases. The only one to lose was Tambov governor A. Ryabov, who fell to his predecessor (whom he had beaten in the previous election). In Moscow region, where the incumbent did not seek another term, the Kremlin backed a "reliable communist," Duma speaker Gennadii Seleznev, in a tough but ultimately losing battle.

Seleznev's loss was an embarrassing defeat for Putin, and it marked the first and last time when he openly and publicly supported a gubernatorial candidate.

In six regions, elections took place in December 2000 (Bryansk, Vladimir, Voronezh, Ivanovo, Kostroma, and Ryazan). In four of these, the incumbent won. In Ivanovo, the communist governor came under intense Kremlin pressure and declined to run; however, his designated successor managed to win. In Voronezh, a Kremlin-backed KGB general easily defeated the highly ineffective and unpopular incumbent I. Shabanov.

Finally, in Kursk, Kaluga, Orel, Tula, Lipetsk, and Smolensk regions, the elections did not fit into larger trends and were driven mainly by local conditions. This provided the Kremlin and the envoy the opportunity to operate more actively and visibly. In Kursk, federal efforts resulted in the demonstrative ejection of the incumbent, Aleksandr Rutskoi, from the race. The okrug authorities described his removal as a victory for the justice system, since it was a decision of the regional court that removed him. Poltavchenko claimed that this decision demonstrated the independence of the regional courts, and he denied playing any role in getting a result favorable to the Kremlin. However, Rutskoi's removal did not lead to the victory of the Kremlin's candidate, the former head of the Kursk regional FSB, whom the envoy had appointed as the region's CFI on the eve of the election. Instead, the leader of the local communists, Aleksandr Mikhailov, won.

In Kaluga, the incumbent governor bowed to Kremlin pressure and withdrew from the race in exchange for a seat in the Federation Council. Despite his departure, he was able to win the election of his deputy as the new governor. In Orel, the Kremlin did not try to intervene because the reelection of Governor Yegor Stroev, who was then also the speaker of the Federation Council,[21] served its interests. In Tula, the Kremlin ultimately decided to back the "red" governor and former 1991 anti-Gorbachev coup leader Vasilii Starodubtsev, who won a second term. On the eve of the Lipetsk elections, Poltavchenko personally resolved the differences between the incumbent whom he supported, O. Korolev, and the rebellious regional oligarch V. Lisin, who then decided at the last minute not to run against Korolev, despite his initial intention to do so. In Smolensk, the Kremlin successfully backed the head of the regional FSB, V. Maslov. Overall, in this group of elections, the envoy used a variety of means to defeat the unwanted governors, and in a majority of cases replaced them with candidates more to the Kremlin's liking.

Thus, in the eighteen elections, eleven governors managed to keep their posts, three lost them through elections, and four were eased out, either by enticements or pressure.

To judge the electoral record of the envoy and his staff on the results of these elections would be somewhat premature. The Kremlin and the PA did not formally assign the envoys the task of achieving "the right outcome" in elections. Also, no one took away the PA's traditional responsibility for overseeing such elections. Therefore I take issue with those who criticize the envoys for being ineffective on the basis of their "poor" handling of the elections. Some also criticize the Central okrug's staff for allowing the victory of communist governors in Tula, Ryazan, Ivanovo, Kursk, and other regions. First, it does not necessarily make sense to assert that the Kremlin and its envoy lost a particular election just because the winner was not their choice. In most cases, their efforts had the effect of considerably weakening the office of governor and strengthening the power of central government, regardless of who the new governor was. Second, the envoy's staff have used the elections not only to affect the outcome but also as an opportunity to conduct a general political inventory of each region—identifying and tracking financial flows as well as establishing ties with various political players. This helps them and the PA to prepare for the next round of elections.

These preparations can be either more or less successful. An example of failure took place in Moscow region, and led to a scandal and the replacement of its CFI. During the elections to the regional legislature in 2001, the CFI, General P. Andreevskii, nominated and backed candidates in all fifty precincts. He also set the goal of electing his candidate as speaker and then backing him as the Kremlin's candidate in the next gubernatorial election. In publicly criticizing the incumbent governor, Andreevskii made reference to the president, who had supposedly set the task of removing the governor. Ultimately, the regional assembly sent a letter to Poltavchenko asking for an explanation of Andreevskii's actions. Meanwhile, the press published numerous articles about the CFI's scheming and violations of electoral law that allegedly benefited the candidates he backed. Later the envoy replaced him with a CFI from Altai, that is, from outside the okrug.

Poltavchenko's Influence over the Choice of Delegates to the Federation Council

An important feature of the federal reforms is the change in the makeup of the Federation Council. Governors and speakers of regional legislatures no longer constitute its members. Instead, the latter—called senators—are representatives chosen by governors and the legislatures. By March 2002, the regions of the Central okrug had appointed all thirty-six of their representatives. Many of the new senators seem like has-beens rather than people who currently wield power. The average age is forty-nine, and about one third are of pensionable or nearly pensionable age.

Their group includes two former deputy prime ministers (V. Gusev, representing Ivanovo region, had this position in Soviet times), four former ministers

and deputy ministers, two former governors, and two former regional first secretaries of the long defunct Soviet Communist Party. As in the previous okrug
delegation to the Federation Council, there are four generals from different ministries. Among the delegates with knowledge of how the body functions are three
former staff members of the council, including the former chief of staff V. Niki-
tov, who represents Smolensk. The delegation includes as many as ten businessmen, most from companies of regional significance, as well as past and present
Communist Party functionaries.

In many cases, one individual occupies more than one of these categories.
For example, V. Gusev led the communists of Saratov during the Soviet era,
then served two terms in the Duma representing Vladimir Zhirinovsky's Liberal Democratic Party, and is now a vice president of the big gas company
SIBUR. And L. Lushkin served in the 1980s as a senior official of Moscow's
young communists, then first secretary of the Balashikha district party committee. In the 1990s he switched to business and rose to be a senior manager
of another gas company, Mezhregiongaz.

In addition, six influential regional bureaucrats became senators: the first
deputy prime minister of Moscow city, the first deputy governor of Orel, the
long-time mayor of Belgorod, and the speakers of the Bryansk, Kaluga, and
Kursk legislatures.

Indirect evidence suggests that the Kremlin had a role in the appointment
of the okrug's fifteen "carpetbagger" senators, who did not have a previous
relationship to the regions they now represent. For at least half of these individuals previously worked in Saint Petersburg, the special services, or the
PA. We should also note that even the most aggressive governors are vulnerable in the months preceding the next elections. Most likely, the Kremlin was
able to exploit a variety of the governors' weaknesses in order to get its candidates selected. In choosing these individuals to back, the Kremlin sets little store on party labels. Rather, it values loyalty to itself. Its candidates can
belong equally well to the communists, the pro-Kremlin United Russia, or to
no party at all.

The example of Lipetsk shows how the Kremlin can use gubernatorial elections to get its allies onto the Federation Council. In the months prior to the
April 2002 elections, it backed the incumbent governor Yu. Korolev for reelection. The apparent payment for this support was handed over in January,
when the Lipetsk legislature adopted Poltavchenko's recommendation to select FSB lieutenant general A. Lyskov for the Senate, even though he had no
previous affiliation to the region. To ensure that no inconvenient forces reversed this deal, Poltavchenko came to the region in March to help Korolev
deal with a serious challenge from local magnate V. Lisin. After his visit, Lisin
agreed to withdraw from the race.

This case, like a similar one in the neighboring Volga okrug,[22] shows how the Kremlin can use the new system of power relationships to pressure the governors and ensure the creation of a compliant Federation Council.

Rooting Out Corruption

Poltavchenko has tended to focus his law enforcement energies on former officials. In contrast to Konstantin Pulikovskii in the Far Eastern okrug, he has not ordered sweeping investigations of the regions he oversees. Unlike Viktor Cherkesov in Saint Petersburg, he has not pursued corruption among selected regional officials who wield considerable power.

Rather than take on the high and the mighty, Poltavchenko has gone after those who have already fallen. In June 2002, nearly two years after the Kursk regional court blocked Governor Aleksandr Rutskoi from seeking another term, thus forcing the governor and his staff out of office, B. Khokhlov, the businessman who had served as his regional prime minister, was sentenced to four years in a penal colony on charges of embezzlement and abusing his power. Six months after Smolensk governor Aleksandr Prokhorov lost his May 2002 reelection bid, Deputy General Procurator N. Makarov filed charges against him and his deputies, accusing them of stealing from the regional road fund.

In examining Poltavchenko's techniques, we should note that his area has some history of prosecuting former governors. For example, former Tula governor Nikolai Sevryugin was arrested in 1997 for taking a large bribe from a Moscow bank. Similarly there is a tradition of threatening sitting governors but never actually acting on their cases, especially if they have strong support within their regions (Primorskii Krai's Yevgenii Nazdratenko was a partial exception in this regard). Here, the best example is Tula governor Vasilii Starodubtsev, whose role in the alcohol business before he became governor is constantly under investigation. But nothing ever comes of it.

The Presidential Envoy's Economic Influence

Forming a Unified Economic Space

To stimulate social and economic development in the Central okrug, Deputy Envoy for Economic Issues V. Kichedzhi has argued the need to go beyond penning yet another development plan, many of which have already been written, and to establish effective mechanisms of coordination.[23] In particular, the envoy seeks to remove administrative barriers to the movement of goods, capital, and labor among regions.

Among the institutions addressing this issue are the Okrug Council, which brings together all of the governors in the okrug, and the Economic Council, which includes all the deputy governors who deal with economic issues. The Economic Council meets before the Okrug Council and prepares issues for it to discuss. To assist them, the federal and regional authorities, working with research institutes in the okrug, are compiling an inventory of the entire economic complex in the area; adding up the value of state property, banks, and natural resources; calculating the demographic prospects; and assessing innovational, infrastructural, investment, production, and consumer potential.

Poltavchenko has also set up an Okrug Investment Agency to even out economic conditions in the okrug's regions to the maximum extent.[24] In addition to seeking financial resources, this agency has the task of helping to improve business conditions so as to attract domestic and foreign capital, and restore and develop interregional economic infrastructure in the okrug.[25] Initially, the disproportionately wealthy city of Moscow tried to control this new agency. However, the mayor's proposal that the regions in the agency have votes proportional to the amount of money they contributed was not accepted, and the agency did not come under his control. By the same token, Moscow was no longer eager to contribute money to it.

So far, the agency has been limited to small matters, such as developing municipal boilers in Tambov and organizing a recycling program for household waste in Belgorod. In this connection, the Moscow city authorities claimed that they invested one billion rubles in the agency in December 2001, and that by October 2002, they had used the capital's funds to support relatively small investments with quick paybacks in the construction sector in a variety of regions.[26]

The Investment Agency is accumulating funds to implement large regional and interregional projects. It is one of the first institutions in any of the okrugs to take the form of a nonprofit partnership established by the okrug's eighteen regions and the External Economic Bank (Vneshekonombank). Future plans call for setting up a leasing company, which would rent out domestic and imported agricultural equipment.

Poltavchenko also takes credit for encouraging Moscow city to work with the other regions of the okrug on a bilateral basis, particularly in the area of housing construction. Moscow signed an agreement with Yaroslavl region to build a half-million square meters of housing and five hotels within the "Golden Ring" area, for a total of $100 million. It has analogous agreements with Tambov, Kaluga, Kursk, Smolensk, and other regions. In Tambov, for example, the companies SU-155, Social Initiatives, Moscow Construction Resources, Main Moscow Construction Investments, and Konti are building new housing using their own investment capital.[27] The program on housing construction in the okrug, adopted in December 2001, calls for investments of $5–6 billion over the course of ten years.[28]

In addition, the okrug's regions established an okrug-level Agency for the Reconstruction and Development of State Property. Its goal is to ensure that the state obtains maximum benefit from the shares it owns in private companies and that wholly state-owned enterprises are working efficiently. The agency is buying up state shares in the okrug's companies to achieve these purposes.

Ultimately, the okrug hopes that the president will sponsor a program helping it to realize its plans. Poltavchenko asserted that his efforts had restored some integrating links between the regions and that he had been able to encourage the city of Moscow to devote more of its attention and resources to the regions. By the end of 2001, Kichedzhi claimed that the okrug had put in place institutional structures to address social and economic problems in the okrug. He also claimed to have pioneered multilateral discussions of multiregional and regional problems. He asserted that this process had also begun coordinating the development programs of the regions and setting interregional economic priorities.[29]

Relations with Business Groups

Many of the presidential envoys have tried to compensate for their lack of economic levers (such as budgetary and licensing power, the ability to give tax breaks, etc.) by offering businesses political cover and by minimizing political risks for domestic and foreign investors. The envoys hope that closer ties to powerful business leaders will increase their own influence. Thus the Central okrug is setting up relations with business groups active in the regions. Within each region it has established a regional coordinating council of manufacturers, industrialists, and entrepreneurs. Planned next steps include creating an okrugwide council.

The envoy can serve as a court of last resort for some investors. A high official in German Gref's Ministry of Economic Development and Trade said that when a foreign businessman complains to them about a violation of his rights, the ministry sends a letter to the relevant envoy.[30] He noted that it is no secret that investors usually lose their cases in arbitration courts at the regional or republic level, but they win at the okrug level.

Poltavchenko provides administrative support for investment projects that he believes are important for the okrug, particularly those that create new jobs and increase the tax base. Poltavchenko claimed that he helped investors by working to reduce all bureaucratic barriers, that he spoke to the governors of the relevant regions to ensure that they pay attention to the project, and that "where necessary" he offered the help of the law enforcement agencies.[31]

One example of such assistance is Poltavchenko's decision to support the construction of a chain of supermarkets under the brand name "12 Months" in the eighteen regional capitals of the okrug. In this case, Poltavchenko backed a firm that is notable more for its powerful political connections than proven business skill. The Central (Tsentral'nyi) company, headed by Rasul Mikailov, is sponsoring the 12 Months project. From 1994 to 1997, Mikailov headed the PA's information department, and thus he clearly has access to people in high places. Poltavchenko supports this company even though it does not have a strong network of stores in Moscow. Companies like Ramstore, a powerful retailer in the capital, believe that they would be better positioned to expand into the regions than a company that does not already work in the capital.[32] The project requires $200 million of investment. The state's powerful Foreign Trade Bank will serve as the coinvestor, while regional branches of Sberbank will provide credits for the construction of the stores. Nevertheless, Poltavchenko's support is the project's best asset, even though formally his backing does not guarantee that 12 Months will have the access to the land it requires, since usually the governors control such permits.

Overall, Poltavchenko has not set up the kind of close relationships with Russia's most powerful companies that are apparent in other okrugs. The main reason is probably that these companies are already strong in the capital and can deal with officials who are much more powerful than he is.

Relations with the Media

Poltavchenko has not tried to create any sort of regional ideology or identity. In contrast to the Volga and Siberian envoys, he decided not to create an okrug information center under the aegis of the Rosinformcenter. He and his colleagues believed that such an effort would be ineffective in an okrug in which all the national media were based. Beyond the extensive competition, such an effort would also be extremely expensive.

Instead, the envoy has limited himself to producing a journal, *Region-tsentr*, which came out three times in 2001 and twice in 2002, along with various inserts to regional newspapers. However, at the end of 2002 the first number appeared of an okrug weekly called *Paper No. 1*, and plans were announced to set up an okrug television channel. Also, the envoy's administration has its own website (www.cfo-regions.ru), which provides quite detailed information about events in the regions.

In November 2002 Poltavchenko organized a conference, "The Means of Mass Communication in the Okrug: State and Corporate Regulation," attended by five hundred journalists from every region. Two goals were announced: first, to facilitate the breaking down of the regions' isolation from one another and promote understanding of other regions' problems; and, second, to start creating a unified information space throughout the okrug. If the goals could be achieved, then the successful model would be cloned for use throughout the country. It was clear that the Kremlin intended to take over the existing regional media, which are fully controlled by the governors, to restructure them and give them a "regional-federal" identity. The new media would help to build up approved parties, would turn out the vote for elections, and would enable the federal authorities to bypass the governors and address the population directly. As Poltavchenko said earlier, "The authorities are keen that their activities should be judged objectively by society."[33]

The citizens' reception rooms are an interesting variation on the KGB reception centers of the Soviet era. It is not surprising that three of the four okrugs in which they have appeared are those run by former KGB officers, the Central and North-West, and by a former MVD officer, the Urals. (Kirienko's Volga okrug is the fourth.) In the past, the KGB centers were used as a way to feel society's pulse, to identify citizens who were discontented, and to recruit new informers for the KGB from the population. Today the reception rooms, which have about thirty staffers and assistants in each location, have some of the same functions, though their proclaimed general goal is a bit different, namely, "to promote dialogue between the authorities and civil society." Besides serving as a two-way channel for information, another aim is to form groups politically committed to the Kremlin that can be mobilized for election campaigns. A further goal is to develop working relations with the local media, which staffers can ask to investigate, for example, citizens' complaints. It is notable that the first reception room in the Central okrug was set up in Moscow in 2000, for businessmen who wanted to complain about abuses by city bureaucrats, far away from okrug headquarters at Staraya Ploshchad'. This put extra pressure on Mayor Luzhkov's administration, and it also made it easier for the okrug and—through it—other presidential structures to establish new links with the business community.

Conclusion

The administration of the Central Federal Okrug has distinguished itself by working energetically without sparking any scandals. While generally relying on old personnel, it has also attracted a wide selection of new people, who are not always from Leningrad/Saint Petersburg and who are not always bureaucrats.

After two and a half years, it is still difficult to say how effective this work is. The okrug holds numerous meetings and conferences, leading some observers to charge that it has little real impact. For example, the Okrug Council, as noted, brings together the envoy and the governors, meets monthly in various cities, and deals with important issues. And highly placed public officials participate in these meetings.

But then what? Do they do anything more than define the problem and discuss it? Often they simply create another coordinating council and adopt some recommendations with little clear effect. After some time the Okrug Council discusses a new problem that is no less important.

These events are reminiscent of the Central Committee plenums held during the Gorbachev era, only the okrug meetings take place even more frequently. Even the "okrug's economic development strategy," which is meant to be less than a program but more than just a topic for informal discussion, is still not ready. Of course, the okrug has facilitated horizontal, interregional ties and has encouraged the exchange of expertise among regions. But beyond these things, it is hard to find any concrete achievements.

Nevertheless, there are tangible results, which can be attributed to the envoy himself and the institution of the okrugs in general. Regional legislation, and particularly that of Moscow city, has been brought closer into line with federal norms—although it is naïve to think that without Poltavchenko and his staff, or the other federal agencies at okrug level, something like this would not have occurred in any case. There are new instruments for coordinating the power ministries at the okrug and regional levels—although at the okrug level there is at best a minimal additional effect. If Moscow had possessed the political will, the technical problems of coordination could have been easily resolved earlier.

At the regional level, the CFIs do a better job of dealing with political realities than the Yeltsin-era presidential representatives did. They have changed the balance of power in favor of the center. During the period from 1991 to 1996, the president appointed the governors. Since 1996, the population has elected them directly. With this transition, the governors were supposed to stop serving as the chief officials to monitor and coordinate the actions of the federal agencies in their regions. In practice, during the latter part of the 1990s, the governors gained control of these agencies because the federal government was politically so weak. Now, the federal government has largely corrected the situation through the new CFIs, whose very name indicates strict subordination.

The federal okrugs have in effect replaced the interregional associations for economic cooperation in addressing the tasks of attracting investment, working with business, and securing the coherence of the Russian market, though it is hard to imagine how people with backgrounds in the military and security sector can be performing these jobs better than civilians did. The okrugs have played an unarguably positive role in helping to renew the ranks of Russia's civil service and rotating personnel through different parts of the country, guaranteeing the unity of an all-Russian elite. The tasks of coordinating the power ministries and establishing a unified leadership with a common infrastructure remain goals for the future. Here, there is some progress, but not very much. Of course, there is little publicly available information about the power ministries, so it is difficult to assess this area in detail.

The activities of the presidential envoy do not seem to reflect the implementation of a distinct and comprehensive strategy. Rather, his work gives the appearance that he is casting about for something to do and simply moving in a circle. What at first seemed to be a dangerous slide to authoritarianism and an attempt to build a martial society, which would evolve in an undefined direction, has turned out to be an even more dangerous paralysis, in which the authorities seem to be standing in place. The envoys have laid out their tasks: bringing regional laws into line with federal norms, dividing power between the three layers of the state, attracting investment to the region, harmonizing relations between the executive and legislative branches, developing entrepreneurship, fighting crime and terrorism, and more. However, when the first task of bringing regional laws into line was apparently almost completed and when it turned out that nothing had changed, a new task was set that was at least two orders of magnitude larger: examining local laws and mayoral acts to see whether they conformed to federal norms.

The mind boggles at the number of topics the president presumably discusses with his envoys. During the course of one day, they can examine issues of dividing power between different layers of government, developing small and medium-sized business, and coordinating the activities of the power ministries.

Although the president hopes that the envoys strengthen the power of the federal government, their activities also point up the weaknesses of the state. One perennial problem is that the Russian authorities do not have enough money to pay for their activities, which forces them to rely on financial support from business. At one point, the Kremlin ordered the envoys to set up National Military Funds to gather "voluntary contributions" from business to be spent on various good deeds. By February 2002, there were fifty-seven regional offices of the fund throughout the country, most of them headed by Chekists. The Presidential Administration is also relying on business contributions to finance the above mentioned reception centers in urban and rural areas where citizens can complain about various problems they face. These centers can serve as a way of collecting information, enabling citizens to let off steam, and demonstrating the responsiveness of the federal authorities. In the future, they could help extend federal power to the local level when Russia eventually implements a municipal reform.

The Central okrug is the most powerful, but also the weakest, most dependent okrug. While all the envoys face a difficult job, in the center there is very little room for maneuver. The hyperconcentration of Russia's socioeconomic potential and practically all its financial resources in the city of Moscow makes it more difficult for the envoy to operate independently. He has a similar problem with the federal agencies: it is not easy to coordinate the power ministries when you are not at the top of them or rooted in the okrug in the way that Viktor Cherkesov is in the North-West okrug. Poltavchenko is an outsider for those both at the bottom and the top of the ministries. The gap between the federal and Moscow city authorities is too small for the envoy to function as a governor-general. He is not in charge and is unlikely ever to be in a position to take over. There is little obvious reason for his entire okrug level of government. Accordingly, only 3 percent of the okrug's residents know his name, while other envoys have achieved a 24 percent rating.

In Moscow, Poltavchenko sounds like a lobbyist for the interests of the neighboring regions. If the distance between the envoys and the main players in the other okrugs makes it seem as if they are somehow "above the fray," then in Moscow the envoy is actually "below the battle," outside the rooms where key political decisions are made and excluded from real political life. The envoy's famous independence has been bought by paying the price of weakness. The result is that he has to exert his leadership on the road—he only feels like a real leader outside Moscow. This situation has also led Poltavchenko to avoid hiring Muscovites; there are none in the leadership of the okrug or even as CFIs in Moscow and Moscow region.

The Central okrug has so far avoided the danger of falling under the control of Moscow city or the Kremlin. The envoy is independent, but weak. Poltavchenko is in a position to know what is going on and to monitor the situation, but he has no real executive authority. Therefore he mainly expresses the corporate interests of the envoys, and—using his close ties to Putin—works to strengthen their institutional power. The envoy's position in Moscow allows him to monitor some of the activities of the Putin-related group from Saint Petersburg, and it provides some access to the authorities; but he is not in a position to build his own machine. He is more like an understudy, a situation that feeds constant rumors that he will be appointed to a more important position, such as chief of the Presidential Administration or prime minister.

Notes

1. Accessed at www.nns.ru/int1862.html.
2. Interview with Georgii Poltavchenko, *Ogonek*, November 14, 2001.
3. These figures come from an article by Orel Governor Yegor Stroev in the first issue of the okrug's journal *Region-tsentr*, no. 1 (May 2001): 20.

4. According to figures from mid-2001, this is the largest staff of the seven okrugs. *Komsomolskaya Pravda*, July 12, 2001.

5. The turnover rate of senior officials on the envoy's staff has recently become quite high. Specially notable changes occurred in the second half of 2002 and early 2003, when three of his deputies departed: A. Esaulkov, V. Denikin, and A. Bespalov, and a third "first deputy" was hired—former okrug deputy procurator general, N. Makarov.

6. Bespalov was also an election consultant to Saint Petersburg mayor Anatolii Sobchak in 1996, working under the campaign organizer, Vladimir Putin. Since the end of 2001, he has been mainly involved in building the new Kremlin-backed party United Russia (Yedinaya Rossiya) and chairing its general council. In June 2002, he left his okrug job on his appointment as a member of the Federation Council.

7. *Region-tsentr*, no. 1 (May 2001): 7.

8. Regions.ru, September 30, 2002.

9. Accessed at www.strana.ru/print/113031.html.

10. An acquaintance of federal general procurator Ustinov from their work together in Krasnodar, Savchenko had been, prior to his promotion to okrug level in late 2002, the procurator for Lipetsk region.

11. Of the eighteen regional police chiefs, we could not find biographical information for two: Kostroma's N. A. Smirnov and Yaroslavl's V. V. Petukhov. Of the seventeen regional FSB leaders, we found information only for thirteen, and none on Vladimir's V. L. Timofeev, Kursk's G. A. Sviridov, Tula's V. P. Lebedev, and Yaroslavl's S. V. Makhrovskii. Additionally, a new FSB chief had not been appointed in Smolensk, following the election as governor in May 2002 of the former office holder V. N. Maslov.

12. See chapter 2 for a discussion of these laws.

13. He has spent most of his twenty-five-year career in his native Ivanovo region, after which he briefly worked in Moscow and in Pskov, where he clashed with a particularly corrupt governor.

14. The Tambov regional police chief is an outlier, since he was born in 1965. Most of his colleagues hail from 1945 to 1953.

15. In Belgorod and Ryazan, the heads of the regional FSBs became the CFIs in their regions; in Yaroslavl the deputy FSB head is now the CFI; and in Kursk the CFI is the former head of the Volgograd FSB.

16. The new governors of Voronezh and Smolensk are the former FSB heads in those regions, while in Kursk the FSB chief failed to win the election.

17. Accessed at www.strana.ru/print/70459.html.

18. Interview with Shchadrin, "Bol'shaya chast' nashikh del svyazana s orgprestupnost'yu," *Nezavisimaya gazeta*, April 12, 2002.

19. *Rossiiskaya gazeta*, 18 July 2002.

20. "I'm Not a Boss to the Governors," interview, *Rossiiskaya gazeta*, July 18, 2002.

21. He was also chairman of the Interparliamentary Assembly of the Commonwealth of Independent States.

22. In the Penza region the governor V. Bochkarev had delegated his representative to the Federation Council in 2001. However, prior to the April 2002 gubernatorial

election he needed the support of the Kremlin and of United Russia's leader Aleksandr Bespalov. With their help, he just won reelection. To repay his debt, the governor recalled his senator, former president of the airline Transaero, A. Pleshakov, and replaced him with Bespalov. At this, Pleshakov took offense and openly told the press that he had lost his job because he "did not provide sufficient financial support to the governor during the elections." An aide of Bochkarev's had informed him of this at an official meeting. See *Nezavisimaya gazeta*, June 11, 2002.

23. V. Kichedzhi, "Tsentral'nomu federal'nomu okrugu nuzhna prezidentskaya programma sotsial'no-ekonomicheskogo razvitiya," *Region-Tsentr*, no. 1 (May 2001): 34.

24. Kichedzhi, "Tsentral'nomu," 9.

25. Region-Inform, July 26, 2002.

26. "Moskovskoe prityazhenie," *Tverskaya 13*, October 19, 2002.

27. I. Telitsyna, "Poltavchenko ukreplyaet vertikal'," *Kompaniya*, October 7, 2002.

28. Interview with Poltavchenko, *Rossiiskaya gazeta*, July 18, 2002.

29. V. Kichedzhi, "Tsentral'nyi Federal'nyi Okrug: itogi goda, plany i perspektivy razvitiya," *Analytical Banking Review* (translated title), December 21, 2001.

30. A. Nikol'skii, "Polnomochnye investory," *Vedomosti*, February 4, 2002.

31. Interview with Poltavchenko in *Vedomosti*, April 18, 2002.

32. *Kommersant-Daily*, October 2, 2002.

33. *Moscow News*, February 29, 2002; *Kommersant-Daily*, February 29, 2002.

5

Southern Federal Okrug

Natalia Zubarevich

THE SOUTHERN FEDERAL OKRUG INCLUDES the republics of Adygeya, Dagestan, Ingushetia, Kabardino-Balkaria, Karachaevo-Cherkesia, Kalmykiya, Northern Osetia, Chechnya, Krasnodar Krai, Stavropol Krai; and the regions of Astrakhan, Volgograd, and Rostov.

Viktor Kazantsev (born 1946) built his career in the military, rising to the rank of commander of the North Caucasus Military District in 1997. In 1999 he led the joint military and police forces in the second Chechnya war. Kazantsev maintains close ties to the armed forces and has brought many officers onto his staff, assuming that soldiers are good managers.[1] He believes in leading from the top, and he tries to personally manage all contacts between his okrug's regions and the federal agencies that seek to carry out the president's policies. He also serves as chief lobbyist for the okrug's interests in the capital. He is a public politician and uses every opportunity to build his image.

"'Chechen' and 'bandit' are completely different synonyms."

—Viktor Kazantsev, Presidential Representative to the
Southern Federal Okrug, Ph.D. in political science[2]

Several factors determine how the new institution of the presidential envoy in the federal okrugs operates. The most important are

1. the functions originally assigned to the envoys and the subsequent changes in these functions;

Southern Federal District of the Russian Federation

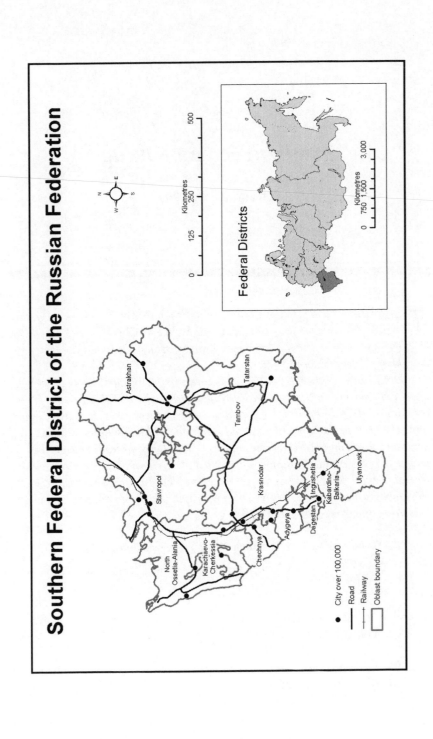

2. the political and socioeconomic conditions in the regions under their control; and

3. the personalities of the envoys, their definition of their priorities, and their ability to achieve the goals set before them.

As this chapter demonstrates, the Southern okrug differs from the six other okrugs in each of these respects.

Okrug Overview

The Southern okrug is home to the most ethnically diverse population of the seven okrugs. Its thirteen administrative units include eight republics—territories set aside for non-Russian ethnic groups, which account for 27 percent of its population. The other units are regions and krais that are predominantly ethnic Russian. Many of Russia's ethnic conflicts are concentrated in the okrug, and in the 1990s some of these disputes erupted into either armed battles (North Osetia and Ingushetia, 1992) or a long-term war (Chechnya, 1994 to the present), thus fostering numerous terrorist acts in various areas and generating hundreds of thousands of refugees.[3]

The Southern okrug is the third largest of the seven and contains 15 percent of Russia's population. Beyond the natural population growth in most of the okrug's republics during the 1990s, large numbers of immigrants came to the ethnic Russian regions from countries of the Commonwealth of Independent States. In Krasnodar Krai, the population grew by 10 percent in the 1990s.

The okrug's contribution to the country's gross domestic product (GDP) is only half of what one would expect, given the size of its population, meaning that local residents generate only half as much as the average resident of the country. The okrug is heavily agricultural, producing 17 percent of Russia's agricultural output (third among the seven okrugs), 29 percent of Russia's grain, but only 6.5 percent of its industrial output.[4] The South's main advantages are its favorable climate, productive soil, and the presence of large ports, which account for approximately half of Russia's foreign trade.

Following the collapse of the Soviet Union, the economy in Russia's South shrank the most of any area in the newly created country. In 1996, Dagestan's GDP stood at only 16 percent of the 1990 level. In the other regions of the South, the figure varied between 23 and 30 percent, with the average for all of Russia a much larger 48 percent. In the ethnic Russian regions of the South, the greatest production drops after 1990 took place in the industrially developed Rostov and Volgograd regions, where their joint GDP declined by two-thirds by the middle of the decade, as compared to 1990. During the period of economic growth between 1999 and 2001, many of the okrug's regions were among the leaders, achieving industrial growth rates of 20 to 35 percent. The main motor was the food industry. During the period 2000–2002, crop harvests increased significantly.

Standards of living in the South are much lower than in the rest of Russia, with personal income only 44 percent of the national average. The share of poor (defined by the number of people with income below the subsistence minimum) is greater than the average for Russia in all regions of the South except Rostov. In nine regions, the poor make up more than half of the population, including in Ingushetia, Kalmykia, Dagestan, and Karachaevo-Cherkesia, where poverty afflicts more than 60 percent of the population. The okrug has the highest level of official unemployment—15 percent of the economically active population, compared to 10 percent for Russia as a whole. In most of the republics, 20 to 30 percent of the economically active population does not have work.[5] Overall, the number of jobless, refugees, and forced migrants in the okrug is about two million people, or 10 percent of the entire population.[6]

The social and economic crises in the Southern okrug (especially in the ethnic, non-Russian republics) are much worse than anywhere else in the country, including the Far East. Chechnya's economy has been almost entirely destroyed thanks to nearly a decade of war. In short, the Southern okrug is the most difficult okrug to manage in the country.

Staffing Policies

Envoy Viktor Kazantsev has an okrug staff of 106, which includes the largest proportion of people from the military and other power ministries of any of the seven okrugs. Kazantsev based his headquarters in the okrug's largest city, Rostov-on-Don, but then set up several branch offices to manage his complex territory. Initially, one of the offices was in Yessentuki (Stavropol Krai), where President Yeltsin's representative had his headquarters in the 1990s. But in May 2001 Kazantsev moved this office to Vladikavkaz, the capital of North Osetia. A second branch office in Volgograd manages the lower Volga regions of Volgograd, Astrakhan, and Kalmykia.

Kazantsev drew on three major talent pools in building his staff. Most of the envoy's subordinates are former colleagues from his time serving in the North Caucasus Military District. Military tradition shapes relations among the staff. There is strict subordination, which leaves little room for employees to show independence and initiative. The army officers who make up the middle level of the staff generally have little of the experience that would have prepared them for their current jobs. The second group of staff comprises officials from the area's elite, mostly former staff members employed by the South's regional leaders. Officials from the ethnic Russian regions of Rostov and Stavropol make up most of this group. The third group is the Muscovites sent to the okrug by the Moscow-based Presidential Administration (PA) or other federal agencies. Except for the Muscovites, Kazantsev picked his staff from people he had known in his earlier work. Most of them, apparently, do not lobby at the okrug level for the interests of their home regions. During the first two years of Kazantsev's work, there was a considerable amount of staff turnover.

Several features distinguish his staff among those of the seven okrugs. First, Kazantsev kept on as a federal inspector only one of the presidential representatives who had served Yeltsin in the 1990s. Overall in Russia, one third of the federal inspectors previously served as Yeltsin's representatives. One reason for the low level of staffing continuity in the South is the fact that many republics during the Yeltsin era simply had no such representative. Thus Kazantsev often had to start from scratch. Second, the okrug management system is relatively complicated: in some cases, a chief federal inspector (CFI) handles two or three regions, while some of the largest regions are divided between several CFIs. Third, Kazantsev took into account ethnic background when choosing CFIs for the ethnic republics. Finally, there is less turnover among the envoy's staff in the regions than in the central office in Rostov.

Kazantsev often tries to calm conflicts among the regional elite by hiring former regional and municipal leaders who have lost elections or quit their jobs in the hope of working on his staff. Usually, they are appointed as CFIs, work in Rostov, or quickly find a different job. Examples include Beslan Gantamirov (the former Groznyi mayor), N. Karpov (former Sochi mayor), Stanislav Derev (the former Cherkessk mayor who lost his republic's presidential election), and Aslan Dzharimov, the former president of Adygeya, who lost his bid for another term.[7]

Strengthening Ties within the Okrug

On taking his job, Kazantsev declared that one of his key tasks would be strengthening the ties between the regions of the okrug. He has tried to stimulate horizontal interregional ties by creating numerous councils and associations. In fact, Kazantsev has created so many new groups that locals speak of this as an "epidemic." Most of the newly created organizations are based in Rostov, increasing the status of the okrug capital, and they are usually chaired by officials resident in Rostov. Some of the organizations work effectively, but many are reminiscent of façade Soviet-era structures. Given the nature of his region, Kazantsev deemed it important to create a council of "elder statesmen," as well as councils for the okrug's religious organizations. He did not create a formal council for his okrug governors, but he brings them together for regular meetings.

With the creation of the okrug, the role of the North Caucasus Interregional Association, a body for economic coordination, has changed. The easterly regions of Astrakhan and Volgograd have both joined the association for the first time, since they were assigned to the Southern, not the Volga Okrug. Formally, the body is more "democratic" now, since the leadership rotates among the governors. Until the reform, Rostov governor Vladimir Chub had chaired the association for several years. In selecting Chub as their leader, the association members hoped that having one person serve as leader over a significant period of time would raise the profile of Russia's least active interregional association.

In 2001, the association named then Adygeya president Aslan Dzharimov as the first of the rotating presidents.[8] Despite the greater formal democracy, the association has, in reality, lost much of its influence, and its discussions are now limited to managerial issues. With increasing frequency, the governors ignore its meetings, which usually take place after sessions with Kazantsev. As Stavropol governor Aleksandr Chernogorov noted, "many of the association's functions have now gone to the okrug."[9]

To bring the regional legislatures into contact with each other, Kazantsev initiated the creation of the Southern Russia Parliamentary Association in April 2001. A. Popov, the chairman of the Rostov legislature, agreed to chair the new association, and eleven of the thirteen regions in the okrug joined, with only Dagestan and Ingushetia declining. Through the association, the okrug authorities try to lobby the interests of the South in both chambers of Russia's parliament. Rostov and Krasnodar legislators were especially active in working to amend federal law regarding the general principles for organizing regional political institutions and drafting a new land code. But the lobbying power of the new structure is sharply constrained by the numerous disputes between the member regions over what issues should take priority. Because of these disputes, the presidents of Dagestan and Ingushetia (until Ruslan Aushev was replaced as president in 2002 by a Kazantsev ally) did not want to join the association, and they prevented their legislatures from joining as a sign of protest against some of Kazantsev's policies.

To further advance his ability to lobby the federal parliament, Kazantsev has also set up an interfactional group of fifty-three State Duma deputies from Russia's South. The chairman of the group, V. Averchenko, set the goal of getting funding for the federal program to develop the South written into the 2002 budget.[10] However, the small amount of federal money set aside for this purpose suggests that this group, too, has little clout at the federal level.

Coordinating the Activities of the
Federal Authorities in the Region

Like the other presidential envoys, Kazantsev took on the functions of an intermediary in relations between the regions in his okrug and the federal government. However, he is probably the most active and public in carrying out these functions. For him, the balance in the okrug between the interests of the center and those of the regions is gradually shifting in favor of the regions, as he increasingly considers himself the head of a "Southern" megaregion. This shift is most clear in his sharp criticism of the federal ministries regarding their contribution to rebuilding Chechnya's economy.[11] The reasons for his shift concern not only the current problems he is addressing but also the deeper transformations taking place in the functions he performs.

First, by the middle of 2001, he had essentially completed the task of setting up okrug-level offices for federal ministries and agencies. Coordination of these offices has taken on a routine character: they operate partly through a council he set up that meets regularly, and they adopt decisions to be carried out by the relevant ministries.

Second, the process of bringing regional laws into line with federal norms is largely complete. All the okrug's regions are ready to renounce the power-sharing treaties that they signed with Moscow in the 1990s. The Justice Ministry found that 1,043 laws violated federal norms, and all but 123 of them had been amended by the middle of 2001. The constitutions of eight of thirteen regions were also amended.[12] The remaining divergences are the most difficult to solve, and most likely will require long-running court battles. To increase pressure on recalcitrant republican supreme courts, the envoy's office filed complaints with a Moscow oversight body charging that justices in seven republican courts were not reacting quickly enough to the procurators' protests.

Third, Kazantsev has a very contradictory role as the coordinator of Russia's policy in Chechnya, reflecting the lack of consistency in the policy itself. In November 2001, he received the authority to conduct negotiations with President Aslan Maskhadov's representative A. Zakaev. But then the meeting did not produce any results. Although Maskhadov was elected president of Chechnya in 1997, the Putin administration no longer recognized him as the republic's legitimate leader. In addition, Kazantsev remains the arbiter of conflicts between the republic's Russian-backed leaders, but Akhmad Kadyrov, Moscow's imposed Chechen leader, is increasingly taking his problems directly to the Russian capital, thus bypassing Kazantsev.

In effect, Kazantsev's powers to manage Chechnya are eroding. Federal Minister for Chechnya Stanislav Ilyasov, appointed in late 2002, coordinates the activities of federal agencies working toward the social and economic development of the republic. Deputy Prime Minister Viktor Khristenko, chairman of the government commission on Chechnya, is responsible for financing the rebuilding. Federal Security Service (FSB) director Nikolai Patrushev directs antiterrorist operations. Interior Minister Boris Gryzlov controls the Chechen police and the guards stationed at the republic's checkpoints. The chief of the general staff, Anatoly Kvashnin, commands the federal military forces in the region. In Chechnya itself, President Kadyrov fought with Prime Minister Ilyasov, until the latter was replaced in late 2002 by another official, with whom Kadyrov also fought. Kazantsev stands above the Chechen authorities, and Putin stands above everyone. But in such a system it is practically impossible to be an effective manager.

Fourth, Kazantzev plays a secondary role in the okrug's foreign political and economic activities. Resolving the issues surrounding Caspian Sea oil and cooperating with the Caspian countries is the responsibility of the president's special Caspian representative V. Kalyuzhnii. Kazantsev's deputy V. Krokhmal only accompanies Kalyuzhnii on inspection trips to oil sites in the okrug. Gazprom and other federal agencies coordinate all of the natural gas projects. Kazantsev plays a more substantial role only in controlling the region's ports. However, the Transportation Ministry is setting up a federal company (Rosmorport) to strengthen the federal government's influence in this area as well. One branch of the company will unite all the ports of the Southern basin, so Kazantsev will have some monitoring powers over this structure.[13]

Fifth, and most important, the envoy has no role in distributing state funds. The problem is not primarily a conflict with the Ministry for Economic Development and Trade over the program for developing Russia's South (this is a major point of conflict for other okrugs). Rather, Kazantsev confronts the firm intention of the Economics Ministry and the entire government to maintain unilateral control over federal finances.

In this situation, the envoy only has one option—to strengthen his role as unifier and as lobbyist for the interests of his okrug's regions. Kazantsev is not only forced to do this, he is obligated to, since his other functions are essentially complete or being performed by other players. He is anyway inclined toward this role by his character and his past experience as a commander who felt himself "a father to his troops."

Coordinating the Power Ministries

Kazantsev believes that, as envoy, he should be the main coordinator of the power ministries in the okrug. He has strong support for this role since many leaders of the local branches of these ministries owe their current position to him. Kazantsev's former deputy in the North Caucasus Military District Gennadii Troshev took over the district after Kazantsev was appointed envoy and served in this post until December 2002.[14] The two generals respected each other, but were not friendly.[15] Kazantsev's relations with General V. Baranov, the commander of the forces in Chechnya, are more hierarchical, since Kazantsev perceives himself to be in charge.[16] Okrug procurator Sergei Fridinskii is also part of Kazantsev's "military team," having earlier served as the military procurator in the North Caucasus Military District. In addition to responding to the criticisms of human rights advocates about the actions of the federal forces in Chechnya, he is busy overhauling the staffs of many republican procuracies. Thus, for example, from mid-2000 to mid-2001, two procurators were sacked in North Osetia.[17]

Currently, the envoy does not have any formal influence over the border guards' service, which so far remains bound to its old structures. In this case, Kazantsev can only send "suggestions" for overcoming operational deficiencies.[18]

The FSB has more autonomy than the other power ministries and did not form real okrug-level offices to work directly with the envoys. Instead, in the Southern okrug it set up a council of the heads of the FSB branches in the okrug under the chairmanship of Rostov region's FSB head Valerii Dyatlenko.[19] New FSB chiefs have been appointed in some of the non-Russian republics (Adygeya,[20] North Osetia), and they are all ethnic Slavs.

The FSB coordinates the actions of the other power ministries in the okrug. After a spate of terrorist incidents, FSB director N. Patrushev usually comes himself to chair a meeting at the okrug's operational headquarters, which includes the heads of all the regional power ministries and often the North Caucasus governors as well. In practice, during crisis situations, Patrushev takes over part of Kazantsev's responsibilities. During the early part of Kazantsev's tenure, deputy envoy and FSB general N. Britvin worked in Patrushev's shadow, and there was little information about his activities in the press. This situation changed dramatically when FSB general M. Zyazikov replaced Britvin and then ran for president of Ingushetia with Kazantsev's support (see a detailed description below). A full-scale media campaign backed Zyazikov's candidacy.

The relations between the FSB and the Ministry of Internal Affairs (MVD) are strained. Patrushev was particularly dissatisfied with the work of the local police in August 2001, when terrorists hijacked a bus, took hostages, and attempted to blow up a car filled with important local bureaucrats.

The MVD delayed forming an okrug level structure until August 2001. In July Deputy Envoy M. Fetisov, the former police chief of Rostov region, recommended that his successor in that job, Lieutenant General Sergei Shchadrin, should head the okrug police structure. However, Shchadrin refused to take this position, preferring to perform the same job in the Central okrug.[21] Instead of Shchadrin, who had relatively good ties to the Rostov elite, an outsider became the new okrug police chief: former Krasnoyarsk krai chief Mikhail Rudchenko.

Rudchenko faces a high crime rate and extensive corruption in the ranks of the police. During 2000, the Southern Federal District registered eighty-two thousand crimes, most of them felonies. Seventy-two percent of them were reported as solved, but the success rate has been declining.[22] It is still too soon to tell how much influence the envoy has on the work of the okrug's police. The police have clearly been dragging their feet with regards to the administrative fine-tuning of their structures. So far, it is the police rather than the governors who are more frightened by the ongoing changes. Thus it is too soon to say if the police have been freed from the governors' control.

Fear among the okrug's top police officers of losing their jobs in the course of the administrative reforms has not reduced the level of corruption in the police. An illustrative example concerns the creation of the Azov-Black Sea Department of Internal Affairs (UVD) for railroad, air, and water transportation. Kazantsev and Krasnodar Krai governor Tkachev lobbied for the new agency "to check the work of the ports, protect tourists, and work with the customs agency, the tax police, society, and the Cossacks."[23] Kazantsev is particularly concerned about this issue and even appealed to Prime Minister Mikhail Kasyanov, complaining about the poor work of the police, the customs, and the tax police in the ports. Subsequently, Deputy Envoy Fetisov, who liaises with the law enforcement agencies, criticized not only the Southern Customs Administration for failing to catch all but a few smugglers, but also the Azov-Black Sea UVD for closing investigations into a large number of criminal cases.[24] However, the statements of the okrug authorities have made little impact, since the Southern ports remain the most criminalized part of the economy.

Only in the fall of 2001 was a member of Kazantsev's staff, the former chief federal inspector (CFI) for Volgograd region, Valerii Napalkov, appointed head of the okrug's Tax Police Service. This was the last of the power ministry appointments at the okrug level. Previously, Napalkov had worked many years in the MVD, before heading the Volgograd region's tax police and then becoming the region's chief federal inspector. The role of the tax police seemed to be growing until Putin abolished the agency in March 2003. Its okrug department had been set up in the premises of the Rostov region's Tax Police.[25] Napalkov, like the other okrug heads of the tax police, had the additional title of deputy head of the Federal Tax Police Service.

Overall, one can reach these conclusions:

- the power ministries have set up okrug structures, though their organizational forms vary from ministry to ministry;

- Kazantsev's influence on the choice of personnel was significant (especially for the military district, the Procuracy, and the Tax Police), but it was not total;
- the dominance of Rostov elites among the power ministries is weaker than among the okrug's civilian and society-oriented agencies;
- the conflicts between the various power ministries remain, particularly during antiterrorist operations;
- the work of the power ministries is most fully coordinated during investigations of terrorist acts, but in these cases, the head of the FSB, rather than the presidential envoy, plays the lead role.

Relations with Governors

In contrast to most of the other envoys, Kazantsev knew almost all of the governors in his okrug from his previous work. These contacts allowed him to establish a competent strategy for working with them. Until the elections in Ingushetia at the beginning of 2002, Kazantsev avoided any sudden, heavy-handed actions against Southern okrug governors, carefully taking into account the existing interests of the various clans and groups, and seeking to stabilize intraelite relations, especially in the republics.[26] Such nonintervention was most likely Kazantsev's personal policy, rather than the result of a direct order from the center. The main goal was preserving stability in the South. A year after taking office, Kazantsev said: "Many feared that we would not find a common language with the governors. Let me say that there have not been any serious conflicts, although there is no fraternization either."[27]

The attempt to find compromises with the governors was particularly evident in the effort to bring regional laws into line with federal norms. In general, Kazantsev did not apply any harsh measures against the regions. By the summer of 2002, after two years of work, the process was continuing in five republics. Dagestan was essentially allowed to keep its divergent laws as an exception from the norm (the republic is the only region that does not elect its president directly and uses ethnic quotas in portioning out seats in the legislature). Only in the cases of Adygeya and Karachaevo-Cherkesia did Kazantsev use more pressure. But even here he largely avoided using his own political capital, by referring cases to the federal judicial system. In many of the most contentious cases, Kazantsev and his deputies generally gave ground so as to reach agreement with the position of the governors. For example, he supported the leaders of the largest grain-producing regions over the regulation of grain prices, even though their position violated federal laws. He took a similarly complaisant position on the regulation of migration in the okrug's resort zone.[28]

Nevertheless, there are clear conflicts in relations between the envoy and the leaders of several regions. It is not easy for him to secure the obedience of the heads of the "Russian" regions. Perhaps his smoothest relations are with the leaders of the lower Volga regions, Volgograd and Astrakhan. These regions are located far from Rostov, and their experienced governors are less ambitious in their battle for autonomy. Volgograd governor Nikolai Maksyuta is the closest to Kazantsev and publicly supports all his initiatives.

Against this general background, Kazantsev has developed a variety of relationships with the ethnic Russian governors of the North Caucasus. His relations with Krasnodar Krai governor A. Tkachev are reasonably rational on both sides. The envoy does not interfere in internal regional affairs. However, Kazantsev and Tkachev work together to address common tasks, of which the most important are economic—monitoring the Black Sea ports and attracting investment. This balance of power between envoy and governor did not appear immediately, even though Kazantsev played a visible role in the negotiations over the transfer of power in the krai from former governor Nikolai Kondratenko, who was unacceptable to the Kremlin, to the more loyal Tkachev. Nevertheless, in some cases Tkachev drops his usual caution and presses the interests of the local elite. Thus, in discussing the Putin administration's law on privatizing land, the governor declared that the Kuban area, which includes Krasnodar, was a separate country and that Putin was destroying Russia with his policy of land sales.[29] Despite rumors that the procurator general then ordered Kazantsev to take measures against Tkachev, nothing is likely to happen. Kazantsev would prefer to maintain stability in Krasnodar than to contest a governor's populist statements that are aimed at pleasing various constituencies among his voters.

There is palpable tension in the relationship between Kazantsev and Rostov governor Vladimir Chub. Beyond their different political views (Kazantsev clearly dislikes liberals and market enthusiasts, and sees Chub as one of them), it is as difficult for the two leaders to coexist in one city as it is for "two bears to share one lair." The governor does not hide his displeasure now that every federal minister coming to Rostov has to meet routinely with the okrug authorities.[30] Chub has also publicly complained that Kazantsev and his team have taken over some of the tasks that the region performed in the past, even though the region still has to foot the bill.[31] The regional administration also tries to prevent the okrug from effectively monitoring it. Thus, after Kazantsev determined that twenty-five regional administrative decisions violated federal legislation, the governor said that he would challenge some of these findings in court. Relations deteriorated even further after an okrug investigation resulted in six new criminal cases against regional officials and the relaunching of investigations into fifteen cases that had been closed.[32] The tense relationship was also clear during the 2001 gubernatorial election, from which Kazantsev distanced himself.

Kazantsev is much more strict with Stavropol Krai's governor Aleksandr Chernogorov and regularly criticizes him publicly. During 2001 Stavropol was the only region in the okrug where Kazantsev conducted two investigations. After the first, the governor was told to reduce the number of krai civil servants by one third (there are more than ten thousand).[33] Following the second one, Deputy Envoy A. Korobeinikov announced that no noticeable changes had taken place following the first investigation, that the data presented by the krai were not accurate or were not interpreted properly, and that the krai lacked coherent management.[34] The governor decided not to contest the results and signed off on the embarrassing and extremely critical report, including its demands that criminal charges be filed against several administration officials. Simultaneously, and not coincidentally, the procurator, the Finance Ministry, and a Supreme Court commission conducted an investigation of the krai court system.[35] Local observers claimed that the reason the envoy was exerting pressure on the governor was that he had tried unsuccessfully to gain control of the local branch of the pro-Kremlin Unity party.[36] More likely, the main reason for Kazantsev's attention was the weakness of the governor and his ineffective management of the krai. The public humiliation of the weak governor allows him to demonstrate his authority and the vigor of the okrug administration. Nevertheless, he does not forget to use the "carrot and stick" approach. While his deputy Korobeinikov was criticizing the Stavropol governor, Kazantsev announced that he was ready to seek the president's help in strengthening Stavropol Krai as Russia's bastion in the North Caucasus.[37]

Kazantsev's relations with the republican presidents are easier to categorize. He has the best relations with the leaders of North Osetia and Kabardino-Balkaria. He is most comfortable with experienced Soviet-style leaders who guarantee stability through administrative methods. Thus, North Osetia president Aleksandr Dzasokhov secured the return of Osetian money to the republic, legalized income from the vodka business, and forced private businessmen to increase the official salaries they pay their employees.[38] In Osetia, all major projects are tied to Dzasokhov, who has a reputation as one of Russia's best lobbyists. It also receives material benefit for the warm ties between its leader and the envoy—for example, getting significant funds from the Federal Program for Developing Russia's South, even though it did not figure prominently in it at the start. Additionally, the federal authorities take Dzasokhov's position into account when making new appointments to the procurator's office and other power ministries. Kazantsev also supported Dzasokhov's reelection, and not just because Moscow ordered him to do so.

Even before he became an envoy, Kazantsev had close relations with Kabardino-Balkaria president Valerii Kokov.[39] Nevertheless, the republican authorities follow warily the actions and statements of the envoy's staff. When disagreements arise, Kokov keeps quiet, and someone on his staff makes a statement. After Deputy Envoy Krokhmal asserted that there were difficult interethnic relations in the republic, the speaker of the republic's upper house protested and denied that such problems existed. He also claimed that the republic had, on its own and without reference to the okrug, brought its legislation into line with federal norms and increased revenues for the budget.[40]

In this case, a relationship of "friendship" that takes account of both sides' interests is viable, because both are ready to compromise. The republican authorities compromised when, under pressure from the envoy, they quietly changed their tax laws before the dispute became public, thereby giving the appearance that there had been no official violations.[41] Both Moscow and Kazantsev value the stability that Kokov provides, as Putin made clear during his visit to the republic in September 2001.[42]

Kazantsev is extremely popular among the population in Dagestan, where he was seen as a liberator after the army successfully expelled the Chechen invaders who attacked the republic in August 1999. Additionally, as mentioned earlier, he did not force any changes in the electoral system of Dagestan, even though it is built on ethnic quotas and violates federal law. He understands the difficulties of maintaining peace in Dagestan's ethnically divided society and is willing to wait while local and Moscow-based legal experts create a system of ethnic representation that fits within the framework of federal law. (Most likely, ethnic groups will be guaranteed representation indirectly, perhaps by using multi-member districts). Public conflict with Dagestan president Magomedali Magomedov occurred only once when Magomedov complained that Dagestan had been assigned little money in the federal plan to develop the South, even though Dagestan was one of the poorest and most problem-plagued regions in the North Caucasus. He also accused federal officials of forgetting about Dagestan.[43] Kazantsev quickly compromised, admitted the oversights, and promised to resolve them.[44] Overall, relations with Magomedov are stable, and Kazantsev urged him to seek another term as republican leader because he did not see an alternative to him.[45] At the unusually advanced age of seventy-two, Magomedov duly secured another term in elections held in summer 2002.

Relations with Kalmykia's president Kirsan Ilyumzhinov are completely hidden and kept to a minimum. Kazantsev does not interfere with Ilyumzhinov's activities and has not conducted any investigations in the republic. He appointed an Ilyumzhinov ally as CFI for the republic. Even though the Ilyumzhinov clan has largely privatized the economy[46] and spends budget money on purposes for which it was not intended,[47] Kazantsev remains neutral. He understands the limits of his abilities, especially after the Accounting Chamber's fruitless inspection of the republic, which found no significant violations. Moreover, the republic long ago brought its legislation into line with federal norms; there is relatively little crime; and there are no visible internal conflicts among the elite. This means that Ilyumzhinov satisfies the main concerns of the federal authorities. In this part of the okrug, the envoy mainly focuses on regulating the land dispute between Kalmykia and Astrakhan.

Kazantsev has essentially conflictual relations with the other republican leaders in the okrug. As early as the beginning of 2001 he would state openly that the then president of Adygeya, Aslan Dzharimov, had got the "wrong people ensconced around him."[48] Additionally, despite the protests of the Procuracy and the Supreme Court, Dzharimov refused to amend the republican electoral law, which prescribed unequal electoral districts for republican elections. The districts favored the indigenous population over the ethnic Russian majority. Thus, in the March 2001 elections the republic's titular nationality won a majority in both houses, even though it made up only a quarter of the population. In response, the envoy only took half-measures, sacking the leadership of the republican FSB and, during the January 2002 presidential election, indirectly supporting the opposition candidate Khazret Sovmen, a wealthy gold magnate aged sixty-four, who ultimately won. Despite their past disagreements, Kazantsev proceeded to take the defeated Dzharimov onto his staff. In doing this, Kazantsev sought to balance the interests of the various clans in the republic and thus divide his opponents.

Kazantsev has very close but also highly complicated relations with the Russian-backed Chechen president Kadyrov. Some members of the power ministries never liked Kadyrov, and from summer 2002 he wrecked his relationship with Kazantsev too. First, Kadyrov squeezed out Chechen prime minister Ilyasov, whose appointment Kazantsev had lobbied for. Second, he began building influence in the federal halls of power and using the differences between the numerous coordinators of Russia's Chechen policy to bypass Kazantsev and win approval for his own policies over the envoy's head. After a personal meeting with Putin in October 2001, Kadyrov was able to merge the Chechen presidential and prime ministerial staffs and place his own person, Yakov Sergunin, at the head of them, making him the second most important person in the republic.[49] Kadyrov also managed to reach agreement with his former enemy Beslan Gantamirov, who had resigned as mayor of Grozny in spring 2001 and joined Kazantsev's staff. In early 2002 Kadyrov appointed him vice-premier of the republic.[50] Although Kazantsev participated in the negotiations and did not publicly oppose the appointment, his deputy S. Yepifantsev had earlier spoken out against bringing the unmanageable Gantamirov back to the republic. The complicated personal and bureaucratic relations between the okrug officials, the various Chechen authorities, and the numerous federal structures make interpretation of these developments difficult. Nonetheless, Kazantsev's lack of independence in personnel decisions concerning Chechnya is clear. On the formal side, in the spring of 2002 Putin issued a decree giving Kadyrov the right to appoint the republican leadership by himself, with only the appointment of the prime minister requiring Kazantsev's approval.[51]

Karachaevo-Cherkesiya president general Vladimir Semenov has poor relations with Kazantsev, even though the envoy did a lot to alleviate the conflict between the Cherkes and Karachai ethnic groups after the Cherkes candidate Stanislav Derev (the former mayor of the republic's capital and an influential businessman) lost the republic's presidential race in 1999. Kazantsev secured the amendment of the republican constitution to make sure that the posts of president and prime minister would be divided between the two main nationalities, and he hired Derev onto his staff as an economic adviser, thereby reducing the intensity of the conflict. However, these efforts soured Kazantsev's relations with Semenov, who thought that the envoy did not have the right to intervene in such matters, and he even expressed the hope that the North Caucasus republics could have their own federal okrug.[52] Additionally, in August 2001, after several terrorist acts in the republic, Semenov protested the fact that the power ministries were not subordinate to him. Another conflict occurred when Kazantsev successfully backed Derev's appointment as one of the republic's representatives to the Federation Council over Semenov's protests.[53]

While it seemed that Kazantsev had reconciled the two sides, during 2001 the number of political murders in the republic grew. A republican law that he backed—on combating the Wahhabi Islamic movement (officially titled "On countering political and religious extremism")—was adopted, but it had no real impact. Although it went beyond federal norms at the time it was enacted, since there was no corresponding federal law, Putin subsequently signed one in the summer of 2002.[54] All in all, despite the various setbacks, Kazantsev's efforts effectively strengthened his influence in the republic.

By the end of 2001, Ingushetia was the most problematic region for Kazantsev. For a long time, he had tried not to make the situation worse. He approved the personnel proposals made by President Ruslan Aushev,[55] and he did not interfere in the clan system of Ingushetia's politics.[56] Also, he did not react to the sharp and reasonably just accusations that he one-sidedly backed North Osetia in its ongoing conflict with Ingushetia, and he did not provide any help in dealing with the floods of refugees from Chechnya and North Osetia.[57] By the end of 2001, the problems reached a critical juncture. Kazantsev's attempt, at Moscow's orders, to resolve the Osete–Ingush conflict quickly failed, and Kazantsev refused to replace the federal bureaucrats whom Aushev considered his opponents (the CFI for Ingushetia and the republic's procurator). Ingushetia president Aushev opted for open conflict. Having stopped attending meetings at the envoy's office in the fall, he started criticizing federal policy sharply at the end of the year, and then abruptly and unexpectedly resigned.[58] At this time the Fourth Congress of the People of Ingushetia sent appeals to the president and the general procurator, saying that "the people of Ingushetia do not trust the envoy of Russia's president in the Southern Federal Okrug, Viktor Kazantsev."[59] The situation was getting out of control, so Kazantsev decided to run his own candidate, newly appointed Deputy Envoy M. Zyazikov, in the republic's presidential election (see below for a further discussion of this election). Thus, toward the end of his second year on the job, Kazantsev decided to follow the examples of the Urals and Far Eastern envoys, whose deputies had competed in gubernatorial elections (the former successfully, the latter embarrassingly).

Overall, the main features of Kazantsev's relations with the governors can be summarized as such:

- His policy of carefully supporting the interclan balances among the regional elites, which he followed for a long time, diversified to include the use of direct pressure on the elites, and then a decision that one of his deputies would participate openly in a regional election.
- The envoy maintained a differentiated approach toward the presidents of the republics who were able to maintain stability in their regions (in these cases, Kazantsev kept his intervention to a minimum) and those who failed to do so (and thus elicited more intrusive interference).
- Kazantsev has monitored the governors of the ethnic Russian regions in a variety of ways. The governors of the lower Volga regions and Krasnodar have managed to preserve the highest level of independence, thanks to their loyalty to the federal government and their ability to conduct relations with the envoy in a rational way.
- The regional leaders have not consolidated around (or against) the envoy. As in their earlier relations with the federal government, they generally act alone. Even lobbying on issues that affect the entire South (such as the new law creating private property for land, or migration policy, or efforts to secure investments) brings together only some of the leaders.
- The regional leaders' ability to act independently of the federal authorities has declined, but the change is not the same in all regions, since Kazantsev treats the regions differently. He has even applied the formal procedures for bringing regional laws into line with federal norms with varying degrees of strictness. In general, the envoy does not possess economic levers to influence the regions. He acts primarily by taking administrative measures.

Gubernatorial Elections and the Role of the Envoy

From the creation of the federal districts in 2000 until the spring of 2002, the presidential representative played only a secondary role in gubernatorial elections. This policy changed when he intervened directly in Ingushetia's elections.

Kazantsev's influence over the first elections in his okrug was minimal. When Volgograd governor Nikolai Maksyuta won reelection in 2000, the oil giant LUKoil and the Communist Party played a much greater role than the presidential envoy.[60] Astrakhan governor Anatolii Guzhvin also won reelection on the basis of his own resources and those of major oil and gas companies. In Stavropol, Kazantsev did not support the reelection of Governor Chernogorov, and the federal authorities' aid to opposition candidate S. Ilyasov was not sufficient to secure his victory. Only in Krasnodar Krai was Kazantsev's role more significant, since he talked Governor Nikolai Kondratenko out of running for a second term.[61] However Kondratenko, who remained extremely popular in his region and was commonly called *"Bat'ka"* ("Father"), was able to choose his successor independently, without any input from Kazanstev.

In 2001, Rostov governor Vladimir Chub succeeded in excluding the envoy from any role in the region's gubernatorial elections. As described above, the tension between him and Chub was significant, and there was some early talk that his first deputy, V. Anpilogov, would run against Chub. However, Chub was able to gain the support of the PA in Moscow, so Kazantsev could not play an independent role. He distanced himself from the elections and did not respond to Chub's request for support.[62] Kazantsev even made a special statement to the media that he did not support any of the candidates.[63] In fact, the envoy's investigation of the administration's work on the eve of the elections and the resulting measures taken against it may have helped the communist candidate Leonid Ivanchenko. Nonetheless, Kazantsev made no clear impact on the election. After the courts disqualified Ivanchenko from the race by ruling that many of the signatures collected in support of his candidacy were forged, Kazantsev met with the former candidate and persuaded him not to invalidate the elections by calling either for a boycott or for electors to vote "against all candidates," which is one of the options on Russian ballots.[64]

In the three republican elections of early 2002, Kazantsev and the Kremlin openly supported only North Osetia's Aleksandr Dzasokhov.[65] In Adygeya, gold magnate Khazret Sovmen won without the envoy's help, on the basis of his personal business success, a talent the voters hoped that he would employ to enrich the republic as well as himself.

Through the spring of 2002, Kazantsev played only a marginal role in the regional elections. All the incumbents who won reelection did so with their own resources, and he did not play any role in bringing new leaders to power. The only contribution by the federal authorities were their efforts to "clear the field" in favor of candidates they supported. Thus, through the electoral commissions and the courts, they were able to eliminate candidates they did not like. However, it was not clear who contributed more to this effort: the relevant PA officials in Moscow or the envoy.

The situation changed in spring 2002 as a result of the political crisis in Ingushetia. In order to weaken the influence of the leading clans and prevent the election of a candidate backed by former president Aushev, Kazantsev, with the backing of other federal authorities, decided to take direct action. He backed the nomination of his newly appointed first deputy, M. Zyazikov, an ethnic Ingush who had headed the Astrakhan regional FSB. He then set out to influence the election by getting the head of the regional television and radio company replaced by a bureaucrat from Moscow; by investigating companies that belonged to the other candidates; by strengthening his oversight of the electoral commission; and by securing a court decision to remove Zyazikov's main challenger Kh. Gutseriev, who had the backing of Aushev. In an effort by the ethnic clans to oppose these manipulations, six of the candidates published an appeal in the national press calling on President Putin to intervene and insure a fair election.[66]

In the first round Duma deputy Alikhan Amirkhanov, who gained Aushev's backing after Gutseriev's candidacy had been annulled through the envoy's maneuvers, won 31 percent of the vote, while Zyazikov took only 19 percent. However, before the second round, the federal pressures supporting Zyazikov increased so much that Aushev resigned from the Federation Council in protest. The maximum use of administrative levers then produced a victory by Zyazikov, after which the new president made clear his loyalty to the Kremlin. At a ceremony marking the second anniversary of the okrugs, he told Kazantsev: "I remain your deputy forever."[67] Most likely, Kazantsev will use the experience he gained in the Ingushetia elections to seek similar victories in other okrug elections.

The Envoy's Influence on the Choice of Federation Council Members

The list of Federation Council members from the Southern okrug at the end of 2002 demonstrates Kazantsev's inability to influence very much the nomination of senators. The okrug's regional leaders have played the main role. Half of the senators represent the regions' elites, including two former governors, Krasnodar's Kondratenko and, briefly, Ingushetia's Aushev. About one fourth of the senators are long-time Moscow residents with their original roots in the okrug. These senators have well-developed contact networks that make it easy for them to lobby the federal government. The third group is the Muscovites who have become senators either as a reward for providing the services of top political consultants to the governor's campaign (e.g., the senators from Rostov region), or thanks to their connections to the regional leader's business interests (the senators from Kalmykia). As for the appointment of S. Derev as the senator from Karachaevo-Cherkessia, Kazantsev arranged this in order to reduce the tensions between the elites of the two main ethnic groups in the republic.

Thus, federal influence in choosing the senators has been small. Political parties have influenced nominations in only three cases, primarily when they have nominated members of local elites (in Dagestan, the Unity party played this role; in Volgograd, the Communist Party).

In contrast to the situation in other okrugs, the influence of big business in the selection process has so far been extremely weak. Corporate ties have been visible only in Stavropol Krai, where the MDM Group lobbied for its favored candidate, and possibly in Karachaevo-Cherkesia, where LUKoil played a role.

Crime and Corruption

Even during the Soviet era, Russia's South had an extensive shadow economy and corrupt authorities. A decade of transition effectively legalized this system, and corruption became the norm for regional and local officials. In most of the okrug republics, there now exists a shadowy system for directing financial flows into the channels of patron–client relations. In Dagestan, the ethnic elites (i.e., the ruling clans) divided up among themselves the various types of legal and black market business. It would be incorrect to call the resulting system of directing financial flows simple bribery, since the scale of the system is much too big for this term to be applicable. In Kalmykia, President Ilyumzhinov and his close allies completely control the republic's business world, and the current system of distributing funds is, again, much more extensive than a mere mechanism of corruption. The president has essentially privatized the republic and turned it into a personal corporation, Kalmykia Inc. Until Ruslan Aushev stepped down as president of Ingushetia, several leading clans there set up a back-channel system of dividing republican money, in which it was impossible to separate the authorities from business. Northern Osetia and Kabardino-Balkaria stand out somewhat because the fusion of the authorities and the business community was accomplished in a manner that was, since the leaders were holdouts from the Soviet period, more covert. But the patron–client relationship did not change because of this: the ruling clans either directly controlled business or received their share of the profits in exchange for creating good working conditions for local companies.

In the ethnic Russian regions of the Southern okrug, the union of the authorities and business takes various forms. Patronage in its most obvious manifestation exists in Rostov, where the governor backed the formation of the largest corporation, Doninvest. In those regions where Russia's biggest businesses are operating, the governors and the firms cement their links through family ties. Thus, Volgograd governor Nikolai Maksyuta's closest relatives work for LUKoil, the largest outside investor in the region. Despite these examples, however, in the ethnic Russian regions the merger of business and politics has not reached the level found in the republics. So corruption in the usual form of bribery is much more common.

The most corrupt forms of business in the South are the production of alcoholic beverages (especially of vodka in North Osetia and Kabardino-Balkaria), the caviar business (Dagestan and Astrakhan), seaports (Krasnodar), construction work in Chechnya, and freight trucking. There is a special system of collecting and distributing bribes in each of these areas. The criminal income from the ports is divided between local (municipal) and federal authorities. For this reason, the Krasnodar regional government, until recently cut off from this source of income, has been fighting hard to take over from them the Black Sea ports. The freight moved by trucks (especially alcohol, fruit, and vegetables sent from the South to central Russia) usually generates income for the police and military units that man roadside checkpoints. The caviar business and a significant part of the vodka business in the North Caucasus republics remain parts of the genuinely black market. The income is distributed among criminal groups (usually ethnic), and the municipal and republican ruling clans.

A system of informal agreements has replaced the official battle against the illegal production of alcohol. If the federal authorities increase the fiscal pressure on the regions—for example, because the budget deficit has begun to grow—the influential leaders of Northern Osetia and Kabardino-Balkaria change the rules of the game to secure their own republics' financial situation. When, for example, North Osetia president Aleksandr Dzasokhov took office, he demanded and secured the legalization of the vodka business to increase the amount of money collected in republican taxes. Corruption in Chechnya is connected to the provision of federal construction subsidies, which attract unscrupulous federal and republican authorities involved in distributing funds for the various projects.

Given the enormous scale of the black market in the Southern okrug, Kazantsev must be selective in picking his battles, and realistically, he can only work in a few areas. Accordingly, he focuses on the following:

- Strengthening monitoring at the seaports and over the activities of the customs service. The federal authorities initiated this work, and it serves the interests of both the okrug and the Krasnodar regional authorities, since most of the income generated by the ports has been taken by the local governments.

- Auditing the distribution of budget funds in Chechnya. This task serves the envoy's interests, since he is trying to control the funding of the restoration work there and extend his economic responsibilities in general. The envoy not only conducts regular investigations but continually informs the federal authorities and the media about the results.
- Exposing individual cases of corruption among the regional authorities. Such cases appear, in particular, when the latter demand a scapegoat or when the envoy wants to demonstrate his leading role in the okrug. One example occurred when okrug procurator Fridinskii presented evidence leading to the removal of Krasnodar Krai deputy governor L. Baklitskii. A special investigation showed that the deputy governor, who had previously served as a mayor in one of the krai's cities, had used budget funds for purposes other than those intended and had illegally handed over land to commercial interests.[68] The real reason for the firing was the need to publicly punish the Krasnodar governor for corruption and his ineffective program to rebuild housing destroyed during the summer 2002 floods. This was the first and only time that the envoy has punished such a high-ranking official since his office was established in May 2000. Analogous investigations in other regions (Rostov and Stavropol) led only to the removal of lower-level bureaucrats. Despite extensive corruption among the authorities in the okrug's republics, there have been no similar investigations there.
- Seeking to improve the work of the police by replacing regional MVD chiefs (though in theory such tasks are the responsibility of the federal MVD, not the envoy). Such personnel actions are essentially political acts aimed at moving the law enforcement agencies out from under the control of the governors. The changes do not reduce the amount of corruption or extortion on the roads, since replacing the leader does not resolve the problem of reforming the law enforcement agencies. Corruption on the roads is a well-established and stable system of bribery that provides income to poorly paid low-level policemen. Without cardinal reforms that increase salaries and without raising the prestige of the traffic police's work, eliminating such bribery will be impossible.

Thus, the envoy's battle with corruption is selective, of little impact, and achieves its purpose only when his goal coincides with the interests of another level of government (either federal or regional). His autonomous activities usually have another purpose—for example, to undermine unwanted governors through various audits and the punishment of lowly officials, or to gain the ability to monitor large financial flows. In these cases, the battle with corruption is not an end in itself, but a way for the envoy to achieve other goals.

The Envoy's Economic Influence

The Battle for Financial Powers

The goal of many bureaucracies is to increase their influence and secure new powers, the most important being oversight over financial flows. The presidential decree setting up the federal okrugs did not give the envoys the right to distribute funds. Nevertheless, the battle to acquire this right continues, though not in all okrugs.

The Southern okrug is a leader in this battle. Deputy Envoy Krokhmal is the key strategic thinker in this effort, but Kazantsev himself is extremely active in trying to implement Krokhmal's plans. The strategy has three goals. The first is to improve the okrug's investment climate by implementing a regional development program. The second is to monitor the rebuilding of the Chechen economy and the money spent to this end. The third is to participate in the management of enterprises in which the state owns a significant stake, so as to ensure that state property is used in the state's interest.

While all the envoys would like to have greater economic influence, the amount of energy they devote to this effort varies. In the Central and North-Western okrugs, the envoys do not play a noticeable role in the economy. In other okrugs, the envoys' priorities differ from Kazantsev's. In the Urals, Petr Latyshev is trying to act as a mediator among large business groups. In the Volga okrug, Sergei Kirienko operates by using innovative mechanisms and developing the okrug's overall infrastructure. Like the South, the Far Eastern Okrug also emphasizes state programs, but it is the influential governors like Khabarovsk's Viktor Ishaev who take the lead in lobbying for them, while the envoy plays little role. Siberian envoy Leonid Drachevskii formally coordinates his okrug's development program, but his deputy for economic issues, backed up by local academic institutions, is actually running the show.[69] In the South, the development program has been dubbed "Kazantsev's five-year plan," given the zeal with which the envoy has been promoting it. Nevertheless, despite his sincere concern for the okrug's development, it would be difficult to give him high marks in the area of economic competence.[70]

The Program to Develop Russia's South

The declared goal of his program to develop Russia's south in the years 2002–2006 is to increase the okrug's attractiveness to investors. In reality, a no less important goal is the intention to secure additional federal financing and the right to distribute these funds through the program. "Kazantsev's five-year plan" resembles previous Soviet programs in that it has a wide range of priorities and is optimistic in terms of what can be accomplished. According to Krokhmal, the program seeks to strengthen the economy enough over the next five years to raise people's living standard by a factor of three.[71] The plan also includes typical Soviet exaggerations, such as the inclusion of major oil pipelines whose construction was actually completed in 2001.[72]

To ensure the adoption of the program in 2001, Kazantsev organized several large exhibitions in Rostov, Krasnodar, and Moscow. In September, he met with members of the State Duma and the Federation Council to lobby for large subsidies for the south in the 2002 federal budget.

Ultimately his program became one of four priority programs included in the 2002 budget. The other three focused on the country's other troublesome regions: Sakhalin and the Kuril Islands, Kaliningrad, and Tatarstan. Initially, Kazantsev dreamed of spending somewhere between thirty and sixty billion rubles (the press reported a variety of figures that changed over time), with 25 percent coming from the federal government and the rest from business projects. However, pressure from German Gref's Ministry for Economic Development and Trade ultimately winnowed the program down to projects of federal and international significance. And the scale of federal financing was cut to 1.8 billion rubles over the five-year period.[73] By comparison, Tatarstan secured more than twelve billion rubles—ostensibly "to implement its development program," but in reality as payment for its political loyalty.

Kazantsev also suffered an even more serious blow beyond simply having funds for his program cut. He had hoped that the program's adoption would enable him to take part in distributing federal funds, and he had planned to set up a directorate for implementing programs, a step that would have significantly increased his power. However, Gref dashed all these hopes in December 2001, when, despite Kazantsev's lobbying power with the federal government, he won for his ministry oversight over the financing of all state programs for regional development. Wise in the ways of power, Gref used the formal reasoning that there was no funding in the budget to set up the kind of oversight directorate that Kazantsev had proposed.[74]

Besides attracting investment, Kazantsev's economic policy has sought to strengthen the linkages between the okrug's regions, thus creating more unity. Among the plan's features were some exotic projects that demonstrated the incompetence and poor management style of the okrug's military-trained leaders, who now had to handle economic issues. Kazantsev sought to increase the number of flight routes among cities in the okrug from the current figure of one (between Sochi and Krasnodar) to seventeen. On the first new route, linking Rostov and Volgograd, Kazantsev demanded that prices be slashed to a third of their market rate. In partial compensation for the losses the airlines would face, First Deputy Envoy V. Anpilogov "convinced" LUKoil's Volgograd oil refinery to supply fuel at discount prices.[75] But the regional governments were supposed to provide most of the subsidies, even though they already relied heavily on federal handouts to cover their existing deficits. This is not the only case in which the envoy used his administrative power to support his unification policy by "twisting the arms" of business and forcing the regions to offer tax benefits. Naturally, the regional authorities and business leaders have not always been happy about his innovations, which they have to finance. But there is no open opposition.

The Program to Rebuild Chechnya

Kazantsev plays no role in the effort to rebuild Chechnya. Moscow finances this program, and the federal minister for Chechnya, S. Ilyasov, manages all the money. Earlier, when he was Chechnya prime minister, Ilyasov tried to get Kazantsev to have the management switched to himself, but he did so without success.

The current system of financing has proven to be ineffective. According to Gref's ministry, in 2001 only 71 percent of the rebuilding program was implemented.[76] According to Deputy Envoy N. Sleptsov, this figure was in fact no higher than 50 percent.[77] The Chechnya authorities and Kazantsev's office believe that the federal ministries are to blame because they hold up payments to construction organizations (although all social welfare support is paid in full). An Accounting Chamber investigation found that for 2001, 12.5 billion rubles of budgetary funds were used extremely ineffectively, including 0.7 billion rubles that either were not used for the purpose intended or were used illegally. Programs for restoring infrastructure received only 20 to 50 percent of the budgeted amounts, while expenditures for personnel were four times larger than planned. Workers overstated the amount of work they did in housing construction by 70 percent, while veterans received only one fourth of the money supposedly given to them. The rest was stolen in Moscow and Chechnya.[78] Putin has already ordered changes in the way these programs are funded and organized. In this connection, Kazantsev's office has been lobbying hard. The envoy is clearly trying to demonstrate that he is irreplaceable as an overseer and could even distribute funds directly. On a separate issue, he has been attempting to cut the illegal export of oil from Chechnya.

Oversight over State Property

The Southern okrug was the first to react to Putin's order to protect and assert the state's interests in companies in which it owns shares. Since the beginning of 2001, the envoy's staff (led by Krokhmal, once a business magnate in Krasnodar) began to appoint so-called commissars to companies in which the state owned at least 10 percent of the shares. Initially, the program involved fifty companies: fifteen river and sea ports, twenty-three electric stations, and twelve oil and gas complexes.[79] However, since the okrug contains about fifteen hundred companies in which the state owns at least ten percent of the shares, Krokhmal faces the daunting task of finding fifteen hundred honest and competent "commissars." But this is not the only problem. The commissars must perform their oversight duties in addition to their regular jobs, and in most cases they are not paid for their efforts. Moreover, the federal property ministry has not clearly defined what powers the commissars should have. On top of all this, Kazantsev has given them the task of increasing labor productivity at the plants they are monitoring by 20 to 40 percent.[80]

It is clear that the sudden launching of this poorly prepared program was motivated by the desire of okrug officials not just to demonstrate the zeal with which they were implementing the president's directives but also to strengthen their influence in the boardrooms of the okrug's most profitable big businesses. This goal is clear from the list of fifty enterprises where the first inspectors were sent. Overall, the okrug's effort to improve federal control over state property, just like its attempts to promote the development program for the South, has proven to be a mixture of rational measures combined with rudiments of Soviet-style thinking and the pursuit of commercial interests by individual staff members.

In economic matters Kazantsev is no different from the governors in that he seeks federal support for money-losing enterprises. During 2001 he worked with the Rostov regional authorities to lobby the PA to place Rostovugol, the region's largest coal company, under special presidential supervision for ten years. The state currently owns a controlling stake in the plant, which is one of the region's biggest money losers. Kazantsev hoped that the government would provide tax breaks that would make the company profitable and preserve miners' jobs. However, his lobbying efforts were not very effective. A meeting with PA head Aleksandr Voloshin did not produce the desired result, and the federal economic ministries strongly opposed the plan.[81]

Kazantsev is extremely cautious regarding the government's agricultural reforms, which have great importance for the South. On one hand, he has worked to ensure the implementation of federal law—for example, by forcing Rostov governor Chub in spring 2001 to remove the barriers to grain exports. On the other hand, he has been relatively mild in handling the opposition of several regional leaders to federal land policy. In February 2002, for example, he did not react to Krasnodar governor Tkachev's statement that the federal law on buying and selling land would not become operative in the Kuban area.

Thus his economic policy follows a relatively simple formula: secure more money from the government; lobby federal agencies on behalf of regional interests; and maximally expand oversight over the okrug's economy, largely using administrative methods. One can only conclude, therefore, that *Presidential Envoy Kazantsev has turned out to be a typical Russian governor*, except that he is presiding over a huge and still fragmented territory, which he is trying to unify into a coherent whole.

Problems of Fiscal Federalism

In the area of fiscal federalism, Putin has implemented policies that generally take more money from the regions and concentrate it at the federal level. Overall, such policies favor poorer regions. The rich regions lose some of the money that they would otherwise keep, while the federal government has more money to give to less well-off regions. The regions of the Southern okrug are among the most heavily reliant on federal subsidies, since they only produce enough revenue to cover 15 to 45 percent of their budgets. Because of the economic conditions in his region, Kazantsev has no choice but to support federal policies that redistribute resources from the rich to the poor.

In Dagestan, federal subsidies make up 85 percent of the republic's revenue, while in the other republics, such funding is near 50 percent. Although subsidies of this size inevitably create tensions between rich and poor regions, such conflict is felt less in the South, where all the regions rely in some degree on subsidies. Even here, though, there is tension between the relatively better off and the real basket cases. The governors of the more highly developed, ethnic Russian regions have asked Kazantsev to lobby for changes in the system of distributing taxes between the center and the regions, seeking to reduce the amount of money they send to Moscow. If they reduced the share of taxes they send to the federal government, the majority of the ethnic Russian regions in the South could get by without federal subsidies.

However, Kazantsev is institutionally excluded from the budgetary process and can only lobby the Finance Ministry to stick to its schedule of distributing subsidies to the regions. In general, therefore, dealing with budgetary matters of this sort is not a major area of activity for Kazantsev.

Relations with the Natural Monopolies

The envoy, with his "administrative-command style," is able to influence the federal monopolies only if they need his support in realizing their plans. Gazprom is one of the most powerful economic players in the okrug, but its construction of the Blue Stream pipeline for exporting natural gas to Turkey gives him a significant lever of influence. When, for example, environmental groups lodged objections to the project, he created a special commission to examine their claims and was thus able to halt construction temporarily.[82] He also asked Gazprom director Aleksei Miller to designate a company official who would work directly with the okrug.[83] Gazprom has to work with Kazantsev, because it needs his support to complete the project, which should yield considerable profits.

Relations with electricity monopoly Unified Energy Systems (EES) are completely different, since the okrug must import electricity from other parts of Russia and since almost all its regions are chronic debtors to EES. Since the monopoly's chief Anatolii Chubais has much greater political influence and self-assertiveness than Gazprom's Miller, he uses all the envoys to reduce the governors' control over the regional energy commissions. His goal is to raise electricity prices to a level he believes to be adequate for recouping EES's expenses. As an experienced politician, Chubais is willing to share power with the envoys, saying: "It is essential for the envoys to monitor the implementation of the state's policy for transforming the electricity sector."[84] In February 2001 Kazantsev gathered all the governors to meet with Chubais and gave him full support. He demanded that the governors pay their outstanding debts for electricity supply. He also declared the current pricing policies of the regions to be unsatisfactory.[85]

Nevertheless, the governors have opposed rate increases, and their efforts have not been without success. In Stavropol Krai a court declared that Chubais's order to cut off electricity to debtors was illegal, and the local law enforcement agencies brought the cutoffs to an end.[86] In Karachaevo-Cherkesiya, a criminal case was filed against the local electricity company, a subsidiary of EES, for not paying its taxes, even though the republic owed it twice as much money for electricity supplies.[87] The regions have also sought to retake assets that had been shifted to EES. For example, the Volgograd regional authorities demanded the return of the Volzhskii Hydro-Electric Station to an energy holding company that it controls, seeking to overturn an early 1990s decision that had transferred the station to EES control.[88] However, the ability of the governors to take such actions is limited, since Chubais has managed to win Kazantsev to his side.

Relations with Big Business

The expansion of big business into the regions has affected the Southern okrug as it has other okrugs. In the Southern regions, Gazprom plays a large role, as do the large oil companies LUKoil and Rosneft (Russian Oil), which are involved in the full range of activities from extracting oil, to processing it, to selling gasoline. YUKOS, Slavneft (Slavic Oil), and the Tyumen Oil Company (TNK) have also recently begun working in the okrug. The MDM Group's influence is quickly growing, in particular at the Volgograd tractor and pipe factories and at Nevinnomyssk-azot; and Alfa Group has started expanding into the region, particularly with the battle for control over the Taganrog Pipe Factory. The Baltika beer company is now working in Rostov; Aeroflot bought Rostov Airlines; NIKoil's Novoship is part-owner of the Novorossiisk and Sochi ports; Russian Aluminum owns a metal factory in Rostov; and the Moscow holding company Sodruzhestvo (Commonwealth) owns the giant combine harvester factory Rostselmash. The list is growing quickly.

Alongside these national companies, two large regional business groups have been formed in the industrially developed Rostov region: Doninvest (which controls the leading regional bank, an automobile factory, and food-processing plants) and Sergei Bidash's group (the Taganrog Pipe Factory and the Krasnyi kotelshchik factory). Bidash is also seeking to control the Taganrog seaport and the Novocherkassk Electrode Factory.[89]

In order for the Moscow-based and regional business groups to expand, they must set up special relationships with the governors. Several of these relationships are well known: Volgograd governor Maksyuta's ties to LUKoil; Astrakhan governor Guzhvin's links to Gazprom; and Stavropol governor Chernogorov's agreement with the MDM Group to take over the giant Nevinnomyssk-azot enterprise. Without the extensive support of Rostov governor Chub, who placed the region's budget accounts in Doninvest Bank, Doninvest could not have become the leading group in the region. These alliances remained in place even after the envoy appeared on the scene. In addition, the governors have preserved their ability to make routine deals with various business groups as regards the governors' assignment to them of control over factories in the regions.

The place of the envoy in the system of relations between the governors and business groups has yet to be definitely determined. However, several tendencies are already clear.

First, and most positive, is the envoy's ability to attract outside investors. After the publication of the *Program to Develop Russia's South,* the number of outside investors grew, including especially those associated with Moscow mayor Yurii Luzhkov (Sistema, the Ochakovo factory, and others).[90] Large investors are also moving into agriculture, often with the help of the envoy.

Second is the establishment of special relations with Russia's largest oil companies working in the okrug. LUKoil is the most active in lobbying for its interests with the envoy. For his part, Kazantsev understands the importance of the oil business for the okrug and publicly supports LUKoil, attending all public events organized by the company. LUKoil won the okrug's "Leader of the 21st Century" contest, which Kazantsev had organized among the okrug's enterprises.[91] In the second year of the okrug's existence, Kazantsev was more evenhanded, seeking to give both of the okrug's leading companies (LUKoil and Rosneft) special preferences in the petroleum products market.[92] He apparently blocked the Russian-appointed Chechen leader A. Kadyrov from gaining control over Grozny Oil (Grozneft), which is a subsidiary of Rosneft.

So far, however, it remains unclear how he will react to the more powerful and aggressive attempts by Sibneft (Siberian Oil) to take over Rosneft's traditional territory in the North Caucasus.

Third is the gradual inclusion of the presidential envoy in the process of regulating the business groups in the regions, a process monopolized in the past by the governors. Initially, Kazantsev simply tried to work out conflicts over property. When MDM gained control of a large fertilizer factory in Stavropol, having got its director sent to jail, Kazantsev ordered his deputy Korobeinikov to create a working group to study the situation. Then Kazantsev worked with Governor Chub to resolve the conflict between the Tyumen Oil Company (TNK), which was aggressively entering the Rostov region with the support of the regional administration, and the weaker Sidanko, from which TNK took over the large retailer Rostovnefteprodukt (Rostov Oil Products).[93] A compromise was found that suited TNK. Seeing that Kazantsev wanted to set up a unified structure throughout the okrug, TNK immediately opened an office in the okrug capital.

In the conflict between Bidash's regional business group and one of Russia's largest companies, the Alfa Group, which sought to gain control of Bidash's Taganrog Pipe Factory with the support of Chub's administration, Kazantsev did not simply try to regulate the conflict but took the side of regional business and opposed the governor.[94] The transfer of shares was blocked and criminal cases were filed against the people involved in the deal. However, in April 2002 Bidash had to sell his shares to the powerful MDM group, and the conflict over the factory shifted to the federal level.[95] *All this shows that the envoy's function is gradually changing—from monitor, to arbiter, and then straight to direct player in the process of transferring property from one owner to another.* This is a dangerous tendency, but of course the majority of powerful federal civil servants have long been such players.

Fourth is the use of large companies as sponsors of the okrug's soccer teams, usually through complex financial arrangements that benefit both sides. Thus, for example, Kazantsev arranged for Rosneft-Krasnodarneftegaz (Krasnodar Oil and Gas) to gain certain tax breaks for its oil processing, so that the profits could go toward supporting the Kuban soccer club.[96] He also wants to expand the program and hopes to elicit "contributions" from Alfa-Eko, Gazprom, and others. The Rostselmash soccer club is likely the next beneficiary of such aid.

The financial arrangements underpinning these sponsorships are opaque, allowing the companies to conceal part of their income and thereby avoid tax payments, while the envoy receives, at a minimum, political dividends by pleasing the area's numerous soccer fans.

Kazantsev has only very limited contacts with foreign investors, since few are willing to brave the high levels of risk and instability in the okrug. Most of the plans to attract foreigners to the Program to Develop the Russian South have remained on paper. Two of the few foreign-owned factories in the okrug that opened in the 1990s are the Philip Morris tobacco factory and the German Knauf construction materials factory in Krasnodar Krai. However, the German investors ran into significant trouble when the Russian managers of the factory tried to oust them with the support of the krai leadership. Doninvest's attempt to assemble cars in Rostov for the Korean Daewoo company failed to turn a profit.

The only major project under way during Kazantsev's tenure has been the Caspian Pipeline Consortium's construction of an oil pipeline from Kazakhstan to the Novorossiisk port. His role in the project, which is supervised by federal ministries, has been minimal, consisting of accompanying federal bureaucrats on inspection tours. Also, he played little role in the conflict that initially surrounded the project: the regional authorities whose territory the pipeline crossed expected to receive tax payments for the flow of oil across their land; however, the federal government cancelled these agreements.[97] Kazantsev did not even try to help the four Southern regions whose leaders appealed to the president to share the revenues.

Relations with Local Government and Civil Society

Local Government

The problems of local government are even more acute in the Southern okrug than in the other okrugs. Here local government lacks autonomy because the majority of municipalities are wholly dependent on financial subsidies from the regional budgets, and also because of the authoritarian style of the regional leaders, especially the republican presidents. Even the traditional Russian conflict between governors and capital city mayors is rare in the South, appearing only in Volgograd region and Stavropol Krai (where the mayors competed against the incumbents in the gubernatorial elections) and in Dagestan (where the capital's mayor is the leader of an ethnic group different from that of the republican president, and supervises business in his city). Initially, the mayors of the capital cities thought that the appearance of the envoy would give them a chance to weaken the power of the regional leaders, but meetings with Kazantsev did not live up to their expectations. The Association of Mayors in Russia's South, created in 2001, does not play a major role, as attested by the location of its headquarters in Krasnodar, where the mayor has no independence. In this region the governor secured the election of his mayoral candidates in the major cities of Krasnodar and Sochi, thereby gaining complete control over local government. Beyond the objective weakness of local government, Kazantsev's lack of initiatives in this area could be a result of his military notion of hierarchy: just as generals should command lieutenants, so governors should command mayors.

Relations with the Media

Kazantsev has an active but traditional media policy. The main okrug newsmakers are Kazantsev himself and those of his deputies who did not serve in the power ministries. The okrug media regularly report on their activities. Besides numerous press conferences and briefings, his staff maintains extensive contacts with journalists in national and regional publications. However, the envoy makes little use of the Internet. The website set up in August 2000 existed only for a few months.

Kazantsev has two goals in his media work. The first is to create a unified information space throughout the okrug. In 2000 he launched an okrug newspaper, *Yuzhnyi federalnyi (The Southern Federal)*, that provides information on his activities. He has also set up two regional media companies, Severnyi kavkaz (North Caucasus) and Yuzhnyi region (Southern Region); approved a plan to set up an okrug television station using Rostov television as its base; established an information agency; and sponsored a press festival for the entire okrug.

The second, and related, goal is to shape the information that the public receives. Deputy Envoy Yepifantsev explained that "from the very start we thought about how to get information about Kazantsev's work to the population quickly and in an objective form, untrammeled by journalists."[98] To put it another way, Kazantsev seeks to disseminate positive information to bolster the image of his troubled okrug.

However, he has encountered great difficulty in spreading his happy message. In the thirteen regions and republics of the okrug, there are more than four thousand print and broadcast media, information agencies, and Internet publications, about 80 percent of which are not state owned. His attitude to the independent local press is not particularly friendly, but to maintain his national image, he has to spend most of his time dealing with the federal-level media. Yepifantsev, who is in charge of media relations, believes that the independent media are much more dependent on the money and political views of certain groups that support them than are the "dependent" state media. However, it has not been possible to find evidence of direct pressure by the okrug administration on the regional media, and Rostov newspapers have often published articles critical of its work. Content analysis shows that the regional press is much more dependent on the regional authorities, especially in the more authoritarian regions like Kalmykia, Kabardino-Balkaria, and Krasnodar Krai.

Kazantsev's Social and Nationalities Policy

Kazantsev's social and nationalities policy focuses on three priorities. The first is limiting migration to the okrug. Here he reflects the preferences of most of the okrug residents. Like the local Cossacks, he supports requiring all foreigners who come to the okrug to have a return ticket home; he wants to limit the rights of those permitted to live permanently in the okrug; and he hopes to set quotas for settling immigrants from other countries.[99] From early 2002 the okrug leadership lobbied to make the new federal migration law harsher, demanding strict conditions for entering the country and receiving citizenship; as well as quotas for foreign and domestic migrants that "take into account national compatibility, the specific psychology of the migrants, and climatic conditions."[100] During the chauvinistic campaign that the Krasnodar Krai authorities conducted in spring 2002 to expel Turkish and Armenian migrants, Deputy Envoy Krokhmal refused to take sides: "We do not plan to take a position, but I earnestly request that [the krai authorities] act more peacefully and adhere strictly to the Constitution and federal law."[101]

The second priority is providing state support to promote the interests of the ethnic Russian population. Kazantsev has actively backed these activities, arguing that "today we see not just a decline in the Russian population, but its exodus from the North Caucasian republics."[102] He claimed that the "the state nationality policy in the North Caucasus can no longer sidestep the problem of the Russian population." He advocated setting up quotas to ensure that ethnic Russians are represented in public office, management, and institutions of higher learning. He claimed that he had already amended four hundred regional laws that circumscribed the rights of Russians in the republics, so as to bring them into line with federal norms. In pursuing such goals, the okrug authorities work with various Slavic societies that have appeared in the South during the last three or four years.

The third priority is supporting the Russian Orthodox Church. Kazantsev believes that the Russian state is predominantly Orthodox and should behave accordingly (this statement comes from a man who is in charge of an okrug in which one quarter of the population is Muslim). At a meeting with Orthodox Church officials, Kazantsev asked them to help make the church a part of daily life for the population. He suggested including a church presence at all events organized by the authorities at all levels and in all North Caucasus regions. Further, the Southern okrug was the first to start meeting the wishes of the church to participate actively in the public education system. However, an element of balance is maintained. The okrug administration plans to facilitate the return to the Muslims of a mosque in Stavropol that has been an art gallery.

Kazantsev is cautious in his relations with the Cossacks. He did not support the appeal by the Council of Atamans of the Terek Cossacks that demanded the return of the Naurskii, Nadterechnyi, and Shelkovskii districts of Chechnya to Stavropol Krai, as well as the introduction in these districts of direct presidential rule.[103] He does not see the Cossack organizations as capable of "becoming guardians of stability in the complicated situations that have been developing in the Southern Federal Okrug." The atamans of the Southern regions criticized both the federal authorities in Moscow and the okrug staff for not implementing the Priority Federal Program to Support the Military Cossack Societies. Nevertheless, the Cossacks maintain working contacts with the okrug authorities and hope that the envoy can help them get this program extended.

Kazantsev considers the Caucasus national movements to be an even more destabilizing force. In April 2001 the okrug authorities resisted the holding in Ingushetia of a congress of the peoples deported during World War II, blocking a delegation of Karachais from entering the republic, and advising Cossack organizations not to participate.[104] Kazantsev sharply denounced the idea of merging Ingushetia and Chechnya, justifiably arguing that it would be destabilizing. In true Soviet style, he has assigned every region in the okrug responsibility for rebuilding one administrative district in Chechnya. He divided the capital Grozny among four "mentors," designating the four largest Russian regions in the okrug to provide aid to the Chechen capital.[105]

Overall, Kazantsev's ethnic and religious policy contradictorily combines elements of great power thinking and attempts to preserve the okrug's fragile stability. He sincerely wants peace in the Caucasus, but he acts on the basis of his military experience and his personal understanding of the problem. Thus he relies on numerous councils, but does not take into account the advice of qualified specialists.

Conclusion: Kazantsev's Overall Influence

The first two years of the envoy's work provide sufficient grounds to draw some preliminary conclusions. Let us examine the successes and failures of the envoy in the context of the tasks he was assigned.

The process of bringing regional laws into line with federal norms is nearly complete in the ethnically Russian regions, but to a lesser degree in the non-Russian republics. Here Kazantsev combines the tactics of applying pressure to secure a compromise and of transferring the most difficult part of the work to others, including the Supreme Court. He has yet to start working at the municipal level.

Formally, he coordinates the activities of the federal agencies working in his okrug, but the collegium of federal agencies he created functions like a party coordinating body from the Soviet era. Thus, he has partially returned the okrug to the administrative-command system. The effectiveness of this type of coordination is not great.

It is too early to say if Kazantsev has successfully removed the law enforcement agencies from the governors' control, since it took a long time to set up the okrug-level police structure. However, the okrug's work in relation to the regional FSB and a majority of the procurators is now close to being finished.

The reconstruction of Chechnya is moving extremely slowly, but the envoy is not responsible for this problem, because the evolving system of governing the republic is slowly reducing his influence.

It is impossible to reduce interethnic tension significantly over the course of two years. However, beyond the lack of time, one can point to the absence of effective mechanisms to resolve conflicts apart from the personal intervention of the envoy as an intermediary and peacemaker (in the Osetian-Ingush and Karachaev-Cherkes conflicts). As a result it has only been possible to establish a relative level of stability. Among Kazantsev's successes are reducing the tension in Karachaevo-Cherkesia and Dagestan, and strengthening federal influence in Ingushetia. His failures include instability on the border of Stavropol Krai and in Karachaevo-Cherkesia (despite the limited progress) and increasing ethnic tensions in Krasnodar Krai.

There has been some unification of the regions, but only through using administrative methods. This unity is unlikely to last long, because the interests of the regions differ greatly. The numerous councils and associations remain largely decorative and bureaucratized. Created from above at the envoy's direction, they are not able to become genuine parts of civil society.

Kazantsev's activities are in line with Russian big businesses' growing desire to work in the South. But instead of working to improve the investment climate and reducing entry barriers for investors coming into the market, the envoy is effectively creating a personalized system of guarantees to investors ("I promise that they will not bother you"). In other words, he is re-creating at the level of the okrug the system of informal personal patronage that the governors set up earlier in the regions.

The envoy's level of influence varies from region to region according to the following factors:

1. The economic strength of the region: In the larger and more developed regions (Rostov and Krasnodar), he must take into account the position of the governors.
2. The type of political regime in the region: In the republics with the most authoritarian regimes (Kalmykia, Kabardino-Balkaria) or a delicately balanced elite (Dagestan), he focuses more on monitoring the situation than intervening in the numerous internal problems.

3. Distance from Rostov and the envoy's familiarity with the region: Astrakhan is the most peripheral for him, and his influence there is the weakest.

4. Each governor's degree of loyalty and his willingness to accept authority. The governors of Volgograd and Stavropol are the most obedient.

The envoy conducts a differentiated policy toward the various regions in his okrug. These differences are partly functional (the need to resolve various problems) and partly subjective (depending on his relationship with the different regional leaders). Because the most important task facing the Southern okrug is resolving military and ethnic conflicts, the envoy devotes most of his attention to the regions that are most problematic in these regards. Inconsistencies appear in his policy because he is much softer on regions where he has trust-based or friendly relations with the leader.

Notes

1. "Military men are as suitable as civilians for public office! If everyone worked like the military, there would be order." From a Kazantsev interview, "Nado razbirat'sya c Baranovym," *Volgogradskaya Pravda*, June 16, 2001.

2. L. Yuzhnyi, "Kak by eto skazat' po-russki . . ." *Rostov ofitsial'nyi* (Rostov-na-Donu), no. 44 (September 26, 2001).

3. According to the demographer V. Mukomel, during the first Chechen war (1994–1996) alone there were more than 350,000 refugees.

4. *Sotsial'no-ekonomicheskoe polozhenie Rossii 2001*, no. 12 (Moscow: Goskomstat, 2002).

5. *Rossiiskii statisticheskii ezhegodnik, 2001* (Moscow: Goskomstat, 2001), 134.

6. According to a speech by Kazantsev quoted in "V. Putin peredal pozdravleniya zhitelyam Kabardino-Balkarii," *Gazeta Yuga* (Nal'chik), September 6, 2001.

7. E. Stroiteleva, "Polpredy," *Izvestiya*, March 5, 2002.

8. "Cherez sotrudnichestvo—k miru i blagopoluchiyu," NIA "AKTsENT" (Kuban'), February 6, 2001.

9. "Regiony i okrug: brak po raschetu," *Parlamentskaya gazeta*, August 16, 2001.

10. Interview with V. Averchenko, *Vremya novostei*, April 10, 2001.

11. "Nado razbirat'sya s Baranovym," *Volgogradskaya Pravda*, June 16, 2001.

12. "Namestniki Putina: god spustya," interview with Kazantsev, *Komsomol'skaya Pravda*, July 12, 2001.

13. Ye. Gaidanskaya, "Klyuch k morskim vorotam," *Russkii fokus* (Moscow), June 14, 2001.

14. Troshev served in this post until December 2002 when the Ministry of Defense announced that it was going to rotate him to the leadership of the Siberian Military District. Troshev publicly said that he would not accept such an appointment and was

fired for insubordination. In his place, Putin appointed V. Boldyrev, who had previously served as the commander of the Siberian Military District.

15. Excerpts from General Gennadii Troshev's book in "Mat ego ne glushili dazhe dubovye dveri," *Kommersant Vlast,* July 24, 2001.

16. "*Moskovskie novosti* in its last issue wrote about illegal oil exports from Chechnya. 'I know. I get reports. Everyone is stealing: the police, the military, and the local population. What can I say? I need to have it out with Gen. Baranov: why do the columns go past the check posts at night without being challenged? I'm going there soon—to get to the bottom of it all.'" Interview with Kazantsev, "Nado razbirat'sya s Baranovym," *Volgogradskaya Pravda,* June 16, 2001.

17. G. Varzieva, "Protsess vseleniya—bez khaosa i spekulyatsii," *Severnaya Osetia* (Vladikavkaz), May 25, 2001.

18. "Podvedeny itogi, opredeleny zadachi" (speech of deputy presidential envoy V. Anpilogov to the collegium of federal agencies in the okrug), *Yuzhnyi federal'nyi* (Rostov-na-Donu), July 25, 2001.

19. "Proshlo pyat mesyatsev: chto sdelano?" *Yuzhnyi federal'nyi* (Rostov-na-Donu), October 1, 2001.

20. "Skol'ko stoit FSB," *Versty* (Moscow), April 21, 2001.

21. Yu. Bykova, "Na Donu net glavnogo militsionera," *Gazeta Dona* (Rostov-na-Donu), July 26, 2001. For more information on Shchadrin, see the chapter on the Central okrug by Nikolai Petrov.

22. REGIONS.RU, June 24, 2001.

23. "Podvedeny itogi," *Kubanskie novosti* (Krasnodar), December 8, 2001.

24. G. Yarygina, "Viktor Kazantsev podbrosil ugol'ka gosudarstvu," *Rossiiskaya gazeta,* July 17, 2001.

25. "Glavnyi nalogovyi politseiskii—v Rostove," *Rostov ofitsial'nyi* (Rostov-na-Donu), August 8, 2001.

26. A. Serenko, "Yuzhnoe oko gosudarevo," *Nezavisimaya gazeta,* April 19, 2001.

27. "Nado razbirat'sya s Baranovym," interview with Kazantsev, *Volgogradskaya Pravda,* June 16, 2001.

28. A. Bykov, "Regiony i okrug: brak po raschetu," *Parlamentskaya gazeta,* August 16, 2001.

29. "Kubanskii kazak okazalsya v chernom spiske," *Patriot* (Moscow), November 20, 2001.

30. M. Bondarenko, "Don v ozhidanii 'parashyutista,'" *Nezavisimaya gazeta,* August 7, 2001.

31. I. Burakov, "Nalichnost' za stolichnost," *Vremya novostei* (Moscow), August 17, 2001.

32. Ye. Kharitonova, "Dali khod ugolovnomu ochku," *Gazeta Dona* (Rostov-na-Donu), June 21, 2001.

33. S. Medvedev, "Polpred pripret 'negodyaev' k stenke?" *Gazeta Dona* (Rostov-na-Donu), May 31, 2001.

34. A Volodchenko, "Raznoglasiya ostayutsya," *Stavropol'skaya Pravda* (Stavropol), November 20, 2001.

35. "Sudebnyi departament pod kolpakom," *Vechernii Stavropol'* (Stavropol), November 21, 2001.

36. M. Glebova, "Na koi sdalas' im eta duma?" *Vechernii Stavropol'*, October 11, 2001.

37. Ye. Rybalko, "Tochka ne postavlena," *Stavropol'skaya Pravda* (Stavropol), November 17, 2001.

38. Dmitrii Sviridov, "Osetinskie varianty," *Versiya* (Sovershenno sekretno) (Moscow), November 27, 2001.

39. Interview with V. Kokov, Radio Mayak, May 11, 2001, 19:05.

40. "Zaurbi Nakhushev obratilsya k Viktoru Kazantsevu," *Gazeta Yuga* (Nal'chik), March 8, 2001.

41. "Normativno-pravovye akty dolzhny publikovat'sya," *Gazeta Yuga* (Nal'chik), March 1, 2001.

42. Ye. Sarkisova, "Severnyi Kavkaz—ne zona riska," *Stavropol'skaya Pravda* (Stavropol), September 8, 2001.

43. V. Lezvina, "Tainy poslednei voiny," *Stavropol'skaya pravda* (Stavropol), August 23, 2001.

44. V. Moskalenko, "Chtoby ne poluchilos' 'kak vsegda.'" *Delovoe sodruzhestvo* (Rostov-na-Donu), September 1, 2001.

45. "Federal'naya vlast'' za kandidaturu M. Magomedova," *Novoe delo* (Makhachkala), July 26, 2001.

46. Ilyumzhinov's brother bought the state's controlling stake in Kalmneft for almost nothing.

47. The republic spent 70.2 million rubles to support the Uralan soccer club, a sum that is more than two-and-a-half times what is spent on all educational institutions in the republic, including payments for child subsidies. I. Slavutinskaya, "Kirsanes" *Profil'*, July 2, 2001.

48. "Skol'ko stoit FSB," *Versty* (Moscow), April 21, 2001.

49. A. Makarkin, N. Manvelov, Ye. Ignatova, "Chechnya: vlast, den'gi, krov'," *Delovaya khronika*, no. 7 (2002).

50. Ye. Chubarov, "Gantamirov stal vitse-premerom Chechni," *Izvestiya*, February 8, 2002.

51. A. Petrosyan, "O chrezvychaike v otpuske," *Izvestiya*, May 11, 2002.

52. B. Akhmedkhanov, "V Rossii poyavitsya 'nekhoroshii okrug,'" *Obshchaya gazeta*, August 23, 2001.

53. See B. Lyauv and A. Barakhova, "Polpred Kazantsev podaril cherkesam parlamentariya," *Kommersant*, July 3, 2001; and "Rost Dereva," Vesti.ru, November 19, 2001.

54. "Ne sravnivaite menya s Maskhadovym," *Moskovskie novosti*, April 3, 2001.

55. For example, Aushev himself appointed the military commissars. "Mat ego ne glushili dazhe dubovye dveri," *Kommersant Vlast*, July 24, 2001.

56. The president's brother, Bagaudin Aushev, was secretary of Ingushetia's Security Council; Abdulkhamid Aushev headed the Ingushetia National Bank; Abdulkhamid's son was the finance minister. The president's cousin Magomed Aushev was head of the clearing center. M. Yevloev, "Kto stoit za pokhishcheniyami lyudei na Severnom Kavkaze?" *Komsomol'skaya Pravda* (Moscow), September 4, 2001.

57. N. Gorodetskaya, "Zhizn' na obochine," *Vremya novostei* (Moscow), August 24, 2001.

58. Interview with R. Aushev, Radio Liberty, December 28, 2001, 18:00.

59. "S"ezd naroda Ingushetii vyrazil nedoverie polpredu i prokuroru," Strana.ru, December 25, 2001.

60. V. Tseplyaev, "Kak regiony vybirali nachal'nikov," *Argumenty i Fakty* (Moscow), no. 4 (January 24, 2001).

61. This is the opinion of most Moscow-based observers. A. Barakhova, "Otstrel zakonchen," *Kommersant*, January 16, 2001.

62. E. Shchukin, "Udachlivaya khitrost'," *Gorod N* (Rostov-na-Donu), December 19, 2001.

63. "Zayavlenie Viktora Kazantseva," *Molot* (Rostov-na-Donu), no. 107-108 (September 21, 2001).

64. M. Fedorov (Rostov-na–Donu), "Chub ostaetsya gubernatorom," *Novye izvestiya* (Moscow), September 25, 2001.

65. Z. Khisamova, "Dzasokhov ustraivaet vsekh," *Ekspert*, no. 5 (2002).

66. "Otkrytoe pismo," *Izvestiya*, March 12, 2002.

67. A. Zaitsev, "Tsitata nedeli," *Izvestiya*, May 27, 2002.

68. E. Stroiteleva, "Prokuratura obvinyaet krasnodarskogo vitse-gubernatora," *Izvestiya*, September 25, 2002.

69. M. Shandarov, "Federal'nye chinovniki pytayutsya redaktirovat' strategiyu razvitiya Sibiri." *Rossiiskii regionalnyi byulleten'*, November 5, 2001.

70. In "Nado razbirat'sya s Baranovym," interview with Kazantsev, *Volgogradskaya Pravda*, June 16, 2001:

> We must unite to fulfill the chief task, which Putin has defined: increasing people's standard of living. You don't know why the south has the lowest life expectancy? I do. People are stealing at all levels of power. I would like to gather the bureaucrats together and say, "Let's declare a six-month moratorium on the plunderers of state property." . . . We will flush out the thieves and expose their activities. Let the people know who their "heros" are.

71. "V stolitse Adygei sostoyalsya festival' pressy yuga Rossii," *Kubanskie novosti*, 26 September 2001.

72. I. Burakov, "Investitsionnye pripiski," *Vremya novostei* (Moscow), November 15, 2001.

73. Vedomstvennaya struktura raskhodov federal'nogo byudzheta na 2002 g.

74. Gref used an even more "elegant" method to deal with the Far East's development program, which had been prepared by local authors and lobbied by Ishaev. The minister ordered the authors of the South's program to write an alternative program for the Far East, forcing the two groups to "butt heads." O. Novak, "Pod Grefom 'sovershenno sekretno,'" *Tikhookeanskaya zvezda* (Khabarovsk), September 22, 2001.

75. S. Kolbasin, "Polety vo sne i nayavu," *Rostov ofitsial'nyi* (Rostov), electronic version, April 23, 2001.

76. Ye. Chubarov, "Chechenskii goszakaz postavili na vid," *Izvestiya*, February 21, 2002.

77. I. Burakov and N. Gorodetskaya, "Vsekh uvolit!" *Vremya novostei*, October 19, 2001.

78. S. Popova, "Spisali na voinu," *Izvestiya*, April 27, 2002.

79. "Edut komissarskie brigady," *Kavkazskaya zdravnitsa* (Stavropol), January 24, 2001.

80. Vitalii Kolbasin, "Zachem komissary polpreda prishli na zavody i fabriki," *Rossiiskaya gazeta*, May 15, 2001.

81. Igor Burakov, "Zaboinye reformy," *Vremya novostei*, May 25, 2001.

82. "Zorkii kontrol'," NefteGaz.ru, July 30, 2001.

83. Kazantsev speech during a briefing in Krasnodar, RBK, November 3, 2001.

84. O. Gubenko, "Polpredov podklyuchili k vysokovol'tnoi politike," *Izvestiya*, January 30, 2002.

85. N. Abramovich, "Dorogoe nashe teplo," *Vechernii Volgograd*, March 13, 2001.

86. S. Bazyl'chik, "Pyatnadtsat' deputatov obldumy," *Novye delovye vesti* (Volgograd), July 7, 2001.

87. "Neobkhodimy antikrizisnye komissii," *Izvestiya Kalmykii*, June 8, 2001.

88. Ye. Sharkova, "Lukoil: lokomotiv dlya regiona," *Delovye vesti* (Volgograd), July 3, 2001.

89. "Osobennosti Yuzhnogo federal'nogo biznesa," *Delovaya khronika*, March 12–18, 2002.

90. L. Valer'eva, "Na Marse zhizni net, zato pivo-na 'Saturne,'" *Kubanskie novosti* (Krasnodar), November 9, 2001.

91. Ye. Kaluzhenkova, "Triumf v triumfal'nom zale," *Oblastnye vesti* (Volgograd), October 20, 2001.

92. Ye. Sharkova, "Lukoil: lokomotiv dlya regiona," *Delovye vesti* (Volgograd), July 3, 2001.

93. S. Petrovich, "Zrya toropilis' khoronit' 'Rostovnefteprodukt,'" *Molot* (Rostov-na-Donu), December 11, 2001.

94. D. Sobakina, "Patriarkhal'nost' i gibkost'," *Delovaya khronika*, no. 9 (2002).

95. Ye. Stroiteleva, "Trubnyi zov," *Izvestiya*, April 29, 2002.

96. "S miru po nitke," *Volgogradskaya Pravda* (Volgograd), March 13, 2001.

97. V. Volgin, "Prezident Kalmykii vyskazalsya po actual'nym voprosam politiki i ekonomiki," *Rossiiskii regionalnyi byulleten'*," April 22, 2002.

98. "Kazantsev k shtyku priravnyal pero," *Volgogradskaya Pravda*, March 27, 2001.

99. Strana.ru, December 18, 2001.

100. A. Petrosyan, "Ne poddayutsya schetu," *Izvestiya*, January 19, 2002.

101. V. Ivanov, "Na kubani novyi glavnyi federal'nyi inspektor," *Yuzhnyi federalnyi* (Rostov-na-Donu), April 29, 2002.

102. According to the presidential envoy's data, ethnic Russians make up only 2 percent of the population in Ingushetia and 6 percent in Dagestan, where they constituted 12 percent of the population ten years ago. In North Osetia, the share of ethnic Russians among the capital Vladikavkaz's population dropped from 50 to 30 percent over the last ten years, and in the Chechen Republic, where there were four hundred thousand Russians before the beginning of the wars, there are almost none today.

103. "Terskoe kazachestvo namereno dobivat'sya vozvrashcheniya raionov Chechni," RIA-Novosti, January 27, 2001.

104. N. Gorodetskaya, "Istoriya s prodolzheniem," *Vremya novostei* (Moscow), May 8, 2001.

105. "Mediki okazyvayut pomoshch' zhitelyam Chechni," Interfaks, August 18, 2001.

6

Volga Federal Okrug

Gul'naz Sharafutdinova and Arbakhan Magomedov

THE VOLGA FEDERAL OKRUG INCLUDES *the republics of Bashkortostan, Chuvashia, Marii-El, Mordovia, Tatarstan, Udmurtia; the regions of Kirov, Nizhnii Novgorod, Orenburg, Penza, Perm, Samara, Saratov, Ulyanovsk; and the Komi-Permyak Autonomous Okrug.*

Sergei Kirienko (born 1962) rose from being the head of the Young Communist League in Nizhnii Novgorod's Krasnoe Sormovo shipbuilding factory in 1986 to becoming—against intense parliamentary opposition—Russia's prime minister in 1998 at the age of thirty-five. He had served only three months when Yeltsin fired him after the major Russian financial collapse of August 1998. Before becoming prime minister, he served as head of the Garantiya Bank, president of the Norsi Oil Company, and minister of fuel and energy. In 1999, Kirienko ran against incumbent Moscow mayor Yurii Luzhkov for the mayor's seat, winning a respectable 11 percent showing against the popular and powerful incumbent. Kirienko won a seat in the State Duma in 1999 as the number one candidate on the Union of Right-wing Forces (SPS) party list.

Okrug Overview

Like the Southern Federal Okrug, the defining feature of the Volga okrug is its multinational character. It contains six national republics: Tatarstan, Bashkortostan, Marii-El, Mordovia, Chuvashia, and Udmurtia; and the Komi-Permyak Autonomous Okrug. Moreover, the okrug includes some of Russia's most assertive regional leaders, among them Tatarstan's Mintimer Shaimiev,

Volga Federal District of the Russian Federation

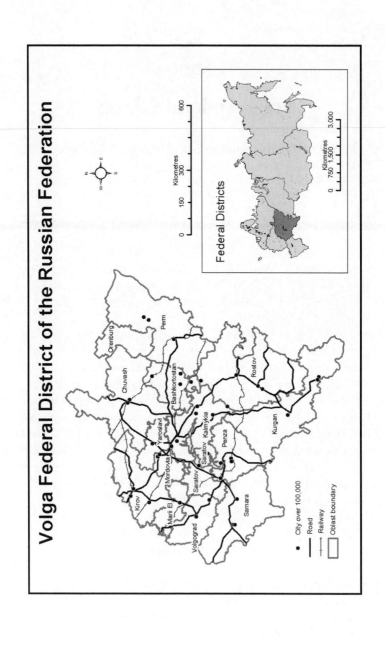

N
W · E
S

Kilometres
0   150   300   600

Federal Districts

Kilometres
0 750 1,500   3,000

Perm

Orenburg

Chuvash

Bashkortostan

Rostov

Yaroslavl

Kalmykia

Kurgan

Mordovia

Saratov

Penza

Kirov

Mari El

Samara

Volgograd

• City over 100,000
── Road
┼─┼ Railway
▢ Oblast boundary

Bashkortostan's Murtaza Rakhimov, Chuvashia's Nikolai Fedorov, Samara's Konstantin Titov, and Saratov's Dmitrii Ayatskov. Before Putin's rise to power, these men made a name for themselves by demanding greater rights for their regions from the federal government.

The fifteen regions of the Volga Federal Okrug constitute 7.27 percent of Russia's territory and 22.1 percent of its population. More than 70 percent of the okrug's population is ethnically Russian. About 70 to 75 percent identify themselves as adherents of the Russian Orthodox faith, and more than 20 percent are Muslims.[1] The okrug includes two regions that are usually considered part of the Urals (Perm and Bashkortostan), while several traditional Volga regions (Astrakhan, Volgograd, and Kalmykia) were included in the Southern Federal Okrug.[2]

Economically, the Volga okrug houses about 80 percent of Russia's machine-building enterprises, a significant part of the fuel and energy complex, and numerous petrochemical plants. The okrug produces 23.9 percent of Russia's industrial output and more than a quarter of its agricultural production.[3] However, the okrug ranks only sixth of seven in terms of per capita income.

One of the most significant peculiarities of the okrug is its envoy, Sergei Kirienko. While all the presidential envoys bring unique qualifications to their work, Kirienko stands out from the crowd. First, he is a so-called liberal reformer, while the other six envoys are representatives of the power ministries, or in the case of Siberia's Leonid Drachevskii, a federal bureaucrat of the "Soviet school." Kirienko is a well-known politician who served as Russia's prime minister prior to the August 1998 economic crisis; he is also a Union of Right-wing Forces political party leader. The style of his work differs from that of the other envoys in that he seems relatively open and accessible to the press.[4] In fact, Kirienko has stated that he sees working with the public as one of his most valuable tools.[5] But, despite his efforts to create a media-friendly image, Kirienko's real political strength lies with his extensive ties to politicians and representatives of big business, both in Moscow and in Nizhnii Novgorod. Therefore his openness to the public is better viewed as a form of public relations aimed at defining the Kirienko image than as an example of real transparency.

With his appointment as presidential envoy, Kirienko experienced a political repatriation, returning to the region where he launched his political career. Many of the other envoys are working in regions where they have little experience or knowledge of the local scene. In Nizhnii Novgorod, Kirienko essentially plays two roles: on one hand, he is an external actor, representing the federal government; on the other, he is one of the regional elite. He left Nizhnii as a young manager and promising politician, and has now returned as a presidential envoy who sees himself as part of the president's team—in fact, he even might be entertaining some hopes of moving to a higher-positioned federal job.

At the very least, even if we do not impute such career goals directly to his actions, Kirienko's deep involvement in the internal politics of Nizhnii Novgorod region, and his activities aimed at expanding his control over the energy sectors in several other regions of the okrug, have the effect more of building a power base for Kirienko than of promoting Putin's agenda of strengthening the federal hierarchy of power. Kirienko's innovative personnel policy—and the successful placement of his associates and teammates in the most important economic and political institutions—testifies further to the idea that his policies are leading to the expansion of his influence beyond the confines of his okrug.

Kirienko's working style is that of a technocrat: he aims at identifying and addressing the problems confronting the Russian state and society by developing problem-solving "technologies." In fact, he is one of the most innovative envoys who comes up with new, sometimes original, ways of addressing various issues. He and his staff, for instance, have been actively promoting the idea of cooperation among the state, civil society, and businesses. Under this general framework, they have organized three big exhibitions for social projects, seeking to stimulate new ideas for addressing some of Russia's most intractable social problems. Kirienko even used his wide business connections to raise funds for the actual implementation of some of these projects. Additionally, Kirienko has successfully realized his earlier plan of introducing a new, competition-based system for civil service recruitment. Filling vacant slots on his staff based on the results of open competition has made it possible for young and competent people to join his team.[6]

The Volga okrug's envoy has also been original in having the famous (some would say notorious) culturologist Petr Shchedrovitskii as a close adviser. Shchedrovitskii played an active role in Kirienko's 1999 campaign to unseat Moscow mayor Yurii Luzhkov. After the creation of the federal okrugs, he set up the Center for Strategic Research (TsSI) in Nizhnii Novgorod, which became the envoy's main brain trust.[7] The results of the center's work have not been too impressive so far. It presented its report "On the Threshold of a New Regionalization" in May 2001, and then "The State: Dividing Responsibilities" in May 2002. Both were widely discussed throughout the okrug.

Few doubt that these documents are the fruit of a political order (*politzakaz*) from the federal authorities and that they aim to provide an ideological basis for weakening the power of the regions. The documents are extremely abstract and schematic, and have little to do with the interests of the regions in the okrug. Their language and style are inaccessible to most readers—a complaint that was most eloquently expressed during a discussion at the Trade and Industry Chamber in Tatarstan on June 13, 2002, when one of the speakers compared the latest report on dividing powers to Dostoyevsky's novel *Demons*. Indeed, despite Shchedrovitskii's close relationship to

Kirienko, his center has had little real impact on the okrug's activities. Officials in Samara were among the very few that expressed an interest in the documents the center produced.[8] Given the lack of practical application of Schedrovitskii's work, the center's continued existence appears to confirm that Kirienko is himself inclined to such abstract and schematic thinking and that he finds such ideas useful as an ideological tool for promoting his larger political goals.[9] Some of his speeches convey a similar impression.

Kirienko's political partisanship and his inclination toward public political activities have made him a contradictory figure on the okrug stage. From the beginning, the envoy was supposed to be a manager, a neutral and impartial figure. But, as Nizhnii Novgorod researcher Andrei Makarychev has pointed out, Kirienko is too closely involved in regional politics and this has stimulated a vocal opposition. Groups like the People's Will (Volya naroda) have, in fact, called for his resignation. Likewise, the press frequently discusses critically his close relationship with Nizhnovenergo director Aleksei Sannikov, one of the most powerful businessmen in the region. Given the contradictory signals sent out by Kirienko's activities, analysts at Makarychev's Institute for Socio-Political Psychology argue that he has little real public support.[10]

Staffing the Okrug

Kirienko's political style has had a strong influence on the makeup of his 112-member staff. The main strength of his team stems from his ability to hire highly qualified personnel who share his general philosophy and approach. Many are young, have achieved considerable success before coming to work in the envoy's office, and see taking a position on the okrug staff as a step up the career ladder. Many sought the job because they were attracted by Kirienko's public persona.[11] In selecting from this pool, Kirienko used methods that were not traditional for Russian bureaucracies. He set up an open competition, publicly announcing openings and forcing job seekers to pass through a number of tests, before, perhaps, being hired. Kirienko claimed that such a recruitment system created state institutions that were accessible to society and helped him find the most qualified candidates for leadership positions. The "usual" recruitment in the state bureaucracy has mostly relied on informal connections and has been riddled with nepotism and corruption.

Following the first competition in 2000, the envoy's staff continued to conduct such competitions in 2001–2002 to fill vacant chief federal inspector and federal inspector slots and create a list of qualified personnel who could be hired as vacancies appeared.[12] In an interview given to the readers of the e-newspaper "Gazetu.ru," Kirienko noted that the success rate of this competition-based system has been 90 percent and that this figure has exceeded his expectations.[13]

Kirienko's team is made up of several groups. In the top rung are people who worked with Kirienko in Nizhnii Novgorod's Young Communist League, or Komsomol, during the late Soviet period; and his old friends from the Krasnoe Sormovo shipbuilding company, the Garantiya Bank, the Norsi Oil Company, and the Fuel and Energy Ministry. Key members at this level are First Deputy Envoy Sergei Novikov (who handles some economic issues, oversees the okrug monitoring agencies, and coordinates the chief federal inspectors) and Chief of Staff Viktor Ratnikov, both of whom worked in the Fuel and Energy Ministry; Deputy Envoy Sergei Obozov (economic issues and investment development), who worked with Kirienko at Krasnoe Sormovo; and Leonid Sukhoterin (the envoy's public relations chief before he became a short-lived senator from the Komi-Permyak autonomous okrug[14] and then transferred in December 2001 to the Kirovenergo utility as a deputy director), who worked with Kirienko at Garantiya and Norsi Oil.

Obozov and deputy presidential envoy Lyubov' Glebova hold special places in Kirienko's team. Glebova is Kirienko's closest adviser: she has worked with him since they were in the Komsomol together. Within the envoy's staff, she handles the important political portfolio, including elections, the choice of personnel in the regions, and political coordination within the okrug and with Moscow. Glebova resigned a seat in the State Duma to take this position and is an influential member of the Union of Right-wing Forces (SPS) faction.[15] She organized Kirienko's party New Strength (Novaya sila), which later merged with SPS. Kirienko trusts her with all organizational questions, including financial ones. Obozov also worked with Kirienko in the Komsomol and retained close personal ties with him, though he did not work for Kirienko until the latter became Putin's envoy. Other influential players include Valentin Stepankov, a former Russian procurator general, who organized the process of bringing regional laws into line with federal norms.

The rest of Kirienko's top advisers are people he recruited from Moscow and elsewhere. They are either former federal civil servants or specialists in particular areas. A good example of the latter is Deputy Envoy Leonid Gilchenko, who handles local government issues; he joined Kirienko's staff relatively late and does not intervene in political issues.

Some of Kirienko's staff work in Moscow on permanent assignment to the presidential administration.[16] This arrangement provides evidence of Kirienko's close ties to presidential chief of staff Aleksandr Voloshin and to the presidential administration in general.

Kirienko's Main Activities

In his numerous interviews, Kirienko has defined his main tasks in different ways. He has, first, focused on the tasks common to all envoys, such as restoring federal power in the regions, setting up a unified legal and economic space, and dividing responsibilities clearly among the different levels of government. He has also defined specific tasks, such as taking action in crisis situations; making an inventory of the whole country's property as a basis for future policy making; and innovating new working methods, including the analysis of problems, setting priorities, and seeking new solutions.[17]

From the moment the institution of presidential envoys was created, Kirienko talked about it as temporary, as being an "instrument for implementing current strategy" and for "changing the model of management," rather than being, in itself, a new model of management.[18] He stuck to this idea for almost two years and seems to have abandoned it only as it gradually became clearer that—with the envoys being few in number and, more important, close to the president—this new layer of bureaucracy was probably here to stay.[19] We should also note that despite Kirienko's assertions that the envoys would exist only temporarily, the range of his activities has continually increased. Two years after Putin set up the institution, Kirienko was actively participating in questions of local government, economic integration, and operational anticrisis measures, measures that required his constant intervention in the affairs of crisis-prone regions such as Ulyanovsk. This expansion into new spheres corresponds poorly with Kirienko's often stated expectation about the temporary nature of the institution.

Creating a Unified Legal Space

One of the envoy's first projects was bringing regional laws into line with federal norms. This was part of Putin's policy of implementing a "dictatorship of law." Despite the extensive campaign to create a unified legal space in the okrug, and despite the numerous changes in the regional laws, the achievements in this area have only been formal and have not affected the way the regional and federal elites interact with one another. The norm of informal interelite agreements as a basis for resolving all problems has remained unchanged in the Volga okrug.

Overall, procurators in the okrug found 853 regional laws that violated federal norms, with the largest number of transgressions in the republics of Bashkortostan and Tatarstan.[20] Kirienko claimed that he had resolved 99 percent of the problem by the beginning of 2002.[21] In his opinion, it was important that disputes over laws among different levels of government should be decided by the courts. Achieving this would be an important step on the way to establishing a rule-of-law state. The envoy played the main role in the campaign to bring regional laws into line during the first phase, when it was necessary to set the process in motion. Then he simply monitored the process as it advanced. According to Tatarstan federal inspector Denis Akhmadullin, Kirienko played the role of catalyzing changes for which everyone was already prepared.[22]

Putin clearly hoped that the campaign to bring regional laws into line would create an atmosphere in which newly adopted laws would not violate federal norms. However, Tatarstan and Bashkortostan's adoption of new constitutions did not meet these expectations. Bashkortostan made significant changes in its constitution in November 2000. However, many observers came to the conclusion that the amendments not only failed to bring the republic's basic law into line with federal norms, but to the contrary, strengthened several aspects of the republic's special status. For example, the prohibition on the republican president's serving more than two terms in office disappeared from the text.[23] The new version of the constitution did remove passages in which the republic identified itself as a subject of international law, declared its laws superior to federal laws, and corrected the definition of republican sovereignty. However, it elevated the status of the 1994 bilateral agreement between the republican and federal governments by including its text in the new draft.[24] Shortly after Bashkortostan adopted its new constitution, the procurator filed a protest against it because approximately twenty provisions of the revised draft violated federal norms.[25] Ultimately, yielding to increasing pressure from Moscow and Nizhnii Novgorod, Bashkortostan adopted a third version of the constitution on December 3, 2002, which did not include the power-sharing treaty, although the republic's president, Murtaza Rakhimov, said this did not mean that the treaty had been annulled.[26]

In Tatarstan, the question of amending the constitution dragged on until 2002.[27] To discuss amendments, the republican authorities and Kirienko's staff set up a conciliatory commission. However, this commission was unable to reach a final agreement on several key questions, leaving them for Tatarstan president Mintimer Shaimiev and President Putin to resolve in a one-on-one meeting.[28]

After adopting 357 amendments, the Tatarstani legislature approved the constitution at the end of February 2002.[29] The revised Tatarstani constitution incorporated the text of the 1994 power-sharing agreement between the federal and republican governments, a concept of limited sovereignty for the republic and limited provisions for republican citizenship. In all these cases the text thwarted the Kremlin's intentions. However, removed from the text were assertions of international status for the republic, of an associative relationship with Russia, and of the superiority of Tatarstani laws over Russian laws.

As the work on bringing the republic's laws into line with federal norms showed, neither the conciliatory commission nor court procedures resolved the main disputes over the republican constitution. Final agreement required the personal intervention of the presidents of Tatarstan and Russia, and their willingness to compromise.[30] The fact that the two presidents had to resolve key conflicts in an informal and personal meeting shows that nothing has changed in the way politics work. In this sense, the relations between Shaimiev and Putin differ little from the relations between Shaimiev and Yeltsin.

Thus, an interelite agreement paved the way for Tatarstan's entry into the (only partially) unified legal space. The gist of the compromise was that the Tatarstani authorities secured financial assistance from Moscow in compensation for the republic's losses in making the required concessions to the federal government. The republic's tax losses turned out to be significant. In the past, the republic was able to keep all fees derived from oil production and about 75 percent of all taxes. Under the new system all fees and value added tax went to Moscow, while all taxes were divided so that the larger share went to the federal government. According to deputy minister for economic development and trade Mukhamed Tsikanov, Tatarstan had to give sixteen billion rubles (about $50 million) more to the federal government each year than in the past. However, in July 2001 the federal government adopted a so-called targeted federal program aimed at the socioeconomic development of Tatarstan in 2001–2006 that would cost 306 billion rubles, sixty-one billion of which would come from the federal budget.[31] Thus, with the adoption of the federal program, Tatarstan was able to soften the blow of its lost status as a privileged taxpayer. The real impact of these changes, however, remains to be seen, since the federal government often, notoriously, fails in practice to provide the funds for such programs.

Although the federal government apparently had to pay dearly to entice Tatarstan to bring its laws into at least partial conformity with federal norms, the adoption of a new tax system that does not make room for exceptions like Tatarstan is a clear success for Moscow. At the same time, one should not underestimate the ability of regional governments to change the structure and number of taxes they collect by devices such as integrating regional enterprises, setting up holding companies, and other accounting tricks.[32]

Overall, the campaign to bring regional laws into line with federal norms was little more than a formality. Not addressed were the causes that make such laws possible, including the growing inequality among regions and the inability of the federal government to effectively address the great and growing variety of regional problems, some of which are further exacerbated by the growth of inequality. Moreover, the very process of bringing the laws into line demonstrated to all observers that key decisions came as the result of deals cut between the heads of the republics and the federal government. This showed that the main mechanism for resolving serious problems remained unchanged.

Coordinating the Activities of the Federal Authorities in the Regions

In general, the Volga okrug presents an example of successful cooperation between the envoy and the federal ministries, due largely to Kirienko's personal preference to avoid conflict, and to his extensive contacts in Moscow. However, Kirienko does not seem to coordinate the ministries, preferring rather to play the role of intermediary between the regions and individual federal ministries. For example, the former Nizhnii Novgorod governor Ivan Sklyarov asked for such help.[33] Additionally, and perhaps, most important for the okrug, Kirienko works as a lobbyist at the federal level for okrug interests, pushing for various megaprojects aimed at fostering greater economic integration.

Beyond his personal ties, Kirienko's oversight over personnel policy is one of his most important resources, allowing him to influence the management of federal ministries in the regions. In particular, Kirienko tries to ensure that federal employees implement the president's policies rather than those of the governors. More than half of the okrug's top regional procurators have been replaced, presumably by new procurators who are not as beholden to the governors as were their predecessors.[34] However, in powerful regions like Tatarstan and Bashkortostan, Kirienko has had only limited autonomy and has been forced to secure the agreement of the republican leaders for key federal appointments.

Kirienko also tried to get the public involved in direct oversight of federal and regional officials by setting up public reception rooms, where ordinary citizens can file complaints about the actions of federal bureaucrats or their failure to implement federal laws. Throughout the okrug, he opened fifty-six such centers and attracted about two thousand volunteers to man them.[35] How well or badly they are working is not yet clear. In another innovation in April 2002, Kirienko was the first to set up an okrug-level Accounting Chamber. The agreement he signed with Sergei Stepashin, the head of the Russian Accounting Chamber, envisions that the body will oversee budget expenditures and salary payments in the Volga regions and that it will also conduct joint inspections in coordination with the envoy's okrug office.[36] Additionally, Kirienko set up numerous councils and coordinating bodies, but these have had little more function than bringing together various officials at the okrug level and trying to build an okrug identity among them.

The Envoy's Relations with the Governors

The evolution of relations between the presidential envoy and the governors is a crucial topic because it addresses the question of how effectively the institution of the federal okrugs has developed and whether it has produced greater compliance by the governors in regard to federal policies. Thus, this section examines how the introduction of the envoys has affected the behavior of the regional elites.

The okrugs' creation and appointment of the envoys have—in the context of other aspects of the federal reforms—definitely influenced the regional elites. Above all, these innovations have changed the psychological atmosphere and the degree to which the regional elites feel the presence of the federal authorities in the regions. The governors' reactions to the Kremlin's new policy have differed greatly, depending on the level of effective control the governors have had over their regions and the quantity of power resources they have possessed. Bashkortostan's Rakhimov, Tatarstan's Shaimiev, and Chuvashia's Fedorov have criticized the federal reforms and continued to take initiatives independently of the okrug authorities.[37] Fedorov, in particular, openly opposed the Kremlin by filing a case with the Russian Constitutional Court, questioning whether several of Putin's key initiatives were constitutional.[38] At the same time, several observers questioned the sincerity of Fedorov's opposition, suspecting him of playing some sort of game with the Kremlin.[39]

In general, the stronger regional leaders prefer to avoid the okrug leadership and continue to deal directly with federal officials in Moscow. Rakhimov on his own, for example, worked out a deal with Deputy Prime Minister Ilya Klebanov on creating an aviation holding company that would unite the engine factories of Yaroslavl, Rybinsk, and Ufa, even though Kirienko had publicly announced that this sort of integration should, as a priority aspect of his economic strategy, be worked out at the level of the okrug.[40] Moreover, at least one regional observer pointed out that relations between Kirienko and Rakhimov deteriorated further after Bashkortostan adopted a new version of its constitution, which did not conform to federal law.[41]

The variety of attitudes among the governors to the presidential envoy has also shown through at the level of symbolism. For example, the weaker and more dependent governors, like Udmurtia's Volkov and Orenburg's Aleksei Chernyshev, greet Kirienko at the airport personally. More powerful figures like Shaimiev and Rakhimov meet one another personally at the airport, but they usually send the chairmen of their regional legislatures to meet Kirienko.[42]

Several governors have taken steps to win Kirienko's and the Kremlin's favor. At various times the heads of Perm, Nizhnii Novgorod, Ulyanovsk, and Saratov regions; the Komi-Permyak Autonomous Okrug; and the republic of

Marii-El requested that the president tear up their regions' power-sharing treaties with Moscow that had been signed during the Yeltsin era, thus anticipating the intentions of the Kremlin.[43] In contrast, the leaders of Tatarstan and Bashkortostan have consistently fought to preserve their treaties.

The regions of the okrug differ in the degree to which they accept external influence. The envoy's real impact depends on how many interest groups there are in the region that are able and willing to oppose the authorities. In closely integrated political systems like those of Tatarstan and Bashkortostan, where the republican government controls all power resources and any opposition is easily neutralized, Kirienko's ability to act is minimal. The republican authorities in these two republics even control the regional branches of the federal law enforcement agencies, such as the Ministry of Internal Affairs.[44] Often media controlled by republican authorities do not want to cover the activities of the presidential envoys because they fear the negative reaction of the regional executives.[45] In those regions where there are real opposition groups or where the situation of the governor is unstable because he lacks the powerful resources needed to exert his authority, the presidential envoy can find a base within the system and use it to influence the course of events. Thus, for example, Kirienko intervened in Orenburg region after Vladimir Gorbunov, the mayor of Abdulino, was fired and the regional authorities were preparing for a new mayor to be elected by the district legislature. Discussions in the okrug offices led to Gorbunov being restored to his position.[46]

Usually, Kirienko tries to avoid open conflict with the regional leaders. Only in the Marii-El presidential elections and the battle over Udmurtia's television (described below) has he entered into open battle with governors. Instead, elite-level agreements resolve the majority of conflicts. For example, Kirienko used this approach in resolving the dispute over Russia's internal passports in Tatarstan and Bashkortostan. Since 1997 the leaders of these republics had refused to give out Russian passports since these no longer identified the bearer's nationality. The compromise that Kirienko achieved stipulated that each passport would include two coats of arms (Russian and republican) and inserts in the republic's national language. However, the republics did not succeed in requiring the passports to identify the bearer's national identity.[47] Additionally, the opening of the federal treasury in Tatarstan in March 2001 was partly the result of Kirienko's efforts.[48] At the same time, however, Kirienko lost out over the issue of allowing the governors to run for a third term because the State Duma adopted a law permitting this despite Kirienko's initial negative reaction.[49]

How Kirienko's relations with the governors have actually worked in practice can be seen by looking closely at some individual regions. In Ulyanovsk, Governor Vladimir Shamanov is a newcomer. He came to power relying on outside sources of support, and he lacks a strong regional power base. Consequently, Kirienko gained considerable influence over the region by working with external political and economic interests. For example, he was able to appoint the chief federal inspector to the region without any input from the regional administration.

Among the region's major economic interests, Kirienko has close relations with Northern Steel (Severstal), which recently bought the Ulyanovsk automobile factory and which draws on Kirienko's support in its battles with the governor. As regards the energy sector, the reforms initiated in this sector and the creation of the Middle Volga Interregional Energy Management Company (SMUEK), have given Kirienko substantial influence, as elaborated below. In the case of Ulyanovsk, its persisting financial problems have resulted in a continuous energy crisis and taken it to the verge of bankruptcy. Thus it is seen as one of the main candidates to undergo one of Kirienko's new "technologies" on "political bankruptcy," whereby the region is taken under complete federal control.[50] Ulyanovsk could also become a target for the federal government's much discussed plans to reduce the number of regions, since economically and geographically it is now essentially a satellite of the much more powerful Samara region.

The situation has been very different in Saratov, where Governor Dmitrii Ayatskov has a much stronger control over the region. His influence operates through a patronage system involving most of the major regional interests and limiting the autonomy of those actors who have not been co-opted. His regional dominance has been very much aided by his high-level connections in Moscow, including such notable national politicians as Lyubov Sliska, deputy speaker of the Duma; and Vyacheslav Volodin, head of the Fatherland–All Russia faction in the Duma and a member of the General Council of United Russia. In contrast to Shamanov, Ayatskov has felt secure enough to criticize Kirienko and to conduct a policy independent of him. Accordingly, he was able to delegate "his own" people to Kirienko's staff to be the chief federal inspector and the federal inspector for Saratov. The former, Renat Khalikov, was Ayatskov's former regional minister for construction, and the latter, Pavel Grishin, was the region's former deputy economics minister.

However, in late 2000 and early 2001 Ayatskov began to lose some of his influence. One of the reasons was a progressive shift in Khalikov's and Grishin's loyalties: they began to see themselves as clients more of Kirienko than Ayatskov, and therefore they started supporting the envoy more than the governor. Furthermore, Ayatskov seemed to be losing his relationship with Vyacheslav Volodin as well, who also appeared to be shifting his allegiance to Kirienko.

In this new political context, the Saratov legislature, which controls the regional budget and its electoral districts, became a primary playing field in the battle between the governor and the envoy. To further weaken Ayatskov,

Kirienko tried to establish a political alliance against him with Speaker Aleksandr Kharitonov. The envoy was also able to convince the Saratov legislature to appoint Chubais's deputy in the electricity monopoly EES, Valentin Zavadnikov, as a member of the Federation Council. Absolutely unacceptable to Ayatskov, Zavadnikov represents the united interests of Kirienko and Chubais (elaborated further below) rather than any regional interests.

However, Kirienko's gambits did not last long, because Ayatskov was able to mend his relations with Volodin and ultimately reestablish control over the regional legislature. In April 2002 he removed Kharitonov as speaker, and subsequently, in the September 2002 elections, Ayatskov's candidates secured a majority of the seats in the legislature. Ayatskov's domination was a result of his renewed alliance with Volodin, who was responsible for United Russia's participation in the elections.

And lastly, Kirienko's unstable relationship with the communist governor of Nizhnii Novgorod region, Gennadii Khodyrev, revealed the limits to the governor's autonomy in a region experiencing acute financial crisis. Kirienko had worked against Khodyrev's election and supported the incumbent governor Ivan Sklyarov. In exchange for this support, Sklyarov agreed to create— ahead of the election—parallel institutions of regional government. Sergei Obozov, Kirienko's teammate, was put in charge of the new regional government, in effect leaving Sklyarov with little more than ceremonial powers. Sklyarov, however, lost the elections despite Kirienko's support, and the unexpected winner was Khodyrev.

Announcing early on "I do not need a nanny," Khodyrev tried to implement policies independent of Kirienko.[51] However, the reality of the region's economic crisis and huge financial deficit meant that it was heavily dependent on the federal government's subsidies. As a result, the federal authorities ultimately gained the ability to monitor regional finances. In February 2002, the Nizhnii Novgorod regional government signed an agreement with the Russian Finance Ministry, according to which Moscow would provide financial aid only if the region made its budget transparent and if it spent no less than half of its income on public sector salaries.[52] Thus, Nizhnii Novgorod is an example of a region where the federal authorities have been able to strengthen federal control by obtaining the power to monitor region-level budgets.[53]

Gubernatorial Elections and the Role of the Presidential Envoy

One of Kirienko's most important jobs has been implementing the president's personnel policy, which includes overseeing the gubernatorial elections to try to secure the Kremlin's interests. Kirienko has had mixed results in this effort. He succeeded in Marii-El, Ulyanovsk, and Penza regions; and he carried out one of the main tasks set for him in Nizhnii Novgorod, namely, to prevent the election of Andrei Kliment'ev, who had a criminal record. Additionally, he blocked attempts to change the election dates in Tatarstan and Marii-El.[54] In Nizhnii Novgorod, the victory of communist Gennadii Khodyrev was a defeat for Kirienko;[55] and in several regions with powerful governors, Kirienko made little impact on the elections.

Kirienko played the biggest role in the Marii-El presidential election. The Kremlin wanted to block incumbent president Vyacheslav Kislitsyn from running for a second term. Nevertheless, Kislitsyn stayed in the race despite Kremlin pressure, and Kirienko was given the job of preventing him from winning. A team of Nizhnii Novgorod election consultants organized a two-pronged campaign of pressure: the federal law enforcement agencies launched an investigation into his activities as governor, seeking compromising material that could be used against him; and the specialists organized a PR campaign against him. Kislitsyn then reached an agreement with Kirienko to withdraw from the campaign, but soon changed his mind and went on the counterattack, seeking support in Moscow. However, Kirienko managed to convince the presidential administration of the need to continue the battle against him. Despite Kremlin pressure, Kislitsyn managed to reach the second round, though he ultimately lost to Leonid Markelov, the deputy general director of the Russian state insurance company, Rosgosstrakh, who beat him by 25 percent.[56] Markelov openly acknowledged that he owed his victory to the Kremlin and especially Kirienko.[57]

There was no similar intervention in other regions. Kirienko had almost no impact on the elections in Tatarstan. When he visited the republic right before the elections in March 2001, he praised the republican government's work, which was seen as a sign of support for the incumbent president Shaimiev. Shaimiev's earlier concern that Kirienko would speak out publicly against him turned out to be unwarranted.[58]

Kirienko also did not intervene in the Chuvashia election, allowing the re-election of Nikolai Fedorov. In Perm, Kirienko supported both major candidates, first incumbent Gennadii Igumnov and then Perm mayor Yurii Trutnev, even though Igumnov was considered the Kremlin favorite (Trutnev ultimately won). In Samara and the Komi-Permyak autonomous okrug, Kirienko did not intervene in the elections; and in Udmurtia he supported Volkov only at the end of the campaign, when it was obvious who would win.[59]

Appointments to the Federation Council

However, Kirienko exercised a powerful influence over the Volga regions' appointments to the Federation Council, with many of the new senators coming from his staff. Thus, Mordovia delegated Kirienko's former deputy for economic issues, German Petrov; Komi-Permyak, after the short-lived service of Kirienko's associate Leonid Sukhoterin, delegated former Perm chief federal inspector Vladimir Solomonov; Ulyanovsk chose former Ulyanovsk chief federal inspector Valerii Sychev; Yamal Nenets selected former deputy envoy Aleksandr Yevstifeev; and Marii-El appointed Aleksandr Torshin.[60] In some other cases, he was also able to secure the appointment of candidates who were much closer aligned with his interests and goals than with the interests of the regional authorities. The aforementioned case of Valentin Zavadnikov's election as a senator from Saratov is a good example.

Such successes can be explained by several factors. First, Kirienko cleverly uses the debts owed to him by various regional players—for example, for his active support of Markelov in the gubernatorial elections in Marii-El. Kirienko also excels in political strategizing, as demonstrated by his political alignment with Kharitonov, Saratov's speaker, which enabled him to convince the legislature to appoint Zavadnikov. And, most important, Kirienko must be credited with a consistent and careful personnel policy, in the framework of which he secures promotion and career development for his close associates. His personal involvement in such promotions undoubtedly contributes to their continuing support for him.

Crime and Corruption

Corruption in Russia has become systemic, in that the state bureaucracy itself is actively involved in corrupt activities that undermine the state's crucial role as provider of uniform rules for the society. According to the procurator general Vladimir Ustinov, about 80 percent of state bureaucrats are implicated in corruption.[61] Understandably, then, establishing a unified set of rules for federal bureaucrats was among the tasks assumed by the presidential envoys.[62] However, despite the widespread understanding of the importance of such rules, the federal reform has not had a major impact on corruption among the authorities, the various forms of which are not limited to bribery but also include informal agreements among different levels of government, deals regarding various types of privatization and property distribution, and efforts to falsify election results.

Corruption in Russia is not only widespread; it has also, not surprisingly, become a weapon in political battles. The greatest demand for information about corruption among politicians and civil servants appears during episodes of intense political conflict. The apogee of such battles in the regions is reached during gubernatorial elections. Thus in Perm, Pavel Anokhin, a challenger to Governor Gennadii Igumnov in the December 2000 elections, initiated an attack on the law enforcement agencies. In particular, a procurator's investigation had discovered that agents were illegally pressuring businesses to contribute to a "Law and Order Fund," which the agents used for illegal purposes.[63] Likewise, before the presidential elections in Tatarstan, republican television broadcast information about the alleged criminal activities of Sergei Shashurin, one of Shaimiev's opponents, who supposedly was illegally selling KamAZ cars.[64]

Envoy Kirienko's appearance on the political scene as a new player at the okrug level has not changed this pattern. His staff has not been very original and has often made information about corruption available for its own political purposes. Thus, for example, to prevent the reelection of Marii-El president Kislitsyn, Kirienko inspired a series of investigations examining the links between the republican authorities and the criminal world.[65] One result of a Moscow commission's work in the republic was the procurator's decision to file charges against the chairman of the republican electoral commission Yurii Petrov and the businessman Aleksandr Odintsov, who was described as the governor's chief enforcer in the republic.[66] In summarizing the work of the law enforcement agencies in the republic, Kirienko's deputy Valentin Stepankov sharply criticized the republican leadership and effectively declared the republic bankrupt.[67]

Additionally, Kirienko's active involvement in the okrug's political and economic life has attracted opposition, and the envoy himself has become the center of scandals. The most serious attack on him was the appearance in the Duma of material from an entity calling itself the Russian Academy of Sciences' Institute for Studying Public Opinion, which asserted corruption on Kirienko's part. As it turned out, such an institute did not exist. However, Duma members Sergei Shashurin and Vyacheslav Olen'ev called for an investigation of Kirienko's involvement in creating a "determined criminal group, whose activities are undermining state security and causing significant damage to the economy of the region and of Russia as a whole."[68] Observers believe that this material came either from the communist Viktor Ilyukhin, who had run in the Penza region gubernatorial elections, or from Kirienko's former ally turned opponent Dmitrii Savel'ev, who was seeking to win as many seats as possible in the Nizhnii Novgorod legislative elections that were taking place at the time.[69]

The Presidential Envoy's Economic Influence

As Kirienko himself has pointed out, the effort to set up a unified legal space is only the first step in setting the stage for implementing economic reforms.[70] Indeed, the economic field is where the envoy has been most active. Observers have even singled Kirienko out as practicing an undesirable hyperactivity in

the economic sphere, especially concerning questions of property redistribu-
tion. This, they hold, sullies the image of the institution of presidential envoy.[71]

Kirienko has intervened most actively in the economy of Nizhnii Novgorod, as one would expect given his extensive ties in the region. As mentioned earlier, using the uncertainty generated by the region's gubernatorial
elections, Kirienko gained effective control of the political system by inspiring
the creation of a regional government structure, which existed in parallel with
the staff of the governor. However, the head of the new government Sergei
Obozov had to resign when Kirienko's plans for Sklyarov's victory failed,
whereupon the victor Khodyrev promptly took the region's political system
back out of the de facto control of the presidential envoy.

However, the results of the region's legislative elections partially compensated Kirienko for his defeat in the gubernatorial vote. The right-center bloc
made strong gains, getting seven members of the Union of Right-wing Forces
(SPS) elected, plus five other candidates supported by the right.[72] (There are
forty-five deputies in all.) The Kirienko allies among the new deputies include
LUKoil Volga region director Vadim Vorob'ev and Nizhnovenergo general director Aleksei Sannikov. In addition, the legislature elected SPS member and
Kirienko's personal friend Yevgenii Lyulin as its speaker.[73]

Beginning in the second half of 2000, the presidential envoys across Russia
set up consultative councils on entrepreneurship designed to conduct dia-
logues with regional business people. This effort to replicate a federal pattern
at the regional level turned out to be less effective than the federal model. In
the regions, business corporatism is weakly developed: regional businesspeople tend to deal with the authorities on a one-on-one basis and do not foster
corporate solidarity to protect their interests. Thus Kirienko's relationship
with the regional business communities is not so much with associations as
with individual representatives of regional big business (this is elaborated
below).[74]

Strategic Development Plans

The envoy's staff has done some exploratory work on strategic programs to
develop the okrug. It has avoided large-scale and ambitious projects, the realization of which often leads to conflict with the federal government and regional leaders, as the experience of the Siberian and Southern federal okrugs
has demonstrated.[75] The envisioned plan for the strategic development of the
Volga okrug represents an integration of the strategic development programs of
the individual regions and of various interregional megaprojects. Toward this
end, Deputy Envoy Obozov chaired a meeting of the Greater Volga Economic
Cooperation Association's Committee on Economic and Investment Policy to

discuss the okrug's strategic development through 2015. The final draft of a Volga strategic plan was expected to appear in the beginning of 2003.[76]

Kirienko has been quite successful in lobbying in Moscow for the interregional projects, which, along with the individual regional programs, will form the core of the strategy. These projects cannot be realized within the framework of one region and can therefore most logically be implemented at the okrug level. The program for the automobile industry's integration is the most notable effort of its kind, since the okrug contains 80 percent of Russia's automobile construction. In June 2001, the problems of automakers were discussed at a meeting with the president. However, the decisions taken then were more concerned with limiting the competition from used foreign cars imported into Russia than with integrating various regional production units.

Additionally, there have been discussions at various levels about integrating the aircraft production facilities in the okrug, including enterprises based in Ulyanovsk, Samara, Nizhnii Novgorod, and Tatarstan.[77] Samara governor Konstantin Titov suggested uniting three enterprises (the Kazan Aircraft Construction Association [KAPO], Samara's Aviakor, and Ulyanovsk's Aviastar) into one company.[78] So far, however, this idea has gone nowhere because some of Samara's neighbors are not keen to facilitate Samara's aggrandizement. It is indeed hard to imagine that the government of Tatarstan, which controls the KAPO, would agree to give up its authority over this factory. At the same time, Chuvashia, Mordovia, Ulyanovsk, Orenburg, Saratov, and Samara have all announced their willingness to set up a unified company.[79]

Another sphere intended for okrugwide integration is the petrochemical industry. Here the envoy's staff has convened many meetings, determined strategic goals, and declared the need to join forces; but little has actually happened. In all these sectors, the biggest obstacle to integration is the issue of ownership and control of property. It will be, at best, extremely difficult to reconcile the interests of federal economic elites and regional elites, especially those in Tatarstan and Bashkortostan, which control the major economic entities on their territories. In the past decade, the federal and regional elites have mostly faced each other as competitors, not as partners.

Among these megaprojects, the plan to develop a North–South international transportation corridor, which would unite Europe and Russia via the Volga and Caspian with the countries of southeast Asia deserves special mention. Kirienko successfully lobbied for the inclusion of several parts of this project in the federal program for modernizing Russia's transportation system.[80] And in spring 2002, the Russian government ratified plans to move ahead with the corridor. However, Kirienko will face many "peace-keeping" challenges in actually implementing the program. Even before Russia decided to proceed with the project, several regions announced that they deserved a priority role. Shaimiev's adviser

Rafael Khakimov even declared that the "Volga Trade Route" would be the "new philosophy" of Tatarstan. Saratov region also hopes to receive part of the $5–6 billion expected to go into the project. Regions like Samara and Nizhnii Novgorod, which have significant transit potential and ambitions to strengthen their position, will also likely lobby for a share. Finally, the prospect of a corridor being built has already caused a prolonged conflict between Astrakhan region and Kalmykia in the Southern Federal Okrug.[81]

Relations with Big Business

The close links between the envoy and Russia's big businesses distinguish the Volga okrug from the others. Since the creation of the okrugs coincided with the arrival of these businesses in the Volga area, Kirienko—as a former prime minister, a leader of the probusiness Union of Right-wing Forces, and most important, a presidential envoy—was in a strong position to try to set new rules for how these businesses should behave in the okrug.

Kirienko used his position to the maximum to negotiate with Siberian Aluminum over drawing up an anticrisis program for the Gorky Automobile Factory (GAZ), to resist the sale of shares in the Krasnoe Sormovo shipbuilding factory,[82] and to play an active role in reforming the Unified Energy System electricity monopoly (to be discussed in greater detail below). Kirienko's staff expected to participate in all deals and were in fact quite irritated when confronted with a secret purchase of the Trans-Volga Engine Factory (ZMZ) by Northern Steel's Aleksei Mordashov. In the words of one of Northern Steel's top managers, "we were told that we had acted in an uncivilized way when we bought the factory without consulting anyone."[83]

Kirienko's staff has often acted as an arbiter in the relations between various economic interests and state agencies in Nizhnii Novgorod region. At the end of 2000, for example, Deputy Envoy German Petrov played a role in regulating the relations between the region's electricity company Nizhnovenergo and the region's tax service, while the federal inspector for the region monitored the situation at Nizhnii Novgorod Airlines, where the workers were planning to strike.[84] The envoy's staff was also actively involved in negotiations with the new leadership of the Gorky Automobile Factory (GAZ) on the factory's role in developing the region's social services,[85] and they participated in resolving a conflict between GAZ and its main engine supplier, the Trans-Volga Engine Factory.[86]

Kirienko seeks to work with all the major players in the economy. He has extremely close ties to the major Russian businesses Alfa Group, Northern Steel, Siberian Aluminum, and United Machine-Building Factories, among others. His interest and participation in the buying and selling of the okrug's largest enterprises have gone far beyond what observers have considered normal, and they have been widely commented on in the media. There is every reason to believe that, in one way or another, Kirienko has sponsored, guided, monitored, or at least intently tracked the strategic deals completed in the period 2000–2002 in the okrug, deals that have radically changed the structure of ownership in the okrug economy. In particular, Oleg Deripaska's Siberian Aluminum (subsequently renamed Basic Element) purchased Nizhnii Novgorod's largest enterprise, the Gorky Automobile Factory (GAZ) and the Pavlov Bus Factory; Kakha Bendukidze's United Machine-Building Factories bought a controlling stake in the Krasnoe Sormovo ship-building factory; the Alfa Group acquired the Balakhna Pulp and Paper Mill; the KASKOL financial–industrial group strengthened its position at the Sokol aviation factory; and, as mentioned, Aleksei Mordashov's Northern Steel bought the Trans-Volga Engine Factory (ZMZ).

Kirienko monitored, tracked, and regulated the arrival of big business in the Volga okrug. However, he was not always an independent player. In helping Siberian Aluminum to gain control of GAZ, Kirienko was probably fulfilling a direct order from the Presidential Administration. Also, the ownership of such federally important enterprises as GAZ and the Ulyanovsk Automobile Factory are not simply economic questions; decisions about their fate require political sanction. In such important cases, Kirienko has expected to play a major role, since he has such close personal ties to the presidential administration, and his staff functions as an institutional extension of it.

The expansion of big, national business groups into the regions has inevitably led to changing relationships between political and economic elites in the regions. In the past, the directors of large enterprises worked in close contact with the regional governments. But the new national-level economic players are more independent of the governors. Naturally, the oligarchs prefer friendly relations with governors, but there is not a symbiosis or an intimate mutual dependence between these actors. This is well illustrated by the situation in Nizhnii Novgorod, where the new GAZ owner, Oleg Deripaska, avoided getting directly involved in the gubernatorial campaign in summer 2001, saying that he preferred to focus on the region's economic development issues and stay out of politics.[87] Other leaders of big businesses who are newcomers in the region, such as Bendukidze and Mordashov, have also been able, so far, to avoid getting involved in its internal political struggles. However, this new feature of government-business relations clearly does not characterize regions where the local elite still control the main enterprises, as in Tatarstan and Bashkortostan.

Relations with the Electricity Monopoly

Kirienko has a special relationship with Russia's electricity monopoly, Unified Energy Systems (EES). At the highest level, Kirienko and EES chief Anatolii

Chubais are two of the three coleaders of the Union of Right-wing Forces, which gives them a link most politicians do not have. Moreover, Kirienko has very close personal ties with the electricity company Nizhnovenergo's director Aleksei Sannikov. Some of Kirienko's detractors even claim that the utility provides a source of income for the envoy's team.[88]

These close ties have been manifested in Kirienko's collaboration with Chubais in starting to implement the much discussed reform of the electricity industry. The ultimate shape of the reform is expected to have enormous consequences in redistributing political and economic power in Russia. The Volga okrug has become a testing ground for EES's national reform.[89] Kirienko's staff and EES have been drafting legislation to create new kinds of market entities that will shape the future of the reform.[90] Specifically, on the basis of several EES subsidiaries in the okrug—including Samaraenergo, Penzaenergo, Saratovenergo, and Ul'yanovskenergo—reformers have already established the new joint energy company, the Mid-Volga Interregional Energy Management Company (SMUEK), headquartered in Samara.[91] Another company, the Volga Hydroelectric Cascade, was set up in Nizhnii Novgorod to unite all the Volga's hydroelectric stations.[92] Kirienko and the other initiators of this plan claimed that merging regional firms into supraregional conglomerates would increase productivity and make the new firms more independent of the regional authorities than their regionally based predecessors were, thereby reducing the governors' grip on the electricity utilities.[93] And indeed, if the reform is adopted throughout Russia, the governors will effectively lose control of a very powerful economic instrument.

The next step in reforming the electricity monopoly is a plan, reportedly drawn up with Kirienko's participation, to create the Kama Electricity Generating Company. This would bring together four hydroelectric stations (in Perm, Konakovo, Cherepets, and Pskov) and the Votkinsk and Kama hydroelectric stations, with the Perm station as the base. Kirienko himself participated in negotiations with EES chief Anatolii Chubais over the creation of this holding company.[94]

In addition, Kirienko sometimes plays the role of intermediary between the regions and EES. In the case of Ulyanovsk, for example, Kirienko participated in meetings between Chubais and Shamanov, and he backed EES and SMUEK's policy of forcing the region to pay for the electricity it consumed.[95] He has also been active in other regions dealing with the electricity issue. Vladimir Lebedev, a close friend and the former financial director of Nizhnovenergo, was appointed the head of Kirovenergo, which led to a deterioration in relations between the Kirov regional governor and the utility. In January 2002, Lebedev brought an entire team of deputies with him from Nizhnii Novgorod, including Kirienko's trusted ally, media magnate Leonid Sukhoterin.[96]

Relations with Local Government and Civil Society

Local Government

Kirienko's adminstration has devoted considerable attention to the question of dividing power among the different levels of government. Tatarstan president Mintimer Shaimiev initially developed a plan to address this problem within the framework of the State Council, but the presidential administration chose to ignore Shaimiev's suggestions. In June 2001, President Putin set up a commission under the leadership of Presidential Administration deputy head Dmitrii Kozak to devise a plan for addressing the issue. Interestingly, the initial focus on strengthening federal authority evolved into devoting more attention to the strengthening of local government. Local government in Russia is extremely weak, in terms both of the resources provided for it and of its status in law. In many regions, there simply is no autonomous local government.[97] At the same time, there has been some realization, at least on the rhetorical level, that this layer of government is the closest one to society. Kirienko has pointed out, for example, "the key problems in the strategy for developing the country are at the local level."[98]

The federal government's recent attention to local government is probably a result not so much of its understanding of local government's importance, but more of its desire to recruit local government as an ally in its battle against the regional authorities. Thus in May 2001, at a meeting with the mayors of six large cities in the Volga okrug, Kirienko, catering to their interests, noted that the problems of such cities were also the problems of the federal authorities. He further asserted that the mayors of cities with more than one million inhabitants should participate in preparing policy documents at the federal level.[99]

However, despite the problems that clearly require a reform of local government, the political imperative to balance the interests of the regional and federal authorities may yet prevent real change in the local government sphere. Tatarstan presents a good example of the contradictory nature of federal policy. On one hand, during 2001 and 2002, the influence of Kazan mayor Kamil' Iskhakov increased thanks to the Kremlin's giving him access to the enormous sum of sixty-five billion rubles to spend through 2005 on celebrating the one-thousandth anniversary of the founding of Kazan.[100] It is possible that Moscow is—or is considering—backing Iskhakov as a potential opponent to Shaimiev. On the other hand, the federal authorities have been practically ignoring Shaimiev's July 2001 decree, which essentially abolished local self-government in Tatarstan and thereby violated, blatantly, the Russian Constitution. It did so by placing virtually all local governments in the cities, towns, and districts of the republic under the authority of the republican government.[101] Kirienko seems to have given his advance consent to this decree at a meeting with Tatarstan State Council chairman Farid Mukhametshin, an action that confirmed again the federal government's inability to dictate conditions to strong regions.[102]

A systematic resolution of local government issues in the direction of democracy depends ultimately on whether or not local government is going to be supported with financial resources. In late 2002 this question remained under consideration by the Ministry of Finance and the Kozak Commission on administrative reform.

Policies toward the Media

President Putin laid out his administration's media policies in the official document entitled *Doctrine on the Information Security of the Russian Federation,* which he signed in September 2000.[103] The main problem in relation to the regional media was the lack of resources for developing information providers that would be independent of the governors. The governors controlled many regional media outlets and used them to express their point of view. Therefore the envoys were assigned the task of creating a so-called unified information space. Initially, the plan was to create federal information centers in the okrugs as subsidiaries of a central Russian Information Center. However, this project was not implemented for lack of resources. Only the Siberian and Volga okrugs made much progress in creating okrug-level media holding companies.[104] In the Volga okrug, an information center was set up on the basis of journalists from the Russian Information Agency–Novosti (News).

Kirienko did not have much success on this front even though he devoted a considerable amount of energy to creating an okrugwide information policy. Initially, he sought to set up an interregional media network in the form of a consortium of regional newspapers. However, this project failed. Somewhat more successful was the creation of an okrug television show called Volga News *(Vesti Povolzh'ya).* According to the envoy's conception, this show should have played the role of an okrug supplement to the national news show *Vesti,* put out by RTR (Russian Television and Radio Company), whose television output goes out on Russia's number-two network. But the idea was only partially implemented, since the show was broadcast in only three regions: Nizhnii Novgorod, Kirov, and Penza. Kirienko also arranged for RTR to broadcast a show called *A Seventh Part (Odna sed'maya)*—a reference to the okrug's being one of seven that make up Russia. This tracked the envoy's activities in a servile way.[105]

In November 2000, Kirienko's office set up the okrug newspaper *Vmeste.*[106] Newspapers from all the regions of the okrug participated in the project, along with the okrug's information center. During 2001, the envoy's office held several conferences and festivals to bring local journalists together. In November

2001, a branch of the Media Union (Mediasoyuz) was opened in the okrug.[107] As many observers have pointed out, this organization exists as an alternative to the Russian Journalists' Union, to bring together "those who are ready to take orders from above and work in a unified information space."[108]

Kirienko's efforts to control the regional media brought him into conflict with Udmurtiya president Aleksandr Volkov. The battle centered on the Izhevsk mayoral elections, in which Volkov's candidate Viktor Balakin faced off against Kirienko's subordinate, federal inspector Sergei Chikurov. The Udmurtian president used the local affiliate of RTR to back his candidate. Television was one of the few resources left to Volkov, after the republic's procurator, police chief, and the directors of the major enterprises had been replaced against his will. In response, the federal authorities named a new director for the television station, but the former director and his associates prevented him from taking over.[109] Ultimately the conflict was resolved after many Moscow officials had intervened in a deal by which Volkov allowed the new television chief to take over, while Kirienko's candidate Chikurov withdrew from the mayoral race. This incident demonstrated that despite all the reforms passed to strengthen the federal government in the regions, the governors retained certain powers that allowed them to oppose decisions made in Moscow and to force the adoption of compromise solutions.

Kirienko exerted his greatest influence over the okrug's media through the media companies owned by his associate Leonid Sukhoterin. Sukhoterin is a successful businessman in the area, often described as the "Volga's Boris Berezovskii." He recently became a senator representing the Yamal Nenets Autonomous Okrug. His media holding company includes the Nizhnii Novgorod Telegraph Agency; the newspapers *Monitor, MK v Nizhnem, Delo, Sem' pyatnits, Leninskaya smena;* and the Dialog television company. Additionally, the envoy influences the editorial policy of the daily newspaper *Nizhegorodskii rabochii.*[110]

According to local observers, Sukhoterin's media holding company has handled all the envoy's propaganda activities, including his unsuccessful electoral support for Governor Sklyarov.[111] After Governor Khodyrev took office, the tax police discovered about ten firms of Sukhoterin's that had been sheltered from the need to make any tax payments. These findings cast a shadow on Kirienko and called into question his choice of associates, and perhaps also influenced his decision to transfer Sukhoterin to Kirov region as deputy general manager of Kirovenergo.[112]

Overall, Kirienko is having difficulty dominating the information market in his okrug. Despite his love for public politics, he is losing the war for the media. These difficulties are most visible in his homebase of Nizhnii Novgorod. Here Kirienko has run up against the powerful media empire of Duma member Dmitrii Savel'ev, who is one of his main opponents in the region.

Previously Kirienko and Savel'ev were allies. Kirienko appointed Savel'ev to his own former position as the head of Norsi Oil when he left that job to join then prime minister Viktor Chernomyrdin's government as part of Boris Nemtsov's team. At Kirienko's initiative, Savel'ev was later appointed head of Russia's oil pipeline monopoly Transneft'. In addition, they are both members of the Union of Right-wing Forces. In 2002, however, Savel'ev worked closely with Nizhnii Novgorod mayor Lebedev until Lebedev lost the September 2002 election. Lebedev generally opposed Kirienko.

Savel'ev's media holding company includes the Volga and TNT-Nizhnii Novgorod television companies; several influential newspapers, such as *Argumenty i Fakty–Nizhnii Novgorod, Versiya–Nizhnii Novgorod, Guberniya, Leninskaya smena plus,* and others. Equally important, it also includes a network of newspaper kiosks throughout the city to sell his publications. In these kiosks, it is difficult to find the newspaper *Monitor,* Kirienko's main publication, and also other publications in which his influence is strong. In contrast to Savel'ev, Kirienko does not control an influential television station.

All of these factors define a certain vulnerability in Kirienko's political standing and also the limited character of his power, especially in Nizhnii Novgorod.

The Third Sector

Their special attention to developing the nongovernmental organization (NGO) sector has become one of the activities that Kirienko's staff are most proud of. In the Volga okrug, they conduct many events seeking to develop active nongovernmental groups. The idea of a social partnership that unites the authorities, business, and society is seen as the basis for a new model of resolving social problems.[113] In implementing this model, the okrug administration initiated three projects: "A Fair for Social and Cultural Projects,"[114] "Guardianship Councils" (focused on helping to raise the level of the okrug's educational facilities), and "Cultural Capitals of the Volga Federal Okrug."[115] In many okrug regions there are various activities focusing on these themes, and efforts are made to encourage society to form new groups and do a better job in organizing itself and raising funds. Such fields as education, culture, and the media are seen as "zones of joint responsibility," where NGOs should come to the aid of the state.[116]

What then are the real results of the state's attention to the third sector? Kirienko has presumably hoped that if the regional authorities could be instilled with enthusiasm for these issues, this could produce some positive results. Activists at the local level, for example, could use the rhetoric of the central elites to justify their activities and counteract any possible opposition from local officials. In pursuit of such goals Kirienko has also been trying to convince national and regional oligarchs to help resolve the okrug's social problems by providing resources for concrete projects. He has had some success—for example, by convincing such companies as Interros, YUKOS, LUKoil, Nafta, MDM-bank, and others to sponsor the Festival of Social and Cultural Projects in Perm in 2000.[117]

However, one should not overestimate the ability of the Russian state to encourage and support civic activities. The divide between the state and society, between the elite and the masses in Russia is so great, and society is so disillusioned, that events such as the Civic Forum or the numerous festivals, expositions, and forums held in the Volga okrug are not able to alter much the reality of deeply entrenched social apathy and atomization.

On the other hand, it should be noted that Kirienko's staff has done little to aid the process of party building in the okrug. After the unification of the pro-Kremlin Unity (Yedinstvo) and Moscow mayor Yurii Luzhkov's Fatherland (Otechestvo) and All Russia (Vsya Rossiya) into Unified Russia (Yedinaya Rossiya) in January 2002, the new party began forming regional branches. According to the party's rules, the regional branches were supposed to elect as their leaders individuals selected by the party's Moscow-based council. In most Volga regions, the centrally approved candidates were approved without hitch. Even in Tatarstan, Unity leader Yurii Nazmeev was elected regional leader, not the head of the pro-Shaimiev All Russia, Nail' Khusnutdinov. However, in Bashkortostan the republican leadership demanded that Mansur Ayupov, a consistent advocate and defender of the republic's sovereignty, serve as the head of the republic branch of the party.[118] In Kirov a conflict arose because the leadership of the regional branch of All Russia complained to Unified Russia's national leadership about the process of creating the party in the region, charging that it violated the rights of Fatherland and All Russia.[119] In creating the Republic of Marii-El's branch of Unified Russia, Moscow and Nizhnii Novgorod backed different candidates to head the party. Ultimately, Moscow's candidate won out and the chief federal inspector for Marii-El, Valerii Yegorov, who was presumably Kirienko's candidate, was removed from the ballot.[120]

Conclusion

The results of Kirienko's activities in the Volga federal okrug are mixed. From the political point of view, his greatest achievement as envoy so far is his success in positioning his institution as a new influential player on the political scene of the okrug's regions. He is a player who participates in developing the "rules of the game" for other politicians and whose interventions in conflicts can sometimes be decisive. The envoy's activities have changed the balance of power and weakened the governors' power. So far, the envoy has contributed significantly to resolving one significant problem: together with the effect of other components of the federal reform like the changed composition of the Federation Council, his efforts have sharply reduced the ability of the governors to intervene in federal politics. Simultaneously, by bringing regional legislation into line with federal norms, the envoy has attempted to strike a blow against the separatist potential of the regions and to minimize confederal tendencies.

However, the completion of several publicly declared tasks assigned to the envoys, which have created a unified legal space in the okrug, has really only been a formal victory. The process of bringing regional laws into line with federal legislation demonstrated that the principles of cooperation among the regional and federal elites in Russia remain old-fashioned in that they are based not on laws, but on personal agreements, or where feasible, on pressure backed by force.

Kirienko's influence over the okrug's governors has not been uniform. Even among the stronger regions Kirienko's policies have had distinct consequences. The republic of Tatarstan, which is more independent of the center, has been able to preserve some of its status differences, specifically reflected in the incorporation of the texts of the 1994 power-sharing agreement with Moscow in the constitution. However, Bashkortostan, which is considered a second "heavyweight" in the okrug's politics, was not able to maintain the same level of autonomy in revising its constitution, and ultimately it had to give up on the attempt to keep the power-sharing agreement as part of the constitution's text.

In some respects, the Volga okrug has been innovative, and has generated and promoted new ideas and projects. However, its innovative ideas and projects, such as hiring staff members on the basis of competitive exams or involving social organizations in resolving numerous social and economic problems, have not been adopted elsewhere, either in society or by the authorities. If one takes into account the closed character of the presidential envoys as an institution, such measures seem to be more public relations stunts than anything else.

Kirienko's achievements in the economic sphere are more palpable, since he has effectively participated in developing new principles of interaction between various businesses, and between business and the authorities.

Ultimately, the envoy's main role lies beyond the bounds of direct interaction with the governors in the name of the federal government. This job is to reduce the regions' economic and political independence. Kirienko prefers to avoid head-on confrontations with the governors in favor of finding ways to work around them. They have lost their former control over important regional enterprises, which, with his help, are now owned by Russia's largest companies. He seeks close contacts with the business community in an effort to turn business into an instrument for President Putin's political regime. Finally, the governors' ability to make important economic decisions has been limited. With the help of the envoy, the power that they have lost is now wielded by Russia's major interregional financial–industrial groups. And however serious the sins for which these groups may one day have to answer, this development creates centripetal forces, which through the groups' far-reaching economic ties, may help to hold Russia together.

Notes

1. Accessed at www.pfo.ru.

2. These regions sought to change their okrug assignment, but no changes were made. See P. Akopov and A. Nikitin, "Korotkie perebezhki," *Izvestiya*, June 9, 2000.

3. "Vdol' po Volge," *Nezavisimaya gazeta*, September 4, 2001.

4. Unfortunately, his staff does not always reflect this openness and did not do much to provide assistance to researchers studying this new institution.

5. Svetlana Babaeva, "Sergei Kirienko: Glavy regionov pytayutsya soglasovyvat' so mnoi remont unitazov," *Izvestia*, June 28, 2002.

6. Kirienko's use of competitions may be introduced more widely throughout the country in the future. In any case, the Presidential Administration has prepared draft legislation calling for such practices. See *Vedomosti*, August 20, 2002.

7. It should be noted that the center is largely a "virtual" think tank for the Volga okrug, since most of its experts work in Moscow offices.

8. *Simbirskii kur'er*, June 27, 2002.

9. This idea is confirmed further by his earlier attraction to Scientology.

10. Andrei Makarychev, "Ot 'rezhima Sklyarova'—k 'rezhimu Khodyreva': institutsional'nye osnovy regional'noi politiki v kontekste nizhegorodskikh vyborov 2001 g.," *Regional'nye vybory i problemy grazhdanskogo obshchestva v Povolzh'e* (working papers presented at the third Congress of Political Regionology at Bol'shoe Boldino, September 21–23, 2001) published by the Moscow Carnegie Center.

11. Author's interview with federal inspector in Tatarstan Denis Akhmadullin, August 2001.

12. Statement of the presidential envoy's press service, July 6, 2001.

13. An interview was given on December 29, 2001. It can be found in the okrug's website at www.pfo.ru.

14. For six months in 2001.

15. In May 2001, she came two votes short of winning the post of SPS executive committee chair.

16. Interview with Sergei Borisov, president of the Nizhnii Novgorod Research Foundation, May 28, 2002.

17. Larisa Aidinova, "Polnomochnyi predstavitel' v Privolzhskom federal'nom okruge Sergei Kirienko: V politike i na gossluzhbe nachinaetsya smena pokolenii," *Vek*, October 2, 2001.

18. Marina Kalashnikova, "Polnomochnyi predstavitel' v Privolzhskom federal'nom okruge Sergei Kirienko schitaet, chto institut polpredov—promezhutochnyi," *Nezavismaya gazeta*, October 25, 2000.

19. He still maintained strongly that the okrugs were temporary in early 2002. Lecture by Sergei Kirienko at Kennan Institute, Washington, January 31, 2002.

20. Statement of the presidential envoy's press service, February 1, 2002.

21. Lecture by Sergei Kirienko at Kennan Institute, Washington, D.C., January 31, 2002.

22. Interview with Tatarstan Federal Inspector Denis Akhmadullin, August 2001.

23. Irina Nagornykh and Gennadii Khodyrev, "Bashkiria smenila konstitutsiyu," *Kommersant-Daily*, November 4, 2000.

24. Nadezhda Vasil'eva, "Tak Konstitutsii ne otsenivayutsya," *Izvestia*, October 10, 2001.

25. Vera Postnova, "Pishetsya 'suverenitet', a chitaetsya 'neft'," *Nezavisimaya gazeta*, April 6, 2002.

26. RFE/RL Tatar-Bashkir Report, December 5, 2002.

27. The republican authorities for a long time argued that constitutional amendments to the republican constitution should be carried out in parallel with amendments to the federal constitution and legislation. They pointed out that Tatarstan adopted its constitution earlier (in November 1992) than Russia, which did so in December 1993. Moreover, the authorities asserted that the vote to approve the Russian constitution in Tatarstan was not valid because only 14 percent of those who had the right to vote took part in the referendum.

28. These issues included key articles of the Tatarstani constitution, determining the status of the republic and its standing under international law (articles 59, 61, 62). Author's interview with Tatarstani presidential adviser R. S. Khakimov, August 2001.

29. Vera Postnova, "Bol'shaya chistka suvereniteta," *Nezavisimaya gazeta*, March 2, 2002.

30. The press center of the Tatarstan State Council announced that the two presidents had reached agreement on January 16, 2002. RFE/RL Tatar-Bashkir Report, January 17, 2002.

31. According to the reports of "Tatnews" news agency from July 13, 2001 (www.tatnews.ru/news/?id=2272).

32. Gulnaz Sharafutdinova, "Concentrating Capital Helps Tatarstani Leaders in Battle with Putin's Centralization," *Russian Regional Report*, October 17, 2001.

33. Statement of the presidential envoy's press service, November 22, 2000.

34. "Namestniki Putina: God spustya," *Komsomol'skaya Pravda*, July 12, 2001.

35. Statement of the presidential envoy's press service, September 25, 2001.

36. Yelena Alekseeva, "Sergei Stepashin vedet prokurorov v regiony," *Kommersant*, April 10, 2002.

37. Gul'chachak Khannanova and Alla Barakhova, "Gubernatory perestali boyat'sya Kremlya," *Kommersant-Daily*, October 18, 2000, and Yekaterina Grigor'eva, "Grefa chut'-chut' popravyat," *Izvestiya*, July 5, 2001.

38. Specifically, Fedorov questioned the provisions of the laws "Ob obshchikh printsipakh organizatsii zakonodatel'nykh i ispolnitel'nykh organov vlasti v sub'ektakh RF," and "Ob obshchikh printsipakh organizatsii organov mestnogo samoupravleniya."

Ultimately, Fedorov backed away from this direct challenge. Valerii Vyzhutovich, "Poslednii romantik," *Moskovskie novosti*, November 14, 2000.

39. Marina Kalashnikova, "Fedorov podygrivaet Kremlyu iz oppozitsii. Chuvashskii lider raschityvaet na post federal'nogo urovnya," *Nezavisimaya gazeta*, November 10, 2000.

40. Igor Rabinovich, "Rakhimov Agrees to Greater Federal Control in Exchange for Aid to Defense Plant," *Russian Regional Report*, July 3, 2001.

41. Igor Rabinovich, "Rakhimov Lays Out Critique of Federal Policy," *Russian Regional Report*, April 2, 2001.

42. Indira Kvyatovskaya, "Kto luchshe znaet Konstitutsiyu. Etot vopros reshayut v Ufe Kirienko, Rakhimov i Shaimiev," *Izvestiya*, December 16, 2000.

43. Petr Akopov, "Dogovor deshevle deneg," *Izvestiya*, July 10, 2000; and Lyudmila Romanova, "Gubernatory ne speshat vozvrashchat' Tsentru kredit doveriya," *Nezavisimaya gazeta*, January 21, 2002.

44. In Tatarstan, the minister of internal affairs is A. Safarov, Shaimiev's former bodyguard. However, in Udmurtiya, President Volkov clearly lost considerable influence over the law enforcement agencies during the dispute over the republican affiliate of the RTR network. See Sergei Krylov, "Udmurtskii bunt," *Novye Izvestiya*, October 12, 2001.

45. From the interview of chief federal inspector to Bashkortostan R. Z. Khamitov to the newspaper *Novye lyudi*, as posted on the inspector's official site. In particular, Khamitov complained that the local television station does not let him broadcast live, and his taped statements are edited to the point where they are no longer significant.

46. Dmitrii Urbanovich, "Abdulinskii eksperiment," *Orenburgskaya nedelya*, November 29 and December 20, 2000.

47. Konstantin Viktorov, "Vnutrirossiiskaya diplomatiya," *Nezavisimaya gazeta*, November 15, 2000; and Yulia Lapina, "Vmesto serpastogo i molotkastogo—orlastyi i barsastyi," *Novaya gazeta*, June 14, 2001.

48. Statement of the presidential envoy's press service, March 19, 2001.

49. Marina Ozerova, "Tretii raz—ne prezident?" *Moskovskii komsomolets*, November 30, 2000.

50. Dmitrii Igumnov, "Sergei Kirienko mechtaet o politicheskom bankrotstve," *Kommersant-Daily*, November 15, 2000.

51. Sergei Anisimov, "Khochesh' zhit'—ne spor' s Minfinom," *Nezavisimaya gazeta*, April 9, 2002.

52. Sergei Anisimov, "Khochesh' zhit'—ne spor' s Minfinom," *Nezavisimaya gazeta*, April 9, 2002.

53. Other regions experiencing serious financial problems, such as Primorskii Krai, have had to sign similar agreements.

54. Marina Kalashnikova, "Politika okazalas' vazhnee ekonomiki . . ." *Nezavisimaya gazeta*, October 5, 2000.

55. Tat'yana Netreba, Konstantin Sergeev, and Vitalii Tseplyaev, "Zyuganov pereigral Kreml'," *Argumenty i fakty*, August 1, 2001.

56. Irina Nagornykh, "V respublike Leonida Markelova vse budet khorosho," *Kommersant-Daily*, February 12, 2001.

57. In gratitude for the help, Markelov nominated Kirienko ally Aleksandr Torshin to the Federation Council. German Galkin, Irina Nagornykh, "Vybory po-kremlevski," *Kommersant-Daily*, March 30, 2001.

58. Author's interview with Rafael Khakimov, August 2001.

59. Irina Nagornykh and Aleksei Chernyshev, "Primorskii uzhastik," *Kommersant-Vlast'*, June 26, 2001, 7.

60. Yekaterina Burg, "PFO—zolotoi kadrovyi rezerv Sovfeda," *Monitor*, no. 2 (January 21–27, 2002); and German Galkin and Irina Nagornykh, "Vybory po-kremlevski," *Kommersant-Daily*, March 30, 2001.

61. Igor Klyamkin, "Byurokratiya i biznes v Rossii," 1 (unpublished manuscript).

62. Author interview with federal inspector for Tatarstan Denis Akhmadullin, August 2001.

63. Nikolai Ivanov, "Groza nad Kamoi. Vybory gubernatora Permskoi oblasti razvivayutsya ne po tomu stsenariyu, kotoryi predpolagalsya," *Nezavisimaya gazeta*, October 20, 2000.

64. Yurii Nikolaev, "Trinadtsat' mgnovenii vesny. Sopernika Mintimera Shaimieva pokazali v kino," *Segodnya*, March 23, 2001.

65. It turned out that about ten members of Kislitsyn's staff had criminal records. Boris Fedotov, "O pravykh delakh i nepravykh dolgakh," *Nezavisimaya gazeta*, August 31, 2001.

66. Boris Bronshtein, "Vremya i steklo," *Izvestiya*, February 7, 2001.

67. Sergei Shcheglov, "Ioshkar-Ola poluchit svoego Rutskogo," *Kommersant-Daily*, November 3, 2000; "Kreml' sobiraet kompromat na prezidenta," *Kommersant-Daily*, October 24, 2000; Boris Bronshtein, "Tol'ko pulya kazaka . . ." *Izvestiya*, November 1, 2000.

68. Sergei Yevgen'ev, "Kompromat dlya blagorodnykh chitatelei," *Nezavisimaya gazeta*, February 9, 2002; and "Kompromat na polpreda," *Vyatskii nablyudatel'*, February 9, 2002.

69. "Kompromat no polpreda," *Vyatskii nablyudatel'*, February 9, 2002.

70. Statement of the presidential envoy's press service, October 26, 2000.

71. Andrei Dmukhin, "Koridory vlasti. Lichnaya laboratoriya prezidenta: pervyi 'vyvodok' polpredov," *Novaya gazeta*, May 20, 2002.

72. Irina Tikhonova and Yelena Alekseeva, "Nizhegorodskii parlament ukrepilsya oligarkhami," *Kommersant-daily*, April 2, 2002.

73. Sergei Anisimov, "Dva medvedya v byvshem obkome. Nizhegorodskii gubernator i privolzhskii polpred delyat vlast' v regione," *Nezavisimaya gazeta*, April 18, 2002.

74. For an elaborate and detailed discussion of changing relationships between the state and business in Russia and the policies and institutions created by Putin as regards this matter, see A. Zudin, "Neokorporatizm v Rossii? (Gosudarstvo i biznes pri Vladimire Putine)," *Pro et Contra* 6, no. 4 (2001).

75. *Obshchaya gazeta*, February 28–March 6, 2002.

76. Accessed at www.kirienko.ru/main/press.

77. Statement of the presidential envoy's press service, December 9, 2000.

78. Andrei Fedorov and Leonid Zavarskii, "Gubernator ob"edinyaet aviazavody," *Kommersant-Daily*, March 2, 2001.

79. Sergei Obozov, "Regiony zayavili o namerenii uchastvovat' v sozdanii ob'edinennoi aviakompanii Privolzh'ya," *VolgaInform*, December 20, 2001.

80. Statement of the presidential envoy's press service, May 23, 2002.

81. For an elaborate discussion of this issue see Arbakhan Magomedov's "Kaspiiskaia neft' i rossiiskie regiony: Meniaiushchaiasia priroda lokal'nykh interesov vdol' nefteprovoda Tengiz-Novorossiisk (sravnitel'nyi analiz), *Acta Slavica Iaponica*, no.19 (March 2002): 19–70.

82. Aleksei Sinitskii, "Neizvestnoe yuridicheskoe litso. Vokrug 'Krasnogo Sormova' nazrevaet novyi skandal," *Izvestiya*, January 11, 2001.

83. Pavel Apletin, "Uroki GAZa," *Birzha*, February 22, 2002.

84. Statement of the presidential envoy's press service, November 29–30, 2000.

85. Statement of the presidential envoy's press service, December 4 and 9, 2000.

86. Roman Zhuk, "Delovye novosti: GAZ razobralsia v motorakh," *Kommersant-Daily*, May 11, 2001.

87. Rustem Bikmetov, "Rol' sredstv massovoi informatsii v vyborakh gubernatora Nizhegorodskoi oblasti 2001" (unpublished manuscript).

88. Svetlana Isaichenko, "Kompromat na polpreda," *Vyatskii nablyudatel'*, no. 9 (February 2002).

89. Olga Gubenko, "Privolzhskaya energetika gotova stat' podopytnym krolikom," *Izvestiya*, July 20, 2000.

90. Statement of the presidential envoy's press service, December 21, 2001.

91. Olga Gubenko, "Srednevolzhskie stradaniya. Reforma energetiki nachnetsya na Volge," *Izvestiya*, November 17, 2000.

92. Svetlana Trifonova, "Upravlyat' energetikoi budut otlichniki," *Nizhegorodskie novosti*, July 13, 2001.

93. Andrei Fedorov and Irina Rybal'chenko, "'Samaraenergo' menyaet odnogo direktora na tseluyu kompaniyu," *Kommersant-Daily*, February 17, 2001.

94. Statement of the presidential envoy's press service, October 29, 2001.

95. Statement of the presidential envoy's press service, December 29, 2001.

96. "Sukhoterin uzhe v Kirove," *Vyatskii nablyudatel'*, no. 3 (January 2002).

97. For example, in Tatarstan and Bashkortostan the republican presidents personally appoint urban and rural mayors by decree.

98. Statement of the presidential envoy's press service, November 26, 2001.

99. Statement of the presidential envoy's press service, May 25, 2001.

100. Dina Shagiakhmetova, "Shaimievu nozhei ne daryat," *Vostochnyi Ekspress*, no. 2 (January 18–24, 2002).

101. Yelena Tokareva, "My i nashe pravo. Ochen' mestnoe samoupravlenie," *Obshchaya gazeta*, September 20, 2001.

102. Yelena Tokareva, "My i nashe pravo. Ochen' mestnoe samoupravlenie," *Obshchaya gazeta*, September 20, 2001.

103. "Doktrina informatsionnoi bezopasnosti Rossiiskoi Federatsii," *Rossiiskaya gazeta*, September 28, 2000, 4–6.

104. Olga Tropkina, "Okruzhnye SMI poka ne sozdany," *Nezavisimaya gazeta*, August 10, 2001.

105. Archive of the Nizhnii Novgorod Research Foundation.

106. Statement of the presidential envoy's press service, November 28, 2000.

107. Statement of the presidential envoy's press service, November 13, 2000.

108. Marina Tokareva, "Obsluzhivat' vlast' ili sluzhit' obshchestvu," *Obshchaya gazeta*, May 31, 2001.

109. Maksim Glikin, "Kak ukroshchali Volkova," *Obshchaya gazeta*, October 18, 2001.

110. Nikolai Viktyukov, "Vlast' i pressa. Kardinal iz polpredstva," *Novaya gazeta*, December 4, 2000, and interview with Nizhnii Novgorod Research Foundation president Sergei Borisov.

111. Nikolai Viktyukov, "Vlast' i pressa. Kardinal iz polpredstva," *Novaya gazeta*, December 4, 2000, and interview with Nizhnii Novgorod Research Foundation president Sergei Borisov.

112. Igor' Tel'nikov, "Kto est' who. Povolzhskii Berezovskii," *Novaya gazeta*, August 10, 2001; and Vera Yakubovich, "Kindersyupriz dlya Vyatki," *Vyatskii nablyudatel'*, no. 51 (December 2001).

113. Tat'yana Bateneva, "Gosudarstvo—drug cheloveka," *Izvestiya*, December 1, 2001.

114. The first exposition was held in 2000 in Perm, and the second a year later in Saratov. In 2000 Kirienko handed out eighteen million rubles worth of grants at the event and thirty-five million rubles at the second. Olga Kopsheva, "Uroki partnerstva na gorodskoi ploshchadi . . ." *Nezavisimaya gazeta*, October 5, 2001, and the statement of the presidential envoy's press service, May 10, 2001.

115. Ulyanovsk was the first cultural capital.

116. Marina Kalashnikova, "Na etot raz v Davose Rossiya ne sdavala ekzamena," *Nezavisimaya gazeta*, January 31, 2001.

117. Marina Kalashnikova, "Vnebyudzhetnyi manevr polpredov," *Nezavisimaya gazeta*, November 28, 2000.

118. Igor Rabinovich, "Moscow, Bashkortostan Return to Political Trading," *Russian Regional Report*, March 27, 2002.

119. "Politkonflikt: Vsya Rossiya 'ukhodit iz Vyatki'?" *Vyatskii krai*, March 14, 2002; and V. Savinykh, "Tsel' opravdyvaet sredstva, ili kak sozdaetsya mestnaya 'Yedinaya Rossiya,'" *Vyatskii krai*, March 15, 2002.

120. "Slovom," *Mariiskaya Pravda*," March 12, 2002.

7

Urals Federal Okrug

Sergei Kondrat'ev

---

*T*HE URALS FEDERAL OKRUG INCLUDES *the regions of Chelyabinsk, Kurgan, Sverdlovsk, and Tyumen; and the Khanty-Mansii and Yamal-Nenets Autonomous Okrugs.*

Petr Mikhailovich Latyshev (born 1948) worked his way up through the Ministry of Internal Affairs, the national police force, ultimately becoming chief in the Perm and then Krasnodar regions. In 1994, he reached the rank of deputy minister for internal affairs and in 1999–2000, served as deputy head of the Federal Anti-Terror Commission. Among his other duties, Latyshev led the MVD group that investigated the murder of Galina Starovoitova and studied the criminal situation in Saint Petersburg, where he demonstrated the extent of corruption in the mayor's office. Latyshev generally avoids publicity and is the type of person who expects to receive clear orders from above and tries to implement them. He requires the same of his subordinates.

Okrug Overview

The Urals Federal Okrug is not the biggest, most populated, or richest okrug among the seven. It is, though, the most "compact," with only six members. However, these six include the Yamal-Nenets and Khanty-Mansii Autonomous Okrugs, which, respectively, produce 90 percent of Russia's natural gas and more than 60 percent of its oil. Therefore the okrug has one of the highest export potentials, but also the highest crime rate in Russia. More than one third of the crimes committed in the okrug occur in Sverdlovsk Region.

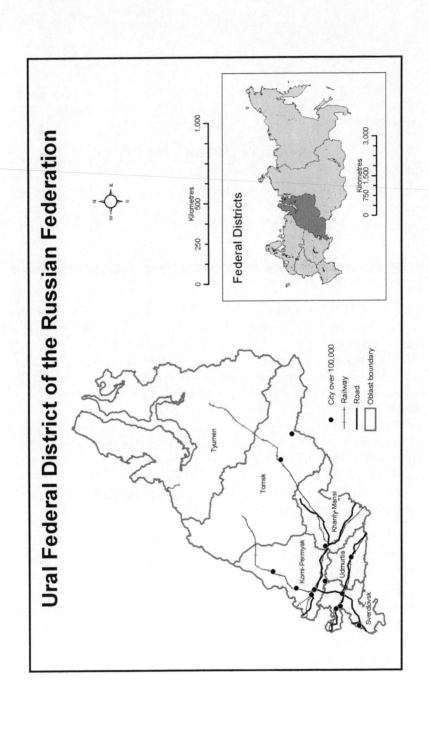

Ural Federal District of the Russian Federation

Federal Districts

Tyumen

Tomsk

Khanty-Mansi

Komi-Permyak

Udmurtia

Sverdlovsk

• City over 100,000
+— Railway
— Road
☐ Oblast boundary

Kilometres
0   250   500   1,000

Kilometres
0   750   1,500   3,000

The okrug straddles the line where Europe meets Asia. The trans-Siberian railroad and numerous wide-diameter oil and gas pipelines cross its territory, connecting Siberia to western Russian and Europe beyond.

The okrug also has a thirteen-hundred-kilometer border with Kazakhstan. The international frontier opens up opportunities for cross-border trade, but it also creates new problems. Various contraband goods flow across the border, including narcotics headed for the okrug's relatively rich northern regions.

The Urals' standard of living is one of the highest in Russia. The local population consistently earns the highest salaries among the seven okrugs, with wages more than 50 percent higher than the Russian average. At the same time, there is a wide range in income levels within the okrug, as salaries in the resource-rich regions are much higher than those in the relatively poor agricultural Kurgan Region.

In contrast to some of the other okrugs, the Urals does not face complicated ethnic or religious problems. While there are more than twenty ethnic groups in the okrug, about 80 percent of the population is Russian and almost 10 percent Tatar and Bashkir. The main religions are Russian Orthodoxy and Islam. Conflict among these groups is not a prominent problem.

The Presidential Envoy's Staff

Latyshev was the first envoy to appoint all five of his key deputies. In contrast to Kazantsev, who took many top staff members from the Southern okrug capital of Rostov-na-Donu, Latyshev did not appoint any officials from Yekaterinburg, the Urals okrug capital, to important positions on his team. In fact, his five top deputies do not have roots in the city and were not connected with the local elite. Instead, three of Latyshev's aides came from Tyumen: Sergei Sobyanin (social and economic issues), the former speaker of the Khanty-Mansii legislature; Mikhail Ponomarev (media outreach), the former deputy governor of Yamal-Nenets; and Anatolii Antipin (relations with the power ministries), the former head of the Tyumen Region Federal Security Service (FSB). Of the other two, Vyacheslav Tumanov (responsible for legal issues, personnel policy, and the envoy's staff) served as Pskov governor from 1992 to 1996 and then in the Russian Ministry for Nationality Affairs and Federal Relations. Sergei Vakhrukov (coordinates the federal inspectors) previously had been the speaker of the Yaroslavl Regional Duma.

Dealing with the Ural economy, however, required hiring a local with extensive experience. For this position, Latyshev chose Viktor Basargin, a resident of Yekaterinburg, who has a stable relationship with the Sverdlovsk region's business elite and who during the 1990s worked in the various state offices dealing with privatization and managing state property. He joined Latyshev's team in August 2000, with responsibility for economic development.

Latyshev's three deputies from Tyumen (Sobyanin, Antipin, and Pono- marev) were opposed to then Tyumen governor Leonid Roketskii. As a result, their appointment to the envoy's staff seemed to be a temporary measure, since they immediately started looking for a candidate to run again Roketskii in the Tyumen gubernatorial elections set for December 2000. After long dis- cussions, Sobyanin himself became the candidate, unofficially but clearly sup- ported by Latyshev, and he subsequently left the position of first deputy envoy after his victory in the election. Following Sobyanin's departure, Antipin re- signed in the hopes of being appointed deputy governor, but he ultimately had to accept a position as one of the heads of the Yuzhno-Russkii oil deposit.

After the departure of Sobyanin and Antipin, two of the other deputy en- voys divided up their responsibilities. Tumanov took responsibility for social issues, while Vakhrukov took over legal issues and relations with the regions. In November 2001, Latyshev appointed a new deputy, Leonid Kuznetsov, to handle relations with the law enforcement agencies and security issues. Kuznetsov is a career FSB officer, who had long worked in Yekaterinburg. Be- fore joining the presidential envoy's staff, he headed the FSB branch in Kras- noyarsk but had difficult relations with then governor Aleksandr Lebed.

Of the six chief federal inspectors, one previously worked in the FSB (Khanty-Mansii), one in the MVD (Yamal-Nenets), one in the military (Chelyabinsk), one as a judge (Sverdlovsk), one as a public official (Tyumen), and one as an agronomist (Kurgan). Overall, Latyshev's staff differs little from the staffs of other envoys. Looking at Latyshev and his eleven top assistants, five come from the power ministries. In total, Latyshev's staff comprises sixty- three individuals.

Part of the envoy's task has been to counter the spread of the regionalist trend, stopping and rolling back the governors' seizure of extensive political and economic control of their regions. The envoys have been supposed to demon- strate that the federal authorities are working in the regions and can intervene in regional affairs if necessary. Doing this required "waking up" the armies of federal civil servants in the numerous ministries working outside Moscow.

However, the Ural Federal Okrug staff is too small to carry out effective co- ordination of the federal agencies or even to monitor the federal and regional authorities. Moreover, the federal agencies in the regions remain heavily de- pendent on the governors, who wield many more resources than the presi- dential envoys. Accordingly, the federal agencies are often loyal to the gover- nors, overlooking legal violations, which they are supposed to counter.

The envoy and his staff work out of offices given to them by the governors. The office of the chief federal inspector in Yamal-Nenets, for example, is located in the governor's building, a situation also found in the neighboring Siberian okrug.

Overall, the staff of the presidential envoy more often makes a show of imposing federal authority than actually imposing it. Unable to act on their own, they overload the federal agencies and regional administrations with numerous inquiries, demanding an accounting of what is going on and the right to participate in organizing various events.

The presidential envoy's staff simply pass on to relevant agencies the numerous complaints and requests for help that they receive from citizens. In 2001, these totaled more than fourteen thousand. Lacking the authority, much less the organizational or financial resources, to respond to these pleas from ordinary people, the envoy simply profanes the idea of paternalism that this institution represents and thus undermines his own authority.

Latyshev's Main Functions

Latyshev has, in the main, followed the key priorities set by the president in establishing the office of envoy, though he has also sought to reduce crime and stimulate federal investment. Of course, the top priority was bringing regional laws into line with federal norms. By the beginning of 2001, he had managed to remove most of the offending regional laws. During that first year, the six Urals regions updated 350 laws and each amended its charter, or "regional Constitution."

The central contentious issue was the right of regional authorities to exercise control over the natural resources on their territories. In particular, the Yamal-Nenets and Khanty-Mansii Autonomous Okrugs were forced to renounce their ownership of the extensive oil and gas deposits on their territories.

The key tasks in 2001 and 2002 focused on dividing responsibilities between federal, regional, and local governments. By analogy with the federal Kozak Commission, which Putin set up to address this issue, the okrug set up its own group to examine the local situation. The membership included many key regional leaders, such as Chelyabinsk governor Petr Sumin, Yekaterinburg mayor Arkadii Chernetskii, and Tyumen governor Sergei Sobyanin, but, in line with federal desires, it recommended centralizing power. Latyshev was naturally pleased with this outcome, dubbing the okrug commission's work "historically significant."

One of the key questions in redefining Russian federalism is what to do about the power-sharing treaties that Yeltsin signed with many of the regions during the 1990s. Sverdlovsk governor Eduard Rossel has declared his region's treaty a "holy cow" and has refused to give it up. Latyshev, in contrast, announced that it was illogical to elevate the treaties to such a sacred status and declared them obsolete. He drew a distinction between federations based on treaties and those deriving from constitutions, emphasizing that Russia was a constitutional federation and that the country's basic law regulated all federal relations. However, he also noted that "unfortunately, after the adoption of the 1993 constitution, many federal laws necessary to implement its provisions were not adopted, including those dealing with federal relations... [Nevertheless] the treaties between the federation and the regions have lost their relevance, they are not necessary and, in a number of cases, even hinder the process of integration."[1]

Latyshev also sought to deal with the problem of recruiting more qualified people for the federal civil service. However, he did not go as far as Sergei Kirienko in the Volga okrug by organizing competitions for such posts. Rather, in June 2001 he established a special personnel commission, promising that appointments would now be based on merit and would no longer favor those with access to the halls of power.[2] However, this commission was apparently stillborn, and it is practically impossible to obtain any information about its activities.

Beyond these general tasks that all seven okrugs addressed, Latyshev, as a former policeman, made fighting crime and qualitatively improving the activities of the law-enforcement agencies one of his top priorities. However, the criminal situation, despite numerous meetings, organizational restructurings, and critical statements, remains largely unchanged, as Latyshev admits. Summing up the results of his first two years of work in this area, he noted that hopeful tendencies appeared only at the beginning of 2002, a year when crime rates seemed to drop throughout Russia, though the level of crime in the okrug remains the highest in Russia.[3] The envoy pointed out that the corruption within the police force makes addressing the problem extremely difficult and notes that the worst problems are concentrated in the Sverdlovsk and Chelyabinsk regional law enforcement agencies. He is particularly concerned about the okrug's steady growth in drug-related crimes. During 2001, these increased 12.1 percent for the okrug as a whole and 45.2 percent in Chelyabinsk, which recorded the largest growth of the six Urals regions.

Latyshev also made attracting foreign investment one of his chief priorities. Beginning in December 2001, he began to organize investor conferences in Western Europe, including in Great Britain, Germany, and Austria. Usually numerous representatives of the envoy's staff and federal agencies, regional officials, and some businesspeople participate in these presentations. Latyshev has also launched an initiative to encourage entrepreneurship, sponsoring a contest to find the most innovative projects and rewarding the best of them with financial support.

Relations with the Federal Government

Latyshev does not appear to have any special access to Putin. During the first two years on the job, Latyshev met one-on-one with Putin once, in November 2000. Otherwise, Latyshev sees the president in conjunction with larger groups. During this period, Putin visited the Urals twice, coming to Yekaterinburg in the summer of 2000 and to Novyi Urengoi in October 2001. The Urals governors joined in these meetings. Occasionally, Putin meets with all of the presidential envoys in the Kremlin. Additionally, the envoys are all members of the Security Council, whose meetings are chaired by the president.

After Putin issued a decree subordinating the envoys to his chief of staff, Aleksandr Voloshin, rather than to the president directly, Latyshev's contacts with Putin seemed to become less frequent. It is hard to define Voloshin's role in regard to the envoys. In 2001 he announced plans to visit each of the federal okrugs, but by the end of 2002, had only succeeded in coming to the Northwest (September 2001), the Urals (January 2002), and—for a "summit" with four of the envoys—Siberia (November 2002). During his one-day visit to Yekaterinburg, Voloshin held two meetings, with Latyshev and his chief deputies and with the heads of the federal agencies in the okrug. He also met with Sverdlovsk governor Rossel in Latyshev's presence. Latyshev coordinates with the federal agencies in his okrug through the same means as the other envoys: working with the newly established okrug-level offices of the ministries and through a variety of councils that he has set up.

Latyshev has faced difficulties in balancing his obligation both to promote federal policies in the Urals okrug and to ensure a healthy social situation on the ground. The most important issue for the Urals is Putin's new budget policies under which the federal government in 2001 directed a significant amount of resources away from the regions in favor of the center. The three constituent parts of Tyumen Region (Yamal-Nenets, Khantii-Mansii, and Tyumen proper) in particular suffered from these policies because they lost income generated from the use of natural resources. Latyshev worked with the governors to minimize the extent of these losses.

Thus, during the first half of 2002, the envoy did not counter the battle waged by Tyumen Region and its autonomous okrugs against the Natural Resources Ministry over the draft law on resources. In pushing this legislation, the ministry sought the exclusive right to issue licenses to extract resources, eliminating the current "two key" practice, which requires that both the ministry and the regional authorities sign off on licenses. In interviews, Latyshev made clear that he supported giving the regional authorities a voice, especially since decisions on resource use had important labor and environmental consequences for the regions whose resources were being used.[4] By the end of 2002, the "two key" system remained in place. However local observers believed that the Natural Resource Ministry would be able to take over the process exclusively in 2003, with the backing of Prime Minister Mikhail Kasyanov.

In March and April 2002, Latyshev frequently said that he would push through the Russian government a special program to provide more funding for the poverty-stricken Kurgan Region, by far the worst-off region in the Urals okrug. He stressed that the government should consider the matter before approving the 2003 federal budget so that it could take into account his request for additional funds.[5]

In these ways, Latyshev became less an implementer of federal policy in the Urals than an advocate of Urals interests in Moscow. He acted to help Urals governors retain the control over natural resources they had acquired in the 1990s, and sought to direct federal aid to some of the okrug's poorest citizens.

Coordination with the Power Ministries

In mid-2001 Latyshev set up a Urals Security Collegium under his chairmanship to coordinate relations with the power ministries in the okrug. With its emphasis on "security," the name of the new body suggests parallels with the federal Security Council. Like its federal analogue, the collegium includes representatives of all power ministries in the okrug and conducts regular meetings. Its sessions provide a forum to discuss security issues broadly defined, including the work of the law enforcement agencies, drugs, corruption, and so forth. At these meetings, Latyshev has constantly criticized the work of the police. But other issues come up as well, such as preparations for winter, particularly in the northern part of the okrug, and the ability of the Urals authorities to respond to potential floods.

The creation of okrug-level offices within the power ministries gave Latyshev an important lever of influence on these ministries. The presidential envoys, rather than the governors, now have a say in who is appointed to various positions. With the establishment of the new offices, it is much more convenient for Latyshev to meet, for example, with the okrug procurator in Yekaterinburg than with the six procurators who work in the okrug's regions. The federal government definitely had a strong interest in replacing many of the power ministry chiefs in the Urals since the governors had succeeded in co-opting many of them during the 1990s.

Latyshev's influence over the power ministries varies depending on the ministries and individuals involved. Latyshev secured the appointment of an ally as deputy general procurator for the Ural Federal Okrug in Yurii Zolotov. He also seemed to have a say in the appointment of the head of the Tax Collection Ministry's okrug office, Gennadii Bezrukov, who formerly served as an adviser on Latyshev's staff in the area of socioeconomic development.

In contrast, Latyshev seemed to have little influence over the Ministry of Internal Affairs' decision to appoint Aleksei Krasnikov to head up its okrug office. In fact, Latyshev had used his influence to remove Krasnikov from his previous position as the head of Sverdlovsk region's branch of the ministry (where he presumably had close ties to Governor Rossel). Nevertheless, two months later Krasnikov took over the okrug police. At the ceremony appointing Krasnikov to his new position, Deputy Presidential Envoy Sergei Vakhrukov explained Krasnikov's unexpected promotion by saying that he had "promptly drawn the appropriate conclusions," after losing his previous position. Possibly, the then newly appointed minister of internal affairs Boris Gryzlov found the drawing of these conclusions more persuasive than Latyshev's case against Krasnikov. In any case, given Latyshev's long career in the police, one would have expected him to have more influence over this particular appointment.

There have been numerous personnel changes in Sverdlovsk Region, which seem to suggest that Latyshev has had a major influence there, though there is no direct evidence describing his exact role. Sverdlovsk Region's FSB chief Gennadii Voronov, who was closely associated with Governor Rossel, lost his position to Boris Kozinenko, who was not loyal to Rossel. Rossel also lost a loyal ally as the head of the Urals Military District. The following appointments may also reflect Latyshev's influence: Aleksandr Zaborov became the new head of the local branch of the Ministry of Internal Affairs, and Vladimir Krysov secured a position as head of the local branch of the Federal Securities Exchange Commission. Boris Kuznetsov became Sverdlovsk Region procurator. At the head of the Sverdlovsk Region branch of the Tax Collections Ministry, Viktor Semenikhin left to become an adviser to the governor on questions of illegal capital flight, making way for Sergei Dobrovol'skii, who had served as the president of Uralretsept insurance company.

Latyshev did play a direct and well-known role in the personnel policies of the Tyumen Region office of the Ministry of Internal Affairs. He helped regional police chief Valerii Borisov keep his position in 2001 even after the department's work had been found unsatisfactory, according to informed sources.

However, it would be naïve to argue that with the creation of the institution of the presidential envoy, the influence of regional leaders over the police, procurators, and judges has become a thing of the past. For example, during the summer of 2001, Chelyabinsk governor Petr Sumin intervened in the property dispute surrounding the Karabash Metallurgical Factory and was able to bring in federal officials on his side. In this battle, the Sverdlovsk Region–based Urals Mining and Metallurgical Company (controlled by Iskander Makhmudov and Andrei Kozitsyn) claimed that it had purchased a controlling stake in the Karabash factory, an assertion disputed by the Chelyabinsk governor, who argued that the region was the rightful owner.[6] Sumin publicly summoned representatives of the Procuracy and other federal agencies to meet with him and ordered them to conduct a number of investigations to resolve the situation in favor of the region. Deputy Presidential Envoy Viktor Basargin publicly blasted the governor for influencing the federal officials in this way. Additionally, he described the behavior of the federal officials in carrying out the governor's public instructions as "caving in."[7] However, his words had no effect.

Thus, while it is possible to say that the governors' influence in appointing federal officials in the regions has been undermined significantly, one should not exaggerate either the role of the presidential envoy in the sphere of personnel appointments or the extent of his effective, rather than declared, oversight over the law enforcement agencies.

Relations with Governors

The authors of Putin's federal reforms never explained why they put together the Urals Federal Okrug the way that they did. Clearly geography was not a consideration: the "Urals" Federal Okrug contains at least half of western Siberia by including Tyumen Region, and the Khanty-Mansii and Yamal-Nenets Autonomous Okrugs; the traditional parts of the Urals, such as Perm Region and the republic of Bashkortostan, are not included. The most obvious explanation for the inclusion of some regions and the exclusion of others is that the purpose of the okrug is to strengthen the power of the federal executive and destroy regional power bases that developed during the 1990s. This logic in managing the okrugs is the same whether it is applied to the seven federal okrugs or to Russia's military okrugs.[8]

One likely target in the establishment of the Urals Federal Okrug was Sverdlovsk governor Eduard Rossel, who had tried to establish a Urals Republic in the early 1990s and had apparently not given up on these plans by 2000. Thus Perm and Bashkortostan, traditionally Urals regions, were purposefully included in the Volga okrug to keep Rossel from gaining control of them, according to the Perm Region's chief federal inspector Nikolai Fadeyev.[9]

The establishment of the okrug works to complicate communication between regional leaders and destroy ties between them. Before the creation of the okrugs, the governors of the Urals and Siberian regions met regularly within the frameworks of the Urals Interregional Association and the Siberian Agreement Interregional Association. The appearance of the okrug, however, has practically wiped out the Urals association and complicates meetings of the Siberian association, which is, however, still functioning.

The Urals okrug brings together governors who have a history of not getting along with one another. The governors of the resource-rich Yamal-Nenets and Khanty-Mansii Autonomous Okrugs do not trust Rossel because of his efforts to establish the Urals Republic, which they have interpreted as an attempt by Rossel to aggrandize his own power at their expense. The governor of Tyumen Region also has come into conflict with Rossel because he supported the losing candidacy of incumbent Leonid Roketskii in the region's December 2000 gubernatorial elections, while the Yamal-Nenets and Khanty-Mansii governors supported Sobyanin's successful candidacy. (As mentioned above, because of Russia's complicated federal system, Tyumen Region technically houses three governors: the regional governor who oversees the whole territory and the two autonomous okrug governors who rule over parts of the larger region.) Likewise, the governor of Kurgan Region fears his fellow governors, who govern much richer regions and continuously discuss the possibility of annexing his relatively poor region into a new, though currently undefined, structure.

In 2001, there were serious confrontations between the governors of Chelyabinsk and Sverdlovsk regions because they were active participants in the battle between shareholders in a number of Urals metallurgical enterprises, such as the Karabash and Zlatoust factories. In these cases aggressive companies based in Sverdlovsk were trying to take over firms located in Chelyabinsk. After these conflicts were over, Chelyabinsk governor Petr Sumin made a point of not attending the celebratory meeting of the Urals Economic Association, which took place in Yekaterinburg, the capital of Sverdlovsk Region, in October 2001. Considering that the federal government is planning to sell a 23 percent stake in Chelyabinsk's giant Magnitorgorsk metal plant, and locals fear that wealthy Sverdlovsk financiers will play a major role in the battle for control of this plant, it is unlikely that relations between the two governors will improve in the foreseeable future.

For these reasons, Latyshev will have great difficulty implementing the idea he announced in March 2001 of setting up a Urals Federal Okrug Council that would include all the governors and legislative speakers of the okrug. The presidential envoys to other okrugs usually create such councils to structure their formal relations with the governors in their jurisdiction.

Although Latyshev publicly characterizes his relations with the majority of governors as normal, constructive, and businesslike, he nevertheless admits that none of the governors were happy with the appearance of new structures that monitor and supervise them. Despite the general wariness, however, none of the governors, except Sverdlovsk's Rossel, has dared to challenge Latyshev openly. The rest have preferred not to enter into public conflict with the federal authorities.

Latyshev had poor relations with Rossel from the very beginning of his term. Rossel struck the first blow against Latyshev by giving the envoy a building used by a children's educational facility to serve as his office space. The resulting media scandal, in which local newspapers denounced the envoy for his inconsiderate appropriation of the facility to house a bunch of federal bureaucrats, gave Latyshev a public relations black eye as children studying at the school demonstrated against the envoy's attempt to take it over.[10] Rossel also leaked information to the media about the allegedly large sums Latyshev was spending on apartments for his staff. In October 2000, Rossel joined with Bashkortostan president Murtaza Rakhimov in a joint denunciation of the creation of the federal Okrugs. Despite this opposition, Latyshev continued to replace federal officials in Sverdlovsk region who had close ties to Rossel and formed closer ties to Yekaterinburg mayor Arkadii Chernetskii, a long-time Rossel opponent. In 2001, the relationship deteriorated to name calling, when Rossel described the presidential envoys as "Gauleiters of fascist Germany" in an interview with *Izvestiya*, while Latyshev responded in kind by commenting that "dogs bark, but the caravan has moved on."[11]

During the height of the conflict, the work of the Sverdlovsk Region Duma was practically paralyzed because of the conflict among the legislature's factions, which reflected the battle between the governor and the mayor. In the conflict a group of deputies supporting Rossel tried to remove regional Duma speaker Yevgenii Porunov, who had been elected with Mayor Chernetskii's support, leading to boycotts of the session's work. The Duma's sessions were in limbo for seven months, through the fall of 2001, though Porunov was ultimately able to hold on to his seat. During the heat of the conflict, Rossel threatened that either the deputies resolve their dispute or he would dissolve the legislature. In response, Latyshev held a three-hour meeting with the deputies and argued that Rossel had no basis to make such threats.[12]

Rossel was the only governor who refused to participate in the numerous okrug meetings that Latyshev conducted during the first two years of his work. In his place, the Sverdlovsk governor usually sent the region's prime minister, A. Vorob'ev. Through his nonparticipation, Rossel made clear his opinion that he believed that the envoy was not of his stature and that elected governors had the right to meet with the president directly and did not have to work through intermediaries like Latyshev. Rossel tried to get Presidential Administration head Aleksandr Voloshin's support in organizing such a meeting with Putin, but failed. The meeting that Rossel had planned for February 13, 2002, with the president never took place.

Nevertheless, during the first half of 2002, relations between Rossel and Latyshev began to normalize a little. Rossel no longer actively denounced the presidential envoys as he did in the past. Moreover, he began to participate in events Latyshev organized, particularly the trips seeking foreign investment in London and Frankfurt.

However, the more cooperative tone did not change the gist of the relationship. Rossel continues to assert his right to a role independent of Moscow's policies; he still seeks a personal meeting with the president; and he does not plan to renounce the power-sharing treaty that Sverdlovsk region signed with President Yeltsin. Moreover, Rossel improved his position following the April 2002 regional Duma elections when his For Our Urals Homeland (Za rodnoi Ural) bloc won a majority of the seats in the regional legislature.

Initially, Latyshev had good relations with Chelyabinsk governor Petr Sumin, who generally behaved toward the envoy with great loyalty. Sumin was one of two governors (along with Tyumen's Sobyanin) who joined the okrug commission to prepare suggestions for the Kozak Commission on dividing powers between the different levels of government. In July 2001, Sumin took the initiative in offering to abrogate Chelyabinsk's 1997 power-sharing treaty. The region's legislature approved the move in November 2001, and the governor immediately signed the necessary legislation.

However, after the conflict surrounding the Karabash and Zlatoust metallurgical factories, relations between Sumin and Latyshev cooled. Latyshev only provided superficial support for Sumin's position, and no okrug official attended the International Congress of Metallurgists in Chelyabinsk, marking the three-hundredth anniversary of Urals metallurgy. Moreover, the Presidential Administration did not even send the customary greetings from the president to the event's participants. Later, after Latyshev delicately criticized Sumin's participation in the property dispute surrounding the metals factories, Sumin refused to join the Urals delegation to London, describing the visit as meaningless.

Little is known about the relations between Latyshev and the governors of Tyumen region. Most likely, Latyshev has good relations with Tyumen governor Sobyanin, who previously served as his first deputy. The governors of the northern districts (Yurii Neelov in Yamal-Nenets and Aleksandr Filippov in Khanty-Mansii) publicly acknowledge the importance of the presidential envoy in federal relations and do not refuse to participate in events organized by the envoy. However, to resolve important questions they more frequently deal directly with Moscow, working in close contact with the presidential administration or factions in the State Duma.

Latyshev has difficult relations with Kurgan governor Oleg Bogomolov, whose region is the only one in the Urals that relies on federal funding to meet its expenses. The region is so poor that federal subsidies cover almost 80 percent of its budget, and its standard of living is only 40 percent of that in the rest of the okrug. In recent years agricultural output has declined by 50 percent in the region and by even more for some specific products.[13] These figures naturally spoil the image of the okrug and lead to discussions about incorporating Kurgan into another region. Kurgan's delegate to the Federation Council, Andrei Vikharev, floated the idea of such a merger at the end of 2001, recalling that until 1943, Kurgan was part of Chelyabinsk region.[14]

Latyshev has devoted considerable attention to the problems of Kurgan. In 2001, he ordered the Center for Economic Planning and Forecasting to prepare a program on helping the region exit its crisis. However, in April 2002 Governor Bogomolov sharply criticized the document at a meeting with Latyshev. "I swear with my hand over my heart, that this is not a program. . . . It is an analysis of the situation in the region. We are familiar with its conclusions, but we have no idea how to implement these plans, including who should take what kind of decisions. Such recommendations do not appear in the Institute's material."[15]

The situation deteriorated further in May 2002, when Deputy Presidential Envoy Viktor Basargin publicly stated that in the near future the federal government would impose external management on Kurgan, effectively declaring it bankrupt, because its leadership was unable to overcome the region's crisis. Naturally, Basargin could not make such a statement without Latyshev's prior agreement. Rossel quickly stepped up to defend Bogomolov since he was happy to ally himself with anyone against Latyshev. He pointed out that Basargin's statement could not be implemented since Russia did not have a law making it possible to impose such external management on one of its regions.[16]

To emphasize the growing presence of the federal government at the regional level, the presidential envoys (at the Kremlin's orders) in 2001 began to carry out extensive investigations of personnel in the regions. There has been little public information about the results of these studies. But the envoy's staff express confidence that such investigations will cut the ties between the regional representatives of the federal ministries and regional leaders.

The okrug's current functioning excludes any possible unification of the okrug's governors against the presidential envoy. With the exception of Tyumen Region, where the three governors meet within the framework of a regional council, the governors rarely see one another.

Latyshev's activities as envoy and his relations with the governors make it clear that the federal authorities want the governors to be regional managers, shoveling garbage out of the way when necessary, but in no way to function as politicians who can negotiate with the federal authorities. Latyshev has achieved this goal to a significant degree, even though he has taken a rather differentiated approach toward the six governors in his okrug.

Regional Elections and the Role of the Presidential Envoy

During the first two years following the establishment of the envoy's office, gubernatorial elections took place in three of the okrug's six regions—

Chelyabinsk, Kurgan, and Tyumen. The elections took place in December 2000 and January 2001, when the envoy was still setting up his staff. Latyshev's office had little influence on the campaigns in Kurgan and Chelyabinsk regions, where incumbent governors Bogomolov and Sumin secured additional terms.[17]

Tyumen Region was a different matter since Latyshev ran his own candidate in the person of his first deputy, Sergei Sobyanin. Sobyanin only entered the race three months before the elections. Prior to his entry, the envoy conducted long negotiations with Khanty-Mansii Autonomous Okrug governor Aleksandr Filippenko. Only Filippenko's ultimate decision not to participate in the elections led Sobyanin to join the race and eventually emerge victorious in January 2001, winning 52.7 percent of the vote.

During the campaign against incumbent Tyumen governor Leonid Roketskii, Sobyanin benefited from the resources of Tyumen's two autonomous okrugs and the Urals branches of key power ministries. Several days before the election, media broadcast the tape of a telephone conversation between Deputy Presidential Envoy Anatolii Antipin, who until the fall of 2000 was the head of Tyumen Region's Federal Security Service branch, and the head of the Urals branch of the MVD's Regional Administration for Combating Organized Crime (RUBOP), Valerii Borisov, from which it was clear that RUBOP supported Sobyanin in the race.[18] After the elections, the Urals RUBOP leader took over the Tyumen Region police department, an appointment that requires the support of the presidential envoy. Additionally, during the campaign, Latyshev's deputy Sergei Vakhrukov devoted his full attention to the effort.

Latyshev's staff justified the envoy's participation in the elections—which was not authorized by his job description—by explaining that Roketskii was a "conflict-prone governor," who was unable to find a common language with the governors of the northern autonomous okrugs that were also part of the region. Latyshev said that he was working to replace Roketskii with someone who could better facilitate the integration of these regions.

The presidential envoy paid much less attention to the regional legislative elections. Latyshev had no influence on the Chelyabinsk and Tyumen regional Duma elections that took place in 2001. The April 2002 elections in Sverdlovsk Region were expected to activate the envoy's staff because they offered an opportunity to weaken the position of Governor Rossel. Latyshev's frequent statements about the need to remove regional parties from the political scene suggested that he would indeed make such an effort. But the envoy either chose not, or was unable, to turn the elections to the regional Duma to his advantage. Rossel's team ran a highly effective campaign, partly by criticizing Yekaterinburg mayor Chernetskii's decision to increase prices for housing and municipal services.

Ultimately, the gubernatorial bloc For Our Urals Homeland won the most votes (29 percent), while the pro-presidential bloc uniting the Unity (Yedinstvo) and Fatherland (Otechestvo) parties, scored less than 19 percent. Nikolai

Voronin of For Our Urals Homeland became the legislature's speaker, and members of the bloc became chairmen of a majority of the committees and commissions.

Beyond participating in regional elections, the federal government has been trying to extend its regional influence by establishing powerful federal parties. However, the population has little knowledge of these new organizations. An opinion poll conducted by the Tyumen Center for Social Research in April 2002 demonstrated that the pro-Kremlin party of power, United Russia (Yedinaya Rossiya), had the support of only 14 percent of the population. The most popular party affiliation was "none," which scored 57 percent.[19]

In the Sverdlovsk regional elections, United Russia did not do well even though it was led by the successful businessman Sergei Nosov, the director of the Nizhnii Tagil metallurgical factory. In Tyumen, the Unity party has not even been able to establish stable leadership, with three different leaders during its two-year existence.[20]

Thus, the political parties that existed in the regions in 2002 were far from achieving the hopes of the authors of the new federal law on parties that sought to build a small number of strong national parties. As opinion polls show, the population associates its material conditions much more closely with the work of the regional executives than with the activities of the presidential representatives and parties.

The Presidential Envoy's Influence on the Choice of Federation Council Members

The presidential envoy has had practically no influence over the selection of Federation Council members from the Urals okrug. Two of the new senators virtually appointed themselves: Andrei Smelev from Sverdlovsk and Aleksandr Aristov from Chelyabinsk. Both are big businessmen who have stable relations with their region's economic and administrative elite. Effectively, big business appointed Andrei Vikharev from Kurgan, who secured the post of deputy Federation Council chairman, and Aleksandr Gavrin from Tyumen. To be precise, the Urals businessman Pavel Fedulev backed Vikharev's appointment and LUKoil backed Gavrin.

Yamal-Nenets senator Aleksandr Yevstifeev most likely had powerful supporters in Moscow, since his previous work, as deputy presidential envoy to the Volga okrug, had no connection to the Urals. The regional elites chose the other Urals senators without any interference from the presidential envoy.

Corruption

The growth of crime and corruption are the third and fourth most troublesome problems that the population expects the authorities to tackle, behind only rising prices and low salaries, according to the Tyumen Center for Social and Legal Research.[21] Latyshev himself speaks about the problem of corruption frequently, criticizing the police and other law enforcement agencies for not taking decisive measures to combat this phenomenon. He and Okrug procurator Yurii Zotov criticized as unsatisfactory the activities of all agencies fighting corruption, organized crime, and economic crime.

Naturally, the battle against corruption cannot be effective if the law enforcement agencies themselves are corrupt. As Latyshev has repeatedly emphasized, his efforts have yet to improve the way that they work. For example, the police continue to exclude many unsolved crimes from their records in order to give the appearance that their work is more effective than it really is. In 2000, the procurator found fifteen thousand cases where citizens had reported crimes to the authorities, who then did not include them in their official records. Among the unrecorded crimes were many dealing with the drug trade. The procurator filed fifty-two criminal cases against policemen for corruption and falsifying records during that year. In 2001, investigators found fourteen thousand cases that were not included in the official statistics and filed thirty-five criminal cases against officers for falsifying the records. The same trends continued in the first half of 2002.

There are problems in other law enforcement agencies as well. Customs officials are often accused of taking bribes. Additionally, even though the Okrug Tax Police handed over three-and-a-half times as much money to the budget in 2001 as in 2000, its director held a meeting in Yekaterinburg in October 2001 to point out that his officers were mainly filing cases against offenders whose underpayments were relatively small, while many of the cases dealing with large sums were not prosecuted.

Latyshev has frequently complained that law enforcement officials often take sides in property battles. During 2001, the authorities prosecuted a large number of economic crimes, filing cases affecting more than two hundred industrial enterprises and other companies in the okrug. These cases often focused on individuals who embezzled money or value-added tax payments, disguising their ill-gotten gains as export operations. Latyshev claimed in a June 2001 Sverdlovsk State Television interview that half of Urals taxpayers simply do not file returns or do so with a zero balance. In many cases, people conduct business activities without paying any taxes.

Perhaps the most famous case of corruption in the okrug has been the transfer into private hands of the state's 80 percent share of the fueling service at the Kol'tsovo airport in Yekaterinburg. This business brought the state considerable revenue, but Sverdlovsk deputy prime minister N. Danilov, who served as the state's chief representative on the company's board of directors, signed an order that gave more than 80 percent of the state share to the Urals Ring (Kol'tso Urala) insurance company, headed by A. Venediktov, who also served as an economics adviser to Governor Rossel. Latyshev successfully intervened in this case and got the shares returned to state ownership. Deputy Presidential Envoy Viktor Basargin has made clear that the envoy's office plans to intervene in similar cases in the future.

The Presidential Envoy's Economic Influence

In contrast to other envoys, Latyshev has not made a major effort to increase his power over economic issues, and he has not prepared a plan for the region's development. Rather, he has focused on developing closer ties with the big businesses operating in the okrug. However, since he lacks the authority to help them resolve their most important problems, these relations remain mostly superficial.

The Urals okrug contains a considerable amount of Russia's economic potential. The energy sector is predominant since Tyumen region produces 92 percent of Russia's natural gas output and 65 percent of its oil. Ferrous and nonferrous metallurgy is also important. The okrug also has extensive machine-building and other industrial facilities. The okrug produces 12 percent of Russia's electricity and has a well-developed nuclear power industry.

Latyshev actively meets with his okrug's most important business leaders. He has said that Putin's famous statement that all big businessmen should be held at "an equal distance" from the state is appropriate only at the federal level. Latyshev amended Putin's directive by asserting "for the regional level, it is useful to seek beneficial paths of cooperation [between the state and business] in order to address such concerns as social problems. On this issue, we should proceed from the idea that we need to develop cooperation between the authorities, business, and society."[22] Judging on the basis of this statement and Latyshev's behavior, he is interested in having businessmen appeal to him for help in resolving their problems with the local authorities, rather than turn to members of the law enforcement agencies. Latyshev well understands that by establishing personal relationships with such businessmen, he will be able to monitor, and perhaps influence, their business affairs.

Unfortunately for him, Latyshev lacks the authority to help Urals businesses resolve their problems in Moscow, and he has even fewer resources to assist them in the regions. Several members of the business elite have agreed to meet with him, and at various times he has sat down with LUKoil's Vagit Alekperov, Uralmash's Kakha Bendukidze, Surgutneftegaz's Vladimir Bogdanov, Gosinkor's V. Chernov, Magnitogorsk Metals Factory's Viktor Rashnikov, and others. In August 2002, Latyshev met with the Urals Mining and Metallurgical Company's Makhmudov and Kozitsyn to discuss their strategy for developing the company and its role in implementing the president's domestic policies.[23] Some of these businessmen have joined Latyshev in foreign road shows to present the okrug to potential foreign investors. However, in their daily activity, they focus on the governors and mayors, who wield enormous budgetary resources and the right to distribute property and land.

The economic problems of the okrug are extremely complex and far beyond the scope of the limited resources Latyshev has at his disposal. During the 1990s oil and gas output declined precipitously. Only in 2001 did Yamal-Nenets succeed in stopping the drop in natural gas production by bringing the new Zapolyarnii deposit on line, but its reserves will last only five to seven years.[24] With the exception of Surgutneftegaz, none of Russia's oil companies are looking for new deposits in the okrug. Moreover, the companies are only slowly paying their back taxes to the federal, regional, and local budgets. Reform in the industry will require major technological and structural changes. For example, in the gas sector, reformers plan to introduce more competition so that Gazprom is no longer a monopolist.

In metallurgy, there has been a glut of steel, aluminum, titanium, and nickel on the international market forcing prices down for all producers, including Russia's. Metallurgy makes up more than 50 percent of Sverdlovsk region's tax base, so the difficulties of this industry have a particularly powerful impact on the region. Urals experts believe that if domestic demand for metal does not pick up, and if there is no investment in the local metallurgy enterprises, then the Urals metals industry will continue to decline.

While not apparently playing a significant role in the energy and metallurgy industries, Latyshev has spoken out in regard to some of the other problem sectors of the Urals economy. The okrug has a high concentration of defense plants that are now struggling. Latyshev recommends that the state pick a few priority areas that it will fund, while letting military enterprises in nonpriority areas switch to civilian production or go out of business. He describes the Kurgan agricultural sector as close to catastrophe and is seeking a special government program to support it. He also ordered the development of a plan to address the okrug's decaying transportation system, following a summer 2001 meeting with transportation minister Sergei Frank in Yekaterinburg, but it is not clear how it will be implemented.

Additionally, Latyshev frequently criticizes his okrug's poor performance in attracting foreign investment. He advocates increasing the legal protection provided to foreign investors and reaching out to foreign businessmen to encourage them to make investments. Latyshev claims that he can guarantee investor rights and that his efforts have stimulated foreign interest in the okrug.[25] He has set up a coordinating and consultative council on foreign investment, including representatives of major foreign companies who are investing in the region. The group has organized several presentations in Western Europe, including in London, Frankfurt, and Vienna.

Relations with Local Government and Civil Society

Local Government

Local government in the Urals has been deprived of any independence. After Putin's centralization of the Russian tax system in 2001, the governors' administrations tried to make up for their losses by taking funds from local governments. As a result, these policies have deprived a majority of the municipalities, even those in the relatively well off Yamal-Nenets and Khanty-Mansii okrugs, of the resources they need to cover their own expenses, thus forcing them to rely on federal subsidies.

Sverdlovsk region has the most active civil society in the okrug, but it is an exception in an area where the nonstate sector remains weak and underdeveloped. The average person would have difficulty thinking of any activities initiated by nongovernmental groups. Against this background of indifference, only activists from religious and ethnic groups seem to be asserting themselves.

Relations with the Media

Like the other presidential envoys, Latyshev supports the formation of a "unified information space" in the Urals okrug. In August 2001, he defined his vision of this concept as the presence of independent media, plus "constructive cooperation among the electronic media," and the creation of an okrug television channel. Although he talks about the need for freedom of speech in building a strong state, Latyshev effectively seems to have in mind a broadcaster that presents the president's and his personal views, while the "independent" media simply repeat them.

Latyshev never tires of pointing out that every newspaper, television station, and television company belongs to someone. "Concrete interests stand behind many regional media, whether it is the regional authorities, local authorities, or financial-industrial groups," he notes. He blames the media for not being objective and for accusing the federal government of not being able to improve life in the regions. Even though he recognizes that the media often reflect the opinions of the regional elites that control them, he blames the media for destabilizing society when various media outlets go to war with one another, rather than focusing on the elites that stand behind them.

Latyshev believes that the media should spend more time discussing the social stability that ostensibly has taken hold under Putin's leadership. To that end, in May 2001, he backed the creation of the pro-presidential journalists' union, Media-soyuz, in the Urals okrug. He noted that this organization, headed by A. Lyubimov, works to create a "constructive dialogue with the authorities."

During 2001, all the significant newspapers in the okrug introduced columns entitled "News from the Okrug," which described the envoy's work and discussed events in the Urals. Each of the regions also began weekly *Vremya-novoe!* television shows and *Vmeste* radio shows on the regional State Television and Radio Company (GTRK) channels. The latter also began live broadcasts featuring Latyshev. In 2001 three such joint television and radio broadcasts took place, giving all the residents of the okrug a chance to view and listen to the envoy simultaneously.

In 2001, the okrug began setting up a Urals television channel, following the model of its Siberian neighbors. The project grew out of the existing GTRK network and the Yugra television company of Khanty-Mansii. In July 2002 the Yermak Urals Okrug Television Company was registered and began broadcasts to the entire okrug. The state television companies of the Yamal Nenets and Khanty Mansii Autonomous Okrugs (GTRK Yamal-Region and Yugra) provided satellites to the new broadcaster. These stations own 3 and 5 percent stakes in Ermak, respectively. GTRK and Yekaterinburg's Channel 4 each own a 25 percent plus one share stake, for a total of 50 percent plus two shares. The Foundation for Developing Urals Television owns 41.8 percent. The foundation's shares will be sold in 2003, and the buyers will likely be LUKoil and Yevrazkholding, which have already invested $4 million in the project.[26] The okrug also set up its own website (www.uralfo.ru), which began operating in December 2001.

Conclusion

The significance of the creation of okrugs headed by presidential envoys can be deduced from the functions of the envoys. The envoy is the representative of central authority in the regions, and nothing more. All of Petr Latyshev's activity in the Urals Federal Okrug confirms this. He represents the president at numerous meetings and seminars, in trips to cities and villages, in the law enforcement agencies, at enterprises, in meetings with business-men, and in governors' offices. In Moscow and abroad, he represents his okrug. He does not have the personal strength, staff support, or authority to do more. He can simply strive to fulfill the tasks that Putin's original decree assigned him: coordinating and monitoring. But even these functions may exceed his resources.

The creation of the okrugs and the institution of envoy, as well as the announcement of the policy of strengthening the federal hierarchy of power, led to a short hiatus in the arbitrary rule of federal bureaucrats and regional officials. But their fear quickly passed because no serious measures were subsequently taken. The federal agencies in the regions, and the gubernatorial administrations, quickly adapted to the ways of the envoys' staffs: the federal authorities did not hurry to limit the governors' power to distribute official resources, and the governors are not particularly concerned that they may face any serious punishments.

The only clear accomplishment of the current reforms, it seems, is that the governors have lost their role as federal politicians. The center has defined their job as that of economic managers who help to remove local obstructions. The presidential envoys' position in the new federal structure remains unclear. Currently they seem like a fifth wheel in the federal executive branch because they do not have enough authority. If their level of responsibility is increased, they will gain a respectable place in the power hierarchy. If not, then we can feel sorry for those officials who in 2000 fought for their positions on, for example, Latyshev's staff, who left their jobs in Siberian and Urals regions and erroneously thought that their status and power would thereby increase.

Notes

1. *Uralskii rabochii,* August 22, 2001.

2. *Elita Region,* no. 4 (2001).

3. Latyshev's press conference marking the second anniversary of the establishment of the seven federal districts, www.uralfo.ru/flash.html.

4. *Nezavisimaya gazeta,* April 5, 2002.

5. Accessed at www.ural.strana.ru, April 9, 2002.

6. Yuliya Latynina, "Arbitrazh po-russki," *Novaya gazeta,* June 14, 2001; K. Zabudin, "V mednykh voinakh net pobeditelei," *Guberniya,* June 21, 2001 (accessed at www.echel.ru/press/?page=0&ctgr=2&id=279).

7. Accessed at www.ural.strana.ru, September 24, 2001.

8. In the case of the Urals, the military and federal okrugs never were the same. Until March 24, 2001, the military okrug consisted of Sverdlovsk, Kurgan, Perm, Chelyabinsk, Kirov, Komi, and Udmurtiya. On March 24, 2001, Putin combined the

Volga and Ural okrugs, setting the new headquarters in Yekaterinburg. The new okrug includes Bashkortostan, Marii-El, Mordovia, Tatarstan, Udmurtia, Chuvashia, Kirov, Kurgan, Orenburg, Penza, Perm, Samara, Saratov, Sverdlovsk, Tyumen, Ulyanovsk, Chelyabinsk, Komi-Permyak, Khanty-Mansii, and Yamal-Nenets.

9. Regions.ru, as quoted in RFE/RL Newsline, October 3, 2002.

10. *Kommersant,* August 12, 2002.

11. Accessed at www.postfactum.cityline.ru/2001/03/31125/html.

12. Accessed at http://region.urfo.org/everyday/art/311777.asp.

13. Latyshev used these figures in an interview on March 28, 2001, on Sverdlovsk State Television.

14. Accessed at www.uralinform.ru/detail2.asp?ID=10270.

15. Accessed at www.ural.strana.ru /stories/02/01/31/2440/122004.html.

16. Accessed at www.regions.ru/article/-/id/764006/html (accessed on May 25, 2002).

17. E. Abelinskas and A. Lankina, "Vybory gubernatorov Kurganskoi oblasti: Izbiratel'nye tekhnologii ili voleiz'yavlenie naroda," in *Vybory i problemy grazhdanskogo obshchestva na Urale,* no. 4 (Moscow: Moscow Carnegie Center, 2001), 78–88; and A. Podoprigora, "'Otlozhennaya partiya' na Yuzhnom Urale," in *Vybory,* 72–78.

18. Accessed at http://nsn.net.ru/print.phtml?id=1273&ch=4&sub=10. For the full text of this conversation, see www.compromat.ru/main/roketskiy/sobyaninpr.htm.

19. *Argumenti i fakti v Zapadnoi Sibiri,* no. 22, 2002.

20. Unity (Yedinstvo) was the Kremlin-sponsored "party of power" that boosted President Putin to power in the 1999 State Duma elections. When the party later merged with Moscow mayor Yurii Luzhkov's Fatherland (Otechestvo), it changed its name to United Russia (Yedinaya Rossiya).

21. V. I. Ul'yanov, T. A. Kryuchkov, and A. A. Silin, *Otchet o rezul'tatakh odinnadtsatogo etapa sotsial'no-politicheskogo monitoringa sredi naseleniya Yuga Tyumenskoi oblasti* (Tyumen, 2001), 39.

22. Interview with strana.ru, January 9, 2002.

23. *Kommersant,* August 21, 2002.

24. *Tyumenskie izvestiya,* June 1, 2002.

25. *Nezavisimaya gazeta,* April 5, 2002.

26. Accessed at www.edfond.ru/news080702_5_print.php.

8

Siberian Federal Okrug

Maksim Shandarov

*T*HE SIBERIAN FEDERAL OKRUG INCLUDES *the republics of Buryatia, Altai, Khakasia, and Tyva; Altai Krai, Krasnoyarsk Krai; the regions of Chita, Irkutsk, Kemerovo, Novosibirsk, Omsk, and Tomsk; and the autonomous okrugs of Agin-Buryatia, Evenkia, Taimyr (Dolgan-Nenets), and Ust-Orda Buryatia.*

Leonid Drachevskii (born 1942) is the only presidential envoy with diplomatic experience. His official biography contains unexplained gaps. He gained degrees in chemistry (1966) and physical training (1982), and he rowed for the USSR's national team. From 1986 to 1991 he worked for the State Sports and Physical Training Committee, known as Goskomsport. In 1992 he joined the Ministry of Foreign Affairs, studied at its Diplomatic Academy, and, among other posts, served as consul general in Barcelona, ambassador to Poland, and minister for the affairs of the Commonwealth of Independent States (May 1999–May 2000). He avoids public conflict but can be quite critical in private meetings, according to journalists who have observed him at work.

Okrug Overview

An Okrug of Contrasts

The sixteen regions of the Siberian Federal Okrug can be divided into rich, resource-extracting regions and areas mired in a deep depression.[1] The richest regions, Krasnoyarsk and Kemerovo, boast extensive deposits of coal, iron ore, nonferrous metals, natural gas, and oil. Often a large portion of a region's

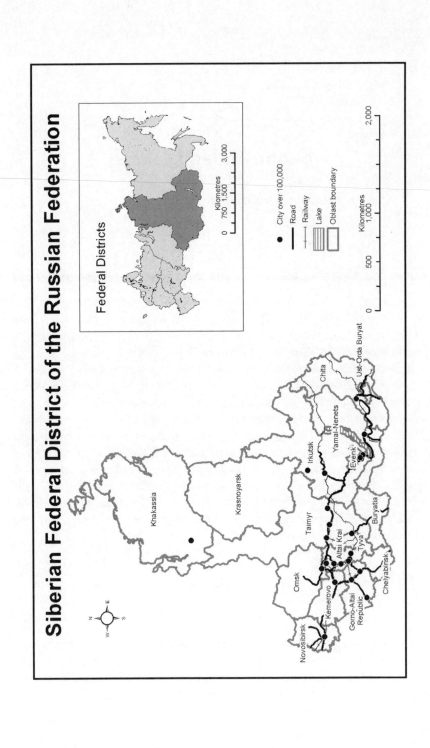

Siberian Federal District of the Russian Federation

Federal Districts

Kilometres
0 750 1,500   3,000

- City over 100,000
- Road
- Railway
- Lake
- Oblast boundary

Kilometres
0   500   1,000   2,000

Khakassia

Krasnoyarsk

Omsk

Taimyr

Irkutsk

Yamal-Nenets

Evenk

Chita

Ust-Orda Buryat

Buryatia

Altai Krai

Tyva

Chelyabinsk

Kemerovo

Gorno-Altai Republic

Novosibirsk

budget comes from one or two resource-exporting enterprises. For example, Norilsk Nickel generates up to 70 percent of Krasnoyarsk Krai's budget, with revenue from enterprises in the aluminum industry, such as the Krasnoyarsk Aluminum and Achinsk Bauxite factories, supplying the rest.[2] Similarly, the budget of Kemerovo region derives most of its income from taxes on mining enterprises (especially coal and iron ore), the chemical industry, and metallurgical plants (Zapsib, KMK). In Omsk the local oil refinery generates most of the region's tax revenue. Likewise, the Irkutsk and Khakasia budgets are based largely on income flowing from the aluminum industry and local hydroelectric plants. Tomsk also has a reasonable quantity of resources.

The concentration on resource extraction and metal exports makes these regions vulnerable to fluctuations in prices on the Russian and international markets. To a significant extent, the economic health of regions like Krasnoyarsk, Kemerovo, and Chita depends on a stable demand for coal. To these regions' detriment, however, many of Russia's utilities are switching to use the cleaner and more practical natural gas. Additionally, many large electricity-generating plants and metallurgical factories that have yet to convert continue to use the Kazakhstani coal for which they were built. The demand for Russian coal has continued to drop in recent years, and many mine and pit owners have been forced to close their enterprises. The coal companies of Chita now work at only half-strength, and a similar situation threatens Kemerovo's firms. The high steel tariffs that the Bush administration imposed on imports to the United States in 2001 have also adversely affected Kemerovo.

Another condition increasing Siberia's vulnerability is the fact that large Russian financial–industrial groups with headquarters in Moscow (or other cities in European Russia) own almost all the profitable enterprises in the area. Vladimir Potanin's Interros controls the extremely lucrative Norilsk Nickel in Taimyr. Siberian Aluminum (now called Bazovyi Element) and the Siberian Urals Aluminum Holding Company (SUAL) long ago divided up the aluminum industry.[3] Large Moscow- and Urals-based companies control the ferrous metal and coal industries, particularly in Kemerovo. The TVEL Corporation,[4] a holding company established by President Yeltsin in 1996 to oversee the state-owned nuclear fuel industry and controlled by Moscow businessmen, owns part of the nuclear energy industry (the Novosibirsk factory for chemical concentrates), while the federal government, through the Nuclear Industry Ministry, controls the other plants in this field (the Tomsk Chemical Combine and the Krasnoyarsk Mining and Chemical Combine at Zheleznogorsk).

Another group of outsiders, namely, foreign investors, own a significant share of resources in the okrug as well. For example, British concerns control the forestry and cellulose industry in Bratsk and Ust'-Ilimsk. Unfortunately, the battles between various financial–industrial groups for the region's resource-processing factories have disrupted work at these plants, threatening the well-being of the regions involved. Examples include the struggle over the Krasnoyarsk Aluminum Factory, pitting local magnate Anatolii Bykov against Siberian Aluminum's Oleg Deripaska, and the long-running skirmishes between Deripaska and Ilim Pulp Enterprise *(sic)* over the Bratsk Timber Mill in Irkutsk region.[5] Despite these disruptive conflicts, Siberia has enormous untapped resources that could guarantee its economic future. There are extensive oil deposits in the area that have yet to receive serious investment. Also, Irkutsk's massive Kovykta gas field remains largely untapped. Extensive discussions of this project at the federal and regional level have yet to lead to action.

The regions that do not have resource deposits fall into the depressed category, where living standards are low and, in some cases, continue to deteriorate. The most prominent members of this group are some of the ethnically defined republics and autonomous okrugs (the republics of Buryatia, Tyva, and Altai; and the Ust-Orda and Agin-Buryatia Autonomous Okrugs). While the situation may be improving in some of the resource-rich regions, the stagnation in many of the poorest regions remains intractable. For example, in Tyva industry lies in ruins; the crime rate is growing by 20 percent a year; and the population either continues to live in poverty or is moving to other regions. Over 90 percent of the republic's budget is made up of federal subsidies. The situation for Siberia's rural population is particularly extreme, forcing many to move to cities while creating a labor shortage in the countryside. The problem of providing the far north with sufficient supplies to survive each winter remains a perennial challenge. Partly as a consequence, the northern autonomous okrugs of Evenkia and Taimyr have difficulty attracting qualified employees for their plants. Even higher salaries are not enough of an incentive.

Siberia's industrially developed, defense-oriented regions also fit into the depressed category. This group includes the somewhat better-off Novosibirsk in the first order and the relatively more impoverished Omsk, Chita, and Altai Krai in the second. Idle defense plants in these regions place a heavy burden on local budgets. One exception is the aircraft factory in the relatively prosperous Irkutsk, which is doing well thanks to export sales. This plant, however, is unusual in the otherwise depressed arms industry. Almost none of the former weapons producers have successfully made the transition to civilian output. The once formidable military giants like Omsk's Transmash tank factory and Novosibirsk's Chkalov aircraft plant remain in deep crisis more than a decade after the Soviet Union's collapse. In addition to the defense industry, Altai Krai, Novosibirsk, and Omsk have large and depressed agricultural sectors.

The okrug's main intellectual resources are based in the regions where the Soviet authorities established branches of the Academy of Sciences and major universities. These include Novosibirsk and the nearby Akademgorodok (Academic Township), Tomsk, Krasnoyarsk, and Irkutsk (which also have their own academic townships). A decade of greatly reduced funding has driven the state-sponsored research institutions into a deep crisis. However, some of the scientists have successfully adapted their research to the new market conditions and now focus on projects that are capable of generating income. Several computer-programming centers in Akademgorodok demonstrate the possibilities in this field. Novosoft, for example, began in 1992 with five people in Novosibirsk and one in Austin, Texas.[6] By 2002, it had more than four hundred employees across Russia, and it is the fastest growing offshore software development company in Russia, according to the company website. It has completed more than four hundred projects for a wide variety of international customers, such as IBM, Hewlett Packard, and Samsung. Recently it opened a branch in the Krasnoyarsk town of Zheleznogorsk, which even today remains closed to foreigners.

In fact, despite the difficult climate and persistence of poverty in many areas, there are signs of progress in Siberia. Business activity is on the rise, and living standards have noticeably improved in many of Siberia's regional urban centers, starting in 2000. Russian and foreign investors have stepped up their activities. The American firm Mars plans to finish construction of a $14 million pet food factory in Novosibirsk, while the Tatarstan-based Krasnyi vostok (Red East) has begun building a brewery in the same city, bringing in an additional $50 million of investment. Sweden's IKEA is also considering investments in the region. The Siberian Machinery Holding Company (Sibmashkholding) now unites many large agricultural equipment manufacturers, making it easier to secure orders from regional governments. And the list goes on. However, the investment ratings of Siberia's regions are often much lower than those of regions in the European part of Russia because they are located far from needed supplies and sales markets, and often lack qualified workers.

Who Is Drachevskii?

Leonid Drachevskii stands out from the other presidential envoys because, unlike Viktor Cherkesov in the North-West and Georgii Poltavchenko in the Central okrug, he is not a personal friend of Putin and does not come from one of the power ministries (as often defined.)[7] Moreover, unlike former prime minister Sergei Kirienko, he was not well known before his appointment. However, he may have made an impression on Putin, when part of his year as minister for the Commonwealth of Independent States coincided with Putin's directorship of the FSB and then his brief prime ministership (May–August, August–December 1999). Apparently Drachevskii has had few personal meetings with Putin and probably sees his boss primarily at sessions with all the envoys present and at meetings of the Security Council. In these cases, it is usually the president or his staff who set the agenda. In 2001 Drachevskii was a member of Putin's delegation to visit Canada, although he did not join him in visiting other countries on the same trip.

On the occasions when Drachevskii has managed to secure a one-on-one session with the president, his lobbying efforts have not apparently been particularly successful. In February 2002 he met with Putin to discuss the strategic development plan for Siberia. After the meeting, he called a press conference to announce that the president supported his position in his current battle with the government. The latter had been trying to reduce the subsidies that Siberia would secure from the plan. However, the published, though not approved, text of the document, which became available later in the year, suggested that Drachevskii exaggerated the strength of his persuasiveness or that the minister for economic development and trade, German Gref, turned out to be even more persuasive in a subsequent meeting with Putin.

Drachevskii's Staffing Policies

The envoy's staff includes just over one hundred members. Half of them work in the central office in Novosibirsk while the rest are based in federal inspectorates throughout the okrug. (The autonomous okrugs of Taimyr, Evenkia, Ust-Orda Buryatia, and Agin-Buryatia do not have chief federal inspectors and are monitored from neighboring regions.)

Drachevskii took painstaking care in choosing his staff. He brought three key deputies from Moscow and then sought out local talent during the first months of his tenure. The core members of his team have stayed with him for the first two years. In cases where staff members left, they often did so to run for public office. Drachevskii has required all staff members who sought such office to resign.

Beyond his Moscow connections, Drachevskii drew most of his staff members from the state bureaucracy. First Deputy Envoy Igor Prostyakov, one of the three who came from Moscow, handles most personnel issues. Several federal inspectors and members of the Novosibirsk office came from the Novosibirsk governor's staff. Additionally, several staff members working for other Siberian governors were invited to join Drachevskii.

The other main source of personnel was Yeltsin's former presidential representatives in the regions and their staff. Several of these representatives kept their old jobs in the same regions where they had previously served, simply changing their title to chief federal inspector (CFI) under the new system (Tomsk, Altai Krai, Altai Republic), while others became CFIs in different regions. For example, Yeltsin's representative to Ust-Orda Buryatia, Nikolai

Kholodov, was appointed the CFI in Tyva, while his predecessor there was transferred to Khakasia.[8]

Several members of Drachevskii's staff have come from the Federal Security Service (FSB). Two of his deputy envoys came from it, as have three of his CFIs (in Omsk, Khakasia, and Tyva). These former FSB officers undoubtedly have significant influence over his personnel policies.

Limited Role for Chief Federal Inspectors

Although evidence is scarce, the CFIs do not seem to be playing a very strong role in the regions. In Irkutsk, for example, Igor Tutevol has yet to find a real niche. He suffers from a lack of administrative capacity, limited funding, and the fact that the CFIs' powers are poorly defined. Apparently the situation is similar in other regions as well.

In a July 2001 interview Tutevol described his job as coordinating federal agencies at the regional level (there are fifty operating in Irkutsk region and forty in Ust-Orda Buryatia, which is also his territory) and promoting social and economic development.[9] He also deals with personnel issues and any threats to the security environment. He has a small staff consisting of a federal inspector and one or two consultants with offices in the regional administration's building. During the campaign for the July 29, 2001, gubernatorial elections in Irkutsk, he said that his job was to monitor developments, but his "principled position" was not to interfere. At least in the way he described it, his job consisted largely of sending information to Novosibirsk.

The main idea guiding Tutevol's effort to coordinate the activities of federal ministries in the region was an attempt to reduce redundancies in the ministries' work and to abolish agencies that were not functioning. He cited some overlapping functions among the Ministry of Justice, the Procuracy, and the MVD, but there seemed to be little progress in addressing the problem.

For the opponents of Irkutsk governor Boris Govorin, Tutevol's policy of "active neutrality" during the July 2001 campaign was not enough. On July 18, a widely publicized raid on Govorin's campaign headquarters revealed that the governor's team had illegally published a newspaper containing negative information about his opponents without clearly identifying the print run of the newspaper or that it was published using funds from his campaign. The governor's opponents charged that the presence of the newspapers in his headquarters provided sufficient grounds to remove him from the campaign. The opposition newspaper *Vostochno-Sibirskie Vesti* asked Tutevol directly, "Will you intervene?" and quoted him as saying earlier that he would do so if one of the candidates broke the law. But he declined.[10]

Unusually Strong Ties with Interregional Economic Association

Siberia is the only one of the seven federal okrugs that has good working relations with the previously existing interregional economic association, in this case the so-called Siberian Agreement (Sibirskoe Soglashenie). In the other okrugs the interregional associations still formally exist but are largely inactive. In a May 2002 interview, Deputy Envoy Prostyakov noted that cooperation with the association is essential because it had a better-informed and more experienced staff than did the okrug.[11] In carrying out his duties, Prostyakov often relies on the association's staff for key support functions. For example, during spring 2002 the okrug and Siberian Agreement staff worked together on issues concerning agriculture, the defense industry, and coal prices. Prostyakov noted that the other okrugs had not properly considered the advantages of working with the interregional associations in their areas due to their ambitions to exert executive power themselves. However, Siberia was unique in that its association had, in the 1990s, been relatively more effective—in creating ties among regions and in lobbying for Siberian interests with the federal government—than the other associations had been.

Critical observers such as Novosibirsk professor Grigorii Olekh suggest, however, that the okrug staff is in fact trying to subvert cooperation among the various Siberian regions so as to prevent them from forming a common front in bargaining with the government.[12] In this way, he says, the creation of the okrug has somewhat limited the independence the interregional association once had.

Resistance to this trend has come especially from Tomsk governor Viktor Kress, who chairs Siberian Agreement and has a generally cool attitude to the okrug's functions. He has repeatedly made clear that the economic decisions that count the most for him are those made by Siberian Agreement.

Relations with Federal Ministries

From the beginning, Drachevskii has never tired of repeating that his two main tasks are to bring local legislation into line with federal norms and to monitor and coordinate the work of the federal agencies in the okrug.

Bringing Regional Laws into Line

In judging the results of Drachevskii's work, one should point out that not one of the projects that he started has been completed. While he achieved some success in bringing local laws into line with federal norms, thus implementing Putin's desire to restore a hierarchy of authority, it quickly became clear that it would be impossible to eliminate all the discrepancies. The problem was not simply reluctance to adopt amendments to existing laws and normative acts, as occurred, for example, in Altai Republic, where the parliament long declined to take any action. Only when the okrug and the Procuracy began to threaten to disband the whole parliament did the situation change. A more worrying trend was the continuing adoption by regional and local legislatures of laws that did not conform to federal norms.

The republic of Khakasia provides interesting examples of this. In 2001 it adopted a series of amendments to its constitution, which drew protests from the republican procurator who pointed out that they violated a number of federal laws. However, he only made his objections known after the republican parliament had approved the changes. As a result, the republic had to reconvene its constitutional commission to rewrite the amendments that had just been adopted. Additionally, in February 2002 the republican procurator asked the executive branch to withdraw the draft 2002 budget that it had sent to the republican parliament, charging that it violated about forty Russian laws. Through this budget, republican leader Aleksei Lebed had sought to implement his long-held dream of abolishing local budgets and strengthening his grip on local government. The procurator's protests left the republic without a budget for an additional month, while the authorities tried to sort out the mess.

More ominous problems occurred in other regions. In Tyva, President Sherig-ool Oorzhak used the process of bringing local laws into line with federal norms to rewrite the republican constitution in a way that expanded his personal power. However, Drachevskii and the Kremlin chose to ignore his power grab in the interest of preserving stability. Likewise, Novosibirsk region failed to rewrite legislation that allowed the governor to appoint mayors, even though federal law requires that they be elected (see further discussion in the section on local government).

Coordinating Federal Ministries

The federal government has approximately fifty major agencies working in Siberia, giving Drachevskii a formidable task in coordinating their work. He uses the newly established okrug-level offices in some of the ministries to facilitate this effort. One of his most important tasks is to oversee the activities of what is now called the okrug branch of the Main Monitoring Department (MMD) of the Presidential Administration (PA). The MMD had offices in the Siberian regions before the okrug was set up, but then, with the appearance of the envoy, the offices became part of the okrug administration. According to administration sources, the okrug branch of the MMD now specializes in investigating how officials in the regions use state property and federal funds. By spring 2002, the sources said, the branch had drafted thirteen laws and regulations, caused five officials to be punished, and identified embezzlement losses amounting to 74.1 million rubles.

Drachevskii also established several councils that seek to address various problems in Siberia. The main forum for discussing broad issues is the Siberian Federal Okrug Council, which includes Drachevskii, some of his staff, the sixteen regional chief executives, and the speakers of the sixteen regional legislatures. The group meets at least once every two months and usually concentrates on a single problem that Drachevskii chooses for discussion (natural disasters, regional legislation, housing issues, etc.). Usually one of the governors makes a presentation on the topic at hand, which is then discussed. Initially, all the governors attended, but over time many of them began finding excuses to skip meetings that did not directly interest them.

Drachevskii has also set up a number of councils dealing with specific problems. For example, there are groups dealing with the power ministries, small business, and security issues. This latter committee, set up in early 2001, has addressed such matters as the civilian use of former military bases, the living conditions of soldiers, the drug trade, border issues, and illegal imports. While the councils provide convenient arenas for discussion, the actual impact of their discussions is extremely difficult to determine.

Supervising Appointments

Another very important aspect of Drachevskii's personnel duties is to approve all the individuals nominated to run the okrug-level offices of the fifty federal agencies that have established or are establishing such offices in Siberia. According to Deputy Envoy Prostyakov, who oversees all personnel matters, immediately after the okrug was created "there were two or three cases when there was no approval process. We found out about these cases and appealed to the relevant agencies and the prime minister. As a result, not one person has been appointed without the envoy's approval."[13] Moreover, on the second anniversary of Putin's decree establishing the okrugs, the Okrug Information Center issued a release saying that the staff had "set up a database of personnel qualified for appointment to state nomenklatura positions in the federal executive branch, consisting of 1,450 individuals."[14]

There have been several cases in which the envoy has opposed an appointment sought by a governor. Among the most important positions that have provoked conflict are the regional heads of the federal State Property Ministry. The person in this post manages state property, state-owned shares in enterprises and organizations, and many questions of land use. Novosibirsk governor Viktor Tolokonskii wanted to appoint his former deputy, the powerful businessman Valerii Bashkov, to head the Novosibirsk branch of the ministry (most likely, with the support of the minister, Farit Gazizullin). Bashkov heads the KSK company, which is involved in housing construction, trade, freight transportation, and other types of business. According to reports in the Novosibirsk media, Bashkov had contributed to Tolokonskii's campaign and received the position of deputy governor as a token of the governor's gratitude. However, Drachevskii did not support Bashkov's appointment and sought instead the appointment of Yurii Zaitsev, a senior member of his staff and an adviser to former Novosibirsk governor Vitalii Mukha, whom Tolokonskii had defeated in the region's 2000 gubernatorial elections. Informed sources believe that Zaitsev is close to the law enforcement agencies. In any case, the appointment of one of the envoy's staff to this position shows that Drachevskii has no intention of giving up his oversight over property rights, one of the most important areas of activity for the federal authorities.

Interacting with the Power Ministries

The envoy has several channels for working with the power ministries. Deputy Envoy Vadim Goncharov, who built his career in these agencies, handles this portfolio on a day-to-day basis. The heads of the okrug branches of several ministries also work directly with Drachevskii, including the Siberian chiefs of the Ministry of Internal Affairs (MVD), the General Procurator's office, and the Justice Ministry. Drachevskii and his deputies frequently meet with such officials in his office.

While the envoy claims to oversee all appointments at the regional level in the power ministries, it is difficult to say how effective these approvals really are. Since his appointment, there has been little turnover among regional police chiefs, a situation analogous to what obtains in the Central okrug. Putin does not seem to be willing to use his power over appointments to force change.

In the case of the okrug's relations with the FSB, these seem to consist more of cooperation than of intrusive supervision. Direct links have been facilitated by the fact that, as mentioned earlier, two deputy envoys and three CFIs previously worked for the FSB. By hiring these people, Drachevskii undoubtedly gains access to inside knowledge about how the FSB functions. However, he also gives the agency he is supposed to be supervising access to his own decision-making processes. Evidently, this is deliberate (see page 307, this volume).

Even though the Ministry for Emergency Situations does not have an okrug office in Novosibirsk, Drachevskii maintains particularly close ties with it. Detailing his office's response to emergencies is one of his favorite themes. Thus an okrug briefing claimed that close cooperation between him and the ministry prevented floods from damaging several Siberian regions in spring 2001. Drachevskii also lists cooperation with the Federal Border Guard Service among his activities. In particular, his office helped organize additional oversight of checkpoints along the border with Kazakhstan, through which many illegally imported Chinese goods enter Russia.[15] However, it seems that these measures have had no effect on the flow of smuggled goods into Siberia.

Tensions Grow with Increased Federal Concentration in Novosibirsk

Novosibirsk is increasingly becoming the main base for federal operations in Siberia and some federal offices previously located in other regions are moving to the city. In summer 2002 the Ministry of Foreign Affairs opened an office in Novosibirsk, with the envoy's staff actively facilitating the operation (earlier, the ministry's closest office was in Barnaul). Most likely, only the Ministry for Emergency Situations will remain in Krasnoyarsk because that city has a large air base and is centrally located.

The increasing importance of Novosibirsk as the "capital of Siberia" is fostering discontent in other powerful regions (Krasnoyarsk, Irkutsk, and Tomsk). It is re-creating at the Siberian level the kind of feelings that many Russian regions have toward Moscow. In both cases the location of administrative power does not correspond with the centers of revenue-generating economic activities (although Novosibirsk, like Moscow for Russia, certainly serves as the region's financial and intellectual hub). This tension undoubtedly limits the envoy's effectiveness in such a vast area. Of course, the problem of interregional rivalry is not unique to Siberia; it is also apparent in other okrugs, including the Far East (Khabarovsk v. Vladivostok) and the South, where many regions are jealous of Rostov's new prominence.

Relations with Governors

Drachevskii's relations with the okrug's governors are businesslike and free of conflict, at least in public. In stark contrast to the situation in the Urals and the Far East, the governors have never directly criticized his work. The peace and concord result in part from the near absence in the Siberian regions of powerful political figures who are capable of pursuing a political line that differs from the president's. Even the relatively independent and well-known governors, such as Kemerovo's Aman Tuleev and Krasnoyarsk's Aleksandr Lebed (until his untimely death in a helicopter crash on April 28, 2002), refrained from criticizing Drachevskii. Of course, the increasingly frequent decisions of the stronger governors, notably Tuleev, to ignore meetings of the Okrug Council suggest at least implicitly that Drachevskii is not as important to them as he would like to be. And they sometimes criticize the federal authorities, even severely, when, for example, the Ministry of Natural Resources or the electric monopoly EES tries to strong-arm them on issues like the granting of licenses or the amount of money to be paid to a region as rent for the use of a natural resource. But they do not direct their criticism at the envoy, whom they are more likely to try to attract to support their region's cause.

Perhaps the most important reason for the envoy's peaceful coexistence with the governors is that he does not interfere with the local elites' key interests. In other okrugs, such as the Urals and the Far East, there has been more open tension between the governors and the envoy because the latter's policies have been less conciliatory than Drachevskii's. However, in Siberia bringing regional laws into line with federal norms hardly affected the status of the regional authorities (in contrast to the situation in regions like Sakha, Tatarstan, and Bashkortostan in the Far East and Volga okrugs). The only place where the regional elite expressed dissatisfaction with the process of bringing regional laws into line was in the Altai Republic, where the parliament vociferously opposed the campaign to change the republic's constitution. But even this situation was probably the result of internal republican politics, where the parliament sabotaged all the initiatives of the unpopular (now former) governor, Semen Zubakin. In most other cases, the regional parliaments and governors, under pressure from the procurator and the Justice Ministry, corrected their laws and regulations without making complaints.

The leaders of the poor regions, which are dependent on federal subsidies for their survival, naturally treat Drachevskii with great reverence. Even though he does not directly control the disbursement of federal funds, the leaders whose constituents depend heavily on Moscow see him as an ally in securing access to the federal budget. During the rare trips by Drachevskii or his deputies to these regions, the locals' expressions of love for the envoy can reach comic proportions. When he visited Ust-Orda Buryatia, Governor Viktor Maleev gave him a Buryat robe, dagger, and hat, and then brought him a roasted sheep's head at a banquet, a honor reserved for the most respected guest. During the visit, Maleev constantly referred to the envoy as the "Governor-General of Siberia."

In at least two cases, Drachevskii intervened in the internal political battles of specific regions. For years, Omsk Region (and particularly the city of Omsk) suffered from the conflict between Omsk governor Leonid Polezhaev and Omsk mayor Valeriy Roshchupkin. Ultimately—with, it is widely believed, Drachevskii's involvement—Roshchupkin was appointed a deputy minister in Moscow and later became first deputy minister for natural resources. In this case the conflict was resolved by removing one of the key participants. Of course, changing the individuals does not remove the underlying problem that both region and city are fighting for scarce resources. However, the arrival of new blood could pave the way for innovative ideas.

In the other case, the members of the Irkutsk regional legislature could not for a long time elect a speaker, largely because Governor Boris Govorin wanted to place a loyal ally in the post but did not have enough deputies on his side to do so. Ultimately, on the recommendation of Moscow—probably of the PA—the legislature elected the director of the Irkutsk electric company Irkutskenergo, Viktor Borovskii (one of the governor's opponents) as the speaker. Observers believed that the envoy had played a role, and certainly, at an informal meeting, Borovskii named Drachevskii as his "godfather."[16] Within a year, though, Borovskii lost the post, as well as his position at Irkutskenergo, and the governor was able to secure the election of one of his allies.

In exchange for loyalty to the federal authorities, Drachevskii is willing to overlook various gubernatorial transgressions, provided they do not visibly harm the president's overall line. For example, during Siberia's gubernatorial campaigns there have been numerous violations of the electoral law when incumbents use the extensive resources they command to unfair advantage. Even more flagrant are the attacks on the freedom of the media in several Siberian regions. For example, there has been no free press in Omsk and Kemerovo for a long time, and most independent journalists were forced either to leave their profession or to move out of these areas. The Tyva president does not even permit opposition journalists to enter his office building. In some cases, regional officials have not allowed journalists critical of them into press conferences given by Drachevskii. The envoy's staff has not intervened in these cases, even though they likely knew what was going on.

Regional Elections and the Role of the Presidential Envoy

In contrast to most of the other envoys, during his first two and a half years in office Drachevskii has assiduously avoided publicly supporting any of the candidates in Siberia's gubernatorial elections. Moreover, whenever a staff member has announced plans to run for public office, he has immediately asked for a resignation. For example, Yevgenii Vasilev had to leave his post when he competed (unsuccessfully) in Evenkia's gubernatorial election. At least two other staff members had to quit after announcing plans to run for seats in regional legislatures.

Drachevskii's neutrality in these elections is certainly commendable, in that he has avoided using his public office for political purposes. Even in the high stakes gubernatorial elections of fall 2002 in wealthy Krasnoyarsk Krai, he limited himself to declaring both of the candidates worthy. The battle pitted the

speaker of the Krasnoyarsk legislature Aleksandr Uss, backed by Oleg Deripaska's Russian Aluminum, against Taimyr governor Aleksandr Khloponin,
who had the support of Vladimir Potanin's Interros. The envoy merely sent
one of his deputies to observe the campaign. By contrast, the envoy to the Far
East okrug, Konstantin Pulikovskii, certainly damaged the prestige of his office during his unsuccessful intervention in the Primorskii Krai elections following Governor Nazdratenko's resignation.

During the period between Drachevskii's appointment and the end of 2002,
twelve of Siberia's sixteen regions held gubernatorial elections. Overall, the
political situation in the okrug was relatively stable. In eight of the twelve cases
incumbent governors won another term. Only the weak governor of Altai Republic, Semen Zubakin, lost his post to an experienced Moscow politician,
Agrarian party leader Mikhail Lapshin. The Kremlin could not have been
happy about this victory, since the leftist Lapshin replaced the only governor
with ties to the Union of Right-wing Forces. Further, Lapshin is a relatively independent and unpredictable figure, who, even though elderly (born in 1934),
might in the future cause the Kremlin trouble.

In most cases, the incumbent politicians aggressively used their administrative resources to secure victory. If Drachevskii had wanted to, he could easily have found numerous violations of the country's electoral laws during
these campaigns. But he did not. Apparently the Kremlin was happy with the
status quo, or it did not believe that an intervention would be successful. Regardless of who is governor, the Kremlin has strong controls over most of
Siberia's regions, since they are dependent on federal subsidies. For example,
the budgets of Tyva and the Altai Republic rely on federal funds for more than
90 percent of their income. Most regional leaders do not want to risk losing
Kremlin money by making political waves.

The real change in Siberian elections, reflecting broader changes throughout
the country, is the new and often open struggle for top political posts between
various financial–industrial groups, mostly based in Moscow. In Taimyr,
Evenkia, and Krasnoyarsk, former top executives of key regional enterprises
now head the regional administrations and are—obviously—not entirely independent from the vested interests of their former employers, who may indeed, in some cases, keep them covertly on the payroll. This trend started with
the election of Roman Abramovich as governor of Chukotka and continued
with the victories of Norilsk Nickel's Aleksandr Khloponin in Taimyr; YUKOS
executive Boris Zolotarev in Evenkia; Khloponin again, in fall 2002, in Krasnoyarsk; and then, to replace him, another Norilsk Nickel nominee in Taimyr. Of
course, powerful companies have for some years supported specific gubernatorial campaigns. Siberian Aluminum backed the election of Aleksei Lebed in
Khakasia, and Anatolii Bykov's Krasnoyarsk Aluminum Factory supported

Aleksandr Lebed's election in Krasnoyarsk. But now some of the business executives themselves are seeking public office.

Overall, in the more than seventy gubernatorial elections conducted in Russia between the beginning of 2000 and the end of 2002, eight businessmen took the top regional office.[17] Thus businessmen make up about 10 percent of Russia's governors. This is an important minority, but one that only tells part of the story. Below, we will examine Drachevskii's relations with Russia's most powerful financial–industrial groups.

As regards elections to regional legislatures, in the future the envoys will have to pay more attention to them. According to a new federal law, beginning in July 2003 all such elections must fill at least half the seats by party list (Krasnoyarsk was one of five regions that already employed this system). However, political parties are, as elsewhere in Russia, poorly developed in Siberia, and the party list approach to elections is virtually unknown. Thus, with the pro-Kremlin United Russia enjoying little popular support and with the better organized, though less visible, Communist Party enjoying more, the envoy's staff will have to work hard to secure respectable representation for the main pro-Kremlin party in the regional legislatures.

The Envoy's Influence on the Selection of Federation Council Members

The reform of the Federation Council, begun in 2000, further undermined the already relatively weak position of the Siberian governors in Moscow. Broadly speaking, the council's new leadership is closely allied with the president. Most of its Siberian delegates are either Moscow politicians or people loyal to the Kremlin. This situation is partly a result of Drachevskii's efforts.

The best example of the envoy's influence was the November 2001 attempt by the Buryatia republic's parliament to appoint the former federal General Procurator Yurii Skuratov as its representative to the council. Yeltsin had fired Skuratov because his investigations of Kremlin corruption were hitting too close to home. However, because the constitution gives the council a decisive say in the general procurator's appointment and dismissal, and because the old council supported Skuratov, he was not forced out until Putin came to power.

In Buryatia, when the republican procurator protested that parliament had elected Skuratov in violation of its own procedures (he was the only candidate on the ballot), it soon fell into line and chose another senator. During the uproar surrounding these events, Drachevskii did not say anything publicly. However, it seems that the "block Skuratov" maneuvers were carried out with his quiet involvement and following instructions from the PA.

Another example, concerning Tyva, also illustrates how the Kremlin has been able to get its allies appointed to the Federation Council. The new senators from that region were initially the former head of the republican FSB, Chanmyr Udunbara, and the former head of Mezhprombank (International Industrial Bank) and a personal friend of Putin, Sergei Pugachev, who had no relationship to Tyva before his selection as senator. In 2002 Udunbara was replaced by Lyubov Narusova, the widow of Putin's political sponsor in the 1990s, Saint Petersburg mayor Anatolii Sobchak.

Pugachev is a controversial figure in Russian politics but one who clearly has extensive political and economic clout. Although he evidently got his post with Kremlin support, the Tyva authorities also stand to gain. With his appointment of Pugachev, President Oorzhak won the gratitude of the Kremlin and also found a generous sponsor for his reelection campaign, which was ultimately successful. It is hard to determine what role Drachevskii played in these events since, on the surface, everything seems to have been arranged between Moscow and the Tyvan authorities.

In other prominent cases, the Federation Council became—at least as far as its Siberian representatives were concerned—both a dumping ground for politicians defeated in elections and a training ground for wizards in the devious art of electoral campaigning who had made a strong impression on the PA. One of Evenkia's representatives is Yurii Sharandin, a former member of the Moscow city Duma and Evenkia governor Boris Zolotarev's top campaign manager. The former deputy chairman of the Saint Petersburg Mayor's Committee on Economic Development, and an acquaintance of Putin, Leonid Bindar, represents Taimyr, as does former Tyumen governor Leonid Roketskii, who shortly before his appointment lost his bid for reelection.

There are numerous other examples. It is hard to believe that these individuals were appointed senators without the support of the PA. It is even harder to imagine they will work uncompromisingly in the interests of the regions they ostensibly represent. In these instances, it seems that Drachevskii's role has been less of an autonomous actor and more of a transmission belt, projecting the power of the Kremlin into the regions.

Crime and Corruption

Despite the Putin-era reforms and the claims of official statistics, the MVD remains unable to cope with what the population feels to be rising levels of crime in the okrug. Of particular concern, the number of gun crimes is widely believed to be increasing.[18] Additionally, there have been several attacks on border guard units working to detain smugglers.

In Tyva especially, crime has seriously damaged entire sectors of the economy, particularly agriculture, where cattle theft is a major problem. Okrug-level meetings seem unlikely to generate solutions because of the prevalence of corruption throughout Russian officialdom. In conditions where criminals are protected at the highest level, none of the power ministries—including the FSB, the Procuracy, the courts, and the police agencies—can secure just punishment for their crimes.

Real change would come to Tyva only if the federal authorities sent in a team of outside investigators to tackle the situation. However, all appeals in Tyva for such intervention go unanswered. Periodic removals of law enforcement officials—such as the dismissal of procurators, MVD ministers, and their deputies that occurred in 2002 in Tyva and Khakasia—make little difference. For the envoy's staff and okrug leaders of the power ministries, it is much more important to send Moscow glowing accounts of their work than to actually attempt to impose order.

Assessing the exact level of corruption among federal officials in Siberia is difficult, but the okrug clearly provides fertile ground for abusing one's office. Its large cities and vast resources are attractive targets for organized crime.[19] Such groups naturally find lucrative targets in the oil, gas, and forestry industries.

The various monopolies in the region are an area where foul play is particularly likely. For example, the oil giant Sibneft has its key refinery in Omsk and sells 100 percent of the gasoline on the Omsk retail market. This company backed Governor Leonid Polezhaev in the region's 1999 elections. Sibneft uses its extensive economic clout and access to political levers to block other companies from entering the local market. One might expect the local branch of the Anti-Monopoly Ministry to investigate the problem. However, the federal officials of this agency have turned a blind eye, either for lack of professionalism or in return for bribes.

There are many similar examples. In Novosibirsk the Moscow firm Video International and companies associated with it control 90 percent of the television advertising market. (In Russia as a whole, this company has managed to acquire 70 percent of this market.) Many believe the charges made by the national media that press minister Mikhail Lesin, who has wide-ranging business interests connected with Video International, which he cofounded, receives substantial profit from this company. Yakov London, the head of the Novosibirsk State Television and Radio Company, who was appointed with Lesin's backing, actively supports the company in Novosibirsk and is often seen with its local executives.[20] To place an ad on state-controlled television now requires working with an agency controlled by the company. Advertising agencies independent of it can only place ads by bowing to its conditions. All attempts by competing agencies to have it declared a monopolist have failed, even though its 90 percent market share is much larger than the maximum allowed by law.

Likewise, Russian Aluminum, which has all of its main production facilities in Siberia and controls 70 percent of Russia's overall aluminum production, has not been declared a monopolist. The federal Anti-Monopoly Ministry approved the merger that created the company in 2000, even though it clearly violated the ministry's goals. The aluminum business is considered one of the most corrupt sectors of the Russian economy.

The Presidential Envoy's Economic Policies and Influence

The Battle over Siberia's Strategic Development Plan

Drachevskii's main tool for influencing economic processes in Siberia is his ability to monitor and coordinate the work of the federal agencies in the regions. In theory, he stands above the territorial branches of the ministries. However, when the interests of the latter and the envoy differ, he is not in a position to dictate to them. The evolution of Siberia's Strategic Development Plan illustrates what happens when the interests of the envoy and the ministries come into conflict. In this battle, Drachevskii defended regional interests against other federal agencies.

When visiting Novosbirsk in November 2000, Putin commissioned a strategic development plan for Siberia that would define the main directions of Siberia's social and economic progress for the next ten to twenty years. He gave the task to a group of scholars at the Economics Institute of the Russian Academy of Sciences in Novosibirsk. In addition, the financing and supervision of their work was assigned to a new Center for Strategic Initiatives, which was specially founded and financed by corporations like Norilsk Nickel; Siberian Aluminum; the Al'yans group; and Yevrazkholding, a vertically integrated holding company with interests in coal mines, ore processing, metal production, and other fields. Not surprisingly, since these large export-oriented companies were sponsoring the project, they used the opportunity to lobby for lower transportation costs for their raw materials and output.

To further complicate things, it was announced that the work would also be performed in close collaboration with a body of different economic philosophy, the Center for Strategic Research. This is the Novosibirsk branch of the Moscow research institute used by German Gref, the monetarist minister of economics and trade.

The scholars sent Putin the first draft of the strategic plan in July 2001, and Drachevskii claimed that he had a positive opinion of it. But winning approval for the plan turned out to be much more complicated.

Shortly after the scholars delivered the plan, officials at Gref's ministry rewrote it in a way that eliminated many of the benefits that the authors had hoped to receive for Siberia. In particular, Gref's team removed suggestions for reducing railroad fees for hauling freight to and from Siberia. The distances between Siberia and its suppliers and markets are very large, making it expensive for Siberians to buy products manufactured elsewhere and raising the cost of their own products so that they are not competitive in other markets. Additionally, the ministry changed the Siberian scholars' proposal to split the tax income derived from the exploitation of Siberia's mineral resources fifty-fifty between the federal and regional governments. It chose to preserve the status quo, under which the federal government received 80 percent of the income from the use of natural resources, leaving the regions with only 20 percent.

As soon as he found out about these changes, Drachevskii gave press conferences designed, as he said, to unmask the "underhanded intrigues" of the bureaucrats in Gref's ministry, who allegedly sought to reduce Siberia to a raw material appendage for the rest of Russia. The battle revolved around who would benefit from the use of Siberia's natural resources: the federal government or the regions themselves. Drachevskii sought to defend regional interests, while the ministry claimed the tax income from the resources should be used to benefit Russia as a whole, including—but not disproportionately—Siberia.

In response to the Siberians' request for special treatment and subsidies, the ministry argued that only enterprises that could operate profitably without such benefits had the right to exist. As a result of these starkly contrasting positions, the adoption of the strategy was postponed indefinitely.

In this dispute, Drachevskii for the first time entered into an open conflict with one of Russia's most powerful ministries, headed by a minister with close ties to Putin. In January 2002 he even made a special trip to Tomsk to meet with Deputy Prime Minister Aleksei Kudrin, who oversaw the work of Gref's ministry and was in the region on an inspection mission. Kudrin and he met behind closed doors to discuss the controversial issues at stake. However, Kudrin refused to yield, and the two sides did not reach agreement.

The next month, Drachevskii met with Putin and tried to win him over. After the meeting, Drachevskii claimed that Putin was ready to sign off on his version of the plan. However, in subsequent battles Drachevskii apparently lost out. In presenting the plan to the government at the end of April 2002, Gref's deputy claimed that he had managed to convert the Siberian authors of the program to the ministry's position. Ultimately, though, as Drachevskii's staff admitted, the key question of dividing the income from the use of natural resources remained unresolved. Moreover, there was no final decision on providing preferences to the Siberian regions in terms of transportation prices.

The battle over the strategic plan demonstrated the vulnerability of Drachevskii's position. On one hand, he must defend Siberian interests, while on the other, as the president's envoy, he must implement the policy of the government. His lack of real power over economic issues, especially control of funding, severely constrained his ability to influence the outcome of the battle. Ultimately, the contents of the plan depended on which federal bureaucrat had greater influence over the prime minister and president. It became clear that even though Drachevskii was able to win verbal support from Putin, the president's words were not sufficient to determine the policy outcome.

Since spring 2002, when the government formally adopted the plan, the document has simply dropped out of public discussion. No final, approved text has been published, and its status is not clear. From the envoy's reluctant and ambiguous comments, it would appear as though some sort of compromise, evidently biased in favor of Moscow, was reached behind the scenes. In reality, though, the plan seems now to be merely a set of nonbinding recommendations that are not supported by any funding.

Relations with "Oligarchs"

Shortly after his appointment, Drachevskii set up relations with key members of Russia's business elite who operate in Siberia. He met with, among others, Norilsk Nickel owner Vladimir Potanin and Base Element owner Oleg Deripaska. Managers of such corporations visit his offices in Novosibirsk regularly.

Like Putin, the envoy seems to have especially close relations with Deripaska, who early on provided financial support to set up an okrug-wide "Siberian Television" (for discussion of this initiative, see the section on the media, p. 238). The Deripaska group's main economic assets are mostly concentrated in the okrug, and they include the Krasnoyarsk, Bratsk, and Sayansk aluminum factories, as well as the Achinsk Alumina Combine. Putin's ties became clearer in the winter of 2001, when he made a trip to Khakasia that he tried to keep secret. He skied at the Deripaska-owned Gora Gladen'kaya resort, not far from the Sayansk factory, and stayed at Deripaska's hunting lodge.

At the same time, Drachevskii's top aides have generally shied away from taking the side of one or another financial–industrial group. Both his first deputies worked in the civil service for many years and have not apparently lobbied on behalf of any business groups in Siberia. One clear exception is that the former head of his Finance and Economics Department, Vasilii Kiselev, had close ties to the management of SUAL. But he left the envoy's staff to run for a seat in the Novosibirsk legislature. Most of the CFIs come from the civil service (including some regional party first secretaries from the Soviet era) or the power ministries, and there is no evidence that any of them have ties to big business.

There may be some connection between the above facts and the noteworthy phenomenon that it is precisely in the Siberian okrug, much more than elsewhere, that a number of oligarchs have taken direct political power. Naturally enough, they have focused on becoming governors of regions with promising economic futures. This merger of political and economic power clearly has big benefits for the companies involved, including, perhaps, making it easier for them to deal with pressures from the envoy and his staff. It remains to be seen, however, whether the businessmen will prove any more adept at ruling their regions than the politicians they have replaced.

Let us look at some specific cases, starting with one briefly discussed earlier. In the Taimyr Autonomous Okrug, Aleksandr Khloponin, the general director of Norilsk Nickel, won the gubernatorial elections in 2001. He had come to Norilsk as a young Muscovite financier. He faced a daunting challenge because the giant plant had accumulated huge debts and was not paying its workers. He turned the situation around, gaining the trust of the workers and building a strong team of managers. After the collapse of the ruble in 1998, the plant became extremely profitable. Through his election victory, Norilsk Nickel guaranteed itself political support in the region where its business is located and also replaced a rather inconvenient governor.[21] However, as governor, Khloponin had to face the problem that Taimyr needed money to address the social needs of its population. Naturally, the only source of such income was his old employer, so he had to turn to Norilsk Nickel for the necessary funds. One complication was that the company was sending most of its tax payments to Krasnoyarsk Krai. Thanks to Russia's complex federal system, although the Taimyr Autonomous Okrug is one of Russia's eighty-nine regions and has its own governor, it is also a constituent part of Krasnoyarsk Krai. As governor, Khloponin waged a campaign for a more favorable distribution of taxes in the krai that would give Taimyr a greater share of this revenue, much of which, after all, was generated in Taimyr.[22] Although he was not able to fully resolve these issues, he did improve the situation by vastly increasing the reliability of the delivery of supplies to his far-north region.

After a brief and seemingly successful tenure in Taimyr, Khloponin went on to win the governorship of the entire Krasnoyarsk Krai in fall 2002, following the death of its governor Aleksandr Lebed in a helicopter crash. From the vantage point of his new job, Khloponin will now need Norilsk Nickel money to deal with the problems of the entire krai. We should note that during a trip to Krasnoyarsk in March 2002 (before Lebed's death) Putin clearly supported the unification of the three parts of Krasnoyarsk into a fully unitary region, a change that would help Khloponin in his new position. However, by the end of the year no progress on this issue had been made.

In an analogous situation, a vice president of the Yukos oil company, Boris Zolotarev, won election as governor of Evenkia in 2001. The region has the smallest and least dense population among all of Russia's eighty-nine regions (twenty thousand residents in a region that is larger than France). However, there are several potentially rich oil and gas deposits for which Yukos holds the development rights. Now Yukos has guaranteed that the region's governor will provide political support for its initiatives.

Following Zolotarev's election, the company stepped up its economic activities in the region. It started developing infrastructure for future work, even though the local offshore zone and the related tax benefits have been discontinued. Thanks to its increased activities during the winter months of early 2002, the tax revenue of the local budget grew ten times, from 10.8 million rubles to 111.9 million rubles.[23]

One way in which Yukos increased Evenkia's tax income was by making several large-scale oil sales through dummy companies registered in the region. On March 31, 2002, the company Samara Oil and Gas (Samaraneftegaz), a subsidiary of Yukos, sold to an entity identified as Ratibor 200 million rubles' worth of oil. The buyer was registered at a wooden house in the village of Tura (Evenkia's capital). Not surprisingly, the local district officials knew nothing about the firms involved or the deal itself, which was several times larger than the district's entire annual tax revenue in the previous year. It seems that this deal was not the first of its kind and will not be the last. Observers believe that Yukos is making such sales through Evenkia to increase the flow of money into the local budget so that these funds can be spent on the development of local infrastructure (roads, housing, energy systems, etc.). In this way, Yukos likely seeks to avoid spending its own money to develop Evenkia's infrastructure while potentially benefiting from such projects as part of its future development plans.[24]

Local and Moscow-based "oligarchs" have long fought over Krasnoyarsk Krai's lucrative assets. Before Putin took office, the most famous conflict revolved around Russian Aluminum's eventually successful effort to wrest away the local businessman Anatolii Bykov's controlling stake in the Krasnoyarsk Aluminum Factory. Despite this loss and his connections with organized crime, Bykov remained popular among the population, as his victory in the 2001 krai legislative elections testified. His electoral bloc took 17 percent in the party-list voting, putting it in second place, and Bykov himself won a seat in a single-member district race.

Also well known is the battle between Russian Aluminum and the Unified Energy System (EES) electricity monopoly over the price of electricity for the Krasnoyarsk Aluminum Factory. The price of electricity is important because it makes up a large share of the cost of producing aluminum. Russian Aluminum has yet to accept EES's claim that it owes the utility 3.2 billion rubles for past consumption, a debt that could conceivably bankrupt the factory. Additionally, Moscow oligarchs, represented by the MDM group on one side, and Mezhprombank and Rosneft (International Industrial Bank and Russian Oil) on the other, have been waging a long-running battle to privatize the 44.2 percent state stake in the Krasugol' (Red Coal) coal company. These conflicts are hardly likely to be resolved soon, especially since Khloponin, and any other Krasnoyarsk governor, faces a daunting challenge in trying to balance the interests of all the major players.

Drachevskii did play a minor role in resolving the conflict around Irkutskenergo, the most important business dispute to be resolved so far during his tenure. This electricity utility is unusual in Russia for being one of four not controlled by EES. The struggle basically involved two disputes in one. On one hand, Siberia's two major aluminum companies (Bazovyi Element and SUAL) wanted to gain control of the utility in order to keep electricity prices down for their aluminum output. These companies were successful, gaining control of a majority of seats on the board at the June 30, 2001, meeting. They have worked since then to keep prices low. Drachevskii has apparently played a peace-keeping role in the process, helping to smooth over disputes.[25] However, he also seems to have given in to corporate interests, since the companies benefit so much from Irkutskenergo keeping the price of electricity low.

The other dispute pitted the federal government against the Irkutsk regional government. They fought over who would control the state's 40 percent stake in the utility. The 1996 power-sharing agreement between Irkutsk and the federal government defined the stake as joint federal and regional property, which meant in practice that the region controlled it. However, toward the end of the 1990s, and especially under Putin, the federal government decided that it wanted to gain control over this property.[26] Ultimately, in July 2002 the Supreme Arbitrage Court ruled that the federal government would have exclusive control over the stake and thereby delivered a major blow to the regional government.[27] However, while the latter no longer has an ownership stake in the utility, it continues to set electricity prices through its control of the Regional Energy Commission.[28] Thus it still has considerable influence. One should note that in this part of the dispute, the court, rather than Drachevskii, played the main role.

One of Drachevskii's early pet projects was to develop closer economic ties between the enterprises of Siberia. His staff suggested that local factories buy equipment and raw materials from Siberian producers, instead of suppliers in distant Russian regions or abroad. In particular, he recommended that the giant Norilsk Nickel reorient its purchasing to local sources. However, the idea has not been implemented. Norilsk managers continue to purchase machinery and supplies where they believe necessary, rather than where he prefers.

Although the envoy does not ultimately have much clout when dealing with big business, he does appear to monitor it carefully and to report regularly to Moscow. Major new business ventures in the okrug evidently have to receive his approval, as suggested by the following episode. Recounted by Vladimir

Kozhin, a deputy director of the PA and head of Putin's personal chancellery, his illuminating story came in response to a journalist's question. Was it true that some firms were using their pull with Putin's chancellery to advance their interests through the bureaucracy? Kozhin replied:

> Recently, envoy Drachevskii called me and said: "Listen, they've brought me a contract written on your note-paper and asked me to support it. The sum involved is several times more than the budget of Novosibirsk region." I say: read on. Soon everything became clear. The document was headed in huge letters "Chancellery of the President of the RF," but down below it read in small type: affiliate company so and so. . . . I told Drachevsky: call the police.[29]

Relations with Local Business Groups

While Drachevskii's press service claims that he actively participates in successful local and Siberian business projects, it is hard to know if this is really true. For example, the service announced that he was closely involved in 2000 in setting up Sibmashkholding, a group of the okrug's largest agricultural equipment manufacturers, including the Krasnoyarsk Combine Factory, the Altai Tractor Factory, and a Barnaul machine-building enterprise. However, whether the venture was successful in a real sense seems doubtful. The purpose of the new entity was to increase local sales of Siberian-produced farm equipment, and it was seeking to expand. Thanks to the lobbying efforts of its managers, several regions purchased large orders of combines made in Krasnoyarsk, even though these harvesters were of low quality and used old designs. For example, Sibmashkholding signed an agreement with the Khakasian Republic, thanks to using the active support of the brother governors (until his death, Aleksandr Lebed governed Krasnoyarsk, while his younger brother Aleksei still rules in Khakasia). The Novosibirsk regional administration also purchased a large order of combines. While the envoy's press service claims that he played a decisive role in facilitating these deals of doubtful value, we should of course bear in mind that its claim may not be accurate.

Drachevskii's efforts to maintain low energy prices for local business were definitely less than successful. In June 2001 he assisted in the conclusion of an agreement among Kemerovo and Krasnoyarsk coal producers, the railroads ministry, and other interested parties. It required all parties not to raise prices before the autumn, to allow the regions to build up supplies of coal at relatively inexpensive summer prices. However, the agreement quickly collapsed. The price of coal began rising in the middle of the summer, partly through the interventions of Kemerovo governor Aman Tuleev, whose region is a major coal producer.

Despite the collapse of this project, Drachevskii's staff claimed that the envoy's efforts made it possible to better prepare for the winter heating season, including supplying the northern regions with fuel. Nevertheless, most observers agreed that the recently elected governors of the northern regions, with much greater financial resources at their command, were responsible for the improved northern deliveries.

The Envoy's International Economic Activity

As noted earlier, Drachevskii is the only envoy with professional experience as a diplomat. In Siberia, he has been particularly active in developing relations with Mongolia, which borders several Siberian regions and has three consulates in the okrug. He has visited the country several times; indeed, it is the only country apart from Canada that he has visited in his capacity as okrug envoy. He has held meetings with Mongolian delegations in Russia, and cosponsored the setting up of intergovernmental commissions on topics including trade, science, technology, and border issues. As a result, relations between the two countries have really improved. Border station facilities are being modernized, and crossing points are being opened to citizens of third countries. Additionally, a cooperation memorandum signed in November 2001 resolved the problem of veterinary monitoring on the border, which opened the Siberian market for Mongolian meat. However, Russian meat producers are now concerned about the increased level of Mongolian imports.

Cross-border relations with another important Siberian trade partner, Kazakhstan, are also improving. The envoy has, for example, pursued talks with the Kazakhstanis on combating smuggling and on the need for Kazakhstan to stop hindering Siberian trade with Kyrgyzstan, which it has been doing by blocking the transit transportation of certain goods. Drachevskii has not been particularly active in regard to China, although he cochairs for Russia the main umbrella group for promoting better relations, the Russian–Chinese Committee for Peace, Friendship and Development in the Twenty-First Century.

In May 2002, the Ministry of Foreign Affairs opened in Novosibirsk an office for liaison with the Siberian okrug, under the leadership of Special Ambassador Nikolai Pavlov. Siberia was the third okrug, following the Urals and the South, to get such an office. The ministry already has three regional offices in the okrug (in Omsk, Barnaul, and Chita), and their number is likely to grow.

Once the new office had been opened, the foreign ministry and Drachevskii announced that they would work together closely to develop political and economic relations with neighboring countries. On June 4, 2002, the envoy held a meeting on international issues that brought together all the relevant federal officials in the okrug and all the deputy governors responsible for foreign relations. He explained to them that from now on the okrug branch of the foreign ministry would coordinate the regional governments' international activities. As his first deputy Anatolii Shcherbinin said, Moscow would strictly monitor the international activities of the regions to make sure that their ties with other countries did not harm Russia's state interests.

Relations with Local Government and the Media

Local Government

Local government in Russia is in bad shape. Mayors usually have few autonomous sources of funding and are often subject to the whims of their governor. Putin's reforms have only increased the level of centralization in the country, in many cases exacerbating the situation. In this regard, the situation in Siberia is typical of the rest of the country. The following case history gives an idea of some of the problems.

The governor of Novosibirsk region continues to appoint mayors by decree, even though federal law requires that they be popularly elected. It is in his interest to retain the existing system at least until December 2003, when he will stand for reelection. Having mayors who owe their jobs to him will naturally make it easier for him to use them in his campaign.

When the regional procurator filed a protest about this blatant violation of the constitution, the governor's administration employed a number of delaying tactics. In particular, he proposed that rural areas in the region elect councils, which would then hire professional managers to serve in place of elected mayors. The procurator then demanded that the law be brought into line with federal norms by August 3, 2002. However, although the legislature now did this at last, only one gesture was made to obey the law. Instead of holding elections throughout the region, new councils were elected in only six towns. The councils were then pressured into confirming in office the mayors whom the governor had earlier appointed. Meanwhile, regional officials say that the law will be fully observed in 2004, when elections will be held everywhere, following the election in which the governor plans to be reelected—with the help of all the mayors he has personally appointed.

Even though Drachevskii is usually a strong advocate of bringing local legislation into line with federal norms, he said at a press conference that in this case everything is proceeding within the framework of the law. Perhaps he is treating Novosibirsk governor Tolokonskii with kid gloves because they have nearby offices in the same city and talk to each other often. Whatever the case, though, since the regional procurator has fallen silent, the lawless authoritarianism of the governor will continue for the time being.

Relations with the Media

Despite its gigantic size, the Siberian okrug has done more than the other okrugs to create a so-called unified information space *(edinoe informatsionnoe prostranstvo)*. The basic goal is to influence, through a variety of incentives and pressures, the content of the regional media so that news stories reflect the point of view of the okrug authorities and thus of the federal government. While the national television networks already present Moscow's views on national issues, the okrug has sought to bring the government closer to the people by presenting federal perspectives on matters of Siberian or regional interest. Naturally, a corollary goal is to reduce the control of the governors over the regional media and make it harder for them to disseminate a message that opposes or diverges from Moscow's. Drachevskii has sought to put his stamp on Siberian information flows by setting up a center to coordinate the work of Siberian journalists and by establishing a Siberian television network.

One of his first steps was the creation of an Okrug Information Center (OIC). Its purpose was to work with journalists across the region, feeding them information in the form favored by the okrug and Moscow. Deputy Envoy Nikolai Reshetnyak, a former Moscow journalist who answered to Drachevsky for issues of the media and public affairs, recruited the following as the OIC's partners: ITAR-TASS; the *Business Tuesday (Delovoi vtornik)* insert to *Russian Newspaper (Rossiiskaya gazeta);* the military paper *Red Star (Krasnaya zvezda);* and several other publications and electronic media. ITAR-TASS now uses the OIC as its base of operations. These partners are owned or controlled by the state. The OIC's employees do not appear on the envoy's payroll, but they do receive their salaries from off-budget sources that are not publicly known. The center uses facilities located in the envoy's Novosibirsk offices and now has branches in Irkutsk and Omsk.

Though Reshetnyak organized several large meetings with Siberian editors during his eighteen-month tenure, he never succeeded in gaining much influence over the media.[30] Despite Drachevskii's attempts to change the situation, the governors continue to control the majority of Siberian publications, especially in the more authoritarian regions like Omsk, Kemerovo, and Tyva. The other papers either belong to local business groups or, like *Kommersant*, which inserts a special section for Siberians, are edited in Moscow. Each Siberian governor has at least one or two regional publications under his control and heavily dominates the local press, which is highly dependent on subsidies from the regional budget. Naturally, no governor will give up this ability to manipulate public opinion without a struggle. Regional editors have generally rejected the idea of taking direction from okrug bureaucrats. At one meeting with Reshetnyak, for example, Krasnoyarsk editors demonstratively walked out of the room.

Drachevskii's most ambitious media project has been his effort to establish an okrug television network, Siberia-TV. This aims to give the federal government a mechanism for shaping public opinion about regional events.

During the spring of 2001, as mentioned earlier, aluminum magnate Oleg Deripaska invested about $10 million in the creation of this network, and the envoy's staff officially declared him its main sponsor. The okrug then appointed the head of Novosibirsk's State Television and Radio Company, Yakov London, as the key facilitator for the project. As noted earlier, even before this appointment London had extensive control of the Siberian media. In addition to running the state's electronic media in Novosibirsk, he also managed several commercial stations in the city and had close ties to Video International, which has long monopolized the Novosibirsk advertising market. Earlier, London had set up the interregional NTSC network, broadcasting the same signal to several West Siberian regions, although this network never attracted high ratings.

According to London, the okrug project has a budget of $21 million. Besides Deripaska, the major investors are Roman Abramovich's Sibneft and the Unified Energy System electricity monopoly (EES).[31]

Initially, the okrug television network, with its own broadcast network and news service, was supposed to start working on September 1, 2001, but the launch date was postponed several times. In December 2002, the network started operations, although it could not be viewed in some areas, including Novosibirsk, because of problems with frequency availability.

The okrug used the money received from Deripaska to purchase several television stations in Siberian cities, including Krasnoyarsk, Omsk, and Irkutsk. Before this buying spree, Deripaska's group already owned the TV-7 television company in Khakasia, where his original aluminum plant is located. Not surprisingly, he has sought to exercise control over the stations that the okrug has bought with his money. In this unusual way, his television empire has grown.

The network has encountered various difficulties getting started. A central problem was the difficulty of finding journalists talented enough to present federal views on Siberian issues in a way that would attract a wide audience. In fact, some observers doubted whether such a feat was possible at all. Certainly, the network's initial output was not stellar. Critics panned *News of Siberia*, the first information show that was made available in several Siberian cities. The chief editor of the new network is a Duma deputy from Kemerovo, Pavel Kovalenko of the Kremlin-controlled Unity party. Not coincidentally, he is the brother of a leading pro-Kremlin editor in Novosibirsk, which led some observers to question whether the staff was picked on the basis of professional skill or family ties.

With unappealing programming, the commercial prospects of the new network seem dim. The managers of Krasnoyarsk's Prima-TV, a controlling stake in which had been purchased by the okrug's OIC as a vehicle for the new Siberian network, have complained that the OIC channel is not popular. It has displaced Prima's broadcasts of material provided by the Moscow STS network, which had been increasing Prima's audience share.

Television shows that no one watches will make it difficult for the new network to sell advertisements, even with the backing of Video International. Lacking the ability to finance operations through advertisements, the okrug's OIC will, we may speculate, probably be forced to rely on contributions from business magnates like Deripaska or compete for subsidies from the state's already scarce resources.

Conclusion

Drachevskii has created an institution, which effectively put some distance between the federal agencies working in Siberia and the regional leaders. However, it would be difficult to argue that the envoy has made his office an indispensable part of the state structure. His main contribution has been to make the system work a little better than it worked in the past, though at the cost of adding another layer of bureaucracy.

During the first two and a half years of the okrug's existence, Drachevskii has established many new offices and councils, but it is not clear that these innovations have made a real impact on the way federal agencies work. Since he arrived, fifty federal ministries and agencies have set up okrug-level offices whose work the envoy must coordinate and monitor. He has reduced the influence of the governors over federal appointments since he now has the authority to approve all these decisions. However, he has not felt confident enough to use this power in a proactive way. For example, there has been little turnover among Siberian regional police chiefs.

The limits of Drachevskii's influence have been most clear in the economic area. In working on Siberia's development plan, he took up Siberians' calls for special transportation and energy benefits to help their unprofitable enterprises, only to be rebuffed by the Russian government, which sought to impose greater economic rationality, thereby letting enterprises die if they could not survive without extensive subsidies. His policies have so far had no impact on the level of crime in Siberia, and he has yet to address the issue of the monopolies in the region, which provide fertile ground for corruption. In fact, he seems more interested in working with the monopolists than in breaking up their holdings.

Even though regional laws now conform better to federal norms, governors continue to operate much as they have in the past. Most incumbents were able to win reelection since the envoy did not play much of a role in the elections. In fact, demonstrating just how hard it is to change the status quo, several regional leaders used the process of rewriting regional laws to strengthen their own authority. Governors continue to have extensive influence on economic policy making and property rights. They also maintain a strong grasp on the media, despite the envoy's efforts to influence regional media outlets. Since he is not really hurting the governors' interests, there is not a lot of covert opposition to him or his office. In fact, the governors seem to be increasingly ignoring the okrug, as the declining attendance at okrug gatherings suggests.

The PA and, by extension, Drachevskii influenced the appointment of Federation Council members from Siberia, creating a more compliant national parliament for the president. But the new system seems also to present useful opportunities for the governors. The Tyvan president, for example, appointed a close associate of Putin as his representative to the upper chamber, and he won financial support for his reelection campaign in return.

In regions where new governors have come to power, they have been powerful businessmen representing some of Russia's most influential financial–industrial groups. Drachevskii seems to be building close relations with these groups in order to gain access to the resources needed to carry out his projects, such as setting up a Siberia-wide television network. The state's reliance on private funding in this way will naturally give such businessmen enormous influence over state policies, and it will tend to further entrench the political and economic status quo.

The okrug has played a role in resolving regional disputes—for example, in cases like the long-running and seemingly intractable battles between the governor and mayor of Omsk and the executive and legislative branches in Irkutsk. However, Drachevskii dealt with these issues mostly at the level of resolving personality disputes; he did not address the underlying causes. Thus he has, for example, done little to strengthen the role of local government.

In conclusion, the seven envoys are unlikely to gain much more power than they have now since federal agencies and regional authorities jealously guard their prerogatives. However, Putin is also unlikely to abolish the institution since this would hand the governors a symbolic victory and would signal a relaxation of the president's efforts to strengthen the exercise of federal power at the regional level.

Notes

1. The editors and author would like to thank Alexander Pankov for his expert advice and helpful contributions to this chapter.

2. *Ekspert*, December 23, 2002.

3. A third aluminum company, Alyukom-Taishet, has been building a new, up-to-date factory in Taishet. However, its repeated efforts to obtain electricity from the Irkutsk electric company have so far come to naught, even though the latter produces ample surplus supplies.

4. Accessed at www.tvel.ru (accessed on January 14, 2003).

5. The fact that Aleksandr Khloponin became governor of Krasnoyarsk Krai in 2002 has weakened the position of Deripaska in the krai, and it could be the prelude to a new upheaval in the ownership of major assets.

6. Accessed at www.novosoft.ru.

7. However, the Ministry of Foreign Affairs, for which he worked from 1992 to 2000, is sometimes grouped with the power ministries because, like them, it reports primarily to the president rather than the government.

8. When the latter subsequently joined the staff of the Federation Council, the former head of the Federal Security Service (FSB) in Khakasiya took his position.

9. *Russian Regional Report (RRR)*, July 23, 2001.

10. *Vostochno-Sibirskie Vesti*, July 20–23, 2001.

11. *RRR*, June 3, 2002.

12. *RRR*, June 3, 2002.

13. *Novaya Sibir'*, May 17, 2002.

14. See the official website of the Okrug Information Center, www.sfo.nsk.su/2.htm.

15. Accessed at www.sfo.nsk.su/2.htm.

16. This was said in the author's presence.

17. RFE/RL Russian Political Weekly, January 3, 2003.

18. The official figures claim that the total number of crimes registered in Russia was 14.9 percent lower in 2002 than in 2001. The figure for the Siberian okrug is 16 percent (with felonies dropping by an even more remarkable 25 percent). However, numerous reports have asserted that in 2002 the MVD stopped officially registering certain categories of crimes. See page 203 of this volume.

19. A. L. Repetskaya, "Organizovannaya prestupnost' v sfere ekonomiki i finansov i problemy bor'by s nei," (accessed at www.isea.ru/sait).

20. In 2002 London acquired control of an additional television channel, NTN-12.

21. *Ekspert*, December 23, 2002.

22. *Vedomosti*, April 29, 2002.

23. *Vedomosti*, April 27, 2002.

24. *Vedomosti*, April 27, 2002.

25. See *RRR*, July 23, 2001.

26. *RRR*, May 9, 2001.

27. *Kommersant*, July 12, 2002.

28. *Vedomosti*, July 10, 2002.

29. *Rossiiskaya gazeta*, June 4, 2002.

30. When Reshetnyak departed after eighteen months, Marina Sen'kovskaya, a former deputy mayor of Tomsk, took over his responsibilities, after rising quickly up the hierarchy of the okrug staff.

31. Knews, April 2, 2002, (accessed at http://k-news.ru/allnews/1372/); and *Kontinent Sibir'*, July 19, 2002, (accessed at http://com.sibpress.ru/075/075-45-13.html).

9

Far East Federal Okrug

Elizabeth Wishnick

*T*HE *FAR EAST FEDERAL OKRUG INCLUDES the Republic of Sakha (Yakutia); the regions of Amur, Kamchatka, Magadan, and Sakhalin; Khabarovsk and Primorskii krais; the Chukotka and Koryak Autonomous Okrugs; and the Jewish Autonomous Region. The okrug headquarters are located in Khabarovsk.*

Lieutenant General Konstantin Pulikovskii (born 1948 in Ussuriisk, Primorskii Krai), presidential representative to the Far East Federal Okrug, has served in the army since 1966, most recently as deputy commander of the North Caucasus Military District. He gained notoriety as acting commander in Chechnya when in August 1996 he unexpectedly demanded that all civilians leave Groznii within forty-eight hours, after which federal forces would initiate large-scale combat operations. Pulikovskii's ultimatum found little support in the Russian leadership—Aleksandr Lebed, Yeltsin's emissary to Chechnya categorically opposed it, and Defense Minister Igor Rodionov quickly dispatched Vyacheslav Tikhomirov to replace Pulikovskii as commander of federal forces, although his ultimatum was never formally withdrawn.[1]

Presidential representative to the Far East Federal Okrug, Konstantin Pulikovskii, has stated repeatedly that his main overall task is "to bring presidential power closer to the regions."[2] He has faced many difficult challenges in the process—harmonizing regional legislation with federal laws, securing the removal of governors at odds with the Kremlin, addressing the ongoing energy crisis in Primorskii Krai and floods in Sakha, promoting business development and foreign economic relations, fostering interregional economic cooperation, monitoring the use of federal funds at the regional level, and developing a working relationship with the media and NGOs in the region.

Far Eastern Federal District of the Russian Federation

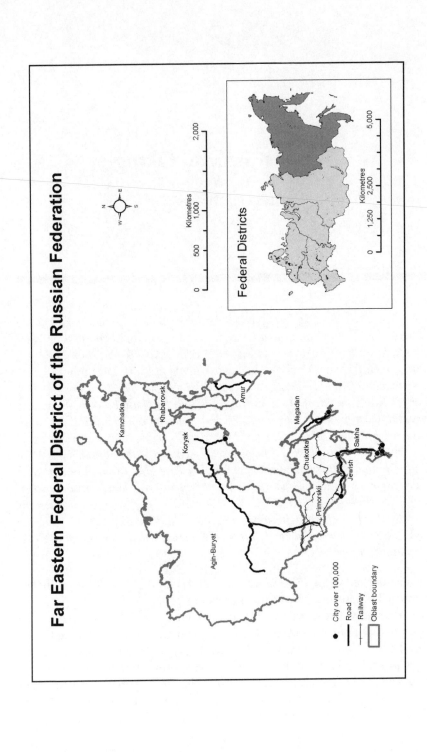

Specifically, Pulikovskii has identified three sets of priorities:

1. ensuring the okrug's energy security through projects such as the Bureyskaya hydropower plant, slated to begin operations in June 2003;
2. improving transportation in the okrug by completing the Chita–Khabarovsk highway by October 2003; and
3. reducing regional autarky by developing a common information space, which would improve communication and cooperation among regions.[3]

This chapter will examine Pulikovskii's record to date in achieving his overall goals and draw some preliminary conclusions about the role of the presidential representative in the Russian Far East and the success of President Vladimir Putin's reforms in the region.

Okrug Overview

The great distance separating the Russian Far East from central Russia has enabled political regionalism to flourish, and political challenges have appeared whenever central control has weakened.[4] At the same time, the Far East relies heavily on federal subsidies, and this dependence limits how far regional leaders can go in their opposition to Moscow's policies.

Center–periphery conflicts have long been a part of the history of the Russian Far East, an area that has proved to be as difficult to govern as to settle and develop. In 1884, Saint Petersburg created the Priamur Guberniia, with its capital in Khabarovka (now Khabarovsk), in an effort to maintain better control over the strategically important Russian Far East,[5] a step Putin replicated by creating seven federal okrugs, including one for the Far East.

Ever since the mid-nineteenth century, when Russian political authorities fixed the boundaries of what is now considered to be the Russian Far East, they have placed a priority on maintaining political control and supporting its economic development due to the region's strategic importance. The Russian Far East constitutes 36.4 percent of Russian territory, with a population of fewer than seven million (6.7 percent of the total population)—these vast territories are Russia's gateway to the Pacific, and they border China, Japan, North Korea, and the United States. During the Soviet era the economy of the Russian Far East served as a key source of natural resources for the domestic market and provided necessary support for the Pacific Fleet and Far East military okrug.[6] Mining, fisheries, timber, and diamonds are the top resource sectors in the Russian Far East, which contains half of Russia's fish resources, one-third of its hydropower, 30 percent of its coal reserves, 25 percent of its timber, and large amounts of nonferrous and precious metals. Defense industries also play a key role in southern areas of the Russian Far East, especially Khabarovsk Krai and Primorskii Krai. Cold War–era tensions in Moscow's relations with China, Japan, and the United States, as well as the location of defense facilities in the Russian Far East served to artificially seal off these territories from the dynamic export-oriented growth emerging as the distinguishing characteristic of the economies of neighboring Asian states. Prior to 1991, 75 percent of goods produced in the Russian Far East were destined for the national market, and only 6 percent were exported.[7]

In the period 1991–1992, the Russian Far East suddenly was cut off from traditional suppliers of food products and consumer goods in European Russia due to interrupted economic links and high transportation costs. Decreased demand for products of the area's defense and consumer-goods industries led to a sharp drop in industrial production. As of 2000 industrial production in the Russian Far East amounted to less than 44 percent of the 1990 level (compared to 54.4 percent for Russia as a whole). Although Russia experienced an average decrease in employment of 16.8 percent from 1990 to 1998, the Russian Far East saw a 22 percent drop. Because costs are higher in this part of Russia, the population's standard of living fell. Regions such as Khabarovsk Krai with more diverse economies reported 28.9 percent of the population living below the subsistence level (slightly better than the national average of 29 percent), while 70 percent of Chukotka residents had incomes below subsistence.[8] Due to the high cost of living and underemployment, the Russian Far East lost 7 percent of its population by the mid-1990s. Although the northern regions of the Russian Far East experienced the most substantial outflows, the population of Primorskii Krai and Khabarovskii Krai declined by 1.5 percent and 3.3 percent, respectively.[9]

Disillusioned by inadequate federal support, the Russian Far East began viewing economic integration in the Pacific Rim as a solution to the area's underdevelopment. Initially, regional leaders focused their efforts on expanding trade and joint ventures with China. Much of the trade with China during this period was barter trade, carried out by shuttle traders from China's northeastern provinces. By the mid-1990s the area's trade partners expanded to include South Korea, Japan, and the United States—currently just 10 percent of goods produced in the regions are destined for the European Russian market. Most of the goods remain within the Russian Far East, and 15 percent are exported.

Attracting significant foreign investment has proven more difficult in the Russian Far East, with the exception of Sakhalin, due to perceived high levels of political risk, onerous regulations, lack of transparency, and crime. Although regional leaders, especially in the southern part of the Russian Far East, expect the Sakhalin offshore oil and gas projects to resolve endemic energy shortages in the long run, interregional competition has made proposed pipeline projects more difficult to implement.

Staffing Policies

Clearly Pulikovskii has a complex set of tasks in handling his job as envoy. He must develop interregional economic cooperation by overcoming the indifference, if not the entrenched opposition, of self-interested governors.[10] He must serve as an intermediary between Putin and the federal ministries and regional administrations. Pulikovskii also must function as the okrug's foreign policy emissary, like the Soviet-era regional party secretaries, who also maintained contacts with foreign counterparts in Asia.

To achieve these tasks, he chose a staff dominated by personnel with military backgrounds,[11] experience that would prove most useful in dealing with foreign policy issues, as well as in maintaining liaison with regional military bases and overseeing defense restructuring in the okrug. According to one Primorskii Krai official, low salaries and poorly defined job descriptions apparently dissuaded top professionals from regional government and most other institutions from seeking employment on Pulikovskii's staff.[12] A lack of economic and civilian management experience on the staff limits its ability to function in economic policy areas.

Putin's chief of staff Aleksandr Voloshin, who supervises the presidential representatives, has monitored the Far East okrug office especially closely, and he reportedly appointed Pulikovskii's main deputy himself, Vitalii Gulii. Gulii, previously Yeltsin's representative to Sakhalin and a reporter for *Rossiiskaya Gazeta* on Far Eastern affairs, serves as Pulikovskii's liaison with Moscow.[13] Pulikovskii's determination to keep the heat on former Primorskii Krai governor Yevgenii Nazdratenko, who was believed to enjoy Voloshin's patronage, may have been a part of the presidential representative's broader effort to assert his own authority over Primorskii Krai and reduce that of Voloshin.

Relations with Federal Ministries and the Governors

Compared to the Yeltsin era, when the Kremlin faced open defiance to its policies in the Russian Far East, Putin has achieved greater balance in center–regional relations.

Unlike Yeltsin, who promised federal subsidies and special privileges to mute opposition from recalcitrant governors in the area, Putin has sought to restore order in center–regional relations by removing troublesome governors, harmonizing regional legislation with federal laws, and acquiring greater control over regional budgets.

Overall, Pulikovskii appears to have played a minimal role in coordinating the activities of the federal ministries and dealing with the okrug's governors. On some of the key problems facing the okrug, such as the energy crisis and flooding in Sakha, federal officials other than Pulikovskii have defined and implemented federal policy. In dealing with the governors, Pulikovskii has lacked the authority to force his will on strong regional leaders, and President Putin has had to step in personally to assert federal interests. Except for his disastrous role in the 2001 Primorskii Krai elections, Pulikovskii has not actively participated in the other gubernatorial elections that have taken place in the okrug during his tenure.

Pulikovskii has played an important role in harmonizing regional laws. By mid-2002, his staff had examined eight thousand legal acts. Of these, violations were found in fifteen hundred; protests were lodged against 740; and ultimately 625 were brought into line. Most of the discrepancies were found in Sakha, Amur Region, and Primorskii Krai.[14] To facilitate the harmonization process, Pulikovskii initiated a new coordination effort, involving treaties among all of the governors in the Russian Far East and the federal Justice Ministry. To prevent the regions from passing legislation that conflicts with federal law, the governors must submit all new laws to the ministry within seven days of their adoption.[15]

In the 1990s bilateral treaties, or separate understandings, many of which contradict the Russian Constitution, governed relations between Moscow and most of the regions. The Kremlin signed power-sharing treaties with the Republic of Sakha (June 1995), Khabarovsk Krai (May 1996), Sakhalin Region (May 1996), Magadan Region (July 1997), and Amur Region (May 1998). In the Russian Far East, only Primorskii Krai, Kamchatka Region, the Jewish Autonomous Region, Chukotka, and the Koryak Autonomous Okrug do not have power-sharing agreements with Moscow. In the case of Primorskii Krai, former governor Nazdratenko preferred extracting individual concessions and privileges in a continual game of high-stakes bargaining with Moscow. Because many of these treaties contradict the constitution, President Putin established a commission on June 26, 2001, to review their utility, but thus far they remain in place in the Russian Far East.

In June 2000, none of the governors welcomed the arrival of Pulikovskii to the Far East, an area known for localism and leaders with strong personalities. Not surprisingly, Pulikovskii has found Khabarovsk governor Viktor Ishaev one of the most difficult governors to work with—Ishaev has seen the establishment of the okrug office in his home region as an attack on his own authority. However, since many regions are dependent on federal subsidies, their governors must cultivate at least viable relations with Pulikovskii. Despite his unsuccessful efforts to achieve the election of his deputy as governor of Primorskii Krai, Pulikovskii claims to get along best with the new Primorskii Krai governor Sergei Darkin, whose region relies extensively on federal support.[16] Governor Mikhail Mashkovtsev of Kamchatka Region, also dependent on substantial federal subsidies as well as support for its submarine bases, even requested that Pulikovskii select a member of his staff to facilitate cooperation between the region's administration and the okrug office, thereby improving the region's access to the corridors of power in Moscow.[17]

The Kremlin's Battle with Primorskii Krai Governor Yevgenii Nazdratenko

Former Primorskii Krai governor Nazdratenko was a thorn in the side of Moscow officials for the eight years he spent in office. The persistent energy crisis that characterized his rule not only inflamed social tensions in the region, but it also proved to be a threat to national security, depriving military installations and power plants of electricity, and an obstacle to commerce, as demonstrators periodically blocked the nation's main transportation artery, the trans-Siberian railroad. Nazdratenko clashed repeatedly and publicly with Yeltsin over China policy—threatening to repudiate the 1991 Sino-Russian border demarcation treaty, opposing any compromises with China involving transfer of Primorskii Krai territory, and using the media under his control to fan fears of China's "quiet expansion" through illegal immigration.[18]

Although Nazdratenko had supported the pro-Kremlin Yedinstvo party in the 1999 State Duma elections, Putin's assumption of the Russian presidency on a platform of restoring federal control over the Russian regions raised doubts about the willingness of the new Kremlin leadership to work with the Primorskii Krai governor. Initially, when the federal okrug was first created, there was hope that Pulikovskii would succeed where previous Yeltsin representatives had failed in forcing Nazdratenko to heed the Kremlin's bidding. Pulikovskii's inability to do more than reprimand Nazdratenko for the energy crisis and salary arrears afflicting Primorskii Krai in the winter of 2000 showed that Putin's new system of federal okrugs and representatives did little to reign in irresponsible regional leaders.

Yet Pulikovskii made it known repeatedly in the regional media and in meetings with Putin that he was holding Nazdratenko personally responsible for the energy crisis in Primorskii Krai—to the point that Nazdratenko sued him for libel.[19] Although Pulikovskii had referred to Nazdratenko's performance as governor as "a classic example of stealing from the state," President Putin, in a phone call on February 5, 2001, allowed the Primorskii Krai governor to save face by resigning for "health reasons" (Nazdratenko had earlier been hospitalized with a heart ailment). According to some reports, Putin threatened to publicize information regarding his participation in criminal activities if he refused to resign.[20] Then, ten days later, the president met with Nazdratenko in Moscow and rewarded his "cooperation" with a lucrative new position, head of the State Fisheries Committee.

In contrast to Nazdratenko's previous struggles with the Kremlin, this time he failed to generate any support among his fellow governors, who already were on the defensive in their efforts to maintain their own power and political prerogatives.[21] Although the Kremlin needed little convincing to remove Nazdratenko and had repeatedly sought opportunities to do so since the mid-1990s, former Vladivostok mayor and current State Duma deputy Viktor Cherepkov claimed that oligarchs such as Sibneft's Roman Abramovich and Interros' Vladimir Potanin played a key role in lobbying Putin to remove Nazdratenko, whom they viewed as an obstacle to the expansion of their businesses to Primorskii Krai.[22]

Reaction in Moscow to the face-saving compromise leading to Nazdratenko's resignation was uniformly negative. Minister for Economic Development and Trade German Gref was categorically opposed to it since his ministry was entrusted with organizing the auctions for fish quotas, which Nazdratenko had criticized as governor.[23] Pulikovskii expressed his concern about the former governor's ability to rejuvenate Primorskii Krai's ailing fishing industry.[24] Putin's decision to compromise with Nazdratenko demonstrated that the 2000 law on removing governors—at least in this case—was too difficult to implement in practice.

The Primorskii Krai Gubernatorial Election

It was during the Primorskii Krai gubernatorial elections in May–June 2001, however, that the weakness of Pulikovskii's position became readily apparent. His deputy, Gennadii Apanasenko, joined the field of candidates, but despite his use of dubious campaign tactics (for example, his effort to monopolize local media coverage), he only received 14 percent of the votes in the first round, giving him a distant third-place finish. Although Apanasenko claimed presidential support for his candidacy, federal law enforcement agencies came out against him and accused him of preparing to manipulate the vote. When the courts on June 17 cited alleged campaign violations and removed Cherepkov from the runoff, even though he had finished in second place to Darkin with about 20 percent of the vote, Apanasenko received an unexpected reprieve and went head to head with Darkin in the second round.[25] Darkin, a local businessman with reported ties to Nazdratenko (and some allege to local criminal groups), soundly defeated Apanasenko with 40 percent of the vote. Apanasenko received 24 percent, while 34 percent of the electorate marked their ballots "against all," an unusually high percentage. Just 36 percent of eligible voters turned out for the election. Taken aback by Apanasenko's poor electoral showing, Pulikovskii blamed Pavel Lysov, chief federal inspector for Primorskii Krai, whom he had entrusted with running Apanasenko's campaign.[26] In November 2001, Pulikovskii dismissed Lysov and promoted his deputy, Sergei Sherstyuk, to the position.

Since his election, Darkin has faced several daunting tasks, including ensuring that the krai did not experience another energy crisis and coping with heightened federal scrutiny, especially from Pulikovskii, who was embarrassed by his deputy's defeat in the election. Although Darkin claims to be his own man, without ties to the oligarchs or regional political elites, questions about the legality of his business dealings continue to dog him.[27] Local observers believe that the Kremlin uses such compromising information against Darkin to force him to toe Moscow's line. In particular, Darkin has apparently taken direction from some groups within the presidential administration to undermine Nazdratenko's economic interests in the krai.[28]

Although working from Moscow as chairman of the State Fisheries Committee, Nazdratenko continues to cast a long shadow over Primorskii Krai, putting him at loggerheads with the new governor. Nazdratenko reportedly harbors some hopes of returning to the krai and has maintained business ties, facilitated by his sons' activities as well as the ties generated by his own patronage in key sectors, such as timber.[29] In his new position, Nazdratenko has been acting in a high-handed way, setting fishing quotas for the krai without consulting Darkin regarding the region's preferences, as is the established practice, prompting the governor to send a letter of complaint to Prime Minister Mikhail Kasyanov, Gref, and Deputy Prime Minister Viktor Khristenko.[30] Nazdratenko also has been stirring up social tensions, for example, by opposing Darkin's move to initiate bankruptcy proceedings at Dalmoreprodukt, which workers have been protesting by striking and blocking traffic in Vladivostok.[31] In June 2002, Nazdratenko's allies won a majority of the seats in the krai legislature and have used the body to support groups within the krai business elite, which oppose Darkin's policies.

Energy Crisis in Primorskii Krai

For several years Primorskii Krai has been plagued with energy crises, leaving many residents without heat and lighting, thereby causing some social unrest. Although the situation in Primorskii has been particularly unstable, the Russian Far East as a whole faces considerable difficulties in the energy sector, which is largely dependent on the coal industry. As a part of a restructuring program, unprofitable mines have been closed, reducing supplies, especially in Primorskii Krai and Sakhalin, two of the regions most dependent on coal for their energy needs.[32] While coal is plentiful in Sakha, the cost of mining in remote areas and transportation to other regions is prohibitive, and much of the coal has been exported to Japan, South Korea, and other Asian states.[33]

Previously Primorskii Krai officials blamed their difficulties on nonpayments by federal agencies or on United Energy System (EES) chief Anatolii Chubais, but in the summer of 2000 Chubais replaced all of the heads of Primorskii Krai energy companies with specialists recommended by the Krai administration. The Kremlin has been increasing fuel subsidies for Primorskii Krai and paying them in full, while outstanding federal debts are relatively minor in the region.

To make sure that the region was fully prepared to meet heat and electricity needs during the winter of 2001–2002, Putin turned to members of his cabinet—Prime Minister Kasyanov and Emergency Situations minister Sergei Shoigu, leaving Pulikovskii once again to play a subordinate role.

Darkin took the credit for having managed his first winter successfully,[34] but until Primorskii Krai, and the Russian Far East as a whole, can achieve energy independence, securing stable energy supplies will be a continual challenge. The Bureyskaya hydropower station now under construction in Amur Region will ameliorate energy supply problems in that region and in neighboring Khabarovsk Krai, but Primorskii Krai can only expect long-term relief should a gas pipeline from the Sakhalin projects be linked to the region and an effort be made to convert its energy system to greater reliance on gas. Pulikovskii has sought to enhance interregional economic cooperation—his ability to broker a deal on energy cooperation would go a long way to developing an economically viable Russian Far East.

Flood Relief for Sakha

Pulikovskii also had to defer to Russia's ministries when flooding on the Lena River in the spring of 2001 devastated the city of Lensk and other neighboring areas in the Republic of Sakha. Once again emergencies minister Shoigu was the point man for aid and reconstruction. In advance of Shoigu's mission to the republic, Pulikovskii traveled there in June 2001 to evaluate the progress of reconstruction, which he found wanting. Pulikovskii criticized the slow pace of rebuilding homes and health facilities in Lensk.[35] Regional authorities and the minister have been trading recriminations over lapses in these efforts. Although Sakha authorities claim they lacked necessary construction materials, an Audit Chamber analysis found evidence of pervasive mismanagement of funds.[36]

Elections in Sakha

The 2002 presidential elections in the Sakha republic presented a tangled tale of center–regional wrangling over political and economic power. There was much at stake for federal and republican authorities: control over 98 percent of Russia's diamond resources; the management of the Alrosa diamond-mining company; and the fate of the ailing Sakha republic, weakened by pervasive corruption and devastating floods in the spring of 2001.

Controversy surrounded the Sakha presidential election for months because of outgoing president Mikhail Nikolaev's interest in running for a third term, a move opposed by the Kremlin although permitted by the 1999 federal law governing regional political institutions.[37] Federal and republic courts disagreed over the legality of Nikolaev's candidacy—the republican Supreme Court rejected Nikolaev's bid three times for violating the Sakha constitution, which prescribed a two-term limit for the presidency.[38]

Pulikovskii failed to keep Nikolaev out of the race, and ultimately it was President Putin who stepped in personally to resolve the matter. In a private meeting with Nikolaev, Putin reportedly offered to withdraw the Kremlin's candidate, Deputy General Prosecutor Vasilii Kolmogorov, and support Alrosa president Vyacheslav Shtyrov's candidacy. Shtyrov was a close Nikolaev ally. Just like Nazdratenko, who was persuaded to resign in exchange for federal office (and immunity from possible criminal indictments), Nikolaev also was offered a deal, namely, a position as one of three deputy speakers in the Federation Council. Nikolaev agreed to forego a third term if Shtyrov ran, and on January 13, 2002, Shtyrov was elected president of Sakha with 59.2 percent of the vote.[39]

Shtyrov's election was only a partial victory for the federal authorities because they were able to remove Nikolaev but not replace him with their own man. Due to its vast mineral wealth, which reduces its dependence on federal subsidies, Sakha has resisted federal efforts (pursued by Pulikovskii's office) to harmonize the republic's legislation with federal laws. While Sakha lawmakers have taken some steps to address federal concerns, they have strongly opposed changes that would undercut the republic's privileged status, especially its sovereignty and ownership over its lucrative mineral and hydrocarbon resources, and the republic's law requiring that speakers of both chambers in the Sakha parliament speak both Yakut and Russian.

Although the Kremlin agreed to Shtyrov as a compromise candidate, he has not been any more amenable than his predecessor to federal efforts to encroach on republican prerogatives. At a March 7, 2002, press conference, for example, Shtyrov downplayed Moscow's concerns regarding conflicts between republican and federal laws, and stated that he saw no need to disband the legislature, as prosecutor Nikolai Polyatinskii had requested.[40]

Moreover, Sakha officials have refused to relinquish control over the republic's enormous diamond resources. The 1992 agreement between Sakha and Moscow grants the republic considerable control over its mineral wealth. On February 5, 2001, Sakha passed an amendment to the republican constitution declaring mineral wealth within Sakha the exclusive property of the republic. This has not persuaded federal officials to concede ownership of the diamonds to Sakha, however, as will be discussed later in this chapter.

Representation in the Federation Council

As in the other federal okrugs, the Far East's representatives in the Federation Council present a mixed picture of federal and regional interests, and of the corresponding business interests to which they are closely related. Several deputies, for example, former Sakha president Nikolayev, clearly represent regional interests. In the Primorskii Krai legislature, the Kremlin had originally been able to secure the appointment of an ally in the person of Mikhail Glubokovskii.[41] However, following the legislature's June 2002 elections, Nazdratenko's allies were able to elect their own representative to the upper chamber in the person of Oleg Kozhemyako, well known in the krai for his connections to the local fishing industry and the former governor.[42] Chukotka's representatives include the former governor—who was offered the spot by current governor Roman Abramovich so that he would not compete against him in the election campaign—and a representative of Sibneft, Abramovich's company. Khabarovsk governor Ishaev appointed his former representative in Moscow to the new senate.

While in general the presidential administration clearly had little say over these choices, in at least one case it made a certain impact. Presumably under the Kremlin's pressure, Sakhalin's governor delegated Valerii Goreglyad, who had no connection to the region but had worked in the Federation Council staff. He proceeded to become the head of the pro-Kremlin Federatsiya faction of Federation Council members.

Nearly one fourth of Russian Far East Federation Council Members have ties to the military, and it is hard to say whether these men represent a Muscovite or Far Eastern point of view. While the strong military presence may reflect the influence of Pulikovskii, a military man, the deputies with military background represent regions where military bases are located, which could also indicate Moscow's or the governors' concern about maintaining political links to military installations in the Russian Far East (which typically attract more communist votes).

Corruption and Crime

The assassination of Magadan governor Valentin Tsvetkov in October 2002 only highlighted that crime and corruption were a major problem in the Far East and brought new attention to the issue. By the end of the year, investigators had yet to identify the culprits or the motives for the crime.

Although even in the Soviet era Magadan and Sakhalin were known as high-crime areas, by the mid-1990s the crime rate in these regions was double the national average, and Primorskii Krai and Khabarovsk Krai were not far behind.[43] Plentiful resources, weapons depots, ports, and a thriving business in fake identity cards and passports have made these regions especially attractive to criminal gangs. Crime and corruption are interrelated problems in the Russian Far East, where rent-seeking federal and regional officials, and an onerous system of resource management, create incentives to siphon off resources in collusion with Russian and foreign criminals.[44] Pulikovskii has been cracking down on egregious instances of corruption, especially in the power ministries—for example, by securing the resignation of the head of the Primorskii Krai Ministry of Internal Affairs, Aleksandr Vasilev.[45]

The Russian mafia reportedly cooperates with the Japanese yakuza in a thriving trade in stolen Japanese cars (valued at $2 billion annually) and works with Chinese criminal groups to illegally export 1.5 million cubic meters of timber annually (at a price tag of $300 million).[46] Illegal fishing is one of the most serious problems facing the Russian Far East, which at the end of the 1980s supplied half of the Soviet catch. For example, illegal exports of king crab, one of the most lucrative but dwindling shellfish variety, amounted to $188 million.[47] By some estimates illegal fishing and unreported fish exports accounted for two-thirds of the Russian Far East's revenue from fishing in the 1990s.[48] Overfishing and illegal sales of fish have depleted fish stocks, reducing employment opportunities in the fishing industry in an area that is heavily dependent on it.[49]

Given the pervasive criminality in this sector—one of the few in the Russian Far East to attract significant foreign investment—efforts to regulate fishing more strictly face considerable opposition from entrenched interests. At times new regulations have resulted in deadly retaliation: not long after the commander of Sakhalin's border guards ordered all small fishing vessels to install tracking equipment, in an effort to crack down on smuggling to Japan, he was killed in an arson attack at his home.[50]

The port city of Vladivostok now boasts Russia's sixth-highest crime rate. In this city Chechen gangs allegedly run several major smuggling operations in fishing and stolen cars. Since 1998, when Iran closed its border with Afghanistan, and Western drug interdiction agencies cracked down on the flow of heroin from Central Asia to Europe, Central Asian drug smugglers began moving their operations to Vladivostok, as evidenced by rising heroin addiction, falling prices for the drug, and increasing instances of drug-related crime.[51]

Inadequate regulation of Sino-Russian border trade, which has been growing rapidly since the early 1990s, has enabled criminals and unscrupulous business people to operate along the 4,300 kilometer border and fueled fears of uncontrolled Chinese migration.[52] Since 1994, new federal rules requiring visas for Chinese traders have been introduced, and regional leaders have been taking steps of their own to crack down on illegal migration. According to estimates from a leading Russian specialist on Chinese migration, there are currently 250,000 to 450,000 Chinese in Russia, including approximately twenty to twenty-five thousand in Moscow and a maximum of twenty thousand in both Khabarovsk Krai and Primorskii Krai.[53]

Anyone visiting the markets outside of Khabarovsk or Vladivostok can see that official figures may understate the number of Chinese residing in these cities. Although regional officials blame the Chinese government for encouraging illegal immigration to the Russian Far East, corruption in Russia makes it possible for Chinese migrants to obtain the necessary legal documents to live and work in Russia.[54] Nevertheless, there has been substantial progress in regulating cross-border traffic.[52] According to regional interior ministry data, in 1994 just 64 percent of foreign visitors to Primorskii Krai left the region within the time allotted by their visas, but in 1997–2000, more than 99 percent left on schedule.[56] Pulikovskii has been asked to contribute to Putin's ongoing effort to reassess Russia's migration policy.[57]

Apart from border control, officials in the Russian Far East face a major challenge in preventing theft and illegal sales of weapons from underfunded military bases in the region. Such activities occur with sufficient frequency to alarm Russia's neighbors about the threat of proliferation of nuclear weapons to rogue states such as North Korea as well as to terrorist groups.[58]

While Pulikovskii's office has added another layer of scrutiny in the struggle against crime and corruption in the Russian Far East, federal level decisions are needed to address fundamental issues, such as resource allocation, control over ports, and adequate funding for border-control functions and military bases. Pulikovskii and his staff contribute to this effort to some extent, for example, by providing draft legislation on regulating the export of key regional resources; but the okrug office alone lacks the wherewithal to resolve a pervasive crime problem, which may in any case be insoluble, given the omnipresent corruption in state institutions.

Economic Activities

Traditionally, the Russian Far East depended on subsidies to attract necessary workers (who received higher than average salaries during the Soviet era) and to cover the increased costs of fuel and transportation. In the 1990s, fewer federal subsidies were available to cope with the rising costs of living and transportation, badly affecting the population and enterprises alike. High transportation costs isolated the region from the rest of the country.

During the 1996 presidential election campaign, Yeltsin unveiled a ten-year presidential program for the economic and social development of the Russian Far East and Transbaikal regions for 1996–2005. However, the Kremlin has shown little intention to implement it. Yeltsin pledged $34 billion in federal funds for the program, but by 1999, only 4.2 percent of these funds had been disbursed.

Relations with the Interregional Association

Despite the failures of past federal efforts, Pulikovskii, like the other envoys, has sought to assert his authority over economic matters, partly by reducing the power of the existing association for interregional economic cooperation. The Far East Federal Okrug overlaps with the jurisdiction of the interregional economic association for the Russian Far East, which also includes the Agin-Buryat Autonomous Okrug, Buryatiya, and Chita Region (parts of the Siberian Federal Okrug). Formed in 1993, the Association for the Russian Far East and the Transbaikal was created to facilitate economic cooperation among the territories of this vast region and to coordinate federal assistance programs. The association has played an important role in mediating between the regions and Moscow, on the one hand, and serving as an intermediary in regional economic cooperation with Asian neighbors, on the other.

After the Far Eastern branch of the Ministry of Economic Development and Trade was disbanded in the fall of 2000,[59] on November 1, Pulikovskii created an okrug committee on regional development to coordinate the activities of the regions in key sectors—including foreign trade, energy, transportation, and fishing—and to bring together representatives of all the federal ministries in the Far East. These efforts by Pulikovskii to put his imprimatur on regional development planning appeared to set the stage for a test of the relative strength of the federal okrug vis-à-vis the regional economic association, controlled by Khabarovsk Krai governor Viktor Ishaev.

In the ongoing saga of the drafting of a new federal program for the Russian Far East through 2010, however, Pulikovskii has reportedly sided with the association and regional officials in their difficult negotiations with Minister of

Trade and Economic Development German Gref. Although the association had played a key role in drafting the first program, Gref commissioned an institute in Rostov to develop a less costly, more narrowly defined blueprint for regional development. According to regional observers, in its initial version the Rostov plan proposed 42 percent less funding than the sum requested by the association.[60] Pavel Minakir, director of the Institute for Economic Research, which drafted an alternative to the Rostov program, noted that the latter's proposed cost savings would come at the expense of key regional needs in transportation and social services, and thus compromise ongoing projects that were counting on federal support to complement promised foreign investment.[61]

Negotiations between central and regional authorities are continuing. During an August 2002 visit to the okrug, Putin said that the federal government would adopt a "policy of preferences" toward the Far East.[62] However, by the end of the year, local observers complained that neither Pulikovskii nor the regional elite had done much to ensure that such a policy was actually implemented.[63]

For his part, Ishaev has been responding to Pulikovskii's challenge to his authority by trying to boost his profile in Moscow, proposing a plan for Russia's development over the next ten years, parts of which President Putin decided to incorporate into Gref's overall economic development plan. Similarly, Sakhalin's governor Igor Farkhutdinov has been successful in using strong foreign interest in his region's offshore oil and gas resources to lobby the presidential administration and the State Duma to approve measures necessary to move forward with energy projects. However, in areas where Farkhutdinov has been less successful, such as the development of the Kurile Islands, there are signs that the Kremlin is trying to reassert its control. These islands now receive development aid from a federal program, in addition to Sakhalin Region funds.

Regions Left to Find Their Own Assistance

The Yeltsin administration's pledges to support a grandiose development program for the Russian Far East were not fulfilled, and, as previously mentioned, Putin has sought to scale back the scope of any future federal development funding. Some smaller projects, such as the Bureyskaya hydropower plant in Amur Region, which will produce 8.7 billion kilowatt-hours of electricity annually, are moving forward and are expected to contribute significantly to the okrug's economy. The first section of the plant is on track for completion in 2003.

Moreover, the Transport Ministry has made the Chita–Khabarovsk highway a priority. The completion of this project in late 2003 will help develop economic links between the Russian Far East and European Russia by making it possible for the first time to drive across the whole country by road. The European Bank of Reconstruction and Development (EBRD) issued a $229 million credit to Russia, part of which will support this project.[64]

Nevertheless, for the most part, the regions have had to find their way to Asian markets largely on their own in an effort to boost development in the Russian Far East. This has meant capitalizing on regional strengths—that is, sales of natural resources, such as oil, gas, minerals, timber, and fish—to pay for items in short supply, especially consumer goods and food products from China. Thus, even though officials in the Russian Far East recognize the necessity of cooperating with China, they express a distinct preference for expanding cooperation with the United States, Japan, and the Koreas—countries that have the investment capital that is desperately needed in the area.[65]

Sakhalin's offshore oil and gas projects drew in $1.67 billion in investment by mid-2001, and the region is second only to Moscow as a destination for foreign investment.[66] Planned infrastructure development for the Sakhalin-2 project (the first of the seven projects on the island to begin operations)—including the construction of a transisland pipeline, a liquefied natural gas plant, and terminal—is expected to bring in $490 million in 2002.[67] In October 2001, Exxon Mobil announced that the Sakhalin-1 project was profitable and outlined the company's plans to invest $30 billion by 2030.[68]

The oil projects are governed by production-sharing agreements (PSAs), providing for the transfer of foreign technology and development techniques in exchange for royalties and resources. For the projects to move forward, the PSAs must be approved by the State Duma, which then must enact enabling legislation. In response to persistent complaints by foreign oil companies and Sakhalin Region officials about costly delays in this process, Putin attended a September 2000 conference on the island to show his support for the PSA process, often a target of criticism in Moscow. In a measure designed to streamline PSA approval and implementation, he entrusted Minister for Economic Development and Trade Gref with coordinating the process—yet another instance when the federal okrug office was bypassed to give a ministry direct oversight over a key project in the Russian Far East.

The decree authorizing Gref's new role was not signed until February 2001, however, and foreign businesses and Sakhalin officials subsequently claimed that Putin's changes actually created more confusion by interrupting established lines of communication.[69] To remedy the situation, in October 2001 Gref put two companies (Rosneft and Zarubezhneft) in charge of PSA approval and preparation.[70]

On November 27, 2002, the Security Council, of which all the presidential envoys are members, held a special session devoted to the Far East's problems, which Pulikovskii termed the most significant event of his two-and-a-half-year tenure.[71] At the session, Putin discussed the possibility of building an oil pipeline from Angarsk in eastern Siberia to Nakhodka. Such a pipeline would improve the Far East's economic prospects, but its routing remains controversial. During their July 2001 summit, Russian and Chinese leaders reached an agreement paving the way for a feasibility study for a $1.7 billion pipeline, running from Angarsk to Daqing in northeastern China. The Russian pipeline monopoly, Transneft, supported by political and economic interests in the Russian Far East, has promoted an alternative routing, which would be less dependent on the Chinese market and instead ship oil from Angarsk to Nakhodka in the Russian Far East and then to the Japanese and Korean markets. Nevertheless, in August 2002, Russian prime minister Kasyanov assured Chinese premier Zhu Rongji that the Angarsk–Daqing project, favored by China, would take priority. If implemented, the twenty-four-hundred-kilometer pipeline could be built as early as 2005 and begin shipping 147 million barrels annually to China. China's National Petroleum Corporation agreed to finance 50 percent of the project through loans to be repaid with oil revenues.

Fiscal Centralization

Putin's changes in the division of tax revenues between the center and the regions have made the regions more financially dependent on Moscow and have thus diminished their bargaining power. Sakha, for example, lost more than half of its tax revenues to Moscow, thereby curtailing the considerable fiscal autonomy the republic had codified in its Yeltsin-era power-sharing treaty with Moscow.[72]

Moreover, the Kremlin has sought to expand its leverage with additional mechanisms, including direct control over regional treasuries and the restructuring of major state-owned industries. After Darkin's election, Prime Minister Kasyanov noted that the new governor "had inherited a very burdensome legacy," but he expressed confidence in his ability to reverse these unfavorable economic trends in the near future. Nevertheless, Kasyanov announced that the federal treasury would fund the region's treasury directly in an effort to reduce the possibility that regional officials could use federal funds in ways that the federal government did not intend.[73]

Darkin has stated that he hopes to reduce Primorskii Krai's dependence on federal subsidies (now accounting for approximately one third of the region's nineteen billion rubles in revenue), but it is unclear where he will recoup the shortfall.[74] He has lowered expectations about the prospects for attracting major foreign investment, particularly from Japan, and instead, as we will see below, he appears to be courting Russian business.

In Khabarovsk, regional authorities are opposing a plan to privatize the Komsomolsk-na-Amure aviation plant manufacturing Sukhoi aircraft (KnAAPO), which brings in billions of dollars in revenues through fighter plane sales to China. On November 26, 2001, Putin signed a decree forming the Sukhoi holding company and calling for the privatization of the Komsomolsk and Novosibirsk factories. Although the Kremlin claims that the change in ownership would not deprive Khabarovsk of revenue, Ishaev has criticized the plan, which is due to be implemented in 2003. Meanwhile in March 2002, Sukhoi managed to divert a long-standing contract to supply forty SU-30MKK fighters to China from KnAAPO in order to concentrate profits in the design bureau and use them to develop a new fifth-generation fighter.[75]

Relations with Business

Despite his lack of business experience, Pulikovskii has sought to make his mark in the okrug's business sector by improving coordination and facilitating foreign investment, especially by Asian neighbors. In an effort to coordinate business activity within the okrug, in July 2001 he created an okrug business council. Although each governor has his own business council, these organizations typically work closely with the region's administration and rarely cooperate with similar associations in other regions. In principle Pulikovskii's council could work to remove administrative barriers to entrepreneurship and harmonize regulations within the okrug, but in practice there has been a great deal more wasteful competition than cooperation among regions.[76] Thus, there is no reason to believe that Pulikovskii's new business council will succeed in promoting interregional cooperation, where the Association for the Russian Far East and the Transbaikal has failed.

In another bid to wrest control over regional investment flows, in October 2001 Pulikovskii announced that a new regional investment company, Dalnevostochnaya investitsionnaya kompaniya (Dalinkom), had been established at President Putin's request. According to Pulikovskii, Dalinkom will serve as a vehicle for his office to acquire a greater say over regional economic issues.[77] Dalinkom director Oleg Mikhailenko believes that the company will help reduce the political risk to investors by enabling them to get help from the okrug office, which can pressure governors to take specific steps to create a more favorable investment climate.[78]

The new company was set up to bring in foreign and domestic investment in priority sectors—including energy, power, communications, mining, timber, and fishing—and to develop the infrastructure needed to implement federal economic policies. Dalinkom began with $10 million in capital. Its shareholders include state-owned companies such as Kosmicheskaya Svyaz (54 percent), Rosneft (26 percent) and Vneshkombank (20 percent). The company immediately met with opposition in Vladivostok, its base of operations, and has faced problems attracting qualified staff.[79]

However, Pulikovskii's greatest challenge is likely to come from oligarchs who are increasingly staking their claim to regional assets and—in the case of Chukotka, where Sibneft tycoon Roman Abramovich was elected governor in December 2000—to regional political power. Abramovich has been taking steps to improve the okrug's investment climate, and his concerted efforts to court foreign investors, especially Americans, have paid off. On February 4, 2002, Sibneft signed a framework agreement with Halliburton (headed from 1995 to 2000 by current–U.S. vice president Dick Cheney) to provide oilfield services in exploration projects in Chukotka, where the company has significant onshore and offshore interests. According to Abramovich, the federal center already overregulates Chukotka: designated a restricted zone in 1996, travel to this region requires approval from the regional government as well as federal immigration authorities, a process hampering the activities of foreign investors and adventure tourists from Alaska.[80]

Since businessman Sergei Darkin was elected governor in Primorskii Krai, major business groups, such as Severstal, Evrazholding, and Novolipetsk Metallurgical Holding, have been moving into the region in an effort to acquire control over commercial seaports and reduce shipping costs to an expanding clientele in Asia. In late 2001, Severstal purchased a 60 percent stake in the Vostochnii commercial seaport, and in January 2002 Evrazholding bought 60 percent of the shares in the Nakhodka commercial seaport, while Novolipetsk is seeking to buy into the Vladivostok commercial seaport.[81] To ensure a federal voice in the ports, Russia's Transport Ministry is preparing legislation ensuring that the federal government will maintain control over the land, property, area of water, and technical buildings, while private companies could operate port services.[82]

For the Kremlin, control over the revenue and assets of Alrosa, the Sakha diamond monopoly mentioned earlier, is a key issue. During the 1990s, the regional authorities were able to run and profit from the company while sharing little with federal authorities. However, since the Russian Constitutional Court ruled in June 2000 that the federal government owns Russia's natural resources, the Kremlin has been seeking to channel to itself as much of the revenue from Sakha's diamond mines as possible.[83]

In June 2001, federal auditors investigated the history of Alrosa's incorporation and Sakha's majority ownership. When Putin took office, the Sakha and federal authorities each owned 32 percent of Alrosa shares, while 23 percent belonged to the workers, 8 percent to eight Sakha okrug governments, and 5 percent to a federal veterans' organization. Thus, Sakha effectively controlled

63 percent of the shares—the 32 percent republican stake, plus the 23 percent belonging to the workers, and the 8 percent controlled by okrugs in Sakha. After Putin asked Prime Minister Kasyanov to take steps to protect state property in the diamond industry, the Property Ministry began investigating ways to increase the federal stake in Alrosa to 51 percent. To forestall any reappropriation of Sakha shares, Nikolaev decided to transfer the republic's 32 percent stake to Sakhinvest, a private fund, at the end of 2001.[84] In November 2002, the federal government took control of the 5 percent previously held by the veterans' organization, strengthening the federal hand but still not reaching the 51 percent.[85]

On December 10, 2001, Putin met with Nikolaev and Shtyrov to discuss the diamond industry's development.[86] The Finance Ministry (which controls the State Diamond Depositary, Gokhran) recommended that Alrosa gradually reduce its diamond sales over the next five years through the South African company DeBeers so that the Kremlin would have more freedom in pursuing its strategy for developing the domestic diamond industry. However, the outcome of Alrosa's negotiations with DeBeers may not have fully satisfied the Kremlin. According to the agreement reached on December 17, DeBeers will market half of Alrosa's annual rough diamond output, valued at $800 million. Alrosa, which signed the agreement with DeBeers for the first time (instead of the federal government), can sell the remaining half of its diamond output to domestic companies, export it, or postpone sales depending on price fluctuations. The firm hopes that the new agreement will help boost production and attract investment, in addition to expanding its marketing options, formerly monopolized by DeBeers.[87]

In March 2002, Vladimir Kalitin, Alrosa's top engineer since 1996, was selected to replace Shtyrov as the company's president. This helped to keep control of Alrosa in the hands of the regional authorities.[88] Indeed, by July 2002, the federal government had made only one further advance: it succeed in having Deputy Prime Minister Aleksei Kudrin named as the sole chairman of the board of directors, instead of having two codirectors, one each for the federal and republic governments, as had been done in the past. Nine of the fifteen board members represent Sakha, with only six favoring the federal government. The Kremlin is also trying to redirect the money Alrosa pays in rent to Sakha for its mines, but negotiations will likely be long and involved.

Thus, leadership changes in Sakha and in Alrosa have not as yet made it any easier for the Kremlin to take control over the republic's diamond wealth, and Shtyrov and Kalitin appear to be standing firm for Sakha's interests.[89] Kalitin has stated that he hopes to provide greater revenue to Moscow in the form of dividends as the diamond industry reemerges from a slump in sales. In the short term, however, Alrosa has had to cut personnel due to a $250 million budget deficit, resulting in a 1.5-billion-ruble budget deficit for the republic (about $50 million).[90] The latter may prompt republican officials to assume a more "flexible" attitude toward Moscow's interest in redistributing diamond assets.

Local Government, the Media, and Civil Society

Local Government

In the Far East okrug, center–regional power struggles over budget resources have found parallels at the local level. These have been particularly striking in Sakhalin, Kamchatka, and Primorskii Krai, where, as previously mentioned, the bitter rivalry between former governor Nazdratenko and Vladivostok mayor Cherepkov became a defining feature of the political landscape. Taking a leaf from Putin's own book, Primorskii Krai's new governor Darkin has sought to assert authority over his region's cities by requiring all local governments to keep their accounts in the krai treasury. This additional financial lever will help Darkin to chip away at Nazdratenko's power base since many of the krai's mayors were elected with the former governor's patronage and continue to support him.[91] Vladivostok mayor Yurii Kopylov, for example, came to power with Nazdratenko's support and has refused to put his city's money into the krai's treasury in order to maintain his political independence from Darkin.[92] As for the federal government, through the end of 2002, it was largely willing to leave local government to gubernatorial supervision, and it took no steps to strengthen its own power in the cities and towns of the okrug.

Media

In the Russian Far East governors dominate the major local newspapers, leaving few independent outlets.[93] Pulikovskii has done little to change this situation. Moreover, he has not built productive relations with okrug journalists. Although he has appealed to the media to "write the truth" about his work,[94] since his appointment, journalists have complained that his excessive concern for secrecy and the lack of information even about routine okrug office activities make it difficult for them to cover him.[95]

Despite Pulikovskii's stated goal of improving information flows among regions, critics allege that he views the media as a political tool. During the gubernatorial campaign in Primorskii Krai in May–June 2002, for example, local observers alleged that the presidential representative helped his candidate, Apanasenko, put his own allies in charge of the two leading television stations. In response to the perceived pressure, journalists sent a declaration to the president, the chairman of the Central Electoral Commission, and the procurator general, condemning Pulikovskii's efforts to dominate the regional media.[96]

Civil Society

In the late 1990s, mass demonstrations and work stoppages were common in Primorskii Krai, where beleaguered citizens took to the streets in desperate protests against persistent wage arrears and energy shortages. Striking miners and public sector employees have periodically stopped traffic along the trans-Siberian railroad, while protests by air traffic controllers paralyzed air travel in Yakutsk.[97] Although trade unions played a certain organizational role in these events, in general they do not represent an effective political challenge to existing power structures.

The development of NGOs in the Russian Far East since the late 1980s has provided some respite for civil society, notwithstanding the weak development of political parties and labor movements and the encroachments of strong governors on media freedom. But even these efforts have little domestic support and must rely on foreign financing and organizational support.

Regional environmental organizations and associations of indigenous peoples have attracted the attention of foreign NGOs, especially in the United States, but also in Japan, Canada, and Western Europe. These have provided financial support and training. Groups from the U.S. West Coast, have been particularly active in forming partnerships with NGOs in the Russian Far East. Senator Ted Stevens of Alaska succeeded in earmarking U.S. assistance money for Russia under the Freedom Support Act to launch a wide-ranging program of economic, cultural, and educational cooperation between NGOs in Alaska and the Russian Far East in the mid-1990s. With the establishment in 1994 of the U.S. West Coast–Russian Far East Working Group as a part of the Gore–Chernomyrdin Commission's Business Development Committee, NGOs working on environmental issues and in a range of other sectors acquired a regular mechanism for contacts and support for new projects through biannual meetings with American counterparts. The 1997 Russian Regional Initiative, launched by the U.S. Department of State, provided additional funds to NGOs in the Russian Far East.

The Bush administration has sought to reduce the role of government in promoting U.S.–Russian economic cooperation by eliminating the Gore–Chernomyrdin framework (although interagency coordination essentially replicates its activities, including support for the Ad Hoc Working Group) and by encouraging the private sector to play a more active role. In July 2001, a new bilateral business initiative was launched, the Russian–American Dialogue. Organized by Russian and American business associations,[98] the new group seeks to enable the private sector to take the lead in developing bilateral economic relations and in supporting economic reform, transparency, and the rule of law in Russia.

Despite the growing ties between regional and foreign NGOs, Russian groups face some additional constraints on their cooperative activities because of the dominant role played by the defense sector in the Russian Far East.[99] Activists seeking to inform the international community about environmental hazards posed by the Russian fleet are sometimes subject to criminal charges. Grigorii Pasko, an ecologist and military journalist, was charged with treason in 1997 for giving Japanese journalists information about (illegal) nuclear waste dumping by the Pacific fleet. Although acquitted in 1999, he was sentenced again on the same charges to a four-year prison term in Vladivostok—despite the fact that the Supreme Court invalidated a secret defense ministry document used to prosecute Pasko and environmentalist Aleksandr Nikitin on espionage charges.[100] In June 2002, the Supreme Court's military collegium upheld the four-year sentence, only for Pasko to be released in January 2003.[101]

Thus, despite the support of the international community, and the efforts by local NGOs and journalists, the development of civil society in the Russian Far East faces serious hurdles due to assaults on freedom of the press by the governors, the military, and now also the presidential representative.

Foreign Policy Role

While all of the presidential envoys have played a role in Russia's foreign policy, particularly trying to attract foreign investment, Pulikovskii has gone much further in this area than any of the others. Accordingly his foreign policy efforts deserve special attention.

Because the regions comprise the okrug border on Northeast Asia, Pulikovskii has played a prominent role in Russia's increasingly active Asia diplomacy, especially vis-à-vis the Korean peninsula, Japan, and China. Moreover, since exports have played a major role in the Far East's modest economic recovery since 2000 and foreign investment is urgently needed to supplement inadequate federal support,[102] Pulikovskii's efforts to promote and coordinate economic cooperation with Asian states reinforce his broader aim of improving the economic health of the okrug.

Pulikovskii also has helped the Kremlin to improve center–regional information flows on foreign policy issues and eliminate the open conflict often seen in the mid-1990s in Russian–Chinese relations, which complicated Russian diplomacy and impeded Sino-Russian economic cooperation, especially on the regional level.[103] Nazdratenko's vocal opposition to the process of territorial demarcation with China in the mid-1990s stemmed in part from inadequate efforts on the part of the Foreign Ministry to communicate effectively with the krai leadership. Thus, one of Pulikovskii's first tasks was to accompany the Russian president on his July 2000 visit to Beijing. As soon as the summit meeting concluded, Pulikovskii was immediately dispatched to Khabarovsk to reassure the regional administration that the Russian and Chinese governments agreed to maintain the status quo of the three remaining disputed islands, including the two located in the Amur River, right across from the city of Khabarovsk. Nevertheless, he has sided with regional officials on this issue and stated unequivocally that the disputed islands in Khabarovsk are Russian territory.[104]

In addition to participating in summit delegations, Pulikovskii travels frequently with representatives of major regional firms to develop economic cooperation between the Russian Far East and Northeast Asia and holds talks with Asian officials on Putin's behalf. He then briefs Putin on the results of these trips, thereby acquiring regular access to the president due to his role as "the Russian Far East's foreign policy envoy." In April 2002, for example, Pulikovskii briefed the president on his recent visit to three of the four Kurile Islands claimed by Japan, and later he told the press that Russia is not opposed to their joint economic management with Japan.[105]

Pulikovskii has gained the most visibility through his engagement with North Korea. When North Korean leader Kim Jong Il took a six-week train trip across Russia to attend a summit meeting in Moscow with Putin in August 2001, it was Pulikovskii who accompanied him throughout the journey.[106] The normally secretive Pulikovskii took the unusual step of publishing a book about his journeys with Kim Jong Il entitled *Orient Express* in the fall of 2002. The memoir provides a detailed description of the North Korean leader's luxurious high-tech compartment—which was fully computerized, air-conditioned, and staffed by a 150-member retinue of security guards, aides, and cooks—and contains mostly vignettes of the day-to-day life on the train, including an arm-wrestling match among Russian and North Korean security guards.

As a result of this experience, Pulikovskii has succeeded in creating an important personal relationship with the even more secretive North Korean leader, who has referred to the presidential representative as "an old friend, who is well-known to the Korean people."[107] Subsequently, the Russian president has taken advantage of this back channel by using Pulikovskii as an intermediary in discussions with Kim Jong Il on a wide range of issues, including regional economic cooperation, the implementation of Russian–North Korean bilateral agreements, and the repayment of Pyongyang's debt to

Moscow. Pulikovskii made a second, shorter trip with the North Korean leader in the Russian Far East in August 2002.

As a member of the Russian Security Council, Pulikovskii also provides briefings on Far East security issues. In a July 2002 interview, he noted that the okrug faces a wide range of potential threats due to its dwindling population, proximity to great powers, vast territory, and rich natural resources. In particular, Pulikovskii stated that the Security Council should take steps to avert a demographic crisis in the Far East by passing legislation to control the presence of foreign workers and by allocating resources to encourage Russian migration from other areas of Russia and the Commonwealth of Independent States (CIS) to the okrug.[108] Unlike many politicians in the Russian Far East, Pulikovskii does not advocate strict controls on foreign workers, whom he believes may be able to make a positive contribution to the regional economy. Instead he has been encouraging governors to contribute to the development of the migration law that is currently being drafted by the State Duma.[109]

Conclusion

Pulikovskii has been largely unable to fulfill the main task assigned to him by President Putin, namely, coordinating the activities of federal agencies based in the Far East Federal Okrug. Federal officials such as Chubais and Shoigu have handled some of the key issues in the okrug since the creation of the envoy's office. As a result Pulikovskii generally has played a supporting role, supplementing high-level actions taken by Putin or his ministers.

In getting rid of unwanted governors, Pulikovskii has also not seemed to be up to the task. President Putin personally stepped in to deal with Primorskii Krai's Nazdratenko and Sakha's Nikolaev. The envoy's effort to replace Nazdratenko with a more pliable governor of his choosing failed, though the man ultimately elected, Darkin, has proven more willing to carry out the Kremlin's policy than his predecessor.

Like other presidential envoys, Pulikovskii has to some extent taken on the tasks of okrug lobbyist in Moscow. However, like Leonid Drachevskii in Siberia, he has not as yet been able to overcome the resistance of Gref's ministry in defining and implementing a regional development plan for the Far East.

Pulikovskii has succeeded in carving out a niche for himself as an intermediary on foreign policy issues. His utility as a go-between on sensitive questions, such as relations with North Korea, has provided him with a channel for access to Putin. Moreover, his Asian diplomacy has helped improve center–regional coordination on foreign policy issues, and it has contributed to regional efforts to promote economic cooperation with Asian neighbors, a key aspect of the Far East's development strategy.

Overall, Pulikovskii has had extremely limited success in promoting regional economic coordination, a problem that has long plagued the Far East. With Pulikovskii's help or through other means, the Far East desperately needs to find a way to ensure reliable and affordable energy supplies and lower transportation costs, without which the okrug's economic recovery will continue to lag behind Russian averages. Pulikovskii is unlikely to succeed in this effort unless he receives adequate economic support and enlightened regional policies from the Kremlin, or the cooperation of the region's governors, who continue to focus more on competing with one another than on working together to improve the economic climate in the Russian Far East as a whole.

Notes

1. Yurii Goltyuk, "The Chechen Crisis Spreads to the Russian Leadership," *Segodnya*, August 21, 1996, 1.

2. Igor' Nikitin and Larisa Larina, "Dalinkom: Investitsiyam dolzhno byt' uyutno," *Dalnevostochnyi Kapital*, no. 10 (October 14, 2001): 40.

3. Oleg Zhunusov, "Konstantin Pulikovskii, polpred prezidenta: Na Dal'nem Vostoke," interview with Konstantin Pulikovskii, *Izvestiya*, July 24, 2002.

4. Intellectuals, such as the historian Petr Slovtsov (1767–1843), were quick to criticize Petersburg's exploitation of Siberia. By the mid-nineteenth century, Siberian regional consciousness was being elaborated in intellectual fraternities or zemliachestva at the university in Saint Petersburg, where Siberian students gathered to discuss the future development of the region. A movement supporting Siberian regionalism or regionnichestvo emerged from these discussions and was developed by influential scholars, such as Afanasii Shchapov (1830–1876), Nikolai Iadrintsev (1842–1894), and Grigorii Potanin (1835–1920). In the 1880s, Iadrintsev wrote *Sibir kak koloniya* (*Siberia as a Colony*), in which he criticized the use of the region as a place of exile, the exploitation of its natural resources, and the neglect of aboriginal peoples. More than a century ago, scholars like Iadrintsev demanded many of the same measures that regional officials in the Russian Far East advocate today, especially a development program taking into account the interests of the region and a well-managed effort to address its labor requirements. See Norman Pereira, "Regional Consciousness in Siberia before and after 1917," *Canadian Slavonic Papers/Revue Canadienne des Slavistes, Tenth International Congress of Slavists*, Sofia, March 1988, 112–14.

5. The first governor-general for Priamur, Baron Nikolai Korf, had powers that the current presidential representative to the Far East Federal Okrug would envy, including command of the police and military forces, administration of justice, tax collection, control over economic development, and diplomacy with neighboring countries. The Priamur guberniia remained as an administrative unit until 1917, although there

were periodic shifts in its composition and briefly, from 1903 to 1905, it was integrated into a newly created Viceroyalty of the Far East, which also included the Chinese Eastern Railroad and was headquartered in Port Arthur. Russia's Far Eastern remote frontiers proved to be difficult ground for revolution. The Bolsheviks took power briefly in a few cities, but Soviet rule collapsed by the summer of 1918. At the time of the allied intervention, a host of autonomous governments competed for control over regions of the Far East. In 1920, a Far Eastern Republic was established in the Transbaikal, complete with its own president. Although it was incorporated into Soviet Russia two years later, it would take much longer for the Far Eastern territories to be integrated into the Soviet system. The Far Eastern territories enjoyed NEP until 1930 and were once again united into a separate entity, the Dalnevostochniy Krai (Dalkrai, or DVK), which existed from 1926 to 1938. The province even had its own army—the Special Far Eastern Army (OKDVA) commanded by Vasilii Blücher. See John Stefan, *The Russian Far East: A History* (Palo Alto, CA: Stanford University Press, 1994), 55, 60, 173, 180.

6. The Pacific Fleet is based in Vladivostok, and the Far East Military District has its headquarters in Khabarovsk. Important submarine bases also are located in Kamchatka.

7. Sergei Leonov, "Russian Far East Economy and North Asia Cooperation Problems," unpublished paper presented to the University of Toronto Northeast Asia Regional Cooperation Conference, November 30–December 1, 2000.

8. Statistics come from Nadezhda Mikheeva, "Social and Economic Differentiation in the Russian Far East," in *Russian Far East: Region at Risk,* ed. Judith Thornton and Charles E. Ziegler (Seattle: University of Washington Press, 2002), 88, 95, 101.

9. Galina Vitkovskaia, Zhanna Zayonchkovskaia, and Kathleen Newland, "Chinese Migration into Russia," in *Rapprochement or Rivalry? Russia-China Relations in a Changing Asia,* ed. Sherman Garnett (Washington, DC: Carnegie Endowment for International Peace, 2000), 351.

10. Raisa Tselobanova, "Besplatnyi obed ot polpredstva," *Tikhookeanskaya Zvezda,* February 9, 2002 (accessed at http://www.toz.khv.ru). As the reporter notes, economic integration will be difficult if regional officials are not interested enough to learn some basic economic facts about neighboring regions. For example, it was revealed at an okrug coordination council session on regional economic integration that Chukotka had been importing soya from Krasnodar Krai, instead of Amur Region, because the Chukotka authorities believed that Amur Region, an agricultural region, was covered by taiga.

11. *Russian Regional Report (RRR),* August 22, 2001.

12. Andrei Kalachinskii, "Vertikal' vlasti utknulas' v polpredov. Polpredstvo Pulikovskogo. Vzglyad iz Vladivostoka," unpublished paper presented at a June 7–9, 2002, Moscow conference on Russia's Federal Okrugs, 3. I would like to thank Andrei Kalachinskii for his permission to cite material from this paper.

13. *Tikhhookeanskaya Gazeta,* September 20, 2000 (accessed at www.toz.khv.ru).

14. Ol'ga Mal'tseva, "Konstantin Pulikovskii: Vladivostok ostanetsya glavnym gorodom Rossii v ATR," *Vladivostok,* October 16, 2000 (internet version); Kalachinskii, "Vertikal' vlasti utknulas' v polpredov," 5.

15. *RRR,* November 7, 2001.

16. *Izvestiya*, May 14, 2002. Reportedly, Ishaev and Pulikovskii time their appearances at Khabarovsk events so as to avoid each other.

17. Interview with Mikhail Mashkovtsev, *Zavtra*, February 2, 2002 (accessed at www.zavtra.ru).

18. Elizabeth Wishnick, *Mending Fences: The Evolution of Moscow's China Policy from Brezhnev to Yeltsin* (Seattle: University of Washington Press, 2001), 158–81.

19. *RRR*, December 13, 2000.

20. *RRR*, December 19, 2001.

21. In July 1997, when Yeltsin sought to transfer most of Nazdratenko's power to Aleksandr Kondratov, the presidential representative to Primorksii Krai, other governors supported Nadratenko to uphold the principle of federalism. *Zolotoi Rog*, July 8, 1997.

22. Kalachinskii, "Vertikal' vlasti utknulas' v polpredov," 11.

23. *Vremya Novostei*, February 26, 2001.

24. *The St. Petersburg Times*, February 27, 2001.

25. Nazdratenko had Cherepkov removed from office in 1994 on trumped up corruption charges. After years of court battles, the Vladivostok mayor was reinstated, only to be ousted again in December 1998 by presidential decree. Cherepkov sought to run for election in 1998, but his name was removed from the ballot due to alleged campaign violations; the results were ultimately declared invalid when a majority of the electorate voted against all. Mayoral elections were postponed, allowing Nazdratenko to appoint his own man, Yurii Kopylov, who was then able to beat Cherepkov in June 2000 elections. For background on the longstanding political battle between Cherepkov and Nazdratenko, see Anna Husarka, "City of Blights," *The New Republic*, December 15, 1997, 14–17; *RRR*, December 17, 1998; Peter Kirkow, "Regional Warlordism in Russia: The Case of Primorskii Krai," *Europe-Asia Studies* 47, no. 6 (September 1995): 936–38.

26. *RFE/RL Newsline*, November 2, 2001.

27. *RRR*, October 10, 2001. For a critical view, see Ivan Korotaev, "Darkin i pustota," *Dalekaya Okraina*, June 8, 2001, 4.

28. Oleg Zhunusov, "Political Struggle Spurs More Contract Killings," *RRR*, January 16, 2003.

29. Oleg Zhunusov, "Byvshii protiv nyneshnego," *Izvestiya*, April 9, 2002.

30. *Izvestiya*, May 14, 2002.

31. RIA, May 17, 2002.

32. Michael Bradshaw and Peter Kirkow, "The Energy Crisis in the Russian Far East: Origins and Possible Solutions," *Europe-Asia Studies* 50, no. 6 (1998): 1047.

33. U.S. International Trade Administration, "Energy Sector in the Russian Far East," April 8, 2002 (accessed at www.bisnis.gov).

34. *RRR*, April 3, 2002.

35. Sergei Suranov, "V chest' nachala senokosa," *Kommersant Daily*, June 25, 2001.

36. Nikolai Seregin, "V Yakutiiu priletel zamgenprokurora Kolmogorov," *Nezavisimaya gazeta*, September 7, 2001.

37. *RRR*, November 7, 2001.

38. Thus, paradoxically, Nikolaev could claim that in seeking a third term he was harmonizing republican legislation with federal law. Although the republican court

kept requesting a clarification from the federal Constitutional Court, the latter refused to provide one on the grounds that the republican elections would have to be postponed for there to be sufficient time to issue a ruling.

39. Accessed at strana.ru, January 14, 2002.

40. *RFE/RL Newsline*, March 8, 2002.

41. Oleg Zhunusov, "Kremlin, Governor Call Shots in Picking Primorksii Legusiature's Senator," *RRR*, February 6, 2002.

42. Oleg Zhunusov, "Political Struggle Spurs More Contract Killings," *RRR*, January 16, 2003.

43. Jacques Sapir, "Economic and Social Trends in the Russian Far East and their Strategic Consequences," Centres d'Etudes des Modes d'Industrialisation EHESS & IRSES-MSH, November 1997, 16. In 1996, Sakhalin's crime rate was nearly 210 percent of the national average, while Magadan's was 165 percent; Khabarovsk, 155 percent; Primorskii Krai, 145 percent; Amur Region and Kamchatka Region, nearly 110 percent. Only Sakha reported a lower than average crime rate, 80 percent of the national average.

44. Judith Thornton, "The Exercise of Rights of Resources in the Russian Far East," in *The Russian Far East and Pacific Asia: Unfulfilled Potential*, ed. Michael J. Bradshaw (London: Curzon, 2001), 95.

45. Oleg Zhunusov, "Byvshii protiv nyneshnego," *Izvestiya*, April 9, 2002.

46. Velisarios Kattoulas, "Crime Central," *Far Eastern Economic Review*, May 30, 2002, 50.

47. Tony Allison, "The Crisis of the Region's Fishing Industry: Sources, Prospects, and the Role of Foreign Interests," in *Russian Far East: A Region at Risk*, ed. Judith Thornton and Charles E. Ziegler (Seattle: University of Washington Press, 2002), 155.

48. Allison, "The Crisis of the Region's Fishing Industry," 157. Nazdratenko estimated that illegal fish sales to Japan alone cost the Russian Far East $500 million in revenue. *RFE/RL Newsline*, April 18, 2002.

49. In the last decade, employment in the fishing industry in the Russian Far East declined by 30 percent, leaving workers with few job alternatives. In Kamchatka, for example, the fishing industry accounts for 50 percent of all industrial jobs and in Sakhalin, 25 percent. Allison, "The Crisis of the Region's Fishing Industry," 148.

50. Reuters, "Fish Smugglers Seem to Reap Grim Revenge on Russian General," *The New York Times*, May 29, 2001, A11.

51. Kattoulas, "Crime Central," 51.

52. Elizabeth Wishnick, "One Asia Policy or Two? Moscow and the Russian Far East Debate Russia's Engagement in Asia," *NBR Analysis* 13, no. 1 (March 2002): 55–60.

53. Vilia G. Gelbras, *Kitaiskaya real'nost' Rossii* (Moscow: Muravei, 2001), 39.

54. A pilot survey of one hundred migrant workers conducted by the public opinion lab at the Institute of History in Vladivostok provides some anecdotal evidence to confirm this. See Mikhail A. Alexeev, "Socioeconomic and Security Implications of Chinese Migration in the Russian Far East," *Post-Soviet Geography and Economics* 42, no. 2 (2001): 127.

55. Some concerns have been expressed, however, that China's recent steps to liberalize foreign trade in compliance with its membership in the World Trade Organiza-

tion could encourage unscrupulous firms to enter the Russian Far East, causing tensions in Sino-Russian regional economic relations to flare up again.

56. Viktor Larin, "Russia and China: Some Regional Dimensions," unpublished paper presented to "Russian Far East and Northeast Asia" conference, Vladivostok, October 10–12, 2001. Currently more than 80 percent of foreign visitors to Primorskii Krai are Chinese tourists: 297,477 out of a total of 379,516 in 1999; and 182,809 out of 252,729 in the first three quarters of 2000. See Igor' Verba, "Polzuchaia ekspansiia velikogo soseda," *Nezavisimaya gazeta*, February 17, 2001.

57. In September 2000, during his first visit to the Russian Far East, Putin met with regional leaders to discuss demographic issues. In June 2001, the Russian Security Council's working group on the Russian Far East announced a new project to develop new approaches to security threats posed by issues such as demographic decline and the "yellow peril."

58. James Clay Moltz, "Russian Nuclear Regionalism: Emerging Local Influences over Far Eastern Facilities," *NBR Analysis* 11, no. 4 (December 2000): 35–57.

59. The Far Eastern branch of the Ministry of Economic Development and Trade had played a key role in negotiations between Moscow and the Association for the Russian Far East and the Transbaikal about the 1996–2005 development plan for these territories.

60. Interviews with Khabarovsk scholars, October–November 2001.

61. P.A. Minakir, "Ekonomicheskoe i sotsial'noe razvitie Dal'nego Vostoka i Zabaikal'ya (korrektirovka 'Prezidentskoy programmy')," *Vestnik Dal'nevostochnogo otdeleniya Rossiiskoi Akademii Nauk (DVO RAN)*, no. 2 (2002): 17.

62. Polit.ru, August 23, 2002.

63. Interview with Professor Mikhail Shinkovskii conducted by Irina Drobysheva, January 2003.

64. *Kommersant*, September 21, 2002.

65. Interviews with officials in Blagoveshchensk, Khabarovsk, Vladivostok, and Yuzhno-Sakhalinsk, October 1999.

66. Sakhalin officials expect another $1 billion in investment in the offshore oil and gas projects by the end of 2002. In 2001 the projects attracted $450 million in investment, double the 2000 figure. Elena Sabirova, "Sakhalin Oil and Gas Update," Summer 2002 (accessed in July 2002, at www.bisnis.doc.gov).

67. Elena Sabirova, "Sakhalin Oil and Gas Update," Summer 2001 (accessed in September 2001, at www.bisnis.doc.gov).

68. Elena Sabirova, "Commercial Update—Sakhalin Region (Russian Far East)," October 2001 (accessed at www.bisnis.doc.gov).

69. Michael Bradshaw, "The Sakhalin Oil and Gas Projects: Obstacles Restrain Sakhalin's Potential," *EWI Russian Regional Investor*, June 21, 2001.

70. Sabirova, "Commercial Update– Sakhalin Region (Russian Far East)," October 2001 (accessed in www.bisnis.doc.gov).

71. *Rossiiskii regional'nyi byulleten'*, December 16, 2002.

72. *Ekspert*, November 5, 2001.

73. ITAR-TASS, June 26, 2001.

74. RRR, April 3, 2002.

75. Mikhail Kosyrev and Aleksei Nikolsky, "Chinese Customers Do Not Recognize Their Partners," *Vedomosti*, March 19, 2002.

76. The routing of pipelines from the offshore Sakhalin oil and gas projects has been particularly controversial, with Farkhutdinov focusing on the Japanese market, and Ishaev and Darkin lobbying for pipelines to the mainland, which would supply their regions and then possibly connect to China and the Korean peninsula. Pulikovskii's focus on economic cooperation has much in common with Ishaev's conception of a unified energy space. V.I. Ishaev, "Strategicheskoe razvitie Rossii do 2010 g. i kontseptsiya regional'nykh preobrazovaniy," in *Vestnik DVO RAN*, no. 2 (2002): 26.

77. Igor' Nikitin and Larisa Larina, "Dalinkom: Investitsiyam dolzhno byt' uyutno," *Dalnevostochnyi Kapital*, no. 10 (October 14, 2001): 40.

78. RIA Oreanda, February 4, 2002.

79. *EWI Russian Regional Investor*, October 3, 2001.

80. Andrew Wilson, "Law Enforcement in the Russian Far East: The Impact of Regional Autonomy on Foreign Investment," unpublished paper presented to AAASS Conference, November 18, 2001, Washington, D.C., 2.

81. *RRR*, January 23, 2002.

82. *Bisnis Russian Far East*, May 1, 2002 (accessed at www.bisnis.doc.gov).

83. *RRR*, March 13, 2002.

84. *Kommersant Daily*, November 30, 2001; *Vedomosti*, November 30, 2001.

85. *RRR*, December 12, 2002.

86. Accessed at polit.ru, December 10, 2001.

87. *The Russia Journal*, December 21, 2001.

88. Republican interests favored Alrosa vice president Aleksandr Matveyev for the position due to his experience as business manager, while Kremlin officials hoped their candidate would help them regain majority control over the company's shares. *Nezavisimaya gazeta*, March 4, 2002, 3.

89. El'mar Murmazaev, "Yakutskoe vremya," *Vedomosti*, August 6, 2002.

90. *Kompaniya*, no. 12 (April 2002): 40–41.

91. Oleg Zhunusov, "Byvshii protiv nyneshnego," *Izvestiya*, April 9, 2002.

92. Kalachinskii, "Vertikal' vlasti utknulas' v polpredov," 18.

93. Two of the rare exceptions are *Arsenevskie Vesti* in Primorskii Krai and *Khabarovskii Ekspress*.

94. Interview with Pulikovskii, *Vladivostok*, October 16, 2000.

95. For example, Pulikovskii's press secretary refuses to talk to the press, and the presidential representative is unwilling to allow journalists to shoot standard footage of the start of his meetings with local officials. Russell Working, "Letter from Vladivostok: Primorye Super-Governor," *Moscow Times*, June 27, 2000. Nevertheless, Pulikovskii has granted interviews to the press on a regular basis.

96. *RRR*, May 23, 2001.

97. Felix K. Chang, "The Russian Far East's Endless Winter," *Orbis* (Winter 1999): 107.

98. Organizers include the American Chamber of Commerce in Russia, the U.S.–Russia Business Council, the Russian Union of Industrialists and Entrepreneurs,

and the Russian–American Business Council. The Ad Hoc Working Group is participating in the new group.

99. Until 1992, Vladivostok was closed to foreigners because of the city's role as a base for the Pacific fleet. Several cities in the Russian Far East remain under federal control because of their defense functions.

100. Nabi Abdullaev and Natalia Yefimova, "Court Nullifies State Secrets Order," *St. Petersburg Times*, February 15, 2002.

101. *RFE/RL Newsline*, June 26, 2002.

102. Minakir, "Ekonomicheskoe i sotsial'noe razvitie," 7.

103. This is not to say that Pulikovskii has eliminated center–regional differences on foreign policy issues. For an analysis of this issue, see Elizabeth Wishnick, "One Asia Policy or Two? Moscow and the Russian Far East Debate Russia's Engagement in Asia," *NBR Analysis* 13, no. 1 (March 2002).

104. Igor Verba, "Konstantin Pulikovskii: 'Migratsiyu nado ne zapreshchat', a ispol'zovat'," interview with Pulikovskii, *Nezavisimaya gazeta*, July 25, 2002.

105. Agence France-Presse, April 22, 2002. Pulikovskii has stated that these islands are Russian territory. See Verba, "Konstantin Pulikovskii."

106. Initially, all of the presidential representatives to Russia's seven federal okrugs were supposed to take turns accompanying Kim Jong Il on his journey, with the appropriate official taking charge once the train entered his okrug. Ultimately, Putin decided only Pulikovskii would accompany the North Korean leader throughout the entire trip to make the security-conscious Korean leader feel more comfortable and to avoid subjecting him to a stream of unknown officials. Pulikovskii had accompanied Putin on his visit to Pyongyang. Portions of Pulikovskii's memoir of the train voyage were published in March 2002 in *Vladivostok*. Ol'ga Mal'tseva and Leonid Vinogradov, "Konstantin Pulikovskii. Po Rossii s Kim Chen Irom [Kim Jong Il]," *Vladivostok*, part I, March 26, 2002; part II, March 29, 2002 (accessed at www.vladnew.ru).

107. Ol'ga Novak, "V Detstve ego zvali Yura" (They called him Yura as a Child), *Tikhookeanskaya Zvezda*, February 16, 2002 (accessed at www.toz.khv.ru).

108. Oleg Zhunusov, "Byvshii protiv nyneshnego," *Izvestiya*, April 9, 2002.

109. Igor Verba, "Konstantin Pulikovskii: 'Migratsiyu nado ne zapreshchat', a ispol'zovat'," interview with Pulikovskii, *Nezavisimaya gazeta*, July 25, 2002.

10

What Do the Okrug Reforms Add Up To? Some Conclusions

Robert Orttung and Peter Reddaway

IN THE CONCLUDING CHAPTER, we sum up the main findings of this first volume of a two-volume book. Volume 1 has analyzed the innovative aspects of President Putin's federal reforms by focusing on each okrug separately, on the envoys, and on the many-sided campaign to reduce the powers of the governors. In volume 2 we shall focus throughout on all the okrugs and examine federal–regional relations through the prism—in each chosen field—both of the federal reforms and of other developments since 2000. The chosen fields include the power ministries, the courts, the natural monopolies, small and big business, fiscal federalism, local government, political parties, the national legislature, health care, and the federal executive as a whole. In this way we hope, in the two volumes taken together, to achieve a multidimensional analysis of Russia's federal system, using a variety of horizontal and vertical perspectives.

In the conclusions to volume 1 that follow, we shall keep in the forefront of our minds broad questions of this type:

- How has the constantly changing balance of power between the federal government and the regional governments evolved since 2000?
- Has the creation of the new institution of federal okrugs and presidential envoys had a lasting effect on Russian politics, or will the impact probably just be temporary?
- What are the prospects that the envoys will be given more power in the future? Or—perhaps more likely—will the institution decline or be abolished?

Specifically, we will examine the impact of the reforms on these topics: the overall functioning of the state, the government's personnel policies, coordination of the federal ministries in the regions, the power of the governors, the locus of economic power and influence, crime and corruption, local government, the media, and civil society.

Institutional Reform

Nearly three years after Putin took office, his federal reforms have weakened some of the institutions that grew strong during the 1990s, most notably the governors and the Federation Council, but his initiatives have not set in place effective new institutions capable of implementing a coherent federal policy in Russia's eighty-nine regions. Although he sits at the apex of Russia's increasingly centralized political system, he has not established a new system that substantially changes the ways that institutions work.

However, his reform of the hierarchy of the presidential administration has significantly changed the tenor of center–periphery relations in Russia. The seven presidential envoys are now a visible part of the Russian political landscape, and they have a certain influence.

Nonetheless, many of the reforms' supposed accomplishments are exaggerated. Putin and his subordinates often argue that they have prevented the disintegration of Russia. This is an overstatement because Russia was not actually disintegrating in 1999. The envoys also claim that they have brought the vast majority of Russia's regional laws into line with federal norms, boasting that the number that do not comply with these norms is now as low as 2 percent. In fact, this change is less significant than such statistics suggest. Many of the laws that violated federal legislation were declaratory and had little effect on the way things actually worked. Changing such laws was largely symbolic and had little or no real impact on day-to-day life, partly because Russia still has a government of men more than of laws. In most cases, this means that informal agreements among these men are more important than written laws.

Personnel Issues

Putin inherited a political system that was in many respects, especially as regards fiscal matters, fairly centralized. His reforms sought to concentrate power further. In these circumstances, the quality of the individuals at key positions in the bureaucracy became extremely important.

Most of the seven men he chose as his envoys moved up the career ladder in the military, security, or police bodies; and they preferred to work behind the scenes, sharing little information with the public. Such professional experience qualified them to deal with the power ministries, some matters of foreign policy, and certain types of personnel issues.

However, they had little of the training or experience required to deal with the complex problems of Russia's economy. Volga envoy Sergei Kirienko was the one exception in this regard. Before his appointment, he was a national politician with extensive ties to other politicians and big business. He had experience in public relations, banking, and industry. In contrast to his new colleagues, he used competitions to recruit staff members, and he came up with original ideas for promoting cooperation among state bodies, civil society, and business. However, outside his okrug these innovations were little applied in the new envoy system.

In many cases, the president and his envoys relied on personnel from the power ministries, and especially the Federal Security Service (FSB), to fill such key positions as deputy envoys, chief federal inspectors (CFIs), and even as favored candidates for gubernatorial elections in some regions. They also drew on existing members of the Presidential Administration (PA) and some regional elites. However, while these jobs did attract some former governors and other high-level officials, in several okrugs talented local analysts reportedly did not want to work on the envoys' staff because the job had poorly defined functions and placed too many restrictions on their freedom of thought.

The PA seemed interested in returning to a pre-Brezhnev policy of shifting federal officials outside their native okrug, hoping thus to keep them loyal to the center and prevent them from developing close ties to regional interests. But again there was no real consistency in applying the policy. Kazantsev relied heavily on Rostov-based personnel for his staff, while Latyshev largely looked beyond Yekaterinburg to fill his ranks. Almost all the CFIs appointed by Kazantsev had done no similar work before, while Poltavchenko and Drachevskii preferred to appoint Yeltsin-era presidential representatives (though Drachevskii often sent former representatives to serve as CFIs in regions where they had no previous experience).

Coordination of Federal Government

One of the most important tasks Putin gave the envoys was to coordinate the work of the federal ministries in the regions. Overall, it appears that they have somewhat improved this "horizontal" coordination, but it is not clear whether this has hindered the "vertical" functioning of particular ministries. Our authors did not find significant reliable evidence on this point. Clearly, though, federal ministries concerned with the economy, and especially financial flows, have strongly opposed any direct involvement by the envoys in the substance of their work and have got their way. Nevertheless, the reform has enabled the envoys to play an active role in personnel monitoring, at least in some ministries, thus compelling governors to work with federal officials whom they did not take part in appointing.

In each okrug, the envoys' staff has been too small to oversee the fifty-plus federal agencies operating in their territory. However, simply increasing the number of staff members would not have had much impact. As in any bureaucratic system, the core of the battle has been for control over resources. No existing federal agency has been willing to give up its power in this regard to the newly created envoys.

Generally, the envoys have set up a variety of councils that include representatives from each of the federal agencies operating in their okrugs. However, these councils appear to have accomplished little more than increased information exchange. The envoys and federal officials meet to discuss important issues, but then there is apparently, in most cases, little translation of the discussions into policy change.

In those agencies like the Ministry of Internal Affairs (MVD) and the Procuracy, which set up okrug-level offices, the envoys have had the best chance of influencing appointments of personnel to the regional level and thereby reducing the power of the governors. In many regions, the governors soon began to find that the federal officials serving in their regions were no longer necessarily their allies but might be individuals who were beholden to the federal authorities for their position and who were sometimes willing to risk confrontation with the regional government. Regional procurators in particular started to become more outspoken in denouncing regional deviations from federal laws. In regions like Bashkortostan, the procurator brought a considerable amount of pressure on the republican authorities. In Siberia, the envoy blocked the Novosibirsk governor from appointing his ally to run the regional branch of the federal property ministry, and instead got one of his own staff appointed to the position.

However, governors—especially powerful ones—have still maintained some say in the process of appointing federal officials in their regions, and envoys' assertions to the contrary should be viewed skeptically. Especially notable is the fact that although the Kremlin has radically increased its ability on paper to replace regional police chiefs, in practice, as evidence from the Central and Siberian Okrug shows, it has made few such appointments. This suggests that in most cases Moscow simply cannot afford to appoint police chiefs who will antagonize governors and thus introduce dangerous conflict into the administration of law and order.

Most important of all, perhaps, with rare exceptions, the federal agencies have remained dangerously dependent on resources from the governors, such as office space, apartments, and other types of infrastructure support. Beyond this, evidence suggests that the governors have lost none of their skill at subverting the loyalty of federal officials in subtle ways by providing them with free or subsidized services like cars, drivers, stays at rest homes, and various domestic conveniences.

Several key federal agencies did not set up okrug offices. These included the Finance Ministry, the Federal Security Service (FSB), and the Defense Ministry. As noted earlier, the envoys have very little influence over federal funds, as the Finance Ministry jealously guards its prerogatives. As regards defense issues, an exceptional situation exists in the Southern okrug, where Kazantsev has maintained a strong influence over the military (since he formerly headed the North Caucasus Military District). As for the FSB, recent evidence shows that it is playing a very special role in the federal reform: this powerful institution actually supervises okrug personnel (from the CFI level downward), rather than vice versa. It does this through the regular FSB offices in each city where okrug staff are located.[1] It appears, therefore, that the okrug dimension of the federal reform is being administered jointly by the FSB and the PA. In the latter case, those who play the key roles include PA head Voloshin, relevant PA departments, and his subordinates in the field, the envoys.

In times of crisis, more powerful federal actors often overshadow the envoys. For example, FSB director Nikolai Patrushev usually takes charge following terrorist attacks. In the Far East, emergencies minister Sergei Shoigu handled the federal response to flooding in Sakha, and electricity chief Anatolii Chubais spearheaded the federal response to Primorskii Krai's energy crisis.

In addition to coordinating the federal agencies in the regions, the envoys have also tried to act as intermediaries between the regions and individual ministries, seeking to help regions in their jurisdiction to extract additional federal resources. This has compensated them somewhat for their inability to directly control the distribution of federal funds. It also means that they are supplementing or duplicating the work of the regions' senators in the Federation Council. Kirienko has been effective in this role of regional lobbyist, thanks to his extensive contacts among federal officials in Moscow.

Several of the envoys have sought to create similar roles for themselves as lead advocates for federal megaprojects that span a number of regions. Kazantsev took this job seriously, helping his Southern okrug to promote a strategic development plan. He also sided with grain-producing regions that wanted to regulate prices, even though such measures violated federal law. In the Urals, Latyshev worked with resource-rich Tyumen Region to minimize the impact of the federal government's policy of directing tax revenues generated by natural resources to the center and away from the regions. At the same time, he lobbied the federal government to send more subsidies to the desperately poor Kurgan Region.

Thus, the envoys may have been less significant as coordinators of federal policy than as advocates of regional interests in Moscow. They seem likely to go on performing this function because it gives them a visible role in the economic and political system. At the same time, since they wield only "administrative," not financial resources, they will often be less valuable to governors than businessmen with funds to invest.

Several of the envoys have tried to encourage more public participation in the process of overseeing the actions of federal officials. These efforts include the opening of public reception rooms where citizens can file complaints about the behavior of officials. It is too early to say how well these offices are working. It is also hard to predict how enthusiastically Russian society will assume the task of monitoring the state officials who are supposed to serve it.

Governors

Putin's federal reforms have reduced the power of the governors in a number of important ways. Nevertheless, the governors remain powerful within their regions.

Relations with the President

Most prominent, Putin has reduced the role that the regional elites play at the national level. By creating the envoys, he put a new layer between himself and the governors. To a large extent, he depersonalized his relations with them. Whereas they often had direct access to Yeltsin, now, if they want to see Putin to discuss matters crucial to their region, they must work through the envoy's staff. Only a few exceptional governors, such as the leaders of Tatarstan, Bashkortostan, and Saint Petersburg, retain the personal clout to deal with Putin directly. However, unlike in the earlier era, these leaders have to maneuver carefully to secure their one-on-one audiences with the president.

By limiting the number of meetings he has with governors, Putin has reduced the role of political deals between the federal and regional governments. He has campaigned ardently to abolish the forty-two power-sharing treaties that Yeltsin or his subordinates signed with the regions between 1994 and 1998. The regions that gained little from forty-six treaties have willingly given them up in an attempt to curry favor with the Kremlin. But powerful regions that derived important financial benefits from the treaties have refused to abrogate them, thus preserving for now some of the formal asymmetry in federal relations. Although Putin has sought to impose a unified system, with equal conditions for all regions, some regions that lack treaties continue to push for special treatment that will differentiate them from the rest of the country.

Relations with the Federal Legislature

By removing the governors and regional legislative chairmen from the Federation Council, the upper house of the legislature, Putin has deprived these leaders of a prominent federal platform for expressing their opinions, and he has also ended their immunity from prosecution. He has also removed them from participating directly in writing national legislation, including the country's budget, and he has taken away an arena where they could potentially form a united front against federal policy, as they did periodically in the years 1997–1999. In sum, he has reduced their status from federal to merely regional politicians. Following the completion of this reform in early 2002, the Federation Council has been much more willing to cooperate with the Kremlin than the body was that existed from 1996 to 2001 and consisted of the regional leaders.

However, while Putin has succeeded in reducing the governors' overall clout at the national level, the reform has also provided them with new lobbying opportunities in Moscow. This conclusion flows from our analysis of the process of appointing the new Federation Council members. This reveals no clear pattern regarding who, overall, wielded the most power—the regional authorities, the PA, or big business.[2] The process worked differently in different regions and depended on a large number of variables. In some regions, the PA and the envoys were able to dictate their nominees for the Federation Council to weak governors who depended on federal subsidies. Even aggressive governors from rich regions were vulnerable to such pressure in the months preceding their reelection, when they needed to parade the extensive ties they had in Moscow for developing their region. In other regions, governors appointed Federation Council members primarily to serve their own interest, whether this was to have a trusted ally in Moscow to lobby the federal government or to remove a potential rival from the local political scene.

In general, the days are over when the Federation Council banded together to support a crusading general procurator investigating Kremlin corruption, as it did for Yurii Skuratov in 1999. It is equally unlikely that the new body will serve as an arena for organizing a party opposed to the Kremlin, as it did for the formation of Yurii Luzhkov's Fatherland party prior to the 1999 Duma elections. In some cases, in fact, it may not matter much whether a senator is originally appointed as an ally of the governor, the PA, big business, or some combination, because once he is in Moscow, he may anyway come under the powerful influence of the PA or take bribes from the highest bidder.

The election of Sergei Mironov as Federation Council speaker on December 5, 2001, replacing Yegor Stroev, marked the culmination of the upper chamber's shift of loyalty toward the Kremlin that had been apparent throughout 2001. In contrast to Stroev—who was a compromise figure between Yeltsin and the communists—Mironov, an associate of Putin's from Saint Petersburg, was the president's clear choice for the job. He quickly consolidated his authority through the adoption of the upper chamber's new rules. These prescribed how many deputies he would have and the use of slate voting for choosing new committee chairmen and first deputies.

The PA's influence over the composition of the upper chamber is clear. As much as 40 percent of the new body are individuals from Moscow with only tenuous connections to the regions they ostensibly represent.[3] Backgrounds associated with Saint Petersburg, the power ministries, and the PA are also common among carpetbagging senators. Many senators are regional politicians whose careers were derailed, such as governors who lost their reelection bids, making them susceptible to the PA's manipulation. Putin's seven presidential envoys are also well represented: the Volga's Kirienko managed to engineer the appointment of two of his deputies, two CFIs, and several key allies; Siberia's Drachevskii did the same for two CFIs; and the Northwest's Cherkesov did likewise for one staff member. By contrast, in the South, the Urals, and the Far East, the greatest say in making appointments seemed to belong to the regional elites.

One way in which the PA and the envoys influenced the membership of the upper chamber was by torpedoing the appointment of controversial figures before they were finalized. When Buryatia's legislature tried to appoint the above-mentioned Skuratov, the republican procurator protested the procedure by which he was chosen. Acknowledging what was clearly a signal from the PA and Drachevskii, the legislature then chose a different representative. Similar events occurred in the North-West when the Leningrad regional legislature tried to appoint the controversial Chubais protégé, Alfred Kokh, to the upper chamber in 2002.

Despite the enormous influence of the PA on the Federation Council's composition and operation, the extent to which its new members serve various regional and business interests remains unclear and certainly deserves further study. Approximately one in five senators previously worked for either large or medium-sized companies.[4] Two former CEOs are Sergei Pugachev of Mezhprombank (International Industrial Bank) and Aleksandr Pleshakov of the airline Transaero. Other businessmen–senators come from the ranks of second-tier executives, including two vice presidents from Mikhail Khodorkovskii's companies, two more from Oleg Deripaska's Base Element, and one from Vladimir Potanin's Interros. The Unified Energy System electricity monopoly and Gazprom each have two representatives. The oil companies Sibneft, Transneft, and Slavneft have one each, while LUKoil and Alfa Group do not have any known members. The Pervouralsk New Pipe Factory in Sverdlovsk region holds the record, with close ties to three members. Corporations have also contributed money to the campaigns of dozens of other senators, but these individuals are not necessarily going to support the corporations on all issues. Among other considerations, they may have received additional, perhaps greater financial support from governors and/or the PA. Also, large-scale bribing of senators and Duma deputies goes on to influence the casting of votes on particular pieces of legislation.

Although Putin gained considerable control over federal legislation through this reform, the governors remain enormously powerful in their home regions. Thus, if they dislike a bill he has signed, the Kremlin may not be able to implement it for lack of an efficient mechanism to enforce its power across the country. The governors can often avoid effective monitoring by the short-staffed presidential envoy, or, if harassed, they can use the lobbying power of their senators in Moscow to minimize any consequences of their actions. The future orientation of the Federation Council will likely reflect, first, the evolving relationship among the regional elites, the Kremlin, the power ministries and big business; and, second, any more permanent method of choosing council members that may be devised in the future.

The Overall Impact of the Envoys and Other Federal Measures in the Regions

As noted earlier, the appearance of the envoys has changed the atmosphere in which the governors work. While their interests may often diverge, the envoys and the governors generally have amicable enough relationships, with open conflict appearing in relatively few cases.

Although it was not their intention, Putin's reforms, while authoritarian in spirit, have in some regions created the conditions for greater institutional and political pluralism. During the 1990s, many governors coordinated their actions with the regional legislature, the business community, and the media to create a monolithic system in which there was very little room for dissenting opinions. By establishing an alternative power center in the office of his envoy, Putin's reform opened up a wider space for differing viewpoints than existed before. His intention was to establish strong federal control to replace strong gubernatorial control. In reality, however, he weakened the governors by introducing a rival. Thus independent-minded politicians, businessmen, and journalists can now maneuver between the federal and regional authorities to pursue their various goals. Such freedom did not exist when the governors held almost exclusive authority.

Since the envoys have few resources of their own, their impact in a particular region often depends on how many groups exist that are willing to stand up to the authorities. Where such groups exist, the envoy can work with them to restrict the governor. In more closed regions, where such groups are not prominent, the envoy has less room for maneuver. Kirienko, for example, can exert much greater control in Ulyanovsk, where outside business interests are strong, than in Tatarstan, where the authorities control much of the republic's business. In Siberia, Drachevskii has intervened in regional politics when the players were locked in conflict and could not resolve their disputes. In particular, he stepped in to address long-running disputes between the governor and mayor of Omsk, and the executive and legislative branches in Irkutsk.

The governors have so far failed to unite against the envoys. Nor, it seems, within a single okrug, have they done so against one envoy. Such an outcome is not particularly surprising. Even at the height of the governors' power during the late 1990s, they failed to form an enduring coalition against the federal authorities. Also, some okrugs seem to have been specially designed to help maintain this status quo. The Urals okrug in particular was apparently assembled to prevent Sverdlovsk governor Eduard Rossel from reviving his ambition to create a Urals Republic that could exert itself against Moscow. Likewise, the envoys seem to have buried or undermined the eight interregional economic associations that worked in the 1990s to bring regions together to lobby Moscow and reduce trade barriers among them. Of the eight, only the Siberian and Far Eastern associations are functioning more or less effectively three years after the reforms began, while the status of the North-Western one is not clear.

Governors' autonomy from the envoys' supervision is sometimes aided by sensitive ethnic factors. In ethnically divided or border regions, the federal government often prefers to maintain stability rather than push governors to obey federal laws. However, in the operational, as opposed to the legal, sphere, the envoys have naturally intervened less in stable regions and more aggressively in unstable ones—to try to restore stability. And while they have interfered in a minority of regional elections, as discussed below, they often overlook governors' use of state resources when they seek reelection, and they rarely object to gubernatorial manipulation of the regional media. Since the envoys have a large number of regions to deal with, many governors seem to escape their attention and therefore feel less impact from the reforms than is evident in other regions.

In the field of fiscal federalism, Moscow has tried to tie its financial support of the regions to increased transparency in regional budgets. Although large areas of nontransparency remain, such changes have forced greater accountability on the regions.[5]

Firing Governors, Replacing Them, and Disbanding Regional Legislatures

Putin has yet to test his new, heavily circumscribed power to remove governors who violate the law and then ignore court orders to correct their mistakes.[6] However, he has successfully used less formal power to get rid of some of the governors he finds most objectionable and, in certain cases, replace them with more pliant individuals. Thus, he secured Governor Yevgenii Nazdratenko's "resignation" over the phone, in part, apparently, by threatening him with potentially damaging revelations that might have led to criminal prosecution and also by enticing him to head the State Fisheries Committee, a position that put him in charge of a lucrative industry.[7] As Elizabeth Wishnick shows in her chapter, Nazdratenko was one of the most troublesome governors for the Yeltsin administration. Additionally, in a Kremlin meeting, Putin persuaded President Mikhail Nikolaev of Sakha (Far East okrug) not to seek a third term in exchange for the position of deputy Federation Council speaker and presidential support for one of Nikolaev's key allies to succeed him. Presumably the new Sakha president's ties to Nikolaev will prevent him from investigating any abuses of power that occurred during Nikolaev's long tenure in the 1990s. The PA also had a hand in securing Ingushetiya president Ruslan Aushev's surprise resignation in the Southern okrug, as well as the decision by the director of the Novolipetsk Metallurgical Combine, Vladimir Lisin, not to enter the April 2002 gubernatorial elections in Lipetsk (Central okrug).[8] In several less publicized cases, the Kremlin successfully pressured governors not to seek reelection (Ivanovo, Kaluga, Kursk, and Krasnodar).

As a method for putting in place pro-Kremlin governors, this manipulative sort of approach to regional politics has had mixed results. After Nazdratenko left office, the local voters ignored Pulikovskii's exhortations to vote for his deputy as governor. However, even though the Kremlin did not support the campaign of Sergei Darkin, a young businessman with no political experience, the new governor has proved to be open to Kremlin guidance in a way that Nazdratenko never was. Darkin reportedly consults with Moscow regularly on important decisions. However, the Kremlin suffered a black eye in the election because of Pulikovskii's poor campaign skills and because many local observers linked Darkin to organized crime groups in the region. In Ingushetia, the Kremlin won a victory with the election of Deputy Envoy M. Zyazikov in place of Aushev. However, in this case the Kremlin had to use heavy-handed election-rigging tactics to ensure that the voters made the right choice, including having the courts disqualify the leading candidate. In Sakha, by contrast, where the new president seems to be just as aggressive as the old one in pushing to maintain republican control over the local diamond industry, Putin's manipulations may have been to little avail. Meanwhile, in regions like Krasnodar (Southern okrug), the former governor was able to pick his successor without any apparent input from the federal authorities.

Putin may have hoped that the law allowing him to remove governors would serve as a weapon that he would never have to use. Its mere existence would encourage the governors to behave appropriately, so as to avoid its potential use. This subtle presumed impact of the law is hard to measure since it is difficult to assess the various influences on a governor's behavior. Most governors go out of their way to proclaim their loyalty to the popular Putin, but their sincerity cannot be accurately gauged.

Although it received much less attention in 2000, the federal law allowing for the disbanding of regional legislatures that violate federal law seems to be having more impact than the legislation aimed at the governors. The Kremlin has threatened to disband legislatures much more often than it has threatened governors. In September 2001, for example, it coerced the Komi legislature (North-West okrug) to renounce the republic's right to sovereignty and forced the Kursk legislature (Central), on paper at least, to strengthen local governments. Federal officials have also threatened regional legislatures in Sverdlovsk (Urals) and several Siberian regions. While the government has yet to disband any legislatures, the threat of doing so seems to be working well enough. Naturally, though, the question remains as to whether regional legislation adopted under such threats will ever be implemented.

Gubernatorial Elections

The role of the envoys in the gubernatorial elections has been one of the most complex issues for the authors of this book. The president's actions have been contradictory. While he has clearly wanted to install new regional executives whom the PA favors, he made an enormous concession to many incumbent governors by ceding to their pressure to run for third and, in some cases, fourth terms.

The Kremlin and its envoys have had a mixed record in the elections. In a majority of cases, powerful governors won reelection regardless of its position. Here it had little choice but to go along and support the incumbent. However, it did succeed in getting some of the most notorious governors defeated at the ballot box, such as Vyacheslav Kislitsyn in Marii-El (Central) and Leonid Gorbenko in Kaliningrad (North-West). But the Kremlin also suffered some embarrassing defeats, especially with the election of a communist governor in Nizhnii Novgorod (Volga), a supposed "bastion of reform" where Kirienko had been particularly active.

Some analysts have criticized the envoys as being ineffective because of their inability to engineer the election of more PA-favored candidates. However, Nikolai Petrov considers this criticism to be exaggerated. He argues that since the reforms have weakened gubernatorial power considerably, it matters much less than in the past which individual is serving as governor. Moreover, he plausibly suggests that the envoys are analyzing each election to build their understanding of regional politics so as to use it in future Duma and presidential elections. In other words, they have an electoral agenda that goes beyond simply trying to get specific candidates elected in particular elections.

This raises an important question, the answer to which our authors have found elusive. One of the main tasks of the envoys is to collect and analyze a wide range of political, economic, and social information about the regions. They reportedly have staffs—inadequate in size and quality, no doubt—for doing this. But most of the work is conducted in the style of an intelligence agency and remains secret. Thus we face many unanswered questions: How good is it? Which topics are researched most intensively? And how effectively do the envoys use the analysts' output? Equally interesting: How much does the PA use it? Do PA analysts collate it across the okrugs? And do they integrate it with research by other state agencies so that policy can be based on their overall findings? Or is the PA too pressured, too internally divided, and/or too short of staff to perform some or all of these functions effectively? We have little idea.

The Governors' Remaining Strengths

Despite the Kremlin's ability to limit the governors' power in the ways just discussed, Putin's reforms have fairly clear limits. Russia's governors remain extremely powerful within their home regions. Unlike the envoys, they can distribute state funds through the regional budgets. They also issue a wide range of licenses for businesses seeking to work in the regions and sign contracts. Governors continue to wield enough resources to have considerable influence over court proceedings and the appointment of some federal officials. They have extensive control both over the regional media, where the envoys' sway is usually weak, and over local governments, where it is minimal. And, as in the past, most businesses have considerable difficulty operating in a region, unless they have the governor's support.

Overall, though, more important than the role of the envoys in gubernatorial campaigns—and probably more indicative of how power streams are now flowing—has been the recent trend of businessmen seeking to become governors. The fact that they have run and been elected in a number of Far Eastern and Siberian regions provides proof that the governor's office remains important despite Putin's reforms. In fact, the virtual fusion of business power and political power in these cases may—especially given the ineffective separation of the three traditional branches of governmental power in Russia—present one of the most serious new challenges to the Kremlin. The combination of regional political power with the economic resources of some of Russia's largest companies could put severe, if largely invisible, constraints on certain sorts of action by the federal executive. In particular, the ability of businessmen–governors to quietly subvert the loyalty of key federal officials in their regions is clearly greater than that of governors who are not backed by an oligarch with billions of dollars in assets.

Economic Power

Since the establishment of the okrugs, the envoys have asked the president to give them extended powers to monitor state money flows. So far, he has rebuffed them. However, they have not accepted this setback passively. Instead, they have sought to increase their economic influence and power by lobbying the government to finance interregional megaprojects, by building ties with Russia's big businesses, and by working to expand foreign investment in their okrugs. The main constraint on their actions in this sphere is the personnel who make up their staff. In most cases, military and secret service agents dominate, and these men have little experience dealing with economic issues.

Kirienko has gone the furthest of the envoys in this field, even seeking to gain extensive control of the economy in one of his okrug's regions. As described in the chapter on the Volga okrug by Gulnaz Sharafutdinova and Arbakhan Magomedov, in his native Nizhnii Novgorod he took advantage of the political uncertainty before the gubernatorial elections to get his deputy put in charge of economic affairs for the regional government. However, his efforts suffered a dramatic defeat when a communist challenger outpolled the region's incumbent governor and forced Kirienko's man out of office. Of course, since the region is heavily dependent on federal subsidies, Kirienko retained considerable influence despite this humiliation.

Other envoys did not intervene so intrusively in the economic affairs of a particular region; rather, they focused on developing interregional ties (trying to increase their personal influence as well as improve Russia's economic system). For example, Kazantsev encouraged more flights between Southern okrug cities, while Drachevskii pushed big Siberian enterprises to buy more parts locally. However, since these particular efforts lacked a sound economic base—there were no passengers for Kazantsev's flights, and the Siberian enterprises could find better deals elsewhere—they were extremely short-lived. They also, no doubt, gave the federal ministries a good basis on which to denigrate the envoys' meddling in economic affairs in general. And indeed, it is not clear what proportion of the envoys' other efforts of this type have had greater success.

Extracting Money from the State

The envoys in the South, Siberia, and the Far East developed ambitious strategic plans for the development of their particular okrugs. These naturally required extensive federal funding and therefore ran into strong opposition in Moscow. In all three cases, Minister for Economic Development and Trade German Gref staunchly opposed the plans, confronted the envoys, and drastically cut the proposed developments. As a result, the envoys were reduced to being regional lobbyists rather than active coordinators of federal policy. Most elements of these plans are unlikely to be implemented. Ultimately the federal government only funded programs to aid the South and the regions of Kaliningrad, Sakhalin, and Tatarstan. Also, in the case of the South, it provided much less funding than Kazantsev originally sought.

Kirienko may have pursued a more effective strategy by eschewing such an ambitious program in favor of more targeted projects, such as developing the large proportion of Russia's automobile industry that is based in his okrug. However, like the larger projects, these plans also have yet to be realized and may never actually bear fruit. Similar plans for the aircraft industry have not taken off, partly because several Volga regions fear that they will only help Samara to expand what they see as its already excessive power. In the Far East, smaller-scale projects do seem to be moving ahead, though it is hard to say whether they are doing so thanks to the envoy's support. For example, the completion of the Bureiskaya hydropower plant in Amur Region is expected to contribute significantly to the okrug's economy. In the Center, North-West, and Urals, the envoys have never even tried to prepare a regional development plan, focusing instead on other approaches such as developing ties with big business and encouraging foreign investment.

Several of the envoys have tapped private funds to set up okrug investment corporations, seeking to attract additional money to their okrug and funnel it into projects they deem worthy of sponsorship. The Center's Poltavchenko and the Far East's Pulikovskii seem to have gone the furthest in this regard. Pulikovskii has also set up his own company in North Korea, trying to take advantage of his special ties to that country's leader. However, the agencies have so far focused on small projects, lacking the funds to do more. Also, their activities would appear to be highly conducive to corruption.

Relations with Big Business

With the prospect of securing additional money from the federal government for their own deployment being extremely slim, many of the envoys began to seek funds from big business. To increase their contact with these corporations, they tried to mimic Putin's approach of herding the oligarchs into the Russian Union of Industrialists and Businessmen by setting up business councils that would bring together the major players for regular consultations. However, these efforts have not been as effective at the okrug level as they have in Moscow. Businesses in the regions do not see themselves as having at least some corporate interests in common, as do the businesses at the federal level, and thus prefer to operate individually.

The envoys have also offered to help businessmen overcome various barriers they face from regional officials or courts. However, these efforts are not aimed at making systematic changes that would improve the overall business environment. Rather, the envoys seem interested in making the existing system work better for specific kinds of projects (especially those that create jobs and provide social benefits) or for specific businessmen whom they favor. Unfortunately for the envoys, they usually lack the kind of authority and resources that can benefit businessmen. Although the latter have periodically set up meetings with the envoys, on a day-to-day basis they deal directly with the governors and mayors. In those Siberian and Far Eastern regions where businessmen have themselves become governors, the problem is of course easier for them. In these cases, the envoy has little to no economic influence, and one of the goals of Putin's reform is directly undermined.

The arrival of big business in the regions has been one of the defining changes in the Russian economy in the wake of the 1998 financial crisis. Kirienko has taken the lead in trying to influence how the regions and the okrug develop relations with these new arrivals. He became envoy to the Volga okrug at the very moment when many of Russia's largest companies were starting to buy up major enterprises in the area. In collaboration with the PA, he has played a significant role in monitoring, sponsoring, and guiding these deals, thus influencing how big business behaves in the okrug. His extensive business connections make it easier for him to operate in this environment than it is for the other envoys. Nevertheless, other envoys can point to some useful activity. Kazantsev, for example, has played a role in helping some big businesses move into the Southern okrug's agricultural sector.

Several envoys have had much less success in setting up such relationships. In the Central okrug, big business does not really need Poltavchenko, since it can deal directly with Moscow bureaucrats, though he appears to have helped some smaller businesses.[9] Cherkesov also played only a small role in the economy of the North-West. However, he apparently helped favored companies like LUKoil to develop their business in the okrug.

Critical observers have pointed out that the envoys seem to have become steadily more involved in many of the property changes wrought by the arrival of big business in the regions. The envoys' role appears to have evolved from monitoring the processes taking place, to arbitrating in disputes, and ultimately to being players of some sort in the process of redistributing property, with the attendant risk that they themselves or their staff may be corrupted. Rather than change the way the Russian system works, the envoys have apparently become a part of it.

In the past, there was often a close synergy of interests between the regional business elite and the governors. Such close ties remain in places like Sakha, Tatarstan, and Bashkortostan, where the republics' leaders retain tight control over their territories' most important economic assets. But in other regions the governors have lost considerable power. They are no longer so closely associated with their regions' most important property owners because, after buying large enterprises in the regions, big business often tries to stay fairly clear of regional political battles. The new owners seek to maintain smooth business relations with the governors but do not always support their political ambitions. In general, the rapid post-1998 expansion of big business beyond Moscow and a few resource-producing regions has limited gubernatorial power more than the arrival of the envoys.

Because of the extensive resources at its disposal, big business is also directly influencing some of the ways in which the federal government operates in the regions. Thus, for example, in order to set up an okrugwide television network in Siberia and the Urals, the envoys turned to contributions from, among others, Russia's largest aluminum company, Oleg Deripaska's Base Element. Naturally, in exchange for their contributions, the companies want a strong influence over what is broadcast.

Overall, the Russian political and economic systems remain deeply intertwined. The envoys simply cannot imagine holding positions of their rank without having influence over economic decisions in their okrugs. Thus, they are constantly striving to supplement the weak economic levers they were given at the founding of the new institution. Not surprisingly, though, given their lack of financial resources, they have had rather little success. Kirienko's personal business connections make him a partial exception to this conclusion.

Crime and Corruption

Putin's federal reforms have done little to address the country's rampant crime and corruption problems. Not surprisingly, many of these are focused in its most lucrative industries: natural resources, alcohol production, and ports. The envoys speak frequently about the problem, but the reforms undertaken to date do not confront the underlying causes.

In the area of corruption, the envoys have simply continued the time-dishonored practice of launching anticorruption campaigns for specific polit-ical purposes. Kirienko stressed antigraft efforts in his campaign against Marii-El president Kislitsyn, inspiring several investigations to probe his links with the criminal world after he persisted in seeking another term. Poltavchenko has mainly gone after retired regional officials. Cherkesov launched a vendetta against Governor Yakovlev of Saint Petersburg, getting charges filed against four of his deputy governors. However, these were dropped in the wake of Cherkesov's departure. Finally, things went even worse for Kirienko, who himself became the object of a campaign of incriminating evidence (*kompromat*), when his opponents sought to discredit him.

In regions like Kalmykia, where political and business interests are com-pletely merged in the leadership, the door is open for unlimited corruption. However, as long as the leaders are able to preserve stability, the federal gov-ernment, in its chronic weakness, pays little or no attention. In distant regions like Tyva, cattle thieves have been able to paralyze much of the agricultural sector. In such cases, only external intervention can hope to tackle the prob-lem. But federal officials have no stomach for a crackdown, regarding it as too difficult to be worth attempting, given their meager resources.

In Siberia, several regions shelter powerful business monopolies. The oil giant Sibneft, for example, sells 100 percent of the gasoline in the Omsk retail market, making it specially vulnerable to price gouging and corruption. In theory, the antimonopoly ministry should take action, but it has not. Like-wise, Video International, founded by Media minister Mikhail Lesin, controls much of Russia's television advertising market, and Deripaska's Base Element produces about 70 percent of Russia's aluminum. Naturally, such monopolies create fertile ground for corruption.

Given the bountiful natural resources of Siberia and the Far East, crime and corruption flourish there, as greedy officials cooperate with foreign and domes-tic crime groups to sell off Russia's energy, metals, and fish for personal benefit. Poachers on Sakhalin Island, for example, stop at little, even killing the head of the border guard service when he tried to limit illegal fish sales to Japan.

Since the okrug authorities lack adequate resources, they mainly take action in cases where other state agencies stand to benefit and are willing to contribute to the effort. Thus, Kazantsev can help to launch a crackdown on port corruption in Krasnodar Krai (Southern okrug) because the regional authorities will benefit from the increased tax yield if trade is conducted legally.

In the area of police reform, Putin has greatly increased the government's formal power to appoint regional police chiefs independently of the governors. However, he has not used this power to overhaul the regional branches of the Ministry of Internal Affairs, or MVD. To date, his new appointments seem to be largely aimed at influencing the outcome of regional elections. As a result, law enforcement agents often take sides in related property disputes, helping unscrupulous businessmen to expand their property holdings. In short, extensive and persistent corruption in police ranks makes tackling crime and corruption in society as a whole close to impossible.

Local Government

Despite high-level expressions of support for local government during the years 2000–2002, this layer of government continued to lose ground. And it is too early to say how the reforms that were proposed in early 2003, which may not improve the situation, will eventually turn out. Local governments in Russia still largely lack independent sources of financing and remain heavily dependent on regional governments. Mayors who hoped that the appearance of the envoy would help them in their struggle with the governors were largely disappointed. Putin's centralization of tax revenues only exacerbated the situation, as regional authorities tried to replace the money they lost to the federal government by extracting equivalent sums from the local level.

In terms of action, the federal government has largely ignored local government, even turning its back when authoritarian regional authorities illegally abolished mayoral elections, as they did in Novosibirsk, Tatarstan, and a number of Southern regions like Kalmykia. Governors would rather appoint mayors than let the population elect them because dependent mayors will work loyally to reelect the governors. This will preserve their own jobs. The governor of Novosibirsk has been specially defiant, saying that he will continue this illegal practice until after the next round of gubernatorial elections in December 2003.

Media

Putin's envoys have sought to create a "unified information space" within each of their okrugs, but their efforts to set up media outlets that reflect an okrug point of view have been largely ineffective. Also ineffective is the little known newspaper *Rossiya,* which attempts to interest its minuscule readership[10] in the affairs of all the okrugs. Generally, the governors or various business interests control regional media, using them to spread their own point of view and often opposing positions taken by the envoys. The latter have hardly ever risked trying to censor such publications.

In Siberia and the Urals, where the envoys have been able to secure private funding to get okrug television programs made, they have had trouble getting stations to broadcast the shows in all regions. Even when they have had access to stations, the production teams have often had difficulty preparing material interesting enough to win viewer attention. The okrug-based shows tend to feature the statements and activities of the envoy and his key deputies, and are hardly thrilling enough to compete with Hollywood movies dubbed into Russian. The envoys have also set up their own official newspapers to spread their point of view, but these are not widely read. While Siberia, the Urals, and the Volga okrugs have been relatively quick to establish basic media and PR systems, the others are following suit with similar programs.

As noted above, the envoys have had to rely on contributions from rich businessmen. Presumably the latter have been willing to support their media activities because they expect preferential treatment from the federal authorities in return. Drachevskii has relied heavily on Deripaska, Roman Abramovich's Sibneft, and Chubais's UES electricity monopoly. Latyshev has courted contributions from LUKoil and Yevrazkholding, while Kirienko has depended on the media empire of his associate Leonid Sukhoterin. In Siberia, the employees of the Okrug Information Center receive their salaries from off-budget sources that have not been publicly identified and are suspected of being businessmen. This direct and often visible cooperation between the federal authorities and big business inevitably makes the public skeptical about the objectivity of okrug media.

And indeed, the envoys' media policies as a whole have provoked many complaints from journalists and advocates of a free press. Reporters seeking to cover the envoys have often complained that the latter are so secretive that it is difficult to write about them objectively. Other critics have pointed out that they often use media stations for political purposes. In the Far East, for example, Pulikovskii got his allies appointed to head two Primorskii television stations in order to promote the candidacy of his deputy in the gubernatorial election that followed Governor Nazdratenko's departure.

In general, Russians living outside of Moscow have access to news and information about their own region that is provided by national sources, but they are poorly informed about events in neighboring regions. The envoys have discussed the need to address this problem by stimulating better information flows. The most successful action was taken in the North-West, where the influential Rosbalt news agency was set up. The envoy's wife, Natalia Chaplina, a prominent journalist in her own right, ran this organization, which naturally distributed news with Cherkesov's slant, at least until he departed for Moscow in March 2003.

Civil Society and Political Parties

In the wake of seventy years of Soviet rule, the gulf between state and society in Russia is still enormous. Under Gorbachev, civic organizations designed to deal with a range of problems from environmental degradation to fostering education and the arts began to take off, but they have found it difficult to develop. It remains unclear how far federal and regional governments want—and are ready—to promote such activities, especially if they lead to criticism of the authorities. Kirienko has given considerable attention to these issues, including the organization of fairs to showcase some of the most innovative groups in the Volga okrug. He has also encouraged big companies to sponsor such activities.

Naturally, the federal government could benefit politically from some of these efforts, especially if it could mobilize the public to monitor and then halt some of the more egregious activities of regional and local officials. As discussed above, the planned establishment of three thousand citizens' reception rooms in the okrugs, rooms that began to open in 2002, seems to have this purpose, among others of a more secret police type. Examples of public activity that the federal authorities find useful have occurred in Primorskii Krai, where angry citizens have protested wage arrears and heating outages, even blocking rail traffic on the trans-Siberian Railroad. Moscow has exploited these incidents, citing them for example as justification for forcing the resignation of the region's governor.

However, it remains unclear to what extent the state can foster such grassroots activities without unduly jeopardizing its own interests. The thrust of Putin's centralizing reforms suggests that he wants to mobilize society only in support of his own policies. His administration appears to have little interest in a society that would behave independently. True, in many cases foreign foundations and governments have stepped in with funding to help Russia's civil society. However, Putin and his associates have made clear they are wary of such aid. Symptomatic was the denial of entry in December 2002 to Irene Stephenson, an American who had worked in Russia for many years, helping independent trade unions with their organizational problems.[11]

Of course, some forms of state support for *approved* NGOs carry major risks. For example, Kazantsev, holding that the Russian state is primarily Orthodox, has strongly supported the Russian Orthodox Church, even though one quarter of his okrug's residents are Muslim. He has also backed church plans to allow it to play a greater role in public schools. However, he has been more cautious in his relations with xenophobic Cossack groups and with ethnic minorities, realizing that strife between them already exists and is politically dangerous. Thus his policies combine, contradictorily, elements of great power thinking and efforts to maintain stability.

Regarding political parties, Putin has, during his tenure, had federal laws rewritten to help promote the merger of a large number of small parties into a small number of large ones. Parallel to this, the Kremlin has tried to build up a strong Unified Russia party that would support its goals.[12] However, this party had, by March 2003, won only very limited popular support, and it was unclear how enthusiastically the governors, overall, would back it in the December 2003 Duma elections. In particular, by imposing tight top-down controls on the party, even to the extent of dictating to regional branches who their chairman should be, the national leadership caused numerous disputes with the regional political elites. In conclusion, it is not yet clear what effect the new laws will have on the structure and performance of the party system across the regions, once they come into force in July 2003.

Conclusions

None of the authors of this volume has seen the creation of the seven federal okrugs as a clear success for the Kremlin. At best, they see the results as "mixed" or as having made the existing system work a little better. Nikolai Petrov warns that the reforms have created a "dangerous paralysis." Sergei Kondratiev sees them as little more than a fifth wheel in the federal executive branch. Elizabeth Wishnick concludes that they have had little impact on the critical issue of promoting regional economic coordination. And most of the authors convey a sense that the envoys' activities often have something of a "campaigning" character to them and recall the numerous campaigns— inevitably temporary—that were a familiar feature of government in the Soviet period.

Generally speaking, the envoys and the okrugs have not become an indispensable part of the state. Their impact has been relatively modest. Abolishing the okrugs now would not make a dramatic impact on the political system. However, Putin is unlikely to do this because it would be a symbolic victory for the governors. On the other hand, his assignment in March 2003 of the political lightweight Valentina Matvienko to be his new envoy in the North-West okrug looked like a signal that the envoys were losing status. Whether the okrugs will survive much beyond Putin's presumed departure from the presidency in 2008 is not clear. In our opinion, their functions could quite easily be handed back to the institutions from which they were appropriated in 2000.

In some contexts, the envoys have become significant players on the Russian political stage. However, their power is largely informal and contingent, since its main source is their direct relationship with the president. They have occasionally been able to influence how the rules of the game develop, as Kirienko did when big business moved into the Volga okrug. Also, they can sometimes intervene decisively in conflicts among other players.

The reforms have also achieved some less "opportunistic" results. The CFIs have probably reduced gubernatorial control over some of the key federal officials in the regions, although the governors are undoubtedly using their formidable array of blandishments to try to resubvert their loyalty. Indeed, it seems clear to us that as long as this practice is not effectively outlawed—an immensely long and complex task that can hardly be separated from truly radical political reforms that we cannot at present imagine occurring—these federal officials will never be securely under Moscow's control.

Putin is also slowly introducing a policy of rotating personnel within and between important ministries, another step that, if seriously pursued, could give the federal government greater control over its employees in the field. Additionally, the governors now have less power to intervene in federal politics than they did in the past.

However, the modest improvements that the envoys have probably brought to the coordination of federal agencies might have been achieved more effectively through coordinated action within the ministries. To put the same idea differently, the grafting of okrug offices onto the existing hierarchy of a number of ministries has added an extra layer of bureaucracy, while producing gains that may or may not be worth the price of doing so. An alternative and plausible view—held by Nikolai Petrov and others—is that the okrug reform, or something like it, was essential because only through the shock of presidential power being directly projected below the federal level, via the specially created structure of the okrug, was it possible seriously to assault the formidable powers accumulated by the governors through the 1990s. This view also holds, less plausibly in our opinion, that at least most of the elements of the okrug system will need to be maintained for the indefinite future, and might indeed be developed, in order to move Russia in a more authoritarian direction.

As they try to increase their economic influence, envoys often serve as regional lobbyists. But they usually lack economic knowledge and judgment, and can easily end up trying to subsidize unprofitable local enterprises. As a result, the federal ministries tend to block their efforts and feel angry at these "amateurs on parade." If the current balance of power between Putin and the

Cabinet of Ministers remains unchanged, it seems inconceivable that the envoys would be able to actually implement any increased economic powers that Putin might give them in the future. Thus, if his representatives would simply be impotent in the aftermath of such a move, it is unlikely that he would give them such powers in the first place. If this line of reasoning is correct, then the scenario just mentioned—that he might use the envoys as one of several instruments for introducing a more authoritarian political and economic system—appears implausible.

The envoys' impact on the governors has not been consistent. The regions that are more powerful and have good negotiators have usually been able to extract satisfactory political and economic deals for themselves from the envoys. Weak regions, by contrast, cede more to their wishes. In general, governors have figured out how to live with the envoys and can work with or around them.

What has become painfully apparent is that the government is not willing to fund the envoys' activities adequately. So they have had to go cap-in-hand to big business. The unintended message to the oligarchs and the governors could hardly be clearer. As a result, big businessmen, with their extensive financial resources, have become new and powerful players in regional politics, and the governors usually have to pay much more attention—and cede more power—to them than they do to the envoys.

To some extent, then, big business has done what the envoys aimed to achieve but could not do adequately. It has reduced the power of the governors, and by extending the operations of their firms across the country, it is building the sort of economic networks that will not only create a more unified (if unhealthily monopolized) national market but may also, gradually, tie Russia's disparate regions together in wider ways. On the other hand, big business has a strong incentive to collaborate with governors at the expense of the Kremlin. Above all, businesses want to minimize their liability to federal taxation, and quiet deals with governors can greatly facilitate this.

Thus we come to our final attempt to distill the findings of this book. The governors are—at least for now—considerably less powerful than they were, and market integration is making progress. However, many of them have powerful new associates who scarcely have the Kremlin's best interests at heart. Thus, on balance, the Kremlin's direct control of the regions—through its ministries and envoys—may no longer be increasing. Also, the "campaigning" nature of most of the envoys' activities suggests that when their campaign loses steam and fades away, so too will much of whatever beneficial effect their work has had.

How well Putin's envoys learn the skills needed to maneuver in this constantly evolving arena, where economics and personal relations count for more than institutions or laws, will determine how much progress they can make toward achieving their goals. However, given their present meager resources and their poorly qualified personnel, they are at a severe disadvantage, especially in the economically stronger regions.

Notes

1. See the revealing interview in the appendix to this volume, also Peter Reddaway's introductory chapter, note 10.

2. More extensive work on the Federation Council is under way now than can be summarized here. See, for example, the chapter by Darrell Slider in volume 2 of this book, and forthcoming studies by Thomas Remington.

3. *Izvestiya*, January 30, 2002.

4. *Kommersant Vlast*, February 26, 2002.

5. See the chapter on this subject by Philip Hanson in volume 2.

6. On the formidable restrictions, see the chapter by Alexei Trochev and Peter Solomon in volume 2.

7. The Russian media variously estimated that his personal income from the job would be $1–$10 million dollars a year.

8. *Kommersant Daily*, February 19, 2002.

9. See the chapter by Lynn Nelson and Irina Kuzes in volume 2.

10. This paper, which appears twice a week, claims a countrywide print run of seventy thousand copies.

11. See the article on this episode by Marina Kalashnikova, "Udar FSB po mezhdunarodnoi rabochei solidarnosti," *Novye Izvestiya*, January 16, 2003.

12. On these and related topics, see the chapter by Henry Hale in volume 2.

Appendix: Interview with the Chief Federal Inspector (CFI) for the Perm Region, Nikolai Anatolevich Fadeyev[1]

P RIOR TO HIS APPOINTMENT IN JANUARY 2002 as CFI for the Perm Region of the Volga Federal Okrug to work under Presidential Envoy Sergei Kirienko, Fadeyev had been a long-time resident and worked as an economist for Perm city. He gave this interview in December 2002, when he was in his early forties. It is notable for the frankness and the detail with which he describes many aspects of a CFI's and an envoy's work, the nature of which normally has to be inferred by scholars and other observers.

INTERVIEWER: You're a federal official. In the regional hierarchy . . . what position would you say you occupy? . . .

FADEYEV: Kirienko said [when he presented me to the Perm regional leaders]: "The chief federal inspector is the third-ranking official in a region after the governor and the chairman of the Legislative Assembly. But he is the top federal official in the region."

From the viewpoint of real power and influence on the process of developing the Perm region, I'm not sure who is first, second or third at the present time: I haven't yet grown fully into my uniform, and it hasn't yet become tight for me. But I'm trying to create levers of influence. My work plan for next year—about how to increase the degree of loyalty to the executive branch among leaders of the regional bodies of the federal agencies—is ready. They won't escape. My plan is tested, correct. . . .

It deals with how the leaders of the federal bodies in Perm region use the funds allocated to them by the federal budget. This has never before been monitored by anyone, except by the Regional Monitoring Division of the Ministry of Finance. But no one has ever checked their efficiency. There hasn't been a single competition. And that's a violation of the law, a matter for the procuracy. This is what I have to do next year, so that I formally grow into this uniform, which should, figuratively speaking, have general's stars on it. Up to now, the uniform hasn't really gone to work.

INTERVIEWER: There are more and more officials in Russia. Now we have the offices of the commissioned representatives of the president. Haven't they too turned into one more official structure?

FADEYEV: Honestly, it's too early to give this question a definite answer. We're still in a developing situation. To say how it'll evolve—at best we'll be able to judge that in one and a half to two years. Why? We'll have the presidential elections [in March 2004]. The president will then have to assess how things have gone and pose the question: what has the institution of the envoys done in the time it had to achieve its special tasks?

Various answers are possible. Maybe the envoys' offices will be judged to be superfluous, bureaucratically constructed apparatuses that have not made any substantial contributions to strengthening the hierarchy of executive power. That's one scenario. But today I can say that the likelihood of the institution of the envoys being abolished is minimal. One of the functions that the President assigned to the envoys was the function of monitoring. This function is becoming more important.

INTERVIEWER: Okay, we understand about the President. But what do you yourself think about the productiveness of your organization?

FADEYEV: Everywhere it's different. [When I started] I didn't know anything about a whole group of extremely important responsibilities that I now have: for the law and order agencies and security issues. Where had I come from? I'd been involved in economics, the reform of the city's business activities: I'd been developing various intellectually complex projects. And now I had these completely new responsibilities, and I didn't understand them, I didn't know about them. So I realized: Fadeyev, sit down humbly and study, focus on what you don't know. And thank God, I was helped by Stepankov,[2] who tutored me, just like any regular student who's struggling. I'm very grateful to him.

Today my work gives me satisfaction because I've managed to develop relationships with a majority of the federal organizations. For them, at first, I was just an official who was one rank higher than they, and on whom they depended for various aspects of their careers. But formal methods aren't the way to build relationships. I have already found the instrument for that—not one based on things like compulsion or aggression, but on a normal approach, sitting round an office table—when I'm sitting not at the head of the table, but at a corner. Then the generals and the agency heads and I discuss things, identify the problems, and take the decisions we have to take together. Without any fighting. Sometimes I reconcile them with each other, when one of them has complained to me about the other, because two federal agencies can't reach agreement by themselves, even on a simple matter that only needs them to shake hands across the table. For example, the Pension Fund and the Tax Police.

INTERVIEWER: But we've had to listen to various generals say that Nizhnii Novgorod [the location of Kirienko's okrug office] causes more problems than it solves. They say that a new layer of bureaucrats has been created, who have to prove they've been created for some *reason*. Don't you come across this?

FADEYEV: I do come across it. But the key question is how to decide what there's more of in the barrel—honey or shit? . . . Yes indeed, a new power center is being created. But it has a real purpose. After all, the concept of "Bonapartism" has settled somewhere in our brains. There must be two parties fighting each other [the federal authorities and the governors] and a third one that is capable of "sorting them out." When the institution of the envoys was being created, the goal was, after all, to neutralize the excessive independence of the governors.

And how could they be neutralized? By two methods—carrots and sticks. Make it hard for them to keep contacting Moscow in the traditional ways. Okay, guys, now you've got to go through Nizhnii [Kirienko's office]. And there, a whole lot of barriers exist. It's not just that a highly-placed boss [Kirienko] has appeared. There's also, for example, the head of the okrug MVD [police], with a big staff of 300–400 people. True, the most serious cases don't get referred to him. Every regional police chief tries not to hand over a case that he considers important for his region and thinks he can solve. They won't hand over cases like that. It's the same with the procuracy. There really is a struggle going on. That's what the new system was set up to create.

Now the regional bodies of the federal executive agencies, too, are forced to think like this: "Well, where do we take this? Moscow's the boss now. The wind's blowing from there, but we have to go through the envoy." It's the envoy who'll recommend a promotion, provided the chief federal inspector writes a positive report. And I, of course, will ask five people about this or that general. Do you have any concerns about him? And the comrades will bring his folder, open it up, and let me read it. So I have to take the responsibility and refuse someone a promotion or an appointment. And lay out the reasons, so that some sort of record goes into the file. This whole procedure has now been created.

INTERVIEWER: But isn't that just typical bureaucracy?

FADEYEV: Yes, bureaucracy! . . . Bureaucracy, of course, has its own laws. It's self-contained. It couldn't care less about the ultimate goals of administration. It's a professional layer of administrators. But if it's professional, then you have to apply the criterion: is it efficient or inefficient? So the logic of hiring administrator-bureaucrats on contract—what [Minister of Economic Development and Trade] Gref is proposing, i.e., a reform of the civil service—is normal. Bureaucratism—I speak as a bureaucrat—is a style of work. It's harmful, it's bad. It's unattractive, ugly, revolting. But bureaucracy as a technological machine for administering those common functions that are financed by the budget, that's just something that's essential. And it can and must be good—efficient, well oiled, not squeaky.

If you've noticed, the hierarchy of executive power is not being built as a chain on the model "President—envoy—chief federal inspector." As regards the budget process, the centralization process is already complete. The new Tax Code and the flow of taxes to Moscow—that's the essence of the centralization. The central nervous system of the country's administration leads not to the Kremlin, but to the White House, to the office of Vice Premier [and finance minister] Kudrin.

That's where the country's main money flows are directed from. I simply know the situation from the inside. The process of integrating the country is making real progress. But it's taking place not on the level of personalities. . . .

If the country's political course changes, or I make a mistake, or grow slack, or take any liberties, or become ineffective, then I'll rightly be dismissed from this position. And in that case, I wouldn't have the moral right to take a job in the regional administration, because I'm supervising it now.

INTERVIEWER: . . . Are you for the appointment of governors? Or against?

FADEYEV: An elected governor is not a centrifugal force, everything depends on his personality. . . . Now the presidents of Bashkortostan and Tataria do indeed have the tendency to strive for autonomy. But there's also governor Trutnev [of Perm], whom I respect and who is oriented toward federal interests. . . . But an elected governor has the potential to encourage autonomy and centrifugal forces. He wouldn't get anywhere, though, because he's bound by the law. "Who's behind me, who gave me their mandate?" People gave it, the voters.

INTERVIEWER: So you're saying that if our governor wasn't well disposed to the federal center, you would fight against him?

FADEYEV: Definitely. Definitely. That's what my colleagues in Bashkiria, the Kirov region, and Tataria do. There's a problem. I know what tough conditions my colleagues are fighting in. They're really fighting. One of them was even awarded recently a ceremonial firearm. He was from the special services. It was, of course, a symbolic present. The main tasks are to supervise the actions of the executive branch.

INTERVIEWER: Would you call yourself a member of "Trutnev's team"?

FADEYEV: At one stage that question was considered not only by the people who were discussing my possible appointment but also by you journalists. But above all by Kirienko. Regardless of how well Sergei Vladilenovich [Kirienko] gets on personally with Yuri Petrovich [Trutnev] (and socially they have much in common: about the same age, the same sort of career, sport, business, a whole lot in common, people of the same generation), by definition Kirienko doesn't need someone here who's Trutnev's man. So when people associated me with Trutnev, I had to go to considerable lengths in Moscow to convince everyone that I wasn't the governor's man. I'm a person who respects Trutnev for a variety of reasons, but I know everything. And knew before. Just as they know in Moscow.[3] Every action by a governor or a mayor can be viewed from various points of view. I know that. These are the things I discuss with the president's envoy.

No one has revoked my instructions to be the ruler's eyes on the territory of Perm region. I have everything I need for this. Full independence from the governor within the framework of my career, above all as regards my material requirements. I never had common interests with him when I was in business. . . . So now we work closely together. And since the governor doesn't do any other work, there's no need for me to have him investigated. But if, God forbid, the need arose, then okay—I'd go into action. Otherwise I wouldn't last long in my job. . . .

I can talk only about the basic principles that underlay the replacement [of the Perm tax police chief, General Sergei Ukladov, by General Sinil'shchikov]. That's the essence of the matter. The tax police have extremely wide-ranging powers, from—let's say—the operational methods they use to track people down, to their network of secret agents. They are potentially the most powerful of all the special services. In this pyramid, which has a pretty self-enclosed existence, they're allowed to use every type of police pressure against people. And how these pressures are used depends on who exactly the chief is. What did we have by the end of the time period that began with General Ukladov and ended with Boris Mikhailovich Prilepin? We had within the system a certain sort of "Darwinism": some people were opening criminal cases, others were closing them. Both the former and the latter were taking money for doing these things. I'm not saying this about all the officers, but this practice was going on. Even if there had been only one or two such cases, that would already have been the end for the chief. A self-cleansing from this practice had to take place. And the practice was rather noticeable. Moreover, an experienced law enforcement officer will open a case for money, and close it for money, only if it doesn't have a good chance of being proved in court.

INTERVIEWER: Don't you believe that the reasons for the departure of various chiefs should be publicized, if reprehensible acts have been committed?

FADEYEV: I don't think I can agree with you. Here public opinion runs ahead of the train. Why aren't the facts that lead to the administrative decision to replace a chief publicized? Remember what the presumption of innocence means. . . . I can't consider this person a scoundrel, if I don't have enough evidence and documents. The problem is one of proof. . . . But when we're talking about the head of a federal organization, and we find out that he's building himself a four-story mansion, and we can even guess who's paying for it, then you'd have to put your life on the line to start an investigation. A journalistic one, usually. Because it's hardly likely that anyone else would take on such an investigation.[4]

INTERVIEWER: Would you please comment on the retirement of the Perm regional FSB [security police] chief.

FADEYEV: The only organization for which top appointments are not made in consultation with the chief federal inspector is the Federal Security Service. Among all the federal agencies, this one is special. It monitors the state apparatus—above all the federal apparatus—as regards the plague of corruption. So the FSB's nominees for top posts don't pass through *my* hands for review—*my* appointment passed through *their* hands [emphases added]. Every federal official from the level of chief federal inspector downward has to be continuously monitored by the FSB. This is how it is, and this is right, in case anyone starts down the slippery slope—because the consequences that can follow from incorrect actions are too serious. As they say, don't look only in the front mirror, look in the rear mirror too. You'll go further.

INTERVIEWER: It's not a secret that the federal authorities find it convenient to have governors on whom there's *kompromat*. They become manipulable, compliant, and loyal. Is there any *kompromat* on our governor? . . .

FADEYEV: A genuine, talented politician is always many-colored and many-sided. What can I say about whether there's *kompromat* on Trutnev? On a figure of his stature there are, certainly, materials—in the hands of those people who don't let officials start slipping or putting their hand in the till, the services you asked about. Above all, this is the FSB and the personnel directorate of the Presidential Administration. So there are materials, information about his career path, and documents. This doesn't at all mean that it's *kompromat*. It's material on the basis of which to analyze the strong and weak sides of a leader. I'll give you an example that's far from our region, and without mentioning names. It was 1998. In the White House, I'm sitting in the office of some "high-up comrades," and suddenly someone says: "Well, this is the seventh time this guy's been caught stealing [from the state] (they're talking about a federal minister). Shall we remove him?"—"Yes, remove him!" I was looking like a wide-eyed idiot: "What d'you mean, the seventh time?" They looked up: "Up to now he's been useful." And indeed, if we're frank, this is the criterion. It isn't spoken, but it exists, this main criterion. What's a chief's effectiveness? If he can't, as they say, cover his traces, if his blunders become known to the press, if he allows information to leak and doesn't reach agreement with the law enforcement bodies, so that they understand his actions, if he doesn't "sort these things out," then he's a bad chief. And he can go and run a municipality, where thieving takes the form of climbing over a fence with a sack of stolen goods.

To return to the privatization issue, a special term has appeared recently: "start-up capital obtained in an ethically acceptable way." Have you heard this phrase? The subtle form of ethically acceptable commercial activity is now harder to justify, and is becoming the realm of only a select few.

But raw *kompromat* doesn't exist as such. It takes on a compromising character only if circumstances come together and if certain goals exist. Otherwise, it's all just information.

[A section is omitted here on corruption in the Perm city administration during the three years when Fadeyev was brought in to head the economics directorate. He describes the latter as having been concerned mainly with economic counterintelligence.]

INTERVIEWER: How often do you meet with Kirienko?
FADEYEV: Regularly. And not only during official meetings. There are various issues that require personal discussion. Such questions exist for every chief federal inspector. They're not publicized, and I think that they never will be publicized.
. . .
INTERVIEWER: Do ordinary citizens have a chance to contact you? How do you work with them?
FADEYEV: Let me say frankly that I try to avoid receiving . . . ordinary citizens. We've set up a citizens' reception room, where regular citizens are received. Mostly they have complaints about housing problems and wage arrears. Often, receiving them is a form of psychotherapy. A person gets it all off his chest, complains, cries a bit, then feels better and leaves. But there are a number of cases

which, after they've been filtered by the reception people, I handle myself. Generally these provide evidence of illegal actions by officials. So I write a letter to the procurator. In any case, the citizen's complaint takes on a second life. There are many examples.

INTERVIEWER: What's the idea behind the so-called Kozak reforms? Are they one more experiment with local self-government?

FADEYEV: . . . The principles behind the goals of the reforms are absolutely right. They'll probably be introduced after the presidential election, not earlier. I'm sure the draft will go through the Duma. The point is that at present we don't have local self-government as such. Each municipality has its boss *(vozhd')*, who lives partly on local money raised through local taxes, and partly on transfers from the regional budget—and even sometimes the federal budget. So a local prince presides. How does he run the town? What are his powers? He can't answer in full measure to the citizens who elected him.

Self-government will arise only when people know by face the mini-mayor elected by each local community, and call him by his nickname. Not by his first name and patronymic, but just Mikhalych, for example . . .

INTERVIEWER: Do you have a good salary?

FADEYEV: Good salaries don't exist. Now I have to live on one salary. Before, it was better, because I could combine my work for the state with research work. . . .

INTERVIEWER: The envoy's office took an active part in the elections for governor of Nizhnii Novgorod region. Will you take any part in the Duma and presidential elections?

FADEYEV: I wouldn't say that the presidential election is a basic task, but it's the most topical one, that's for sure. In reality, preparations will start in May of next year [i.e., 2003, for the election in March 2004].

Naturally, the federal authorities have certain views as to who they would not like to see in the Duma—to make sure it works constructively and in harmony with the government and the Presidential Administration. The range of parties is predictable: it seems to me the communists will split, and the democratic wing will compromise with the federal authorities. That's my prognosis. I have reasons for thinking this. But this isn't some sort of scenario. No list of people [to be elected] exists, there's no such thing. And I haven't been tasked to do that. . . .

The deputies [to the Perm city legislature] live on something. I look, they change their cars. The elections happen, and they've changed their cars. Interesting. I made inquiries: what, who, why? In this connection, all of them are taking money on the side.

INTERVIEWER: How do you like [our paper] *Zvezda* and its articles?

FADEYEV: . . . Your paper is one of the few, if not the only one, that apparently doesn't represent some firm's corporate interests. Frankly, I'm fed up with papers that are full of articles paid for by various interests. You often sense who has paid whom, so that one or another article should appear. Thus the autonomy of a group of writers, and having the funds to exist independently, is an extremely important thing. I hope you can carry on like this. . . .

Notes

1. Published in the newspaper *Zvezda*, Perm, December 20, 2002, and translated (by Peter Reddaway) with the permission of Mr. Fadeyev.

2. Valentin Stepankov (b. 1951) rose in Perm through the MVD and then the Procuracy, to become the general procurator from 1991 to 1993. In 2000 he was appointed deputy envoy under Kirienko.

3. These three sentences refer to Trutnev's record in the eyes of the police and security authorities, that is, to the evidence of prosecutable actions (usually called *kompromat*) that they collect on all officials.

4. This section explains why the vast majority of Russian officials who are dismissed for corruption are never prosecuted, let alone jailed. The law enforcement bodies do not dare to investigate them seriously, for fear of armed retaliation from the private security organizations or criminal groups that have been bribing the corrupt officials and are still protecting them. Sometimes the authorities give information to journalists and have them investigate a case and write a story they hope will intimidate the offenders. In such cases journalists are sometimes killed, while the former officials often get well-paid jobs in the private sector—for example, from the groups that were earlier bribing them.

Index

About the Contributors

Alexander Duka heads the group on political sociology at the Russian Academy of Sciences' Sociological Institute (Saint Petersburg). He is editor and coauthor of *Regional Elites of Russia's North-West: Political and Economic Orientations; Power Elites and Nomenklatura: An Annotated Bibliography of Russian Publications, 1990–2000;* and *Regional Elites in Russia: Problems, Approaches, Hypotheses* (all in Russian); and numerous articles dealing with power elites, political discourse, and institutional change in Russia. He is the deputy editor of *Journal of Sociology and Social Anthropology* (Russia).

Sergei Kondrat'ev is the dean of the History and Political Science Department at Tyumen State University, where he is also a professor of history and a reader in early modern history and political and legal thought. He has been a visiting fellow at the Center for Parliamentary History, Yale University; and Linaca College, Oxford University. Among his books are *Lawyers in Pre-Revolutionary England (1993); The Concept of Law in Pre-Revolutionary England (1987); Seventeenth-Century England: Socioprofessional groups and Society* (with S. Fyodorov and G. Pitulko, 1987); and *History of World Civilizations* (with A. Emanow and I. Bobrov, 2001). Since completing his doctoral studies at the University of Saint Petersburg, he has written about the political situation in the Ural and west Siberian regions.

Arbakhan Magomedov, a Ph.D. in political science, is a professor at Ulyanovsk State Technical University, where he chairs the Department of History and Culture. He is the author of *The Mystery of Regionalism: Regional*

Elites and Regional Ideologies in Contemporary Russia (Moscow Social Science Foundation, 2000), and *Regional Ideologies in the Context of International Relations* (Swiss Federal Institute of Technology, 2001). He has contributed chapters to *Regional Economic Change in Russia,* edited by Philip Hanson and Michael Bradshaw (2000); and *Spatial Factors in the Formation of Party Systems: A Dialogue between Americanists and Post-Sovietologists* (Slavic Research Center, Hokkaido University, 2002). His recent articles include: "The Tengiz-Novorossiisk Petroleum Pipeline and Russian Regional Elites," in *Monthly Bulletin on Trade with Russia and East Europe* (in Japanese; Tokyo, December 2000); "Russian Southern Ports in the Inter-relations between 'Center-Periphery'" in *Comparative Economic Studies* (in Japanese; Kyoto, 2001); and "Caspian Oil: Political Stakes in Russia's South," in *La Revue Tocqueville* (Paris, 2002). He has also contributed to *Communist Economies and Economic Transformation* and *Acta Slavica Iaponica.*

Robert Orttung is an associate research professor at the Transnational Crime and Corruption Center of American University and a visiting fellow at the Center for Security Studies of the Swiss Federal Institute of Technology, Zurich. He is the author or editor of *The Republics and Regions of the Russian Federation: A Guide to Politics, Policies, and Leaders* (with Danielle Lussier and Anna Paretskaya); *Russia's 1995 Parliamentary Elections: The Battle for the Duma* (with Laura Belin); and *From Leningrad to St. Petersburg: Democratization in a Russian City.* He is the editor of the *Russian Regional Report.*

Nikolai Petrov is a senior researcher at the Russian Academy of Sciences' Institute of Geography and the head of the Center for Political-Geographic Research. Previously, he directed the regional project at the Moscow Carnegie Center. He is the author or editor of numerous publications dealing with the social and political development of Russia's regions, federalism, elections, and territorial and ethnic conflict, among other topics. His works include the three-volume 1997 *Political Almanac of Russia* and the annual supplements to it. He is the author of the chapters on federalism and regional modeling in the *White Book on Russian Democracy* (Carnegie Endowment for International Peace, 2003).

Peter Reddaway is professor of political science at George Washington University in Washington, D.C. In the past, he taught at the London School of Economics and Political Science, and was the director of the Kennan Institute for Advanced Russian Studies, Woodrow Wilson International Center for Scholars from 1986 to 1989. He has also been a fellow at the Wilson Center, Columbia University, Stanford University, and the U.S. Institute of Peace.

Among his books are *The Tragedy of Russia's Reforms: Market Bolshevism against Democracy* (2001, with D. Glinski); *Russia's Political Hospitals* (1977, with S. Bloch); *Uncensored Russia: The Human Rights Movement in the USSR* (1972); and *Lenin: The Man, the Leader, the Thinker: A Reappraisal* (1967, ed. with L. Schapiro).

Peter Rutland is a professor of government at Wesleyan University and editor of the Jamestown Foundation's *Russia and Eurasia Review*. He has been a visiting professor at the European University in Saint Petersburg. He is the editor of *Business and State in Contemporary Russia* (2001).

Maksim Shandarov is a journalist working for the west Siberian regional edition of the newspaper *Kommersant*, where he specializes in the politics and economics of western Siberia. He contributes to a number of other Siberian and Russian publications, as well as the *Russian Regional Report*. He is the author of numerous articles on politics in Siberia.

Gul'naz Sharafutdinova is a Ph.D. candidate at the George Washington University, currently working on her dissertation dealing with political and economic transformation in Russian regions. She has published in *Problems of Post-Communism* and *Europe-Asia Studies*.

Elizabeth Wishnick is a Fulbright visiting scholar in the Department of Politics and Sociology at Lingnan University, Hong Kong, and an associate at the East Asian Institute at Columbia University. She is the author *of Mending Fences: The Evolution of Moscow's China Policy from Brezhnev to Yeltsin* and of numerous articles on great power relations and regional development in Northeast Asia.

Natalia Zubarevich is an assistant professor in the Geography Department of Moscow State University. She is the editor or author of numerous works, including *The Evolution of Relations between the Center and Regions in Russia: From Conflicts to a Search for Agreement* (a project of RAND's Center for Russian and Eurasian Research and the Center for Ethnopolitical and Regional Research); *Politics and Economics in a Regional Dimension* (2000); and *The Region as a Subject of Policy and Social Relations* (Moscow Social Science Foundation, 2000). She contributed chapters to the following books: *Russia, the Caucasus, and Central Asia: The 21st Century Security Environment* (produced by the EastWest Institute in 1999); *Regions of Russia in 1998* and *Regions of Russia 1999* (Moscow Carnegie Center); and *Explaining Post-Soviet Patchworks, Vol.3. The Political Economy of Regions, Regimes and Republics*, edited by

Klaus Segbers. She authored the book *Social Development in Russia's Regions: Problems and Tendencies of the Transition Period* (2003) and the recent article "Big Business and the Regional Authorities" in the journal *Pro et Contra*. She contributed to the United Nations Development Program's Human Development Report for the Russian Federation (1997–2002). She is also an expert for the Fredrick Nauman Foundation.